# A RICH SOUP

*with additional material*

*To Olivia*
*And for my children and their children.*

ALSO BY BRIAN FARRINGTON

*The Emigrant of a Hundred Townlands*. (Dublin, Poetry Ireland, Dolmen Press, 1968).
*Salt Suds for Keeps and other Poems*. (Aberdeen, Koo Press, 2006).
*Malachi-Stilt-Jack, A Study of W B Yeats and his Work*. (London, Connolly Publications, 1965).
*Words as New as the Hills. Concept Formation in the Field of High Altitude Topography (1750 – 1850).*
French Language Studies, 10. (Cambridge University Press, 2000).

SOFTWARE
*BonAccord, A Semi-intelligent Translation-Learning System for French*. (Aberdeen, Faro Systems, 2007).
*Dominie, Guided Writing Software for English as a Foreign Language*.
(Aberdeen, Faro Systems, 2006).
*Genders. French Vocabulary Software*. (Aberdeen, Faro Systems, 2009).

# A Rich Soup
## with additional material

BRIAN FARRINGTON

LINDEN

Published in 2010 by
LINDEN PUBLISHING • DUBLIN • IRELAND


ISBN: 978-1-905487-38-7

A catalogue record for this book is available from the British Library.


This book is designed and typeset by SUSAN WAINE
in 11.5 on 13.5 point Bodoni
Printed in Ireland by
THE PRINT BUREAU, DUBLIN

# Contents

## Acknowledgements

This book owes its existence to my great friend the late George Watson, who suggested I write it. I also owe thanks to many people for advice, information, corrections, support and criticism, in particular Maeve Black, Una Brown, Graham Davies, Henri Dégoutin, Geneviève Doze, Paul Dukes, Robin Eyre-Maunsell, Olivia Farrington, Tadg Farrington, Jim Flannery, Ruarc Gahan, Nicole Gandilhon, John Heuston, Carolyn Kirton, Norman Lush, Mary Moss, Marie Souviron, David Sowby and Christopher Woods. I must also thank Barra Boydell, Branwen (Diverres) Treiber, George Harvey, Jane (Farrington) Straker , Margaret Synge and Marjorie Wexler for the loan of photos. My friend the poet Irene Leake has been through the text sedulously ironing out inconsistencies and faults of style. Any remaining infelicities are my responsibility alone.

# I

# Home and Family

The earliest memory that I can put a date to is of falling out of the front seat of a car when I was not quite three years old. I know the precise date because it happened in Dartmouth Square in Dublin, where I was staying temporarily and whence my father was fetching me to go and see my newly born brother, Conor. I can remember ladies in black dresses crying out and running down the front steps. Everybody was still frightened of cars in 1928. I wasn't hurt; we were hardly moving when the door flew open. The car would have been the parents' first four-wheeled vehicle, a Peugeot, pronounced p-yew-joe. I can remember them later joking about its having no reverse gear, the teeth having been stripped off a cog in the gearbox, so that they had to devise various ingenious manoeuvres if they wanted to come back the way that they had gone. The only other very early memory I have, which surely dates from before Conor's birth or when he was only a baby, is of the imaginary friends I invented to play with and talk about, and their names: Joddy and Chokkum and little Balleen.

My father, Anthony Farrington, had, in 1928, just been appointed Resident Secretary of the Royal Irish Academy which is a foundation somewhat similar to the Royal Society in London. The term "Resident" distinguished his appointment from that of the Secretary of the Academy, which was an honorary post held by a distinguished academic or scientist, though, many years later, my father acceded to that distinction. Until then he was a civil servant, the salaried administrator of an imposing institution whose Members were all Honorary. But "Resident" meant that we lived above the Academy, which was at 19 Dawson Street, in what had once been a magnificent Georgian town house, known as Northland House. We had a marvellous flat on two floors with more rooms that we could ever use, and many of them interconnecting, so that Conor and I could race from room to room around the apartment on our tricycles. The rooms were

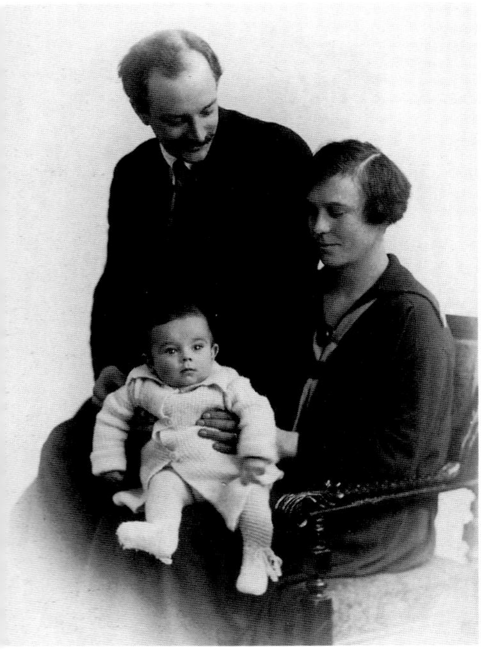

Parents and BF as a baby.

Royal Irish Academy, 19 Dawson Street, Dublin

vast, particularly the one my mother called the Drawing Room whose windows looked out on the Mansion House garden. From there we could watch the comings and goings of Alfie Byrne, who was Lord Mayor of Dublin through most of our childhood, never went anywhere without his gold chain of office, and figured frequently in cartoons in the satirical magazine *Dublin Opinion*, shaking hands with all and sundry.

To reach our flat you had to go through the main front door of the Academy, through the hall, up a magnificent 18th century staircase, with its classical busts and portraits and bas-relief plasterwork, and then up the definitely less splendid back stairs. Visitors would be announced by the hall porter down below with two rings on a bell. One ring announced the delivery of groceries or mail, which were put in a basket hanging down the back stairs on a long rope from a small winch outside the front door of our flat.

Groceries were always delivered. Though my mother would take me shopping for them, in Leverett and Frye or the Monument Creamery in Grafton Street or the butchers in Chatham Street, she never carried them home. An errand boy, with a big basket on the front of his bicycle, would deliver them. And she never paid for anything; the shops would send a bill every week. I enjoyed the shops, especially the grocers, where friendly men in brown aprons would shovel sugar or flour into big brown paper bags and there were hams hanging up and interesting smells. The only place I didn't like was the Bank. I can still remember the sterile boredom of waiting interminably while she did whatever it was people did in those days in banks. The bank was the National City Bank, and the parents were among its first customers, a choice made for patriotic reasons, when it was founded in the early days of the Irish Free State. My mother was furious when, in the seventies, it was taken over by Chase Manhattan.

There was very little traffic in Dublin then. The Peugeot, or my father's motor cycle would often remain parked all day in front of the Academy. The electric trams went rattling up and down Dawson Street with their trolleys hissing on the overhead wires. There was a coal merchant with a horse-drawn dray who would go from street to street calling out "Co-o-o-al Blocks" in a loud voice. There were in fact quite a number of horse-drawn vehicles. I remember the bread vans and above all the most elegant, the prize-winning primrose yellow Court Laundry van, drawn by two beautifully groomed horses. There were several steam-driven coal lorries also.

Life in Dawson Street had its peculiarities. There were no neighbours of course. The only playmates Conor and I, and later, our sister Una, had were the children of our parents' friends, some of whom, when I think back on it, we would not ourselves have chosen as friends. The only way into the building was by the main front door. This was locked every evening with an impressive set of bolts and locks by the hall porter, a burly ex-Royal Navy man called Carroll. Carroll, I never knew his first name, had been a stoker in one of the big battleships at the Battle of Jutland, which he would often describe to us in meticulous and superfluous detail. Any visitor ringing the doorbell after half past five would have to summon this forbidding individual who would put on his uniform with the brass buttons before coming up from his rooms in the basement to answer the door. Visitors to Conor and me, as for example when we were teenagers, were therefore few.

A staircase from the upstairs floor of our flat led to the roof of the building where a predecessor of my father's had installed a greenhouse to grow tomatoes. There a door led out on to the roof itself where you could walk around on duckboards and lean over the low parapet to look down on the street. Conor and I would sometimes bring our friends up there to fly paper darts out over Dawson Street or, once, to try and spit on the passers-by sixty feet below. In later years Una, more intrepid than either Conor or me, would venture out over the roof of the building next door and even, I believe, on to the roof of St Anne's church beyond it.

We were middle class people, though my father's salary was fairly meagre and, as was normal at the time, my mother never had a job. In fact I sometimes wonder now what she did all day, in Dawson Street. When I was little I can remember her going off to play lacrosse. She had a number of friends from pre-war days; she always referred to them by their surnames, Brindley, Dermody, Smyth etc. They may have been lacrosse players also. She had a definite artistic talent and she and my father would go out sketching when we were on holiday. Her pictures were always much better than his. Every summer holiday they made a point of doing watercolour sketches of the house we were staying in.

At that time we always had two maids, Alice and then May, who came and looked after Conor and me, taking us to Merrion Square or to walk along the canal, and, later, Mary. Mary, who came from near Clonmel, lived in a room upstairs beside the kitchen. She did all the housekeeping and cooking. She was an excellent cook and a most likeable person; she was with us for about ten years. She was a very devout Catholic. Mary was paid, I remember, £30 a year. There was also a charlady called Mrs Murray, who was a sort of Sean O'Casey character dressed all in black with a strong Dublin accent. Conor and I used to have our tea in the kitchen every day; the parents of course were served dinner by Mary much later, in the dining room. Mary and Mrs Murray would drink strong tea sweetened with lump sugar, what my Aunt Nancy described once as "Catholic tea". We would crunch up lumps from the sugar bowl and I remember Mrs Murray saying," God, Mary, wouldja lissen to the nise o' them atin' the sugar".

About this time Mary suffered a sad disappointment, though I only heard about it years afterwards. A man named Coggin was working downstairs in what capacity I don't remember, assistant Hall Porter may be. At any rate he and Mary started a friendship which, on Mary's side at least, turned into a serious love affair, probably the first and only one in her life. She came and told my mother that she had accepted a proposal of marriage from Mr Coggin and was going to get married in a few months time. She was supremely happy; I can remember her singing and joking through the day, as I can remember the tears that followed. It turned out that Coggin had been married before, in England, though he had not seen his wife in years. He had been either separated or divorced. That would have made no difference, the priest was quite firm: they could not marry. My father went and argued with him but nothing could be done and in any case Mary would never have gone against the dictates of her religion. But it broke her heart. My mother did her best to console her; I can remember in later years Mary surprising me by the warmth with which she spoke of my mother's kindness and sympathetic nature, and I think it must date from that time. The episode can have done nothing to temper my mother's dislike of the Catholic Church.

Most of the parents' friends were better off than they were. They managed however to have a lot of fun. Both were, so far as I can see, totally indifferent as regards the usual bourgeois preoccupation with social status. He would go around wearing a little French beret though, as you can see in old films, in those days men always wore hats. She, to the end of her life, indulged her taste for bright colours by wearing striking, and often artistically beautiful, but distinctly unusual, combinations of colour. Until they acquired an orthodox Austin A40 after the war, they drove around, after the motor cycles, in a series of egregious vehicles. There was, after the Peugeot I fell out of, a baby Austin, an open tourer of course, since they both scorned what were then called "saloon cars". The baby Austin was painted, by my mother, with a paintbrush, black with bright green mudguards. Later they also acquired, for my father's field work, a three wheeler van with a large motor cycle engine behind the front wheel. When I was at the Dublin High School it was a constant fear that they would come to fetch me after school in this eccentric conveyance. They would both, I think, have been quite indifferent had they realised that Conor and I, and later Una, viewing them through the eyes of our conventional schoolmates, were pained to see them as a pair of freaks.

They had met for the first time at the lonely cottage at the head of Glencree in Wicklow by Lower Loch Bray, where J M Synge is said to have imagined the setting for *In The Shadow Of The Glen*. At the time, and for many years after, teas were served there by a characterful lady by name of Mrs McGurk. The parents and their friends always referred to this place as Mrs McGurk's cottage. They both had motor cycles. My mother rode a Triumph sidecar combination of which I shall have more to tell later. My father had a much more primitive machine with no gear change, the drive being taken directly from a clutch on the main shaft by a belt to a pulley on the rear wheel. Hills could only be climbed if he took a run at them. At Glenmalure he told me how my mother would go and stand at the crossroads to stop any possible traffic on the road at the bottom of the glen, so that he could use the speed gained coming down one side to get him up the hill on the other. It was motor cycles and a love of wild country, in particular County Wicklow, that brought them together. He once told me that he had won my mother's heart, when her Triumph had broken down somewhere above Sally Gap, by retiming the ignition in the dark, by "feel". They were both enthusiastic followers of motor sport, which was an agreeably amateurish affair in those days, and they took Conor and me to watch cross-country motor bike "trials" and road races, of which there were several each year: the 'Skerries 100', the 'Leinster 200' and such like. Once, at Skerries, we saw Stanley Woods, who was a national hero, winner of the TT in the Isle of Man, come round a corner under a bridge, banked over for the next bend, to find a rider and his machine sprawled on their side in the middle of the road. Woods managed, in a second, to right his machine, brake and swerve around the obstruction. On the next lap when he came round, and saw us, the only witnesses of this brilliant, literally, *tour de force*, he gave us a friendly wave which, to use a modern expression, made our day.

Both the parents were very open air people. They would take us on picnics in the Wicklow hills - they had many favourite picnic places - at all times of the year, Conor and I shivering and grumbling in the back of the unheated, unheatable because open, car. Or we would be taken camping, a thing they loved, often in wild and lonely places. It was a fairly spartan business: tents in those days didn't have integral groundsheets, and our sleeping bags were made of blankets which my mother stitched together. Earwigs and small black beetles which could give quite a nasty nip were attracted by the warmth into the bags. The parents bathed and swam, often naked, in rivers, lakes and, of course, the sea, in spring, summer and autumn. They were both, particularly my father, strong swimmers. For a number of years they rented a house at Easter near Brittas Bay in Wicklow, at a place called Jack's Hole. It was a favourite place for picnics and we often went there for the day, starting on St Patrick's Day, when they would have the first bathe of the year. Every year we ate our soggy tomato sandwiches – a speciality of my mother's – sitting on the same rock, and every year my father took a photograph of the rock, as he was interested by the way the level of the sand varied from year to year.

Once at Jack's Hole, on a cold but sunny Spring day, with a north wind blowing, we were walking on the beach and became aware of some excitement nearer the point. A few people had gone swimming and had got into difficulties and were being slowly carried out to sea by the undertow. My father ran to a farmhouse on the edge of the beach and came back with a rope. He tied it round his waist and my mother held it as he went out after the swimmers. He managed to bring two of them to shore but a third was drowned. Meanwhile a small crowd had gathered on the rocks, kneeling and reciting the Rosary. As we walked back to our tent – we were camping that year - my mother vituperated against "those snivelling Catholics, all they could do was pray." My father answered, "Well their prayers were answered, weren't they, since God sent a Protestant with a length of rope?"

Every year we would go away for my father's annual holiday and stay for a month in a rented cottage or house in a different part of Ireland, almost always by the sea. In this way both Conor and I got to know West Cork, Clare and Kerry, Connemara and Donegal as well as places nearer home like Wicklow and Wexford. We rarely went to the same place twice, the parents' idea being that Conor and I should get to know all of our native country. Interestingly we never once went to Northern Ireland. In fact my mother had never been there at all until, in 1960, I drove her across the border in my French car. Her indignation on that occasion at the sight of red letter boxes suggests that politically she was still nearer to De Valera than she probably suspected.

Early in the year they would decide on a place and my mother would write to a Protestant rector or a local doctor asking if there was anywhere we could rent. We never knew what sort of house to expect and it was a game we all joined in, guessing what it would be like as we approached in the car. They varied amazingly, from corrugated iron bungalow to thatched cottage to tumble down mansion. In Dingle where it rained every day for a month the tin roof leaked so we had to have buckets and cans and saucepans all over the floor, and the water

BF age 11.

dripped musically into them all day and all night. In Bantry there was a boat that went with the house, which added a whole extra dimension to the holiday. At another place in West Cork, called Coolkellure, we lived in a few empty rooms in a huge otherwise abandoned Big House, unfurnished except for the beds and chairs etc that we used. If we left the windows open at night bats would come in and fly round the vast echoing bedrooms. "Let them," my mother said. "They eat the midges." At Milltown Malbay there were the rusting remains of a shipwrecked steamer on the rocks to climb over. Also there were nuns on the beach there, spooky figures all in black, but with smiling faces when they came close and offered us toffees. My mother discouraged this, fearful, I believe, that they might whip us off and surreptitiously baptise us. In Donegal when I was 12 there were handloom weavers and when we got back to Dublin I made a loom out of Meccano and wove a scarf with it for Una's teddy. The last time I saw Conor, a few weeks before he died, we talked of those summers, going through, name after name, all the places where we had spent our childhood holidays.

My father came from Cork where his family, who were Congregationalists, had been established since the end of the 18th century. My grandfather, Thomas Farrington, who died the year before I was born, was a chemist, an analyst with a firm called Jennings that made lemonade and other soft drinks. He had discovered a way to extract magnesium, which for some reason was essential to the manufacture of fizzy lemonade at the time, from sea water. The firm had in fact been founded to exploit this discovery. My father would describe visits to a hut on the seashore where his dad would operate this process. He had an agreement with the firm by which, though the secret remained his property, he undertook not to patent it or communicate it to anyone else. When he died Jennings suddenly found themselves in serious financial difficulties because he had never written the formula down, being justifiably fearful, according to my aunt Queenie, that if he wrote it down and they got hold of it they could terminate his employment. A Unionist in politics and a JP, he was, in my father's words, "a sincere Christian but a most tolerant man. He must have been to stand us all, who went pretty much against his whole tradition and feeling". At some time, early in the century, a Turkish lawyer, called Bey, arrived in Cork as a political refugee, asking for help. My grandfather asked what he could do. Obviously there was not much opening in Cork for an expert in Turkish law. "I can make lokoum," he told Thomas Farrington, who lent him enough money to set himself up as a confectioner. In a few years Hadji Bey's Turkish Delight became famous as a Cork *specialité*. But the Bey family never forgot my grandfather's gesture, and for fifty years or more gifts of Turkish sweetmeats would arrive at the Cork Farrington's door every Christmas.

They lived, Thomas Farrington, his wife and five children and various unmarried relatives, in a smallish house in Summerhill Terrace in Cork. My father once described Thomas Farrington and an uncle, setting off to walk across Cork for work in the mornings. They would play chess as they walked. I imagine the dialogue, in singing Cork accents:

"Pawn to K4,"

"No, you can't do that; you're forgetting my Bishop is on K4."

"Sorry, so he is, well then Pawn to K5.

In 1946, when I was in Holland, one of the Dutch students, whose father was a chess enthusiast, asked me was I any relation of the Thomas Farrington who had been European champion of postcard chess twenty five years before. When I told my father this he was surprised. He had never known of his father's international eminence as a chess player.

My grandmother, née Emily Foreman, died when my father was only six. Her brother, Stephen Foreman, whom we called Uncle Dean for some reason, had written several novels and lived in Cork in Redclyffe, a big house on the Western Road which his wife Emma ran as a select boarding house. When I was little we used to go to Cork every year to spend Christmas, and would stay there, in rooms vacated for the festive season I suppose. Aunt Emmy, as we called her, was different from all the other adults that loomed over us as children. She was a Catholic, and Dean had converted to Catholicism to marry her, which had caused no small family upset when it happened but was more or less forgiven by the time I remember. She had been an army nurse at the time of the Somme, had a loud voice and a rich Cork accent. Even though I was very small I sensed, hearing her giving orders to the various servants, a different sort of authority from that exerted by the middle class Protestants I knew in Dublin. Though she bossed them around she was on much more familiar terms than, for example, my mother ever could be with Mary, our domestic.

On one of those Christmas visits to Cork my cousin Rosemary brought me to see a lady who lived down the road from them, called Miss Jack. Miss Jack had been a governess early in the century to the Tolstoy family, in Moscow, but the thing that interested us was the revolver she kept by her bedside. She explained to Rosemary and me that she would never use it since it says in the Bible that "they that live by the sword shall die by the sword," and she "would not want to die that way". Miss Jack spoke with a strong Cork brogue. Twenty or more years later my uncle Ben was in Moscow and visited the Tolstoy museum where he was shown around by Tolstoy's daughter. He was interested to notice that she spoke excellent English but with a distinct Cork intonation.

Thomas Farrington's five children, "Queenie", Stephen, Benjamin, Anthony and Nancy, all distinguished themselves in later life in spite of the fact that their mother died when they were all quite small. My father once told me how, when he was little, he would climb into his mother's bed in the mornings and then suddenly, one day, there was a baby there as well. It would, I think, have been one of twins, both of whom died. And then, a few days later, his mother had died too, of puerperal fever I think. He was six years old. The five children were brought up then by the unmarried aunts. My father told me how, when the time came to give the aunts their morning kiss before leaving for school, as the youngest boy he used to be pushed forward by the others, so that it was always he that got the dewdrop off Great Aunt Debby's nose.

Years later, quite late in his life, my father wrote to me in a letter about his mother:

> I hardly knew her but she left a great tradition of beauty, intelligence and strength, not only in the family but in a great circle of Cork people. I have few memories of her. One comes to mind. I had been for one of my solitary rambles. It was winter and I remember coming up the Wellington Road in Cork, walking in the gutter because the snow was deepest there. Then I got home and was welcomed, no scolding. She changed my shoes and stockings before the kitchen fire. I remember the feel of her warm hands and the long, black, thick, comforting woollen stockings. A few things like that are all I have, and it is now getting

on for sixty five years since she died, but her unfailing tenderness – it comes in all my memories - can soothe me still.

I have many clear memories of all my uncles and aunts. All, that is, except the eldest, Victoria, who was called Queenie for obvious reasons. She married a man called Tom Jacob and lived in Waterford. I don't know why I knew the Waterford people so much less well than the others. I suspect it was because my mother, who had strong and, it seemed to us, often irrational, likes and dislikes, didn't care for them. She certainly didn't get on very well with my Aunt Maud, Stephen's wife, who came from Lurgan in Northern Ireland and was a Unionist. Maud was a highly intelligent woman who wrote a thesis on Calvin in later life, but she was very conventional. Queenie, on the other hand, had a wide range of less orthodox cultural interests and enthusiasms. She had wanted, I learned long afterwards, to leave Tom Jacob and marry his cousin Willie instead, and was talked out of this by her puritanical brothers, Stephen and my father. In the end they formed some sort of *ménage à trois* which must have interested people in the small town of Waterford.

Stephen himself, the eldest uncle, we saw often. He was City Engineer of Cork and came up to Dublin regularly for meetings. He was tall and lean, with a distinctive way of speaking, above all when he was telling a story - he was a marvellous raconteur. Whenever he came Conor and I would sit at the back of the room as he told of his latest *déboires* with the Cork City Council or its General Manager, Mr Monaghan, keeping dead quiet for fear the parents would notice that we were still there and send us to bed. He always had interesting and unusual cars. One, a huge bright yellow Talbot, was, in his words, "so long it wouldn't fit round corners." Another had to be started with a very long starting handle. Threading this object through the various layers of steel sheet was, Stephen said, "like taking up dropped stitches in knitting". Stephen came to stay with us when we were on holiday near Bantry in 1932, in a house the rent for which included use of a boat. Some time not long after this he built the first of a succession of boats. The biggest of these, Craobhin was a 16 foot sailing boat in which I first learnt to sail in Cork Harbour, and on the open Atlantic at Helvick Head where they had a holiday cottage.

Nancy, the youngest aunt, lived in Lisburn with my uncle Bob Clarke who was also a civil engineer. They were politically very much to the left. Though Bob Clarke was never a member of the British Communist Party he was a firm Stalinist, and remained so, a Stalinist fellow-traveller as Ben said, until the end of his life. Nancy, who I got to know better in later life, was a very warm, friendly and amusing person. I remember her describing some over-pious neighbour as "the sort of woman who can't leave her soul alone, she keeps on scratching at it as though it had some sort of spiritual impetigo". But the most memorable thing about her was her voice. Like my father she was a trained singer, with a lovely clear contralto voice and a distinctive style of expression. I believe she broadcast, from BBC Northern Ireland, though I never heard her. But what I do remember, and very vividly, was her unaccompanied singing of Irish folk songs. She was asked to sing at one of Stephen's daughter's weddings, and I can still hear the way that rich voice rang out from the gallery, filling the whole church, singing St Columba's hymn Be Thou My Vision, maintaining the tension all the way through the long phrases of that most beautiful, typically Irish, tune.

But, of my two uncles and two aunts, the one I knew best and was closest to in several ways, was Benjamin, though I was in my twenties before I got to know him. He had been a lecturer in classics in various Irish universities, ending up in Belfast where his political involvement began and he joined Sinn Fein. In 1920 he went to the University of Cape Town. He rapidly became a Senior Lecturer and then Professor of Latin there. About the same time he became involved in left-wing politics in Africa and it was in this context that he got to know, and came to love, a remarkable Jewish intellectual, Ruth Schechter, a friend of Olive Schreiner. Ruth was already married to an eccentric and liberal Member of the South African Parliament, Morris Alexander. Together they all worked out a separation and divorce and Ben and Ruth married round about the time, in 1935, that Ben was appointed Professor of Classics at Swansea in Wales.

Divorce was, of course, in those days a scandalous affair, and Ben received some terrible letters from members of the family in Cork, cutting off all contact with this black, or rather red (both Ben and Ruth had joined the British Communist Party) sheep. My father, I am proud and pleased to say, had no time for this, and, together with my aunt Queenie, maintained a friendly contact with Ben and Ruth all through the row. They came to visit us and I have a memory of a very likeable person with dark red hair, though Baruch Hirson, who wrote a book in 2001 about Ruth Schechter and her circle, knew no other reference to her hair colour. She wrote to my father about my first little book of poetry. I never saw the letter but I remember him saying that praise from her was something special since she had a very high reputation as a reviewer. She died at the comparatively young age of fifty three, in 1942. Ben married again and had a daughter, my cousin Jane Straker, who has inherited her father's dedication to radical causes and is an active environmentalist.

I used to stay with Ben and his second wife, Barbara, on my way to and from France, first in Swansea and then in Lymington where they moved when Ben retired. Ben always had an interested ear for my varied developing enthusiasms and always came up with thought-stimulating comments. I had found it harder to talk to my father in those years for some reason. In Swansea Ben and my aunt Barbara lived a few doors down from Dylan Thomas's parents, who they knew

Professor Ben Farrington

quite well. Ben had, however little time for Dylan's poetry, and criticised *Under Milk Wood* for expressing "just a pub's eye view of the world".

Though Ben was well-known as a classical scholar, an authority on the rationalism of Epicurus and Lucretius, his main interest was the relation of science to practical life. This is shown by the titles of his best known books, which were still in print until quite recently: *Greek Science: Its Meaning for Us*, and *Science and Politics in the Ancient World*. He saw the ultimate weakness of ancient science in its divorce from practical life – it became a way of knowing and not of doing. Greek, and later Roman, society, depending on slaves, failed to see the need to apply knowledge to the development of technology. It was a view that led him in later life to work on Francis Bacon about whom he wrote two books, one with the revealing sub-title: *Philosopher of Industrial Science*.

This was the first of Ben's books that I read. Having to study, and later to lecture on, Bacon's essays I had failed to find Bacon interesting, in spite of the pithy common-sense of his essays, which of course we studied, from a purely literary point of view. Ben highlighted the revolutionary nature of Bacon's observation, in the *Novum Organum*, that: "three things: printing, gunpowder and the magnet have done more to change the world than the conquest of any empire or the emergence of any new religion", this was a revelation to me. Though the subjects of Ben's books might seem at first sight off-putting, they were marvellously easy to read thanks to the clear, unstuffy, style in which they were written. And the gentle humour. As for example, in *Greek Science*, when he described Anaximenes's explanation of rarefied and condensed mist: the air is warm when you blow on your hand with your mouth open but cold when you blow from pursed lips. Ben says : "Anaximenes did not know the true explanation of this phenomenon. Do you?"

There cannot have been many Marxist professors of Greek, I know of only one other. And Ben's membership of the Communist Party obviously made life difficult for him. For one thing it meant that he could not accept any of the many invitations he received to lecture in the United States The first time I stayed with him in Swansea, in 1950, the local paper had on its front page a photograph of a left-wing demo, with Ben in the front rank, bearing a placard saying No to Atomic Weapons. "Another headache for the Vice Chancellor," said Ben, who was at the time, academically, one of the most distinguished members of the university's staff.

Another memory of that first visit. We had been to a performance by his students of a Greek tragedy, I don't remember which. Ben got out the text and explained to me how much of the power of the play hung on the implications of one single word, spoken by one of the characters, which the students had emphasised correctly. And then there was the Sunday evening. We had been for a long walk on the Gower. Just before going to bed, Ben was going round pulling curtains and tidying when Barbara suddenly said. "I haven't had time to look at the Sunday papers, Ben. Was there anything in them?" Ben said, "Well, in the *Observer* there was an article by Edward Crankshaw who was saying..." And there followed a complete résumé of articles and book reviews and the description of a cartoon. I could just remember him vaguely browsing through the papers over breakfast. I never put down a Sunday or other newspaper now without thinking how little I can remember of what I think I've read.

My father was the youngest of the three brothers. In 1914 or 1915, when he was due to start at university, he had some health problem, possibly a primo infection of TB. Or else there was some emotional upset. Anyway he went to work in Portugal as tutor to an English mining engineer's family, where he stayed for several years. He came home as the war was ending and did a degree in University College Cork, in engineering. It was around this time, in 1920 to be precise, that he had an upsetting experience which he only described to me long years after. He became very friendly with a young woman from Denmark who was staying with his sister, my aunt Queenie, as some sort of au pair, a Miss Peterson. She went back to Denmark but returned when Queenie's second child was born. The friendship deepened but with Miss Peterson it became something much more, though my father never suspected this. Then, in his words,

"One day she came to me and poured out a surprising tale; that she was travel-

> ling incognito by the permission of her educators and counsellors; and that she was a pure blooded Hapsburg, by name Countess Jeanne Christine Von Peruthgraz; that she had been brought up with one idea only, that she should further Hapsburg interests by marriage, and finally that her marriage with Alexander of Serbia was being negotiated but that she had changed and had written to Alexander asking to be released. As you may imagine I was incredulous. But some time afterwards there arrived by post a letter from Serbia covered with crowns and seals. I took it and gave it to her. Shortly afterwards she came beaming to tell me that Alexander had released her and that she was free. I still have a series of letters I got from her when, as Countess Von Peruthgraz, she was in Serbia for the marriage of Alexander in the summer of 1922. It was during September that she suddenly broke down and confessed passionate love for me. There were terribly difficult scenes. I could not give way ... perhaps I was a little bit frightened and I had a sure feeling that deep respect and affection was not the right basis for marriage at 26. But I was very torn and was glad to escape to Dublin to the (Geological) Survey where I went in December. I corresponded with her up to the time I got engaged and then by her wish we stopped writing. I regretted this as she was one of the finest people I have ever known."

He trained, as I said, as an engineer. When I was going through his papers after he died I came on a plan of a patch of land. Scribbled across it in his handwriting were the words, "Joe McKinsey paid me 10 shillings to survey this field. The only money I ever earned as an engineer." His first real job however was in Wicklow, on the Geological Survey. I don't know at what point his lifelong enthusiasm for geology started. I am sure, however, that having a job which involved a lot of fieldwork and which called for a high degree of skill in observing and distinguishing natural phenomena helped to focus his interest towards geomorphology. His research in that field ended up by earning him an honorary doctorate from the National University of Ireland. Conor and I were probably a disappointment to him because our interests when we were growing up were purely literary. In later years I at least came to have an interest in science, and to value the scientific attitude to knowledge, when I gave up trying to teach literature and went over instead to studying and lecturing on linguistics.

His basically scientific attitude to life and the broad range of phenomena to which he applied it were apparent all through our childhood. For example when we were little if ever we had hiccups he would take out his watch and time them. Then he would tell us when the next hiccup was due so we could suppress it. It was a cure that always worked; I don't know why because any time I ever tried to time a child's hiccups they didn't seem to come at regular intervals. Then there was his advice when we had mislaid something. "Stop looking for it," he'd say, "Sit down instead, and think." Whenever we were ill when we were

My father and Una's daughter Mary

small he, rather than my mother, took our temperatures, though that, I think, came more from his caring than from his scientific persona.

When we were little my father, who loved children, was great fun to play with and good at thinking up adventurous games. In later years, when we had a week-end cottage at Ticknock, the parents would hold a Halloween party the main feature of which was a paper chase which involved sending a troop of children in unsuitable footwear scrambling through gorse bushes and over barbed wire fences. Once the trail laid by me, who was the "hare" that year, crossed a trail belonging to some totally different paper chase. A chase of paper became a chase of wild goose all over Kilmashogue until my father, who was following the "hounds" to see that no stragglers got lost, noticed that the scraps of paper composing the trail came from some Catholic or English journal that was foreign to our household.

Warm, affectionate and often very funny, he was all the same a very reserved, private person. I have no memory of him kissing me even when I was quite small. His letters to me when I had left home were often quite long, always interesting and thoughtful, but he always signed them Yours A F. One incident stands out. When I was 15 I had a nasty accident. Cycling along a darkened road I ran into the back of some sort of cart and smashed my four front teeth. I made my way home in the tram and my father took me to a dentist he knew who lived nearby, in Stephens Green. As we walked up Dawson Street he briefly put his

My father on Slieve Tuohy

arm round my shoulder and pressed me to him. The memory of that gesture is precious to me, all the more because it was unique.

I tried to read some of his scientific articles but they were too technical for me and I gave up. But in 1964, when he was nearly seventy I several times spent a day with him on the hills in Donegal. He wanted to explore Slieve Tuohy, the ridge of hills that we looked across the bay at from Rosbeg, but thought it was wiser not to go alone. They were long days for he was still a very strong walker; we went over the ridge and right down to the water's edge in one place as well as traversing all the tops. At one point we were finding our way through the peat haggs at the top of the mountain. (Peat haggs are the misshapen banks of peat left standing by the weathering process on a mountain top.) Where the top layer of peat had been stripped off he noticed that the stones on the surface tended to lie in roughly circular patterns. He thought it was probably an effect of alternate freezing and thawing. What struck me, though, was that he should have noticed it. Even after he had described the phenomenon to me I found it hard to see examples until he had pointed them out. It seemed to me at the time an example of the scientific mind being trained to distinguish patterns in nature that the untrained eye doesn't notice. He was of course very observant. It was not just that he noticed so many things, it was the number of fields in which he displayed a degree of specialised knowledge, and above all the way in which he related them to each other. That day on Slieve Tuohy we saw a kestrel and he described - was it a certain rock formation? a type of moss hanging on the face of a cliff? I don't remember - where he had noticed that kestrel's nests were likely to be found. On that or maybe on some other occasion I remember him criticising the overspecialisation of today's scientists. "Geologists nowadays," he said, "never know anything about birds, and the ornithologists are amazingly ignorant about plants." Another criticism he had was of, usually young, scientists who, he said, wouldn't follow up a hunch unless they could get someone to pay them to do it.

At some stage he had been trained as a singer and he had a fine and very tuneful voice. He actually once came very near to winning first place at the Feis Ceoil, the Irish music festival. The judges were undecided between him and another and they got them both to repeat one of the pieces. It was a Purcell aria, *Ye Twice Ten Thousand Deities*, with a lot of runs and repetitions and my father unfortunately stumbled over the words at one point, so he lost. The other singer went on to make several gramophone records and to give recitals. I don't remember his name. Once Eoin O'Mahoney, a picturesque Cork lawyer who knew everyone in the country, was having lunch in the University Club in Stephens Green with Peter Allt, my teacher at St Columba's. Seeing my father, beret on his head, rucksack on his back, heading for the Ticknock bus, O'Mahoney pointed him out, saying, "There goes Farrington, the loveliest voice in the whole of the County Cork." There were not many pianists among the parents' friends but whenever one came they would be persuaded to accompany him. He had a huge repertoire of songs, Elizabethan and Victorian, and also Irish settings by composers like Stanford or Herbert Hughes. In later years Conor, who had an enviable gift for sight-reading at the piano, added to his repertoire, and my father would sing to his accompaniment on Sunday evenings. A lover of chamber music and an enthusiastic opera-goer, connoisseur of *bel canto*, he had little time for untrained folk singers however authentic. In fact I think his opinion was that the more authentic they were the worse they sang.

My mother, Doreen Synge, came from the English branch of an Anglo-Irish Ascendancy family, whose tree stretches back at least to the sixteenth century. The original name was Millington but some ancestor sang so beautifully that the name was changed. There were Synges in Ireland from the seventeenth century. A bishop ancestor refused to ordain Oliver Goldsmith because he turned up for the ceremony wearing red plush breeches, or so the story went. Early in the 19th century one Francis Synge made a lot of money exporting

My mother & Una

My mother in her seventies

goods – I can't find out what exactly – to England, and built Glanmore Castle, a scaled down Scottish baronial style mansion by the Devil's Glen in Wicklow. My mother, who was born in London and lived there with her parents, spent school holidays at Glanmore with her brother Francis who was her elder by four years. There was a possibility that Francis would eventually inherit Glanmore. It was with Glanmore in mind that, when she left school, my mother got some training in horticulture and worked in various places as a "lady gardener". The estate was then owned, and the castle inhabited, by the widow of the first Francis Synge's grandson, Edith, and her second husband a Major Gardiner who, we were told once, believed his bottom was made of glass and wouldn't sit down for fear of breaking it. On Edith's death Glanmore was to go to my grandfather. She lived, however, on and on so that, when she eventually expired, both my grandfather and his son, my mother's brother Francis, were no longer there to inherit Glanmore and it went to some other distant cousin, who sold it. The castle and some of the lands were later bought back into the family by another cousin, Robert Synge, an engineer, who had made a fortune in Argentina. He lived there - I can just remember him - with his daughter Kathleen, who eventually sold it. My mother had mixed feelings about all this. She loved the place, and the Devil's Glen was, and is, certainly a beauty spot, but I can't believe she would have wanted to be a landlord.

I think my mother had mixed feelings about the Synge family. Though she kept in touch with all her close relatives, so far as I remember she only saw the ones she actively liked, such as the doctor Victor or his brother John Lighton, the mathematician. I always felt that she had more in common with her cousin the playwright J. M. Synge, who was something of a black sheep, than with his very conventional family, none of whom went to see any of his plays performed. When, years later, I published a poem in the *Irish Times* about J. M. Synge that was critical of the Synge family, she wrote warmly congratulating me on it.

HOMAGE TO J.M.SYNGE

There was always the imperial Parent, looking on,
Time-honoured know-all, brooking no answer back,
Sagacious, deprecating, self-appointed
Author of our achievements;
Always there, the strict correct paternal
Umpire that his sons would never set on.

You can't have understood what you were doing,
And if you had you'd likely have suppressed it:
[Your brother, evicting tenants in Mayo,
Maintained the family incomes that you lived on.]
You tried to opt out, only half succeeded,
Broke, not poor, you never looked for a job:
Art for art's sake on a private pittance.
And yet, tenebrous mollycoddle with the silver tongue,
It came from you, or through you, it was yours
The stark triumphant image, faked out in prancing words,
The bootstrap myth that made of us the first
New Nation. No wonder they couldn't take it,
The Independent readers in their Pit,
No wonder they tried to chase you from the stage
When you reached for the loy to split that meddler's crown!

I know very little about my grandparents on my mother's side. Her father, Alexander Hamilton Synge, invested unwisely in Russian oil exploration. Unfortunately this was before the drilling at Baku bore fruit and he lost almost all his money. Her mother, Georgina Mary Graves, came from a family whose name, like the Synges, can be traced back to the sixteenth century. The poets Alfred Perceval Graves and, later, his son Robert were distant cousins. My mother hardly ever spoke about her parents. They both died young, she in 1911 and he the year after. When my mother was about 15 she was offered a choice of expensive schools: either Roedean or St Leonard's in St Andrews, Scotland. She told me that she chose St Leonard's because it was a long way away from home. She was very happy there and all her life she had a prejudice in favour of Scotland and things Scottish as a result. Her best friend at school, to whom she remained close all through their lives, though they didn't meet again until they were in their eighties, was a girl called Hilda Gifford. Hilda's father was Rector at Aviemore and Doreen spent holidays there, climbing mountains and riding ponies. I think it was there that she got her passion for wild nature. Aviemore then was just one little Highland village among many. Hilda never married. She had a successful career and was headmistress of a huge girls' school in Liverpool. When I was teaching in Hoylake she invited me out a number of times to her beautiful flat. A kindly person, very cultured with, I could sense, a lot of authority, as befits a headmistress. In 2003 I happened to be in Aviemore with time to kill and managed to locate the house which is still known as the Old Rectory and is now a guesthouse. Its new owner told me he had just that week replaced the century-old wallpaper in the bedrooms, the paper my mother would have slept beside nearly a hundred years before.

When war came in 1914 Doreen joined the V.A.D. – the women's Voluntary Aid Detachment - and was trained to drive and maintain ambulances. She spent the war years in France doing this. Her brother, Francis, was a Captain in the Irish Guards and won the MC. He was killed in action in 1917.

At the end of the war Doreen spent her demob gratuity, to the strong disapproval of all her family, on a 500cc Triumph motorcycle and sidecar. With three speed gearbox, a manual oil pump that you had to keep pumping and belt drive, it was the latest model. I have a clear memory of this vehicle; I used to enjoy watching the engine valves going up and down. She used to take Conor and me to school in it when the Baby Austin broke down. We also used to go for drives with it in the Wicklow Mountains. I can still remember the belt drive slipping and breaking and how cold we were. My mother never felt the cold, or else maybe she liked it. She was very tough. She and my father started the day, all through the year, with a cold bath. They did this all their lives. She only stopped when she was very old because, with arthritis, she found it difficult to get into and out of the bath.

Her first long trip with the Triumph and sidecar after the War was to Ireland, where she arrived, I think, early in 1919. There the Irish War of Independence had started. Doreen found that many of her Dublin and Wicklow friends were involved on the Nationalist side. She joined Cumann na mBan, the women's branch of the movement for independence, where the usefulness to the nationalist cause of this determined young lady with a V.A.D. uniform, a cut glass English accent and a motorcycle and sidecar, was immediately obvious. At one time she was given the job of driving the Countess Markievicz around

Dublin and Wicklow. The Countess – she was Irish, married to a Polish count – disguised herself by wearing a motoring veil over her hat. When they were stopped my mother would explain that she was taking her aunt for a drive in the country. I don't know how long this went on for but it must have been quite a time because she told me that she shared a flat just off Frederick Street in Dublin with the Countess. She remarked once how untidy Markievicz was: she just threw her clothes and things down anywhere, being used to having servants to pick them up. Untidy, but also resourceful. There was the time when they were looking after a lot of politically dangerous papers and were afraid the flat might be raided by the police. The Countess packed all the papers into an antique chest she had and my mother drove with this in the sidecar to a second-hand furniture dealer Markievicz knew. This happened to be just down or across the road from what is now Pearse Street police station. "Put it in the window," said Markievicz. "No one will think of looking there." The chest remained there until the Treaty.

Around the same time my mother was involved in what I think was called the Boycott Britain movement. She drove around County Meath and Louth persuading shopkeepers not to handle British made goods. She told me two stories about this time. Once she was with two girls in County Louth somewhere and they passed a Catholic church. The girls wanted to go in and accomplish some religious duty. "You go on," said Doreen, "And I'll wait for you here." When the two discovered from this that Doreen was a Protestant they simply could not believe it and insisted that she must be joking. And then there was the time she went to Drogheda. She had been given the name of a contact, a person sympathetic to the cause, so she went to him, a Mr Monaghan. He was appalled, said: "Go away, go away! You can't do anything here; the place is full of soldiers and police." "I know," said Doreen, "So is everywhere. That's why we're here." But he wouldn't give any help or advice, pretended he didn't know her when she went about the business of going into shops distributing her leaflets. It's certainly true, they were dangerous times. But years after, when my uncle Stephen was City Engineer of Cork, he had problems getting on with the City Manager, a somewhat small-minded official. It was the same Mr Monaghan, who had probably got the job thanks to his heroic share in the fight for Irish freedom.

There were certainly other stories about her activities, but Doreen never told them, and she only told me these at the very end of her long life. Until then she would never speak of her time with Cumann na mBan, though it is clear she had been active enough to have earned two medals later from the Irish Government. The medals came with the right to travel gratis on all public transport in the Republic, an appreciable privilege that disappeared when free travel was granted to all pensioners.

The reason for my mother's silence was her experience of the horrors of the Civil War that followed the War of Independence. She described to me once in glowing terms the relief and the rejoicing when the Truce was called and, later, the Treaty presented to the Dail. "And then," she said, "It was all spoilt by De Valera, and suddenly people you had trusted with your life had turned overnight into enemies". Though she didn't name anyone when she told me this she was probably thinking of the Countess, who had voted against acceptance of the Treaty. My mother blamed De Valera for the Civil War that followed and she never forgave him for it. Until she died she wouldn't suffer a good word to be spoken about him in her presence and she always voted Fine Gael, though she disapproved of most of the Fine Gael party's policies. In fact she supported radical causes actively all her life. These ranged from a lobbying group that she ran in favour of roadside tree-planting to CND, and included demonstrating in the street, when she was nearly 90 years old, against the ESB who were vandalising the East side of Merrion Square. Her dislike of De Valera didn't, however, prevent her being friendly with some Fianna Fail supporters such as, for example, Erskine Childers, with whose children, Ruth and Erskine B. we used to play. She used to say of Childers, when he was a young TD and they occasionally met, that he was "very bumptious". However she was pleased when he was made President of Ireland on the death of De Valera, described him as "our most appropriate president since Douglas Hyde", and was sincerely distressed when he died at a relatively early age.

A final word about St Leonard's, which is still one of the most expensive schools in Britain. When my daughter Roisin wrote to them about her grandmother's schooldays and they said they were interested in hearing about the lives of past pupils I wrote to tell them how an Old Girl of the school had earned two medals from the Irish Government. They didn't reply.

Dawson Street, however, was too urban a setting to suit either of the parents with their love of wild country and with my mother's enthusiasm for gardening. Some fortunate financial windfall enabled them, in 1932, to buy three and a half acres of land at Ticknock in the Dublin Mountains, and to build what we all called a cottage there, high up – 900 feet - on the side of Three Rock Mountain. The house was designed to fit plans largely drawn up by my mother. Unfortunately the builder got the orientation wrong when laying out the foundations so that it was slightly twisted round, and the window my mother had designed to face the splendid view of Dublin Bay looked out instead on a rock bank. The building was carried out using an original technique patented by an acquaintance of the parents, called, I think, Waller, under the name of Nofrango. Internal and external walls, and even the roof, were built by constructing a framework of timber and hanging sheets of hessian between the uprights, and then daubing the hessian with liquid cement. As the hessian tended to sag with the weight of the cement it was difficult to get the walls straight, and the ceilings and roof had vaguely pagoda-like curves. The technique made for strength and the house is still standing to this day. Unfortunately, it turned out not to be an economic method of construction because daubing the cement onto the hessian was classified by the trade unions as plasterers' work, and plasterers were paid at a higher rate than any other building worker. So the house at Ticknock is one of the only examples of Nofrango in existence. It had, we were told at the time, the only Nofrango roof that didn't leak. It was a reputation that outlived the reality; every winter for many years my father had to clamber around on the roof squeezing some black gooey stuff out of a tube into the cracks.

As the years went by they gradually tamed the wilderness of gorse bushes and thorn around the house. Flower beds, beech hedges, a variety of unusual shrubs and a sizeable vegetable garden appeared. A large quarry hole was lined with cement and filled with rainwater. It wasn't big enough to swim in but made an agreeable open air cold bath. My father built a garage out of two of the crates used for importing motor cars; they could be purchased quite cheaply. He also designed and built an ingenious earth closet. A door opened into an area of about 25 square feet enclosed in high wooden walls. Inside this space a moveable seat, with a small canopy over it against the rain, was placed over a deep hole in the ground. When the time came the hole would be filled in, a new hole dug and the seat moved. My mother planted sweet peas around the walls, which grew marvellously. I often wonder now if the richer dust concealed in this corner of a Ticknock field still produces an unusually luxuriant growth.

All through my childhood we spent week-ends and school holidays at Ticknock, playing in the wild garden or roaming the hills around: Kilmashogue, Tibradden and of course Three Rock Mountain with its big granite tors. My love of long lonely days on the hills, rarely indulged in later life, started at Ticknock. There was no electricity or telephone in the house and there was only rainwater. When we would arrive up on a Friday evening in winter everything was damp and had to be aired. The only heating for this was a turf fire, with a Pearse rotary bellows that Conor and I enjoyed turning, filling the room with steam rising from the bedding. Light was from candles or paraffin lamps.

We were as I have said, middle-class people, and Protestants, though the parents never went to church or saw that we received any religious instruction, apart from what was unavoidable at the schools we went to. When I was about six years old my mother managed to procure a key to Merrion Square and we used to be taken there by Maisie or Mary. There we played with a disparate group of small children whose presence in the Square was probably as illegitimate as ours. We quickly formed into gangs, to play our cowboy and Indian games, and the gangs were Catholic or Protestant. I joined the Catholics for

Ticknock cottage in the Dublin Mountains and the main room

some reason, the name meaning nothing to me. But whoever was in charge of us, Maisie or Mary, quickly told me that I had no choice in the matter, I was born a member of the Protestant gang. If I remember the incident it must be because it had some importance. Certainly from a very early age I saw society as divided into two classes: people like us, i.e. middle class proddy intellectuals, and everyone else. And the "everyone else" tended to be, implicitly though certainly not exclusively, Catholic. Since our family had no religion the distinction was purely social.

A more important social distinction was brought home dramatically to Conor and me by a mishap which occurred when I was about eight, and which I remember vividly. My mother had taken us for a picnic at Portmarnock in the company of one or two other mothers and children. We were on our way home in two or maybe three cars, one of them being a large American Ford belonging to the Borums, an American family whose two children were at Park House School with us. We came into the north side of the city, through some of the worst of Dublin's appalling slums. Coming down Gardiner Street, which in those days was lined on both sides by shabby tenements with front doors hanging loose and stained or broken windows, the Borums' car suddenly had a puncture and we all had to stop. Punctures were a frequent occurrence in those days, but not everyone was as proficient as my mother at dealing with them. She took some time, however, jacking up the Ford and changing the wheel while the other two mothers fussed around talking of getting help from a garage.

What I remember of the incident, however, was the horde of slum children of all ages that quickly surrounded us, sitting on the running boards, climbing over the bonnets of the cars, reaching in and tooting the horn of the Ford, which was operated by squeezing a large rubber bulb, and above all peering in through the windows at us, posh kids with our buckets and spades. I can see them now, many of them barefoot and with streaming snotty noses, their patched or ragged clothes either too big or too small for them, their excited voices. My mother fended them off as best she could while she tightened the wheel nuts and put the jack away. "Mummy," said one of the Borum children, "Why do they smell so?" "Well, I suppose," said Mrs Borum, "It's because their mummies don't have enough money to buy soap." I don't remember being at all frightened by this intimidating mob of alien children. Small as I was, the emotion I remember was intense embarrassment and, yes, something resembling shame.

Middle class we may have been but, regarding our sense of identity, one thing is clear from my earliest memories: we saw ourselves as Irish, and nothing else. In this we were certainly different from many of the children we were at school with, and even from other people we met. For example, May, our youngest domestic, who came to "look after" Una, and who used to regale us with accounts of the films she saw at the Princess Cinema, which she visited three times a week. I remember asking May what old Irish songs she knew, assuming that, being Catholic working class, she would be more Irish than we were. I was slightly shocked to find she didn't know any and had no time at all for "all that oul' Irish stuff".

On the other hand many of our schoolfellows, particularly at Avoca School, had a world view that was distinctly West British, when it wasn't plain British full stop. In his memoir, *Running the Rapids,* Kildare Dobbs, who I knew at St Columbas, describes himself as having been "raised in an already obsolete tradition and educated for a role that no longer existed", i.e. helping to run the British Empire. Nothing could have been further from the self-image that the parents, consciously or unconsciously, helped to form in us. They saw themselves, and us, as citizens of a new, Irish, nation. In fact, now I think of it, I can remember Dobbs, who I admired greatly at school, saying how, playing away matches, it was only at Portora (the public school Oscar Wilde went to in Northern Ireland) that you met people you would want to consort with. I certainly never ever felt anything like that. The boys I met at matches against Blackrock College or Clongowes were slightly different from us, but that was all.

Once when I was eight or nine years old, walking down Kildare Street my mother pointed out a distinctive, unusual, and, now much remembered figure, a tall man with a shock of blue-white hair, a distinctive unusual coat, a big floppy tie and an eye-glass on a black ribbon. He was walking with his head thrown back and not looking about him. I remember all this because my mother told me to. "You must remember this," she said, "always. You have seen W B Yeats, the poet." On another occasion, though it can hardly have been the same day, she pointed out to me an even more strangely garbed personage, a lady all in black, like something in an old photograph, who she told me was Madame Gonne MacBride, Yeats's "loveliest woman born."

In later years I saw Maud Gonne quite often, she was a distinctive and familiar figure around Dublin. She wore Victorian mourning, long black widow's weeds all her life for her husband, John MacBride, the "drunken vainglorious lout" of Yeats's poem on 1916. And that tall figure in a black veil down to her ankles is not easy to forget. My best memory, though, is of sitting beside her at a performance of, of all things, Yeats's play *The Countess Cathleen*. It was during the war, a first night in Dublin's Gate Theatre. The Countess in the play is modelled in many ways on Yeats's idealisation of Maud Gonne, the lines addressed to her by Aleel, the poet in the play, were Yeats addressing Maud Gonne. Not only had I the Countess herself in the seat beside me, but various members of the Yeats family were in the row in front. Surrounded by Olympians I was sure that this would be material for anecdote. But it isn't. When Madame Gonne MacBride dropped her programme and I picked it up she just said Thank you. But I can remember her eyes. "For we have hidden in our hearts the flame out of the eyes / Of Cathleen the daughter of Houlihan."

One thing the parents were brilliant at was organising children's parties. We had one of these colourful and noisy events every year at Christmas, usually in fancy dress. It must have surprised eminent Celtic scholars and scientists when, on their way into the Royal Irish Academy, they encountered a host of little girls disguised as gipsy queens or boys dressed up as pirates in the hallway and on the imposing staircase of that prestigious institution. If it did it never embarrassed my father to have his dignified work-place thus invaded. In the huge drawing room of our flat my mother would organise games. We would not only play the standard repertory consisting of Hunt the Thimble and Nuts in May, but unorthodox activities that she devised herself. In one of these every child had a balloon attached to one ankle with a piece of string. The aim of the game was to burst other children's balloons by stamping on them, while protecting your own. In another a large sheet was held tight by the corners by four adults and a large orange or grapefruit rolled around on it. The children, divided into two teams, stood under the sheet, each team trying to get the orange into the opposing goal by pushing up through the sheet. After tea there would be a conjurer. This was a member of the Academy, I have forgotten his name, a scientist I think, whose hobby this was. I'm not sure if the parents paid him for his performances; I prefer to think he just did it for fun. Though fun hardly seems the operative word, since the distinctive thing about him, and which made him better than any other conjurer I have seen since, was that he remained silent, neither frowning nor smiling, using no patter to distract our attention from what was, usually, pure, brilliant, prestidigitation. For example, he held up his hand with the fingers splayed out, shook it and with each shake a billiard ball appeared between two fingers. When all four gaps were filled he waved the hand again and one by one they disappeared. Afterwards, when all the other children were gone and my father had poured him a whiskey, we all begged him to explain how he did it but he wouldn't say.

Among those invited to our children's parties in the early years were the children of Dr Adolf Mahr. Dr Mahr, a distinguished German archaeologist, was curator of the National Museum. He had three children I think, I can remember two of them, Gustav, a robust, and somewhat bossy, boy some years older than me, and Hildegard, a pleasant lively little girl. We went on picnics with them occasionally. Frau Mahr was a motherly woman who spoke with a very strong German accent. And they would invite us to Christmas parties in return. The highlight of these occasions was the magic lantern show. Dr Mahr would set up this imposing apparatus, made of brass and mahogany, and recount one or more of Grimm's fairy tales as he projected lantern-slide after lantern-slide, putting on the voices of Rapunzel etc in a guttural and heavily dramatic Teutonic voice. The slides were of course not photographs; they were hand-painted in somewhat dingy colours and portrayed scenes from Grimm that were sometimes quite gruesome.

After a few years, however, Dr Mahr's membership of the Nazi party became known and we stopped seeing them. Dr Mahr resigned his post in the Museum shortly before the war and the family returned to Germany. Later my father told me that he sometimes wondered if Mahr hadn't been using funds from the Museum to visit wild places on the south and west coast of Ireland where there was little of archaeological interest but where a submarine could shelter unseen. After the war we learned that he had died in Berlin. Gustav, I heard, was called up in the Wehrmacht and ended the war as a prisoner of war in America.

Other friends and acquaintances of the parents were more congenial. Diarmuid Coffey, Liam and Dorothy Price were friends from the earliest days and typical, like the parents, of those more foresighted members of the Protestant middle class, whose sympathies were more or less actively with the Republicans in the War of Independence. Liam Price was a J.P., his career as a magistrate having started under the, clandestine, first Dail Eireann. He was an expert on toponymy and had published articles on Wicklow place names. He drove a large powerful car that was always very exciting to go in as compared with our black and green Baby Austin. I remember him once asking would I like to go at 60 miles an hour, and watching the speedometer needle creep up to what seemed at the time a fantastic speed. One day we went out to Baldonnel airport where Liam was learning to fly a plane. Unfortunately we never got flying with him since he failed to get his pilot's licence because he could not learn to land correctly on the ground. He would carry out the manoeuvre perfectly time after time, but always 50 or 100 feet up in the air. His wife, Dorothy, was well known as a paediatrician. She was personally responsible for introducing to Ireland the BCG vaccination of children against TB. Childless themselves they were good at playing with us when we were small children and talking to us as adults as soon as we began to grow up. They would join us for picnics in the Wicklow hills or at Jack's Hole and would always come for tea on Christmas Day.

There was one Christmas when the Prices had told the parents that they had got some fairly splendid presents, possibly our first bicycles, to give to Conor and me. These were to have been presented to us over Christmas tea. The parents decided that, in view of this munificence, the rest of our Christmas should be toned down somewhat. Or maybe they just wanted to play a joke on us. Anyway, instead of putting in the stockings, which we hung up on Christmas Eve, the usual toys and surprises, they filled them with things like toothbrushes, pieces of soap, sponges and nailbrushes, each of them wrapped up in Christmassy paper. My mother told me years afterwards that, as I took the paper off each one of these uninspiring objects, I had dutifully exclaimed, "Oh thank you, that's just what I wanted." Conor on the other hand, more honest and more down to earth, undid the whole disappointing collection in silence and, when he had got to the end of it, turned to the parents and said, "I think this is a lousy Christmas."

Diarmuid Coffey came frequently for lunch in Dawson Street. In fact many of my parents' friends used to take advantage of the central situation of our flat, though I don't remember the parents ever minding. Diarmuid was a tall thin man who smoked very strong tobacco in a long pipe and talked interestingly about books and plays and had an enthusiasm for the music of Bach. In fact he once complimented me on my playing which I am sure was very generous of him. He spoke Irish and was the author of a biography of Douglas Hyde, founder of the Gaelic League and first President of Ireland. Though they were very fond of Dermot, as they called him, I think my father considered him a bit ineffectual. I remember once asking,

"What does Dermot do?" He had in fact a job in the Record Office. My father replied, "He draws."

"Draws," said my mother, "What does he draw?"

"Draws his salary," said my father.

It was with Diarmuid Coffey and one or two others that, in 1925, my father had made his only Alpine expedition. With two guides they had climbed the Gran Paradiso in the Italian Alps. We had some fading sepia photographs of them standing on the summit in plus fours with ice axes. The others went on to Zermatt then, but my father had to return to Ireland, since my birth was imminent. His ice axe lay around the flat in Dawson Street for years. As I read the writings of Frank Smythe and Mummery I came to regard it as a prestigious object. But in fact Tony Farrington's times in the Wicklow hills often included much more impressive performances than being guided up a tame four thousander like the Paradiso. He often covered more than thirty miles of rough ground in a day. And he didn't only walk the Wicklow hills, he helped to find out how they had been shaped. Together with my mother he now lies, in the words of a recent book about the geology of the Wicklow mountains, "in the old churchyard on Calary, among the moraines deposited by the glacier ice that spread over that area from the granite hills, and in view of the Great Sugar Loaf Mountain."

# 2 Schools

THE FIRST SCHOOL I went to was called Park House. It was started – I was among the first pupils I think – by a friend of my mother's, Molly Fayle. Miss Fayle was a brisk energetic woman with curly hair and glasses who would arrive at school in the mornings in a green leather coat, first riding a motor bike and later at the wheel of a three-wheeled Morgan car with a big vee-twin engine mounted in front of the bonnet. She had a lot of authority, knew a lot about art and music and inclined politically to the Left. She also had a number of avant-garde educational ideas. The school was situated in one, later two, late Georgian houses in Morehampton Road in Dublin. The day at Park House started with all the children gathered together in the main room for what we called Showing. You were encouraged to bring in some object and demonstrate it to the assembly of about twenty or thirty other children. The object could be a picture or a beloved teddy or something picked up in the country. The teachers also would Show us things, paintings or poems or wise sayings, and get us to talk about what we were shown. Then we would all sing and, though I am not sure about this, recite the Lord's Prayer. Where else, though, could I have got the impression that it started Our Father, chart in Heaven?

Miss Fayle, an unfortunate name for a schoolmistress, though that never occurred to me till now, which may mean something, since success and failure were not things that mattered much at Park House, taught us mathematics. There were little sticks in bundles, or blocks, of tens and hundreds. I can remember being taught Irish and French and, yes, Latin, by a refined lady called Miss Morphy. Morphy, my father remarked, is Protestant for Murphy. There were no men teachers and the mistresses all wore bright flowery overalls. We sang a lot, played in a percussion band and acted plays. I have no memory of school rules, of discipline or punishment of any sort though I didn't leave the school until I was ten, old enough to misbehave. I can remember some disruptive behaviour on the part of one boy and Miss Fayle taking the rest of the class into her confidence and discussing how to treat him, and explaining to us that he was like that because he was lacking one or other of his parents.

Then, in 1935, when I was ten I was sent to the Dublin High School in Harcourt Street. Instead of the thirty or forty girls and boys there were several hundred boys, some of them very tough and intimidating - though I remember no overt bullying - in a huge dusty playground. Instead of Miss Fayle and Miss Orpen and Miss Morphy in their flowery overalls there were men, mostly kindly though some were terrifyingly strict. Some had carefully studied eccentricities, such as Mr Butler, who taught us English and once said, when we were reading Treasure Island and it had been my turn to read aloud: "That boy reads in a way worthy of Robert Louis Stevenson." I have prided myself on my reading aloud ever since, and can still recite the last sentences of Treasure Island by heart. There was Mr Chillingworth, who reviewed books for the *Irish Times* and taught us French, and kept embarrassing me by referring to my "learned uncle" Benjamin Farrington. There was the terrifying Mr Samuel S. Evans, whom we called Sammy. "Yeh can fool Mr Chillingworth, yeh can fool Mr Butler, but yeh can't fool SSE." There was Mr Watson who had taught my father science in Cork, thirty years before, and, in the room next to the science labs, Mr Young who taught French and Irish and never opened the windows. The resulting smell we all associated with "Froggy" Young, though it more likely came from the unwashed little boys in the preceding classes. There was the "School Sergeant", whom we called "Frosty", who would bark at boys infringing some petty regulation in a manner formed on the parade ground, and who came round the classes before Break collecting little blue slips of paper on which were recorded the names of boys to be kept in after school, "stuck" as we called it, usually for not doing, or for copying, their homework. I used to be given pennies to buy two doughnuts to eat at Break. School didn't end until ten to three when I would walk home across Stephen's Green and, I suppose, have a belated midday meal.

At the end of the small playground were the lavatories. I was afraid of not being able to pee in public. I don't think I ever put it to the test; years later, at St Columba's, Brian Boydell told me that it is a common male anxiety. Consequently, though I was often bursting to go, I would wait till the bell went and we were all in class and I could perform unwatched. Then I would put my hand up and ask to "Leave the room." I got regularly told off for this, or else the master – they all said this – would reply: "You may leave the room where it is."

I made no friends at the High School; no one I knew accompanied me on the first day and I knew no one there. Most of the boys came from South Dublin, Rathgar or Rathmines. They bought cap pistols or fireworks at shops in Rathmines that I had never heard of, or went to the pictures at the Stella cinema. They talked a lot about swapping things, about the prices of things, about money in general. None of that meant anything much to me since the parents hardly ever talked about how much things cost or what they were worth. Though I can still put faces on a number of the boys I was at The High School with, I knew none of them out of school and had no desire to invite any of them home. An exception was maybe Steve, but I only really got to know him long after the High School. The teaching was good if a bit authoritarian, and my being able to remember so many of the teachers clearly suggests that most of them were interesting individuals.

I got in disgrace once, though I think it was weakness of character rather than criminality. The class clubbed together to buy a present for our form master and I and a lanky boy called Orgel had the job of collecting the money and purchasing the object decided upon: a tie-press. I didn't know what a tie-press was, so Orgel bought it. The thing cost a few shillings less than we had collected, so Orgel decided the remainder was for us to keep. At least I think he kept it, or most of it, for I have no memory at all of coming home with extra money, though I may have. It's true; money didn't interest me one way or the other. Anyhow, someone did the arithmetic and we were both hauled up in front of the class by "Sammy", who denounced us as "a pair of downright swindlers," and reported the affair to our parents. I heard no more of it, but Orgel told me that he had been severely punished. He was Jewish, which may explain his father's reaction and may not.

There were a number of Jewish boys at the High School; I was only really aware that they were different because they waited outside while the prayers, which started the day in the big hall we called the Clockroom, were going on. I think there were several Jewish children at Park House but, as there were no prayers, I wasn't conscious of them being different. In fact I don't know how I know that the girl called Ruth was Jewish. At The High School if anyone had made anti-Jewish remarks I fancy I would not have attached much importance to it, since I already felt myself to be so different from everyone else at the school. A great friend of my mother's, Estella Solomons, the painter, was a practising orthodox Jew. It was something interesting about her, like her being married to Seumas O'Sullivan, the poet and bibliophile. When I first encountered anti-Semitism, in England, at my first teaching job, I couldn't understand it and I was profoundly shocked. Catholics, on the other hand, in my view then, were a race apart. There were of course, this being Ireland in 1935, no Catholics at the High School.

It was at The High School, though, that I first encountered organised religion. We had Bible Study as a school subject, and everyone in the class was entered for an examination set by the General Synod, at which I came last. And then my mother intervened, which was very unusual as regards anything curricular, and said I was not to be taught the Catechism. She saw it, rightly I think now, as indoctrination. So, when this was going on I was sent to read in the main hall called the Clockroom. I much preferred this, since Catechism sounded boring and scary and the Rev Mr Nowlan who taught Bible Study – "He's worse than Sammy for sticking" - dished out more punishment impositions than any other teacher we had.

While I was a pupil at The High School, Alexander, later known as "Derry", Jeffares, who became an eminent Yeats scholar, was editor of the school magazine and wrote to W.B.Yeats, who had, briefly, been a pupil at The High School long before, - "my father sent me to Harcourt Street and told me to put myself to school" - asking for a poem for the school magazine. Yeats obliged with *What Then?* which duly appeared in the Erasmian. I was, however, in those days, prouder of being at a school that numbered among its alumni Stanley Woods, winner of the TT in the Isle of Man.

I walked to The High School across Stephens Green every morning. One day there was a loud bang during the night and in the morning the gates to the Green were closed. The IRA had blown up the fine equestrian statue of King George - I don't remember which George - that graced the centre of the Green. I have no memory of any discussion of this event, at home. Ireland was a new nation, not fifteen years old and my mother had fought for it. Also, as I only realised years later, it was a political affinity that had brought them together as much as their love of wild nature and their motorcycles. My father had been a fervent Home Ruler, unusual for a Cork protestant, as my friend Christopher Woods pointed out, when he discovered that it was he that had drawn the map figuring as frontispiece in a nationalist pamphlet about the burning of Cork by English soldiers. But I have no memory of them endeavouring to inculcate patriotic feelings in us. Our Irishness was something we took for granted. For example, in December 1936, the school production of *The Pirates of Penzance* at The High School was interrupted so that the audience might listen to Edward VIII's abdication speech from a wireless that was set up on a table on the stage. The parents, that I do remember, had no interest at all in the English royals or their affairs, or, for that matter, in English politics, so they complained about the play being interrupted.

When I went to The High School my brother Conor remained at Park House. After I had been there two years the parents decided that The High School was a bit rough for Conor, who was still a delicate child. Also it was clear that I was not really happy there and our distant cousin Robert Harbord had just started at Avoca School in Blackrock, six miles from the city centre. So Conor and I started at Avoca in September 1937. I was there for two years, Conor for four.

Fraternal jealousy was a feature of both Conor's and my childhood. Though I have no precise or specific memories, I can certainly recall the general feeling of being displaced, of no longer being the unique object of my parents' affection when Conor was born. This was exacerbated by his being a very delicate child and needing special attention. When he was still a baby he was so ill that a night nurse had to be hired to sit up with him and he had to be fed a high protein diet which

BF, Conor and Una

consisted, I seem to remember, of raw liver which they mixed with strawberry jam to make it more acceptable. Though that may be folk-lore. What was very real, however, and to both of us, was our mutual resentment. We squabbled incessantly as little boys; I can remember us sitting in the back of the baby Austin driving to Cork and one or the other of us saying in fury: "Don't sing the same song as I'm singing." Absurd, but this sort of row continued until we were in our teens. In fact the rivalry didn't really end until I had left home. And for a time I used to think that one reason for my leaving Ireland and living in France was to be away from Conor. The cause of our animosity when we were small probably lay in our similarity: we had similar talents and interests and enthusiasms, and this meant that we were constantly competing with each other in some way. As we grew older more important differences between us became more apparent. Conor was more talented than me, more single minded and a perfectionist, which I most certainly am not. Because of this his life had a unity about it, and a dedication that mine lacked. In adult life we became very close, confided in each other a lot and became very fond of each other, enjoying a degree of mutual esteem that would have been unthinkable when we were little boys.

Avoca School was very different from The High School. Above all it was much smaller, and the intake was much more homogenous, the boys – there were two girls – all coming from comfortable middle class families living mostly in Dun Laoighaire or Blackrock. The classes were much smaller than at The High School too and the teaching more informal. Most of the teachers were fairly young too. We played hockey in winter, not football, and a former teacher had been an international hockey player. I played hockey at Avoca, the only team game I ever participated in, at Left Wing because I could run fast. We went to cheer at an international hockey match at Londonbridge Road and I enjoyed that. But I had poor co-ordination and a slow response time so I was not good at hockey or any other physical game, and therefore didn't enjoy it. I got out of playing whenever I could. A more important thing I opted out of at Avoca was the scout troop. My mother thought that scouting would be right up my street but she was wrong. I sensed straightaway the slightly paramilitary nature of the Boy Scouts and declined to join. But the reason I gave was the Promise to "do my duty by God and The King." My father supported me in this. He had never been a Boy Scout. Though I was sorry to miss out on some of the activities of the scouts I felt I was right when I heard that the troop had learnt to sing *Rule Britannia*.

The Headmaster of Avoca, Cyril Parker, had been, I think, shell-shocked in World War I, which explained his nervous uneasy manner and the way he fidgeted a lot while he spoke. He was a strong pacifist. His wife, Cerise, was a daughter of the painter William Orpen. She had been a teacher at Park House, a kindly smiling lady who was heavily pregnant while I was there and one day Parker burst into class and announced that Mrs Parker had just given birth to twins and we could all have a half-holiday. Among the teachers the one I remember best was William Boland because he gave me individual coaching for the scholarship exam for St Columba's, which I failed to get I had been at the bottom of the class at The High School and I don't think I shone specially, academically, at Avoca, but Mr Boland must have found some hitherto hidden intellectual qualities because he was certainly the first teacher to give me any feeling of self-assurance particularly as regards writing in English. I was conscious of this at the time and I am glad to say I wrote to thank him after I had arrived at Columba's. He wrote back thanking me for my description of Columba's and saying that he thought Avoca a more democratic establishment. Which was certainly true. Some years later I heard that he had left teaching to become a Presbyterian minister but I never saw him again.

Though the name might suggest otherwise, St Columba's College, which was founded in the 19th century to provide schooling in Ireland for the sons of landlords, was of course strictly non-Catholic. I started there in September 1939. I will never be sure what possessed the parents to send us to what was in effect a sort of Irish imitation of an English Public School. To begin with, it was very expensive, and my father certainly did not have that sort of ready money. Then, as I have shown, there was his whole family background, his own father's character and career and the fact that the achievements of his two brothers, as well as his own responsible position, were due to hard work and academic success. All this, I feel, should have precluded his sending his two sons to a place dedicated above all by its founder to the formation of gentlemen, and whose academic reputation among Dublin schools at the time was, to say the least, undistinguished. I can only suppose that in this he was swayed by my mother's opinion. She herself had been so happy at her girls' Public School in Scotland that she must have thought that, for Conor and me, St Columba's would be a similar experience, and this must have counted more with her than success with mere schoolbooks. I have to conclude that my father let himself be persuaded because he wasn't terribly interested in our education.

Whatever about that it is certain that leaving home for the first time, at the age of fourteen, and for a place so totally different from my entire world, was the most upsetting and most painful experience I had ever known. In my memory the summer of 1939 and the start of World War II is overshadowed by the foreboding I felt at the thought of leaving home. "How exciting!" my mother would exclaim as we went through the list of prescribed clothing and I tried on outlandish garment after outlandish garment: shirts with detachable collars, starched collars for Sundays, and, oddest of all, and to me distinctly alarming, the white surplice for Sunday chapel. I had to have collar studs and cufflinks and every evening I had to practise fitting the collar studs to the collars until my fingers had learned all the complicated movements.

As the first day of term drew near I grew increasingly apprehensive. When it came, and they drove me out to St Columba's in the family baby Austin and presented me to the Warden or headmaster, a pink faced man in a very black clerical suit and with a marked English accent, it was all like a slightly unpleasant dream. The Warden's English accent seemed typical of the strangeness of the whole place. Calling to a boy with raven black hair, and also an English accent, he said what sounded to me like, "Toeford, this is Farrington, show him around will you." When I realised that the boy's name was in fact Telford I became aware of a distinctive feature of the English spoken in Ireland, my English, namely that it has only one /l/ sound, whereas most English pronunciations have two. I found this fact interesting – it is demonstrated for example by the Irish pronunciation of a word like "film" as "fillum. That is probably why I remember the incident, though I had no idea that I was encountering the world of linguistic science for the first time. Strange that that should be the only thing I can recall of my first day at the College.

Several accounts have been written of St Columba's College as it was when I was there. Michael Campbell's novel, "Lord Dismiss Us", is probably the truest description. The school figures also in stories by William Trevor. Both authors were contemporaries of mine. Neither however, conveys a true impression of how extremely odd the place was, as compared with other Irish schools at the time. The school in Campbell's book, for example, called Weatherhill, is situated in England, so the book ignores one essential feature of St Columba's, namely that it was trying to be an English style public school situated in the foothills of the Dublin mountains, while at the same time contending with a variegated but, for the most part autochthonous, Irish, clientele.

Also, it was September 1939, at the start of the war. Up to then, several of the staff had been Englishmen. These left or were leaving in order to join up. I remember thinking of them as somewhat conventional, English schoolmasters, like the ones in school stories. In their place some of the masters that came to teach us remind me now of W H Auden's lines about his teachers during World War I:

> Many were raggable, a few were waxy,
> One had to leave abruptly in a taxi.

Such individuals came and went. But a number of the teaching staff were Irish, relatively young and enthusiastic. That they also came and went after staying only a year or two suggests tensions that we were only vaguely aware of at the time. The Warden, for all his zeal, and his ideals, some of which were genuinely progressive, was still quite young at thirty seven and had a certain brashness and insensitivity in human affairs. A lot of responsibility for running the College, therefore, devolved upon the two senior masters, G K White and Sandham Willis, and this gave these two an authority which they clung to. It manifested itself, especially in White, in jealousy regarding the more successful, more popular, or simply more intelligent, of the junior staff, so they were never very sorry to see them go. In fact, as I learned years later, they schemed and plotted to get certain of them sacked. Their attitude to the Warden, who had all the same, single-handed, saved the College from total financial disaster, was one which was shared by many of the boys including myself at the time, and consisted, I can see now, mostly of snobbery. Like W.B.Yeats considering himself socially superior to English people seen kissing on station platforms, we Irish looked down on Sowby, seeing him, quite wrongly, as some sort of English parvenu. Though it is true he was a bit of a snob himself there was more to the man than we realised as evidenced by the friendly terms he was on with Eamon DeValera, something I didn't learn about until many years later. At the time I probably wouldn't have believed it.

The oddness of St Columba's, the unfamiliarity of everything about the place that struck me, arriving as a 14-year-old from home, and from the friendly, Irish, atmosphere of Avoca, was seriously disconcerting. I had read countless school stories; now, I suddenly found myself living in one, in an unreal Billy Bunter world of prefects, colours for games, fags and caning, the last named a constant dread, (though I only experienced it once). There was compulsory chapel twice a day, a bizarre routine for me who had never attended a church service in my life, there was a Latin grace before meals and there were Latin terms for the most ordinary things. For example, brothers were major and minor, and the two Sundays during term, when we were allowed home for the day, were labelled Exeats. In my first term I counted the days to the first of these; when it came it was very upsetting. I walked across Kilmashogue - the College was only a mile or two as the crow flies from our week-end cottage at Ticknock - towards the agreed meeting place, suddenly seeing across Taylor's big field my parents in their woolly clothes, Conor and little Una, and felt such a wave of emotion that I burst into tears. In the evening my father walked down with me to the back gate of the College. The chapel bell was ringing; as I said goodbye to him I could see boys in gowns and surplices waiting to go in: my other world.

I soon got used to all these alien ways. On the whole I was very happy at St Columba's, once I had come to terms with it. Though the school was in those days not particularly distinguished as regards teaching or exam successes, and I was in any case a late developer for schoolwork, and was parked in a B stream, there was plenty of opportunity for independent intellectual development. I soon had a place in the choir and learnt to sing the bass part of hymns and chants. This attenuated the tedium of the constant chapel services. There were many out-of-school activities; boys could learn about unexpected things like printing or electronics. And we enjoyed a considerable amount of freedom. Maybe because Warden Sowby had been a parson in the Lake District and was himself a hill walker, we were able to take sandwiches and go off, either on foot or on bicycles into the Dublin Mountains and even into Wicklow, without even leaving word as to where we were going. In my first term I led a reluctant group on bicycles all the way over Sally Gap and into the Liffey valley, and on another occasion walked to the top of Kippure, highest point in County Dublin, now crowned by a TV aerial but then a wild mountain summit made of storm-carved peat haggs. It was a long walk for a fourteen-year old.

One immediate effect of the start of the "Emergency", as the war was called officially by the Irish Government, was the sudden influx, at the start of my first term, of twenty or thirty boys who normally went to English Public Schools but switched to St Columba's in September 1939 for fear of German bombs or submarines. Though nominally Irish, these people were so England-oriented, speaking for example with English accents and talking of Tonbridge, Harrow or Leighton Park, that they made the rest of us more conscious of our Irishness. In fact the one thing that struck me almost immediately about many of the boys at Columba's was how much more Irish they were than the general run of boys at Avoca. No scout troop existed in my time at St Columba's but had there been one I couldn't imagine them singing *Rule Britannia*. We had occasional services in Irish in the chapel and there were even several boys who were openly, radically, nationalist. In contrast to this a number of the boys were, it is true, what we used to call West British, these were mostly the sons of Dublin bourgeois who would like to have sent the boys to English Public Schools but couldn't afford it. There were several other clearly defined categories. Prominent were the sons of Church of Ireland clergy, many of them from country

Farm at St Columbas. Kenny, Madden, Hackett, Warden Sowby and Patterson

parishes. There were the sons of provincial bank managers or small businesses. And of course there was the fag end of the clientele for which the College had been founded in the first place, in 1843, namely the sons of the remains of the Ascendancy, the landed gentry. Finally, there was a small, but important, contingent of boys from the North. All of this made, I realise looking back on it now, for an interesting and intellectually stimulating social mix.

By a fortunate chance I was able to avoid having to take part in the compulsory games that are such a feature of most Public School life. When the parents first visited the school they had told the Warden that I didn't want to play team games. Keen to please a prospective parent the Warden told my mother that I wouldn't have to, and when I got to the school I held him to his promise. I joined the games-players in cross-country running, which I enjoyed. Otherwise I worked on the school farm. It was a pet idea of Warden Sowby's that the College could itself farm some of the land it possessed and that boys could be allowed to work on the farm instead of playing rugby or cricket. A lively and entertaining master, called Sidney Patterson, who taught Irish and maths, made a success of this unusual school activity. We grew potatoes and wheat and other crops and even kept pigs. The only disadvantage in being a farm worker was that one had to come back to the College occasionally during the holidays, as, for example, when it was time to do the threshing. But it was more fun than anything else, to be at the school without being "at school", and to have lunch in the masters' Common Room. And anything was better than being caught up in the competitive games-playing ethos: the blazers, the ties, and the swagger. My present complete lack of interest in, and knowledge of, all team games started then. Conor, on the other hand, though he always said he hated Columba's, was an enthusiastic sportsman and a champion long jumper. Also, Columba's gave him the opportunity to write plays and have them performed at the end of term. I remember one very effective one about two mad lighthouse keepers who murder a third one because he failed in respect for the god, the dazzling idol that they worship at the top of the tower.

Two hitherto unknown phenomena loomed importantly at this time in my life: sex and religion. They seemed to come upon me together and were certainly associated. A few months before leaving Avoca I had experienced my first orgasm. It had happened one night in bed, quite unexpectedly and involuntarily, though I suppose I had been stimulating myself unthinkingly. The sensations were so violent and so totally new and unimaginable that my first reaction was one of shock and fear which quickly turned to guilt. The guilt obsessed me in the months that followed. I cannot imagine why this should have been so, nobody had spoken to me of masturbation, certainly no one had ever told me that it was a sin. I fancy I must have just picked up that idea from the generally puritanical climate that reigned in Ireland at the time. From that moment on, and for years, sex and guilt were inseparably associated in my mind. Masturbation itself was a problem that I could discuss with no one, and it remained so until the Art master Brian Boydell, remarked that the public school ethic was inconsistent since they set such a high value on the physical exercise of every part of the body save one. To hear someone in authority say such a thing was a liberation. It was probably the first of the many things I owed to that exceptional individual.

Religion was an important feature of life at St Columba's. There were several clergy among the masters and we had chapel at least twice a day, though the daily services were very short. The chaplain, the Rev Lynn Millar, because of the cassock he always wore, his theatrical high-church gestures and the florid sermons he preached in which his eloquence seemed to be driven by some parasexual passion, always seemed to me more like a Catholic priest out of Joyce's *Portrait of the Artist* than a normal Anglican parson. The other clerics were much more likeable human beings. There was the Rev C. W. Quin, an unkempt, bearded man with a large shaggy dog called Grayboy, which he used to bring into class and talk to in Irish. He was, actually, an eminent Celtic scholar, but we tended to see him as someone only vaguely in touch with the real world. For example, brief, optional, daily services were held at lunchtime in the chapel, ostensibly to pray for peace, though in fact the key word tended to be more victory than peace. Quin was once asked at short notice to "take" this intercession service. Not knowing what form it usually took, he came in, sat down and looked around. Then, with admirably comprehensive vagueness: "Let us pray," he said, "For the world."

Then there was the Rev Francis Evelyn, a desiccated little man who spoke several languages fluently, and had been chaplain to British embassies all over the world. His sermons used to be based on quotations from St Paul's epistles and he would start by describing, in crisp vivid terms, the places in Greece or Asia Minor from which St Paul had written them. His teaching would often consist of the study or discussion of some text he had taken a liking to, or felt like reading again, chosen without reference to any syllabus or programme. He had a passion for the theatre – he was a friend of Sybil Thorndyke and Lewis Casson - and had written some unreadable plays in classical blank verse. I was one of the boys he liked to take to the theatre in the holidays. We would have a memorably frugal supper in his, temperance, hotel and then go, sometimes to one of the main Dublin theatres, but more often to some suburban hall where he had heard that an amateur company were putting on some little-performed piece. What I remember admiring about Clarence Evelyn, as we called him, was the way, though he had a sharp critical sense and knew a lot about theatre, he always found something to praise in what were often the most drearily lumbering productions. He would come out saying: "Well the lighting was cleverly managed," or "What a beautiful voice that second man had!" It occurred to me then that he regarded the world and Columban society, rife as it was with malicious gossip, in something the same way. I don't think that much remains in me of Columban Christianity, but one thing that does is an ideal of goodness, and often, when I think of goodness, I remember that wry, absurd, dried-up, gold-hearted little man.

Similarly to The High School, where I had been excused attendance at catechism periods, at St Columba's I was spared preparation for confirmation and communion, all what Clement Attlee once described as the "mumbo jumbo part" of Christianity. I don't know how many other boys did the same; I know that there were Methodists and Baptists among us. For the rest, I enjoyed the singing in chapel and selected for belief the bits of Christianity that seemed meaningful to me: the Christmas myth, the Sermon on the Mount and a vague pantheism that I found expressed in some of the choruses of Handel's *Messiah*. When I found in the library the Swinburne poem that starts, "Thou hast conquered O pale Galilean, /The world has grown grey with thy breath!" it seemed to sum up my personal impression of the Jesus we were invited to worship. Since Columba's He has always struck me, in spite of His teachings, as a bit of a drip. If He really was God, I couldn't help thinking, He surely could have talked His way out of the crucifixion. Unless of course He wanted to be crucified. I can't have been alone in being turned off by this meek and mild figure. Once, in a sermon, the Archbishop of Dublin, Dr Barton, who had a special, and much ridiculed, way of talking to boys, said that he could imagine Our Lord as a champion boxer. "Joe Jesus, the Bethlehem Bruiser!" I heard one of the masters mutter, sitting behind me. I continued to believe in God, though vaguely. I didn't become an atheist until ten years later. I was always, however, and still am, quite interested in religion. So I wrote in the Suggestions Book in the school library that it should acquire a copy of the Koran. This eventually appeared, and, since I had suggested that it be purchased, I felt that there was a moral obligation on me to be the first to study it. Unfortunately it turned out to be an even heavier read than the Bible. Years afterwards I learnt that my suggestion had been the hotly debated subject of a specially convened masters' meeting.

The tendency that all schools had - and still have for all I know - to exaggerate out of all proportion the gravity of the most elementary transgressions, was a specially marked feature of life at St Columba's. From time to time there would be one of these crises and the entire school would be summoned and told that in the long history of human depravity such an orgy of sin had never even been contemplated as... what had recently been happening in the changing room. While I was at Columba's two boys were expelled, the event being each time the occasion for just such a mass meeting. In both cases the offence, which in the Warden's view, justified this extreme sanction, would not raise many eyebrows today. The first, which happened in my first term, concerned a boy who had broken into an empty house in the neighbourhood and stolen a piano accordion. The other involved a boy who had the misfortune to have in his possession an exercise book containing several obscene recitations in the style of *Dangerous Dan McGrew*. The book had been circulating among us for some time. If it hadn't been for this I might never have read the full text of the *Ballad of Eskimo Nell*, which I consider a most useful part of my education. I can still remember bits; proof of a definite literary quality:

> But Eskimo Nell she knew full well
> This wasn't a cat to cosset,
> So she gripped his cock like a Chatswood lock
> On a national safe deposit...

Pretty harmless stuff; that it should have shocked the Warden opened our eyes to his quite extraordinarily Victorian ignorance of the ways of the world.

However, apart from such emotion-charged episodes, discipline was a fairly relaxed and informal affair at Columba's. There were some idiotic traditions and privileges, reminiscent of Tom Brown's Schooldays, it is true, but not too many of them. And the school was small, about a hundred and fifty boys. Discipline was handled for the most part by the prefects. As a result the masters were not obliged to spend time and energy supervising the observance of a lot of petty rules. Relations with them could therefore be pleasantly informal. And because, due to the "Emergency", public transport was limited and nobody had cars, though the College was only five or six miles from Dublin, the city seemed much further away. As a result the masters spent much more time in the College and were much more accessible than could be the case now. This was probably one of the best things about St Columba's.

It was something I was able to take advantage of. I owe a lot for example to Joseph Groocock, the Precentor, which was the pretentious name the College had for the music master and organist. He came up to me one day and said that he had noticed that I always came to any musical event; had I ever considered learning the piano? I told him I had tried but was no good. "Well," he said, pushing his hands down into his jacket pockets. "If a thing is worth doing it's worth doing badly." The piano lessons he gave me can't have been fun for him but I have been grateful ever since, not just for my very mediocre talent as a pianist, but for the principle behind those words. The long list of other things that I have enjoyed doing badly include playing the flute, skiing, sailing, singing, electronics, photography, carpentry, engine maintenance, mountaineering, computer programming and speaking various foreign languages. I would probably have dabbled in most of these activities anyway but Joe Groocock's justification of amateurism made it intellectually respectable in my mind. I used to quote it when I lived in France, where the word *versatile* is actually pejorative. I often thought of writing to him to thank him for all this but I never got round to it. I very much wish now that I had.

Another master who was memorable, though I never knew him personally, was Harry Lush, principal teacher of Irish. Since the College received government funding dependent on the number of boys learning Irish it was obviously a subject few could opt out of. A muscular 'broth of a man' - he also acted as a rugger coach - who plastered his curly hair with a pleasantly strong-smelling aromatic compound called, I think, bay rum, Harry Lush, with great energy, force fed the Gaelic language to often reluctant, sometimes recalcitrant pupils. He was a teacher of the old, authoritarian, school on which model he imposed his own distinctly personal style. There were I am sure plenty of textbooks available for learning Irish; what I remember of his classes were bundles of pages reproduced by a thing called a jellygraph, the only sort of copier available to teachers in those days. On the pages, handwritten, were list after list of words, irregular verbs, turns of phrase, bits of grammar, all with English translations and all of which, there was no avoiding it, had to be memorised thoroughly. It was as stark an example as could be found of the much-scorned grammar-translation method of language learning. But of course it worked, quite well, for a very simple reason. I have spent forty odd years teaching and practising Applied

Linguistics in the course of which many methods and ways of learning foreign languages have come and, most of them, gone: the Direct Method, the Audio Lingual method, the Language Laboratory, the Silent Way, the Code-Cognitive approach, Communicative methodologies, Data-Driven Learning, and others whose names I have forgotten. That there should be so many of these, and so divergent, points to one simple fact that none of them mention: the one essential ingredient in any methodology is the teacher's enthusiasm for the subject. With it any methodology will work, more or less; without it none will do any good. Harry Lush's enthusiasm, not only for Irish but for teaching it, means that this far from poetic individual has engraved indelibly in my memory, not aspiration nor slender consonants, but a sizeable chunk of the poetry of Raftery.

But Harry left Columba's under a cloud, a thundercloud of his own distinctive making. We were all assembled in the dining hall for our evening meal when we were shushed to silence. Harry was standing at the end of the hall. "Boys," he said, "There are a few things I want you to know, I want you to know." There followed a long and somewhat rambling account of how and why he had come to St Columba's. In a succession of anecdotes he told how in his early days he had been Warden Sowby's "white-headed boy" but how all this had suddenly changed for the worse. I should explain here that for quite some time we had all been aware of his friendly relations with the Matron, Molly McLoughrey, who was a lively young woman with a good sense of humour whom we all liked. As I say, we had all been aware of the friendship without finding it particularly interesting; we had our own dramas to worry about. Others it appears, Harry told us in anecdote after anecdote, did not share this healthy indifference to his affairs; hints had been dropped regarding the illicit nature of his relations with a "certain person." As he went on it became increasingly clear that he was accusing no less a personage than Mrs Sowby, the Warden's wife, who, he claimed, was the source of a rumour that an illegitimate baby was on its way. "Well I'm telling you now," said Harry, "That there is no baby. That's what I wanted you to know."

The whole performance had lasted a good twenty minutes and in the middle, when we were just realising the aberrant nature of the occasion, there was a sudden rattle at the door. "Don't mind that, boys," says Harry, "I've locked it." And held up the key. At the end someone called out, "Three cheers for Mr Lush," and we all shouted Hooray. Minutes later he was on his way out the back gate of the College, no longer a member of the staff. We thought at the time that he had been sacked on the spot; I only learnt years later that his contract had already been terminated because White considered his presence inappropriate in a school for the sons of gentlemen. And it's not sure how right he was as regards the source of the malicious rumour. Harry and the Matron were married shortly after and almost immediately he landed a job as manager of the Adelphi, a large Dublin cinema, where he remained the rest of his working life. When

Harry Lush (left)
Peter Allt

film stars, Leslie Howard, Anna Neagle, Cary Grant, made a personal appearance to promote a film Harry would present them to the audience with a speech in Irish. And he went on coaching private pupils in Irish to the end of his life, using his office in the cinema for the purpose.

Two other masters became special friends. Peter Allt arrived at the college in my second year there, when my first booklet entitled *Ten Poems* had just been produced by the school Printing Club. I had arrived home for the Christmas holidays when I received a letter from Allt praising the poems and inviting me to dine with him in the Dolphin, which was a pleasantly old-fashioned hotel and restaurant off Dame Street. Michael Farrell, the writer, came and joined us. He had just been giving a talk on what we in those days called the wireless. We ended the evening in Peter Allt's rooms in Trinity, the first time I had ever been in the University. At one moment the talk turned to Sean O'Casey. Michael Farrell described the row in the Abbey Theatre over *The Plough And The Stars*, at which he had seen Yeats "Shaking his lion head at the crowd and shouting, 'Tonight you have rocked the cradle of yet another Irish genius!'"

From then on I saw a lot of Peter Allt. He taught us English and French. I don't think he was a particularly good teacher but that wasn't really the point. For example I can remember a most inspiring introduction to the tragedies of

Racine in which he skated gracefully over the tiresome fact that our clodhopping acquaintance with the language prevented us from understanding the text. He took us, word by word, through unpoetic poems by John Donne, he lent us books by D H Lawrence, of whom we had never heard, and Graham Greene, whose first novels were just then appearing. It was with him that I first heard the name of Samuel Beckett. Most of what he said went right over our heads but the bits that didn't were much more interesting and more thought-provoking than anything that we heard from more conventional schoolmasters.

I don't know why he took an interest in me. For that matter I often wonder why he came to Columba's. I find it hard to believe now that his friendship with me owed anything to the literary quality of my *Ten Poems*. It may have had something to do with my being related to J M Synge, whom he admired greatly. It may have been that I appeared in some way unconventional or unusual and therefore interesting. The most likely explanation is that there was an underlying homosexual attraction. If that was so I was so gullible that it never occurred to me. Whatever the reason I was very fortunate in being able to enjoy the privilege of his company and conversation. I am sure that my appreciation of poetry, above all the poetry of Yeats, which we agreed in admiring above all other, owes a lot to the approach that I learnt from him, which was insightful, analytical, and above all linguistic, and I use the word advisedly. I have never known anyone so sensitive to the sound, the subtle and often very distinctive rhythms, the consonant echoes and the vowel harmonies, of Yeats's poetry. And it wasn't just long sessions discussing and analysing poems. During the holidays I spent many long afternoons with him in a library when he was beginning work on the variorum edition of Yeats, which was, some years after his death, completed and published by another Yeats scholar. I would read one version of a poem while he would check a later version for alterations. I learnt a lot during those afternoons, not only about Yeats and about poetry, but also about the exciting drudgery that is literary scholarship. Though I have spent my whole working life among academics in two quite different cultures I think that Peter Allt was probably the most intellectually stimulating person I have ever known. In the letter I wrote to his mother when he died I said that for many years my whole way of thinking would bear the imprint of his mind. That was true.

On the other hand, when I think about it, I realise now that, though I was very grateful for what he taught me and for what he did for my self-assurance, we had really very little in common. I don't think, if he had not died and if we had met in later life, that we would have had anything to say to each other at all. Apart from literature he shared none of my enthusiasms, and I definitely shared none of his. The last time we met I felt that we had both moved on. His politics were extremely right-wing and elitist. His religion, in so far as it wasn't just a pose, like so much about him, was grotesquely high-church. And he was a very cerebral, city-bound, impractical person. As was shown by the incongruous,

Brian Boydell

tragic, way in which he died while still quite young. He had got into the wrong train in a London station, saw the right train and tried to make his way to it across the tracks, stood on the live rail and was electrocuted.

The other master with whom I became friendly out of school was a very different kettle of fish from Peter Allt. Brian Boydell joined the staff of the college to teach art. He was a resounding success at this, finding or awakening artistic talent in boys who did not know they possessed it, setting self-expression above the mere acquisition of technique. Several boys who "did" art with Boydell became successful professional painters or sculptors in later life. His own paintings were strongly influenced by Surrealism.

But painting was only one of the amazing range of talents the man possessed. He had a science degree and, in his first term, formed a Geological Society in the school. He somehow acquired a large insulated jar of liquid air and performed a number of fascinating low temperature experiments with it to communicate to us the simple meaning that science was fun. He had designed a sort of furnace or retort bolted to the back of his car which made it possible to run the engine on producer gas made from charcoal. Since there was no petrol for private motoring because of the "Emergency" Boydell had formed a company with two friends to market this contraption, which worked quite successfully. He actually sold one to Warden Sowby. This meant that he was able to drive around freely when hardly anyone else could. He was also a trained singer, played the oboe and the piano and organised musical appreciation sessions on Sunday afternoons for which we would cycle down to his house in Rathfarnham. He had a gift for communicating enthusiasm. I never hear Beethoven's seventh without remembering the way he took us through it, singing the themes in a funny voice. In fact music was his principal field of activity and it was as a composer, conductor and professor of music in Trinity that he was best known in later life.

Life at St Columba's was certainly enhanced by his ebullient personality. He wasn't all that much older than we were. So maybe the most picturesque memory I have of him is not particularly surprising. One day in the art room, in the course of some discussion, Boydell explained that intestinal gas was methane, and to demonstrate this he suddenly cocked his leg up on the table, lit his cigarette lighter and farted. The image of one of my respected schoolmasters with a long jet of blue flame coming out of his behind is one of the most striking memories of my time at St Columba's College. Some boys, I heard, endeavoured to repeat this performance but less successfully; as a result they had to go to the Matron to obtain treatment for burns the location of which they had some difficulty in explaining.

Fellow Old Columbans to whom I have shown a draft of this Memoir have made suggestions for corrections or minor changes, most of which I have accepted. In general most agree that I have told it like it was. The reaction of others, who did not know St Columba's in those years, has often been of the order: "My God, what a madhouse!" Norman Lush, who arrived shortly before I left and who ended as Sub-Warden, rightly reminds me of one fact which should go a long way towards correcting this impression. It is the proportionally large number of people who were at Columba's during what G K White described to me as "those crazy years" and who distinguished themselves in later life. Certainly the list of professors, astronomers, QCs, senators, judges, distinguished scientists and surgeons, successful writers, painters and composers is most impressive. It is true we were all middle class boys with relatively educated backgrounds, but the fact remains that the College must be held responsible in great part for this very striking panoply of success.

When I look back and compare Columba's with the schools my own children have been to, Aberdeen Grammar School, a large comprehensive, and the Lycée de Chatenay, and, for that matter, with the multiplicity of Scottish schools that I have known in my capacity as a Visiting Examiner, three things stand out which may help to explain the College's educational triumphs. One, of course is the sprinkling of remarkable individuals that taught us, some of whom I have described. Some of these men, Millar, Evelyn, Quin, Patterson who ran the farm, Allt, Groocock and Boydell were not professional schoolmasters first and foremost, and some had, I suspect, no formal teaching qualification. Not that, in my opinion, this mattered overmuch. Because, when I think of some of the, flawed but memorable, individuals that taught me at Columba's I cannot help feeling that most of the schoolteachers I have met in later life, for all that they were conscientious, very professional, overworked and underpaid, were in comparison somewhat uninspiring people. And I am led to the tentative conclusion that teaching is maybe too important a job to be done just by trained teachers. Instead I imagine a perfect society in which it is customary for any man or woman achieving a degree of success in any career to be obliged to do a stint of a year or two in a school, just talking to children and opening up their horizons.

The second important difference between Columba's and other schools I have known comes of course from its being a boarding school, and from the sense of community that this inevitably creates. In my mind it is about the only thing that can be said in favour of the so-called "Public Schools", but it is not a negligible feature. In the case of my time at St Columba's the sense of community was strengthened by the small size of the school and by the "Emergency" situation, which meant that the six miles or so between the College and Dublin isolated us much more completely than would later have been the case. One effect of this, which may be specific to me – I just don't know – is the number of boys I was at school with that I still number among my close friends. This is not true of any non-Columbans that I know.

But possibly the most significant difference between Columba's and other schools I know or have known is simply a matter of size. In the four years I was at school there were never more than about a hundred and fifty boys. Small numbers means of course that specialised subjects can't be taught. I am inclined to think that that doesn't matter overmuch, compared with the advantage of having a small vibrant community in which everyone knows everyone else. There is inevitably a down side to this: it can get a bit claustrophobic. And this is exacerbated, particularly in a boarding school, by the presence of teachers whose whole life is wrapped up in the school. This was to some extent true of the two senior Masters at St Columba's: Willis and White I personally think that their lives would have been improved, and it would have done the College a lot of good, if they had moved on. The extreme example of this claustrophobia was an individual I met teaching at a school in England. A man in his late fifties, he had been a pupil at the school, had come back as a teacher after a year or two, and had then spent his entire working life "living for the school." When his team failed to win some footling cricket match this man broke down and wept.

# 3 Three Friends

SEVEN OF MY CLOSEST FRIENDS through most of my life had been at St Columba's with me. However, four of these I only really got to know some years after I had left the College. While I was there I was on good terms with quite a number of boys. Three were especially important friends: Will Harvey, Steve (David Stevenson) and Michael Biggs.

Will Harvey and I came together through a mutual interest in machinery and in mountaineering. The College Library possessed – I wonder if it still does – a first edition of A. F. Mummery's *My Climbs In The Alps*, with the original illustrations which, as I remember though it seems unlikely, were engravings. I can still, in my mind, see the pictures of the forbidding North face of Blaitière and of the Grépon that were in that book. Will and I procured a rope somewhere and cycled to Lough Bray in Glencree over which there hung some severely vegetated crags. It wasn't a very glorious bit of climbing, though I boasted about it afterwards, but it was a start. However I don't think that Will and I did any further roped climbing together until we scrambled up the Arrochar Cobbler in Scotland, when we were both in our seventies. Will, however, when he was living in Belfast after leaving school, had done quite a lot of serious rock-climbing in the Mournes and his name is on the first ascent of several routes listed in climbing guides. At school anyway, we walked over the hills behind the College.

The first, and only, big, relatively speaking, mountain we climbed together was when I went to stay with Will at his home in Mitchelstown County Cork in the holidays and we got to the top of Galteemore, a big sandstone Munro with, if I remember rightly, a splendid corrie on the North side. It was a long day, since we had to cycle to the foot of the mountain to begin with. I can still remember the taste of the raisin sandwiches which Will's kindly mother had made for us. Will's father was the Church of Ireland Rector of Mitchelstown. He was also Chaplain of Kingston College, which was not a college but an ensemble of small

Will Harvey and BF at Mitchelstown

houses, founded in the eighteenth century by Baron Kingston for "poor decayed gentlemen and gentlewomen". In a sense the College was sheltered housing, arranged in an attractive square at the gate of what had been Mitchelstown Castle. In a shed behind their house Will was rebuilding an old motor cycle engine, cranking and cranking it in the hope it would fire, which it at last did making a resounding and satisfactory noise, since it had no silencer.

But the high point of that visit to Mitchelstown was exploration of the Mitchelstown caves. I had read about these in a book my father had bought, about caving by E.A.Baker, one of the first British speleologists, and it had started a fascination, which lasted several years, with the subterranean world, but I had never been down a cave. The Mitchelstown caves, which are actually nearer to Ballyporeen than to Mitchelstown, are, or were, the best known show caves in Ireland. There are two, the Old, or Desmond, Cave and the New Cave which was discovered when quarrying early in the twentieth century. The New Cave, which was, and is, much the more extensive, was fitted with electric light and open to visitors for a guided tour. This meant that the old Cave was neglected, for all that it contained the largest subterranean chamber in the country, big enough to hold fourteen double tennis courts.

My father had come by a description and plan of the Desmond Cave which I had brought. It was easy to see why the cave was not developed for tourists. Entrance was by a narrow cleft in the rock and a drop of twenty feet. Will and I inspected this and worked out a way of anchoring a rope ladder at the top of the rock cleft, using an iron bar. We cycled back and set ourselves to fabricating the ladder, which ended up by making a singularly cumbersome bundle to carry on a bicycle. Somehow or other we managed this, installed the ladder and clambered down into the cave. We had none of the equipment modern cave explorers regard as essential. Instead of helmets we had old caps of Will's father's stuffed with rags. Instead of lamps we had candles and pocket torches whose batteries kept running out. In spite of this we managed to visit most of the cave, getting an idea of the impressive size of the main chamber by lighting strips of magnesium and by calling out and listening to the echo.

But the most remarkable achievement of the day was the discovery of an unknown passage on our way back from the main chamber. It was a narrow low-ceilinged burrow, several tens of metres long, which we had to crawl along and which opened out to a small chamber at the end. Whereas in every other part of the Desmond Cave the walls were marked with graffiti, names and initials, here there were none. We looked at each other, taking in the stupendous fact that we, two 16 year olds, were standing, or crouching, in a place which, since the start of time, no human being had ever penetrated. We couldn't go back without leaving some evidence of our having been there, so, with some difficulty, we scratched and pencilled our names and the date on the wall. We crawled back out through the narrow passage, scrambled up our ladder and pedalled wearily back to Mitchelstown. Our faces and clothes were thickly coated with the heavy glutinous clay we had had to crawl through. But we were enormously, and justly, proud and pleased to think of where we had been.

Twenty five years later Will was back in Mitchelstown with his two teenage sons and his daughter. They went to the Desmond Cave, managed to negotiate the 20 foot drop, and found their way, not without some difficulty, to the passage we had discovered years before. Other people had found their way in there since but our names were still visible where we had scratched them, and our date. Will took a photo of them which I have before me as I write.

Will left school a year before I did and went to Belfast to be trained as an engineer with Harland and Wolff. For over 20 years we hardly ever met, though we wrote to each other constantly, exchanging ideas, anxieties, and enthusiasms. We met again when I came to live in Scotland. Will was now living in Glasgow, working for an oil company and at the same time enjoying a reputation in industrial archaeology, a field in which his training as an engineer enabled him to speak with authority. He was largely responsible for making known the Leadhills Library, the first working-class subscription library in the world, founded in 1741, visited by, among others, William and Dorothy

Wordsworth, and for the founding of the Museum of Lead-Mining at Wanlockhead. He also published a large number of articles on, mostly, 18th and early 19th century machinery, and co-authored a book about William Symington, Scottish pioneer of marine steam propulsion. He had to keep quiet about all this activity with his employers, who liked to think that they owned every minute of his time and were too short-sighted to see how this ancillary expertise enhanced the image of the large oil company they worked for. I found that this contrasted depressingly with the situation of certain of my academic colleagues at Aberdeen University, who grumbled constantly about the university's requirement that they produce published evidence that they were engaged in research.

One of the last things Will did was to be very active in a small group of enthusiasts that restored on the Clyde a 19th century three-masted sailing ship, the Glen Lee. He took me over it in 2006, the year before he died. It was very imaginatively set out. For example on the main deck they had a replica of one of the yards fitted with ropes and sail ties and reefing cords, so that school kids could straddle it and tie reefs imagining that they were 80 feet in the air over a heaving sea and not four feet from the floor! On the way to Will's funeral the taxi took me past the dock. Very smart she looked, the Glen Lee, and the flag at her main top was at half-mast.

Steve, David Stevenson, was my oldest friend, as I was his. We were ten years old when we met, sitting together, at the bottom of the class, at The High School in Harcourt Street. There was a plaque on the wall in the Clock Room, in memory of a distinguished old boy of the school: Dr Walter Clegg Stevenson, a pioneer in the field of radiotherapy, and I remember being told that it was Stevenson's father. I had no idea then of the appalling drama of his childhood: the mother drowning in front of the two little boys playing on the beach, followed shortly after by the father's tragically early death. But I knew that there was something special about him, even then. Two years later, on the first day at St Columba's I found myself sitting beside a boy who looked vaguely familiar. "Are you Basil Farrington?" he asked. Years before, at The High School, boys had wanted to know what my forename was, but I was ashamed of "Brian", it seemed to me then pretentious, middle class, a show-off name. When someone asked if the B stood for Basil? I said Yes, to shut them up and because there was a senior called Basil something-or-other who was highly thought of. All our lives Steve never called me anything else.

I had other friends at St Columba's, some of whom Steve disliked; he had strong likes and dislikes. I think we really discovered our affinity for each other when we happened to be together recovering from flu in the Sanatorium. Our friendship grew as we weathered the torments of adolescence together. Steve was looked on by most boys as a joker, an eccentric, someone who never did anything in the standard orthodox way, and who didn't have to be taken seriously. I am afraid I shared this attitude, because he was so funny. I never realised then how much we had in common. We were both desperately unsure of ourselves and hid it in a series of poses. Both intelligent we did very badly at schoolwork: Neither of us was even entered for the Intermediate Certificate. Steve's problems were more serious than mine: I think nowadays he would have been classed, and treated, as dyslexic. He certainly had great difficulty in writing, which made his achievement in entering medical school, graduating as a doctor, and in later life earning a very distinguished reputation as a psychiatrist, all the more remarkable. We both enjoyed the esteem and friendship of some of the more intelligent of the masters at St Columba's. Steve had a distinctive artistic talent and produced some strange, slightly disturbing, paintings. I edited an unofficial school magazine of which more later and had two little booklets of poems printed by the College printing club.

Memories of him come crowding back. Our first experience of alcohol, drinking flagons of cider one Sunday afternoon in a thicket of brambles on the side of Kilmashogue. There was a leaf hanging down and with every swig we would reach out and touch it with a finger until at last we weren't able to connect with it first time. There were the times we climbed out of the dormitory windows at St Columba's and went for long walks in Marlay woods, drinking sherry out of cut Waterford sherry glasses that Steve had procured, and arguing about the purpose of life. There was a lake in the Marlay estate and once when we were drinking our sherry in the boat in the middle of the lake someone started shouting at us from the waterside. It was two or three in the morning. We had to stay in the boat until we could be sure whoever it was had got fed up and gone away. And once we cycled at night all the way down to Dublin and climbed into the house where some of Steve's aunts and uncles lived, in Ranelagh. The table was laid for breakfast, the kettle filled, cups upturned on saucers, porridge, bacon and eggs all laid out ready. We sat down and ate the aunts' and uncles' breakfasts.

Because of his parents' tragic death, home was with two eccentric aunts who lived in Leinster Road, Rathmines. One of these ladies I only knew by sight but the other, Lena, had a memorably strong personality. An accident (she had broken her neck, said Steve) had left her partially disabled. This didn't stop her climbing ladders but it made her speech very hard to understand. "Watch this," Steve would say, whenever some religious fund-raiser or missionary came to the door, "She hates religion." And Lena would bang on the window and squawk inarticulate abuse at the unfortunate Salvationist. The aunts still lived in the nineteenth century; all the furniture, even the kitchen equipment was extraordinarily outdated. Electricity had only been installed in 1939. I remember one evening we took all the family photographs down in one room, removed the sepia portraits of dignitaries in uniforms or frock coats from the heavy Victo-

Steve (R D Stevenson)

rian frames, and replaced them with reproductions of Picasso and, Steve's great enthusiasm of the time, Van Gogh.

In the first year after leaving school both Steve and I missed the closely structured community life of St Columba's very much and we found it hard to adapt to living on our own. It was harder for Steve than for me since I was at Trinity. We had various adventures together. For instance we attended a spiritualist séance. Though neither of us was particularly devout, we were both interested in finding evidence of the existence of some sort of non-physical, supernatural, reality, if such a thing existed. We had seen a notice announcing that an English medium, a Mrs Emilia Clutterbuck would be attending a Spiritualist meeting at a Dublin address. (By the way, I can't think how Mrs Clutterbuck coped with the problems of wartime travel restrictions.) Anyhow she did and we went along. It was actually a sort of religious service held in a private house somewhere near the canal. The door was opened by the somewhat seedy geography master we had had at the High School years before and we were ushered upstairs to a room where about ten or twelve people were singing a hymn while a lady in a long dress, presumably Mrs Clutterbuck, sat facing them with her eyes closed. When the singing ended she opened her eyes and pointed her finger round the room at various members of the audience/congregation, telling them about the presences she saw or sensed standing by them.

"The gentlemen third from the left in the back row, yes, you sir. I sense a person with grey hair."

"Would she be wearin' a green hat?"

"No hat."

"I don't see who it is. Is she a small thin class of a woman?" And so on.

Steve got up suddenly and walked out. He told me he was sure she was going to start telling him she could see his parents. Whether she could or not we certainly did not find there the convincing evidence of Another World that we were seeking. Steve used to do a ludicrously funny imitation of Mrs Clutterbuck.

I can't remember what Steve did with himself during those months but it's likely that the general feeling of *désoeuvrement* we suffered from explains his sudden decision, in 1944, to go to Belfast and join the British Army. I never knew exactly why he did this. In all our arguments and discussions we had never talked about politics, or about the war and a possible personal involvement in it. It's true that a number of old Columbans were joining up. There was certainly a measure of unselfish idealism in this and Steve could well have wanted to follow their example. He was a soldier, in the Irish Guards, for two years, saw action in Belgium and Germany, driving a Bren gun carrier, and then, when the war ended, was sent back to England where he was given the absurd job of helping to guard the Tower of London. He applied for demobilisation on compassionate grounds, saying that his aged aunt in Dublin needed him. The Army authorities had the British High Commission in Dublin send someone round to Leinster Road to check the truth of this, and Aunt Lena, who had been put wise to it, put on such a performance, exaggerating in every imaginable way the gravity of her medical condition, squawking and dribbling, that Steve was home within a week.

Once he was back in Dublin we saw lot of each other. We made another attempt to penetrate the occult world some time after he had come home from the British Army. Together we cycled to near Roscrea, where the ruins of Leap Castle (pronounced Lepp) had the reputation of being the most haunted place in Ireland. The stories told about the place were certainly eerie. Local people told of strange lights and weird sounds. An old friend of my mother's, Dr Helen Boyle, had actually stayed there when it was still inhabited by, I think, the O'Carroll family. The sudden presence of what they called the elemental spirit, accompanied by an appalling smell of rotting flesh, had meant that they had to vacate the dining room in the middle of dinner.

It seemed to Steve and me that if evidence of the supernatural could be found anywhere it would be here. It was the right time of year too, a day or two before All Souls. We climbed into the castle as night fell, and lit a fire. We were in good form and had plenty to talk about, Steve recounting lurid and hilarious tales of Army life. But after some hours we got tired and cold and Steve developed one of his imperative desires (I must have dressed crab, Basil), this time for a drink of milk. We walked for miles along little boreens but it was long after midnight, there wasn't a house anywhere. At last we saw a light in the distance and made our way, with great difficulty across fields, to a thatched cottage. We looked through the window: there was a coffin on the table and people sitting around it drinking, it was a wake. So we made our way back to Leap castle. But it looked so sinister in the moonlight that we couldn't face going back into it and climbed into the hay in a nearby barn to sleep the rest of the night. We saw no ghosts. The only really strange thing, which made a powerful impression on us at the time, happened on the way to Leap, when we were somewhere in County Kildare. I remember it very clearly: we were cycling along the main road - there was no traffic then, because of petrol rationing - when an old tramp suddenly walked into the middle of the road, held up his hand and stopped us. "Two boys," he said, and then, pointing to Steve, "And this one's the better of the two." And then, "Boys," he said, "Ye are going to a dark and an evil place, and may the Mother of God watch over ye when ye get there."

Steve was such good company, so free of all normal inhibitions and the fear of being made fun of that he always made me feel pompous, fussy and materialistic. He had a talent for not taking things seriously and for seeing the funny side of things that I admired greatly. It is true, funny things kept happening to him. There was the time he went to France with a motorcycle and sidecar and got lost in the suburbs of Liverpool and then broke down. He took a bus into the centre of the town to buy a part for the bike but didn't note the number of the bus. So he had to take bus after bus to different suburbs until he caught sight of the wretched vehicle as they went past. Or the time when he was doing his anatomy exams and Mae, the maidservant at Leinster Road who looked after Aunt Lena, got her boyfriend, who was a gravedigger, to bring back bones from the cemetery which Steve used to boil up so that he could study them.

Then there was the saga of his receiving Catholic instruction. Steve fell in love with a girl called Betty O'Mara. She was sensationally pretty, warm and sensual, but a very devout Catholic. It was nineteen forty five: Irish Catholicism was at its most fundamentalist. Steve was obsessed with Betty, who, while she was attracted to him, clearly never contemplated a future with anyone so unconventional, and a Protestant to boot. She criticised him for not being a Catholic so he decided there was nothing for it but to go to the Jesuits in Gardiner Street, take instruction and become a Catholic himself. At that time he was trying, fairly desperately, to get into Trinity, to start a medical degree. I used to cycle out to Leinster Road to give him tuition in Latin and French for Trinity Entrance. The first teaching I ever did.

Steve would regale me with hilarious accounts of his weekly dialogue with the Jesuits. It wouldn't ever have been an easy conversion. He objected to the idea of the Index. "What books do you want to read anyway?" said the priest.

"Well, Voltaire," says Steve, an admirer of Bernard Shaw. The priest sneered at this taste in literature so Steve got up and walked out. But the desire to be like Betty was too strong, so he returned and found that the Jesuits had realised what they were up against and had given the job of instructing Steve to a very sophisticated, smooth ecclesiastic, (in a velvet soutane, said Steve). Week by week Steve would raise an objection to some article of Catholic doctrine: transubstantiation, virgin birth etc. Each time the Jesuit would produce elaborate sophistries to prove that, for example, the miracles were full of deep meanings very different from the conjuring tricks that the ignorant believed in. "In other words," said Steve, "You mean that all that is just for the peasants." The Jesuit would wrap this up in sonorous words and talk about brethren of simple faith. And they would go on. Until eventually they came to what Steve called the Doctrine of the Extraordinary Contraption. ("Not just one pigeon, but generations of pigeons stretching back to the dawn of time.") This time the reverend monsignor's soothing explanations were to no avail. "As far as I can see," said Steve, "Your whole caboodle is just for the peasants." And that was the end of it. But the motivation had been weakening for some weeks: Betty must have begun to feel it was time for her to move on. Mae, the maidservant in Leinster Road, suggested to Steve that if he stopped seeing Betty for a time she would become keen on him again. So he told her he was going to London, and hid indoors in Leinster Road for a week, not daring to go out for fear he'd chance to run into her. When he came back from "London" there was a touching reunion. But it was only temporary. Anyway, during his supposed week away he had missed a session with his instructor. So when he went back to Gardiner Street he said, "I'm sorry I didn't come last week", and, deciding he might as well give the same explanation as he'd given to Betty, said, "I was in London." "I know, my son, I know," said velvet soutane. "Well he couldn't have bloody known," said Steve, "Because I wasn't in London at all."

All these anecdotes just tend to portray the sort of likeable clown that is prone to funny misfortunes. And they show - I can see it now - an inadequacy in our friendship, on my side. There was much more to Steve than this. I could have done more to help him than I did in those early years. He himself was the most loyal and devoted of friends. I shall never forget one example of this. In 1965 I was in Manchester, going through a dreadful personal crisis. I desperately needed to talk to someone. So I rang Steve up at the hospital he worked at, in South Wales. It was late at night. I expected at most an extended phone call. But Steve got into his Mini, drove all the way from Swansea, and spent half the night reasoning with me and talking me out of the slough of despair I had got myself into, before setting off to drive the 200 miles back to work.

I saw him only rarely during the last 30 years, and not at all in the five or six years before he died. Our paths didn't cross, we lived in different countries, Steve never wrote letters, at least not to me. But it might also have been that, each of us having found ourselves at last, we had less need of each other. By the time he retired he was a foremost national authority on alcoholism with an impressive string of qualifications to his name while at the same time he was voted year after year as the most popular lecturer at the Royal College of Surgeons. Of one thing, however, I am sure, for he as good as told me several times. If Steve found himself and was able to embark on so very distinguished, and characteristically unorthodox, a medical career, it was thanks to his triumphantly successful and happy marriage to Martine Hoffet. Disorganised, hypersensitive, lacking dreadfully in self-confidence while at the same time having deep down a sure idea of his potential and his ability, he began to change, to come together, the moment he got married. I can remember one evening, soon after they were married, in the International Bar, where we always used to meet. Martine had said that it was time to go home and had taken Steve off.

"What's up with Steve?" said one of the cronies, "He's not the fun he used to be."

"I'll tell you what's up with him," said another, Jimmy Smith I think, more perceptive than the rest, "He's a happy man." I like to think that the tormented, hilariously funny, uncompromising and unusual person that I shared my boyhood with turned finally into a happy man.

Michael Biggs was a very different person from either Will Harvey or Steve, and our relationship was a phenomenon of a very different order. To put it simply I was in love with Michael that last year at St Columba's and for some time after I left. Romantic, homosexual affairs, on all levels from platonic idealising down to fumbling physicality, were a common feature of everyday life in Columba's. It was a fact which Warden Sowby failed, or refused, totally, to understand, seeing all manifestations of the "love that dare not speak its name" as an abomination about which the last word was to be found in the Book of Leviticus. Some other masters were more comprehending, recognizing that a hundred and fifty adolescent males cooped up in a semi-monastic environment will inevitably find, or devise, an outlet for their emotional energy, not to mention their sexuality.

Michael and I came together when the idea of an unofficial school magazine, to be called *Why Not* and edited by me, was suggested, by Eric Earle of the College Printing Club. I invited Michael to contribute and he came up with the idea of doing caricatures of College personalities. Our limited facilities meant that they would have to be printed by lino-cut, so Michael quickly mastered this craft and produced a handful of brilliantly funny drawings. If ever I look now at the tattered copies of *Why Not* that have survived, the style and the humour of the text seem so embarrassingly puerile as to make me cringe, but Michael's caricatures still stand out.

Michael and I saw each other mostly in the holidays. He was a strikingly beautiful sixteen-year old with his ginger hair and blue eyes. In addition he was highly intelligent, and his conversation was both witty and thoughtful. Our relationship was a very happy one, situated somewhere half-way along the spectrum between the platonic and the physical. It was certainly very different from the jealousy-obsessed love affairs described in Campbell's novel about Columba's, though I think I worried occasionally about how or whether it would end. I needn't have worried, in the event we just grew out of it after a year or two, though we remained close friends for years afterwards. I don't think we ever talked much about the nature of our relationship, but during term-time we kept out of each other's way, if only not to attract the attention of the school gossips. Michael's parents were English, his father, Claud Biggs, was a concert pianist and Professor of Piano at the Irish Academy of Music. He specialised in playing Bach. He and Michael's mother were fairly high church Anglicans and attended church services regularly. I don't know what they thought of Michael and my friendship; they were always very good to me.

I think this may have been because they compared me favourably with Brian Boydell. Once they invited Brian and me around one evening to their house in Rathgar. Brian's inability to see himself as others saw him, usually quite a likeable characteristic, worked on this occasion to his disadvantage. "Would you like to wash your hands," said Mrs Biggs when we arrived. "I never wash my hands," said Brian Boydell, beaming around him, "Because as soon as I put them in my pockets they are dirty again." Later in the evening Brian did a few party tricks. Some of these were very funny, as for example when he sat down at the Biggs's concert grand piano and played things like Annie Laurie in a way that made it sound as though the piano was dreadfully out of tune. But one of these acts was not appreciated. It consisted in taking a death notice at random from the evening paper and improvising a recitative and aria in the style of Handel's Messiah. The recitative consisted of the death notice proper (Mulligan, suddenly at his residence, James Mulligan, 13 Brighton Avenue etc) while the aria used as its libretto the lines of pious doggerel that usually accompanied death notices in the evening paper. Boydell declaimed the name and address and other details to the accompaniment of dramatic Handelian chords. Nobody laughed. And, when he went on to sing the aria, the atmosphere froze. "Sacred Heart of Jesus, Look down upon my dad, " he sang, his powerful voice ringing out, rising and falling, putting in runs and repetitions, "The nicest father any girl ever had..." When he reached the final chords there was a silence which only ended when I said it was late and I must get home. The embarrassment was such that even Boydell must have been conscious of it. "Somehow I don't think they really appreciated my Handel," he said, as we walked back, "I can't think why."

The best times Michael and I had together were when we cycled around the west and south of Ireland. Because of the "Emergency" there was very little motor traffic, hardly any cars and only occasional lorries or buses, which made the roads much more user friendly for cyclists than they are today. Also, in order, it was said, to confuse possible German parachutists, all signposts were removed. In those days there was much less difference than there is now between the major and minor roads. So we ended up quite good at map reading, though the only maps we had were out of date Bartholomew's quarter inch. To begin with we spent quite a lot of time trying to relate the evidence of the landscape around us to where we thought we were on the map. We got in the habit of asking where we were whenever we arrived in a town or village which used to seem, to the inhabitant we asked, a crazy question. There were technical difficulties too; tyres and inner tubes were almost unobtainable. I once had to get a cobbler to repair a tyre by stitching it together.

It wasn't easy either to find places to stay the night, especially as we had very little money. We had joined An Oige, the Irish Youth Hostels Association but there were no hostels where we were going. However, since Irish hotels were suffering from the wartime lack of visitors, An Oige had negotiated an agreement with hotel keepers by which its members could have supper bed and breakfast for a few shillings if they brought their own sheet bag and contented themselves with the most basic of meals. Not surprisingly the accommodation we encountered varied enormously but was usually spartan in the extreme: damp beds, bread and margarine washed down by watery tea in surroundings which had seen better days: mahogany tables in vast dining rooms and huge carpeted bedrooms. Once or twice we had to stay in places where we were asked if we didn't mind sharing the room with one or two "decent gentlemen". There were times when we slept out, sitting or crouching uncomfortably under trees or in some ruined house. If we were in luck we would find the most comfortable solution of all, a barn full of hay.

We started in County Clare, partly because it was the only part of the Free State, as it was called then, that I didn't know at all from holidays with the parents, and partly because of my fascination with caves, underground rivers and other subterranean phenomena. We managed to locate Poulnagollum, which was at the time, and, for all I know, is still, the most extensive cave system in the British Isles. The entrance to it was a much more intimidating sight than the Desmond Cave at Mitchelstown. It was at the bottom of a huge funnel-shaped pot-hole about 80 feet deep. Three sides of this impressive gulf were vertical but the fourth consisted of a steep very slippery slope which we slid down. Holding bicycle lamps in our hands, half climbing half crawling, we entered a passage that wound downwards. All around us we could hear the noise of running water which made the whole place seem alive. In comparison the Desmond Cave at Mitchelstown had been dry, except for occasional stagnant pools. After a while we came to a vertical drop. In the blackness far below we could hear the echoing boom of a considerable waterfall. It was clear that to adventure further called for more equipment, more experience and more courage than either of us possessed. And Michael had neither Will's skill as a rock climber nor Will's taste for adventure. Also, it is only fair to say, he was several years younger than Will. So we turned back. Not without difficulty we managed to get out and up the gluey clay of the slope.

Freudian explanations for mountaineering always seemed to me far-fetched. Regarding the fascination of caverns, underground rivers and the orifices that led to them, on the other hand, the symbolism was obvious, and powerful. Not far from Poulnagollum we found our way to the mossy lip of Poulnaelva, a pot-hole over the same underground river, but an even scarier abyss. No sloping side here, the walls, black with damp, were sheer, and the bottom of the "deep romantic chasm", that slanted far below, was concealed in the shade of the vegetation, trees and bushes, whose roots could be seen clinging to cracks in the rock. And, here also, from the depths could be heard "the boom, of the far waterfall, like Doom".

The sensations afforded by the cliffs of Moher were of a simpler and less poetic order. Though not particularly high, as compared for example with Slieve League in Donegal, the Moher cliffs have the speciality of being completely vertical, in fact they actually overhang in places. There is, or was when we were there, no fence at the brink. You could, and we did, lie with only your head protruding over the edge and look straight down at the water, 600 feet below. The trouble was, when you did that, you got very little impression of the height. So we looked around and found one or two boulders some distance away and, very laboriously, by lying on the ground and pushing them with our feet, we managed to roll them to the edge. Then, lying side by side with a boulder between us, we succeeded in tipping them, one by one, over the brink. They took a satisfyingly long time to splash into the sea and, as each one went down, it dwindled until from being a foot or two across it seemed no bigger than a pea.

Passing through Kerry we managed to scramble up Carrauntuohill, Ireland's highest mountain. I had climbed it when I was 10 years old with the parents, in the mist and rain. This time we had the sort of weather that hill walkers reminisce about. It seemed to us that the whole of Ireland was spread out visibly at our feet like a huge map. Away to the North East I thought I could even see Galteemore. We had reached the top by first climbing a secondary peak, Caher, which is connected to Carrauntuohill by a narrow slightly exposed ridge, my first experience of that unique exhilaration afforded by altitude, described to me many years later in the Pyrenees by old Leon Gassan, as "the sensation that you are visiting the sky". Instead of going down by the way we had come up we decided that the "normal" route seemed easier, so we plodded down interminable scree into the Hag's Glen. Next day, to get back to our bikes, we discovered how much longer and more tedious it is to go around a mountain than to go over it.

During the war, and long before Shannon airport was built, Foynes, on the

Shannon estuary, was the refuelling point for trans-Atlantic air travel, which in those days was always by flying boat. We stayed there in a guesthouse run by a kindly retired railway engineer. He was an insomniac and we sat up late into the night as he described in loving detail features of the Lartigue railway which used to run early in the century to Listowel. The Lartigue was a monorail and the locomotives had two boilers hanging like saddlebags one on each side of the central rail. Cattle and horses could only be transported in even numbers so as not to upset the balance of the wagons.

When we arrived at Foynes a plane had just come in from I suppose Southampton. Important-looking people in expensive clothes were being ferried in from the plane in a large motor boat and men in uniform with English accents were getting them, with great deference, into taxis. Next morning, following our railwayman's directions, we scrambled in a mad rush through bramble thickets to reach a place where we could watch the big Sunderland flying boat taking off. A moment after we had got to the viewpoint it came in sight, lumbering awkwardly over the choppy little waves, gathering speed very slowly. It skimmed then for a moment along the surface, like a speedboat, and, all of a sudden, coming as it were unstuck from the water, seemed to leap into the air. Then, once it was in its own element, it disappeared quickly out over the Atlantic, heading for Gander in Newfoundland.

In Achill we stayed for a week with Brian Boydell, who was spending the summer in the westernmost cottage on the island. Other people came and went while we were there, the painters Thurloe Connolly and David Hone, Brian's eccentric sister Yvonne, others whose names I don't remember. It was a pleasantly bohemian set up. Brian and the others painted; Michael did some drawings. I underlined my lack of artistic talent by putting a curiously shaped piece of bog-wood on the fire to be told afterwards that I had destroyed an *objet trouvé*. Since there was no electricity there could be no recorded music. So Brian suggested we should sing rounds. Oppressed by the musical banality of all of the traditional rounds that we could remember Brian started composing new ones, often with strange interesting modern harmonies. Meals in the cottage happened at indeterminate and irregular intervals. In fact we ate whenever Brian was hungry, but then he was a marvellous cook. I had never seen a man cooking; in those days it was very unusual. My father, who had many varied talents, was only just able to boil an egg. But I have a vivid memory of watching Brian Boydell making a cake of soda bread, admiring his quick deft movements, and thinking to myself that I should like to be like that. I could have chosen a worse role model, though it is true that now, whenever I break a cup or generate some other domestic accident, my wife Olivia always says, "That Brian Boydell has a lot to answer for..."

In the course of our week in Achill Michael and I climbed Craughaun mountain, explored the fearsomely jagged cliffs leading to Achill Head and swam in the Mediterranean blue waters of Keem Bay. Once when there had been a high wind all night Boydell took us all to a savage rocky cove facing the Atlantic to admire the waves. Tucked in among the sacks of charcoal piled in the back of his car, which was a sort of pickup truck, we sang Brian's newly composed rounds at the top of our voices in the teeth of the storm. Brian Boydell was not only amazingly lively and entertaining company but extremely generous. In Achill, as in his house in Rathfarnham, the door was never closed and friends would wander in at all hours, and if their visit coincided with a mealtime Brian considered it quite normal for them to sit down and eat with us. One day in Achill a telegram arrived announcing the arrival of another Columban, Patrick Tenison I think. But the wretched Tenison elected to arrive by train in Sligo, eighty miles away. Brian thought nothing of loading the car up with enough charcoal for a hundred and sixty miles and going to fetch him. This required a very early start and, since early rising was not in the habits of the household, it was decided we would stay up all night. This we did, singing rounds and playing cards until six in the morning. We all trooped out, bleary eyed, to see Brian off. The anti-climax came when the car refused to start and he had to take the carburettor to pieces before eventually leaving at about lunchtime.

On the last day of our last trip together Michael and I covered the hundred miles from Portumna to Dublin in less than ten hours. We had no choice since we had run out of money but it seemed somehow appropriate: to have broken our daily record on our last day seemed in some ways a fitting conclusion to this stage in our friendship. We never spoke of the change in our relationship. Michael left school a year or two later. He did not go to university; instead he went and trained in England having decided to follow in the footsteps of Eric Gill whom he admired. When he came back to Ireland he set himself up as a stonemason specialised in cutting inscriptions in stone. Jobs in Ireland were hard to come by in those days; Michael solved the problem by inventing a trade for himself as a letter-carver. When the Government, setting up a monument to the memory of the men of 1916 at Arbour Hill in North Dublin, looked around for someone to carve their names, Michael was an obvious choice. It took him years. I used to go and see him working on this, marvelling at his patience and the accuracy with which he chiselled into stone never making a mistake. He was wittily scornful of commercial monumental masons who carve lettering on tombstones, using an instrument like a dentist's drill.

In later years, though we remained friends, we met only occasionally and every time we met we seemed to have the same conversation, about the artist's role in society, not a subject about which I had anything very interesting to say. Michael had come to have more in common with my brother Conor: they were both single-minded artists and perfectionists. He died tragically, in 1993, while still in his early sixties, of a rare and little understood nervous illness which affected his hands, causing him such excruciating pain when he moved his fingers that, when he died, they were actually considering easing the pain by amputating his hands, an appalling situation for a sculptor.

By this time he had made for himself a considerable reputation as a sculptor. His finest work, at least the piece I admired most, was, and is, the altar, font and lectern in the Catholic Church at Dun Laoghaire. The altar, one huge single slab of Wicklow granite weighing several tons, was so large and so heavy that they had to open the roof of the church to lower it in with a crane. At first sight it is just a huge more or less rectangular block of stone, but when you look at it and realise that there are no flat surfaces anywhere, you begin to see in it, subtly limned out, the gentle hills and hollows of a human torso. Looking at it I suddenly remembered an argument we had had long years before, when looking at pictures of one of the great cathedrals, Chartres probably, and Michael saying, "I just don't feel it's the right thing to do with stone. You have to let the granite speak."

# 4 College

I ENTERED UNIVERSITY, Trinity College Dublin, TCD, in September 1943. The qualification that most students presented was either the Irish Intermediate Certificate or the English School Cert. I had been in a B stream at St Columba's and had not been presented for either of these examinations. Instead, in my last year at school I had been prepared for an examination, which was called Trinity Entrance and was organised by the University, and accepted as an entrance qualification, but was not used as such by most of the students that sat it. In fact I think I was the only boy in the class that actually went to Trinity. The others joined the Army or went to work in some job. Things were very much easier in those days than they are now and I enrolled without difficulty at Trinity in an honours course in modern languages. I had wanted to do English but Joint Honours was the rule so I put myself down for English and French. I had originally wanted to put down English and Irish, since I knew nothing of France and my Irish was much better than my French, but Peter Allt persuaded me to change, pointing out that I would find French literature more interesting which was certainly true. I often wonder how different my life would have been if I hadn't taken his advice.

On the whole I don't regard my time at university as having been particularly successful. I ended up with a respectable degree getting first-class honours in English and second-class in French, which the university later lumped together as an upper second. But Trinity in those years, at least so far as modern languages and English were concerned, was not a very inspiring place intellectually. I was certainly a very complacent, easy-going but somewhat conceited, young man. St Columba's had given me a veneer of sophistication which concealed, from myself if not from others, an almost total lack of any real self-knowledge. I would have needed, we would all have needed, the sort of rude shock that medical students receive when they first enter the dissecting room. This was certainly not forthcoming from the lectures in English literature that

I attended. Most of these were pedestrian in the extreme. The Professor of English, H.O. White, was a vague, totally un-awe-inspiring man, who carefully cultivated an absent-minded professor image. His colleagues were probably conscientious teachers monologuing away professionally about the standard literary landmarks. But in the course of the four years I spent in T.C.D. there all too rarely happened that special moment, which justifies the whole university set up, when knowledge seems to take fire from a teacher's enthusiasm for his or her subject, and the memory of the occasion remains with you for years. It happened once in English when the Professor of Greek, W. B. Stanford, was invited to talk to us about tragedy. Many years later when, in Manchester, I suddenly had to take a sick colleague's tutorial on Corneille, and on Le Cid which I had, as it happens, never read; I was glad to be able to tap into the long-dormant enthusiasm for classical tragedy that single lecture had generated.

If I could be critical of the lecturers in English it was because, from St Columbas, I was already acquainted with Shakespeare Wordsworth and Milton et al. French was something different. I knew next to nothing about French literature and my knowledge of the language was less than rudimentary. As I puzzled my way through the Balzac short stories that figured on the syllabus for the first examination, searching the dictionaries to translate the names of obscure pieces of furniture or obsolete articles of clothing, it was difficult to appreciate Balzac's literary genius. Fortunately, as I was not the first to find out, the Trinity university library, by virtue of the copyright legislation, possessed translations of all the French classics. I read all that I could in English. But it wasn't always possible to cheat in this fashion. The censorship of publications legislation in force in Ireland at the time had banned most contemporary French writers on grounds of "indecency", including such prominent modern Catholic authors as Mauriac and Bernanos. The ban, however, only applied to the English translations; one was free to obtain and read the French original. So I had to read quite a lot of French and over the years a certain amount of the language rubbed off on me. As Owen Sheehy Skeffington remarked about the censorship, the official view was probably that anyone who was able to read French was damned already anyhow.

Of all the University teachers I had he was certainly the one to whom I owed the most. Not that he was a brilliant lecturer, though his notes on Zola or Balzac or Proust were almost always interesting. He had, I think, written out his lectures in full at some time in the past, which was shown up by occasional anachronisms. As, for example, when he would mention: "Other young writers..." citing a list of middle-aged has-beens. Inevitably there were plenty of dull moments. But he made up for them by talking off-the-cuff about the background, social, historical and above all political, to whatever writer was the subject of his lecture. On these occasions he communicated two things that were to be enormously important, personally, to me. One was an informed, humanist, left-wing view of society; the other was a deep, not uncritical but comprehensive, love of France and things French. Unable, because of the war, to go to France we knew little or nothing about the social or national context of the literature we were studying. In the course of these red herrings, and in the intervals between explaining the Dreyfus Case and the history of the Third Republic, he would also wax lyrical about French wines or Paris cafés where, he said, you could sit all morning over one cup of coffee and where the waiters would bring you newspapers and writing materials at a click of your fingers. (Alas no longer true.)

His francophilia had a dimension that I did not appreciate fully until I met him in a French-speaking context many years later. His spoken French was outstandingly good, not only as regards pronunciation but in his command of vocabulary and turn of phrase. This must have rubbed off on us to some extent but I only appreciated it in retrospect when, years later, I met graduates from Oxford or Cambridge where linguistic skills were not only neglected but positively looked down upon. One such, a colleague I had in Paris, who knew a lot about French literature and read Proust in French for pleasure, was quite unembarrassed in Paris restaurants ordering things like duzz uffs doerz (*deux oeufs durs*) or oon salad nickoyze (*une salade niçoise*). Looking back I think it is a great pity Skeffington didn't lecture to us in French, though at the time the idea would have appalled me.

Once, during our first year, my friend and fellow old-Columban John Heuston, already displaying a journalist's eye for unusual *faits divers*, found out somehow that Skeffington would be speaking at a meeting of, I think, a branch of Sinn Fein. Together we found our way to a somewhat dreary meeting room in N. Frederick Street. Owen told me years later that he had been taken aback to see two students from his First Year French class sitting there, surrounded by hardened republicans. His talk in favour of socialism was cleverly illustrated by a host of relevant quotations from unimpeachable Irish patriots, Padraic Pearse, Fintan Lalor, Wolfe Tone etc. The discussion that followed his talk had nothing to do with socialism and was dominated by bitter recriminations from one speaker accusing other speakers of different degrees of betrayal of the cause.

The French Department was at the time in a slightly curious situation. The Professor of French, Rudmose-Brown, an eminent Racine scholar, had just died and had not been replaced. Sheehy-Skeffington was acting Head of Department but was unlikely to be appointed to the Chair since he had done very little research, his main interest being in politics; he went on to become one of the University's representatives in the Irish Senate, and was described later as a voice of liberalism crying in the wilderness of nineteen-fifties conformism. There was a conscientious but somewhat colourless woman called Dr Orgel (I often wondered if she was related to my fellow swindler at The High School).

And there was Jean Pierre Molinier, an exchange student from the Ecole Normale Supérieure. Molinier had been caught in Ireland by the fall of France. He was an albino with very weak eyesight. You would see him in the library holding a book two or three inches from his face. He was a keen cyclist and I ran into him once or twice on my cycling peregrinations around the West of Ireland. A highly intelligent man his political affiliations were very much to the left. This of course meant that he was persona non grata at the French Legation in Dublin, which, though there apparently were internal tensions, represented, for most of the war, not De Gaulle's government in London, but Vichy. Rudmose-Brown, whose politics were I believe very right wing, had been on very friendly terms with the French Legation, but these friendly relations died with him. Now the frontier between La France Libre and the occupied France of Marshal Pétain passed between the Legation in Ailesbury Road and the School of Modern Languages in Trinity College. Sheehy-Skeffington used to encourage us to listen to Free French broadcasts from London which always started: "*Ici Londres; les français parlent aux français*". He once mischievously set the English version of one of these in an exam for us to translate, so as to catch out those of us that didn't know the French for "London calling" and who wrote something like "*Voici Londres qui appelle.*"

All this is typical of the incidental way in which the War impinged upon our daily life and consciousness. We had very little idea of the reality of the conflict that was tearing Europe apart, not to mention the wider world. I don't think I was in any way untypical in this, though it is true I did know people who suffered a tragic loss through a brother or boyfriend who was killed. But, apart from Steve, no close friend of mine was on active service and, with regard to Steve, I somehow couldn't represent to myself, or be fearful of, the danger that I knew he was in. When, a few years later, listening to my friends Henri's and Jacques' descriptions of life in France under the Occupation, I became aware of some at least of the horrors that my contemporaries in other countries had lived through, instead of feeling guilty at the easy life I had led I just felt glad that Ireland and the Irish had been able to keep out of the War. On the other hand there was no question where our sympathies lay, and I can remember how concerned the parents were in 1940, when there seemed to be a serious danger, not only that Nazi Germany might win, but that the next phase might well involve the invasion of Ireland by German troops.

I had started writing poetry in my first year at Columba's. English being the only subject that I was any good at, it seemed an obvious thing to do. I wrote a poem about the wild landscape of Three Rock Mountain which was printed in the school magazine. This was encouragement enough and I went on writing and my friend Eric Earle produced, with the equipment of the school printing club, the booklet containing, and called, *Ten Poems* that attracted the attention of Peter Allt. Dreadful derivative juvenile stuff, I can't imagine what he found in it to praise. But it is true my Aunt Ruth, Ben's wife, was impressed by the poems and said so to my father. I went on writing and in my last year at school produced a more ambitious booklet entitled Midnight with illustrations, linocuts, by Michael Biggs. I was very proud of Midnight and various friends and relations were obligingly complimentary so I thought it was only normal when a reviewer in the English Poetry Review described it as "the most pellucid poetry so far encountered this year." Then, in my first year in College, I met the Belfast poet Robert Greacen and he took me to meet Geoffrey Taylor, literary editor of the magazine *The Bell*. We sat in a room lined with bookshelves, all of them poetry, Geoffrey told us. I listened as they discussed literary topics. And next day I sent Taylor a copy of Midnight, sure that I had my foot on the first rung of some ladder of literary success.

Because Ben's first wife had spoken highly of my first little book I expected him to be even more favourably impressed by the copy of Midnight that I sent him. I was as surprised as I was disappointed when he wrote back, kindly but very frankly, saying that he found much less to admire in it than in my earlier book, which had seemed to him to express a positive and thoughtful attitude to life, implying that such was not the case in Midnight. I was even more seriously discouraged by the letter I received from Geoffrey Taylor. He said he found my poems, "well written but too talented," and "not autochthonous". When I think about it now I can see that what he meant was that I could write but quite simply had nothing to say, or, if I had, I was just not saying it. I can see now that both he and my uncle were right. Most of the poems in Midnight are just self-indulgent word-spinning. But the problem I had in those years of college and after was both greater and deeper than any question of mere literary expression. Nowadays we would maybe describe it as a problem of self-image. I don't know whence the *angoisse* came but *angoisse* it was. When I thought about it, and I avoided thinking as much as possible, I didn't know what I wanted from life. Other students I talked to saw their future, the jobs they hoped to get, the salaries they hoped to earn, quite clearly, but I couldn't share their modest ambitions: sit on your arse for fifty years and hang your hat on a pension, as MacNeice said; it seemed appallingly claustrophobic. The patrician attitudes I had learnt from Peter Allt, the arrogance I had cultivated in imitation of W. B. Yeats, were an inadequate covering to conceal the diffident, undecided person I was slowly discovering myself to be.

Could I see myself as a poet? It's true that, in spite of the criticisms I received and my own misgivings, writing poetry was, for years, what I liked doing best and what I did best. I realised quite soon, however, that I just didn't have the commitment necessary, I was not single-minded enough, to give myself up full heartedly to writing poetry. Also, though it was what I did best, and though my best poems were, and are, quite good, if maybe technically unadventurous, they were not good enough to justify my setting myself up, so to speak, professionally, as a poet. There was another more powerful, and more important, reason that I was only half aware of to begin with but which became more important with time. It was that I didn't feel that I belonged to a community. Quite early in my life I had adopted a view of the poet's place in society, which was refined and strengthened later by the Marxism I learnt in France. This was that the poet's function was, not only to describe the world as he or she saw it, but to give a voice to, and speak for, a group of people. An important part of my self-image problem was that I couldn't feel myself to be part of any recognizable coherent community. Looking down from the viewpoint of age on the young man that I was then I can see that this was largely imaginary. I was a middle class Protestant Dubliner, I was a bourgeois nationalist, I was a left-leaning intellectual; there were plenty of other labels that I could have found acceptable, groups that I could have identified with. The trouble was that I could not in my heart feel myself at one with any section of the community; when I looked around at my fellow intellectuals, fellow Protestants, fellow students, the dominant feeling I had was how different I was from them. I think I also thought myself, against all the evidence, in some mysterious way superior. Had I been able to see all of this as clearly as I do now, 60 odd years later, I might have been able to make poetry out of an identity problem that was surely not unique among young Irish-minded middle class Protestant intellectuals in the Ireland of the day. But I hadn't the self-knowledge, the intensity or the talent for that. Instead I sedulously avoided any situation in which I was called upon to face the fact that, though I loved my country and my native city, I could not bring myself to feel, wholeheartedly, that I belonged there.

I met Constance Conner in my second year at College. Until then the female sex had played a very small part in my life. My mother's clear preference for boys meant that few girls came to our children's parties. Single sex schools were the norm; to my knowledge there was only one coeducational boarding school in Ireland patronised by middle class Dubliners at the time and that was Newtown School in Waterford. In College we old Columbans, but not only us, tended to regard people who had been at Newtown as slightly unusual. We couldn't see that what was unusual about them was an almost normal attitude to the opposite sex. The attitude prevalent among male students on the other hand was sexist in the extreme. Though Trinity College can claim credit for being one of the first "old" Universities to give degrees to women, the manner in which college life was organised, both officially and unofficially, did little to change traditional ways of thinking. The entire campus was closed to women students at six o'clock; a fairly recent dispensation allowed them access to the Library after six, but only on condition that they did not stray from a strait and narrow path between the Reading Room and the Front Gate. The two main student societies, the College Historical Society or "Hist" and the University Philosophical Society or "Phil", were closed to women students. In the Modern Languages lecture rooms the front rows tended to be occupied by women students who, by the end of the first term, chatted gaily and freely among each other while the six or eight young men, of whom I was one, sat at the back in embarrassed silence. The embarrassment in many cases concealed what a colleague many years later described to me as *une peur et une haine du con* that surfaced nastily in the occasional binges or "blinds" organised by the "Hist" or the "Phil" at which the embarrassed males would release their inhibitions by bawling obscene and obscenely sexist songs and limericks of a sort only to be heard nowadays sung by yobs in their cups. I went along with all this because I didn't at the time know any better.

I was in any case coming to terms with normal social life after the single sex environment of Columba's and the emotional aftermath of my relationship with Michael. For a time I wondered if I wasn't permanently homosexual. I realised in later years that various members of what would now be called the gay community must have wondered the same thing, which may explain certain overtures of friendship I received from mature men which both flattered and puzzled me at the time. I was, however, quite certain that I didn't want to be "a queer", to use the term then current. I became very conscious of this on one specific occasion. It was when my cousin Rosemary came to Dublin to do her obstetrics at the Rotunda Hospital. I saw a lot of her at the time; we talked and argued a lot about all sorts of things. We never mentioned the word homosexuality, or for that matter the phenomenon, it wasn't a thing that anybody ever talked about in mixed company in those days. But I am quite sure that Rosemary understood something of what was going on in my mind. Then, one evening, I was in the Rotunda, sitting drinking with her and other medical trainees, when Rosemary suddenly asked me would I like to see a baby being born. She said that, in theatre overalls and with a mask on, I would be taken for another student and no one would notice me. I hesitated; I think I was frightened of what I might see and how I might react to it. Nowadays everyone has seen childbirth on cinema or television if they haven't seen it in reality. It is hard to realise how awesome it would have seemed to the callow nineteen-year-old that I was in 1944. In the end there was some problem and I didn't get to watch a child being born. But I had come so near to it that it felt as though I had. That, together with the conversations I had listened to in the Rotunda, the general atmosphere of female physicality, all of which might have turned me off had I been genuinely gay, made me profoundly aware of a sexual world that I wanted, however vaguely, to be part of.

The sexual revolution was, however, so far in the future as to be unimaginable. As time went by I managed to make friends with several girl students. It was all very polite and well behaved. Then some time in my second year, at a party in, of all posh places, the Shelbourne Hotel, I met Constance. I had known her by sight for many years. When I was still a schoolboy I had noticed a distinctive-looking girl in a green school uniform and a St Trinians style hat. I used to see her in various places, theatres, a concert by the Glasgow Orpheus Choir, the carol services at St Patrick's cathedral, always accompanied by her father, a heavily built, slow-moving, clergyman who wore a strangely old-fashioned shovel hat. I got to know her because I had joined the University dramatic society, the Players. Constance Conner was Chairman (as we called it then). In those days her great enthusiasm was the theatre. She acted and danced, but her main talent was for production. In the Players we put on a one-act play every Thursday, and Constance produced many of these. She did this very well thanks to a combination of firmness and tact in getting people to produce the effects she wanted. She was three years older than me and, when we met, she had just got a brilliant first class degree in history. She had never received the gold medal that her starred first should have earned her, through, I think, the inefficiency, or, more likely, the sexist prejudice, of one of the history professors, and was angry about this. She was still a student, following a course in Public Administration, and later joined the staff of the University Library.

Constance was my first, and for many years my only, girlfriend. Due to my immaturity, to my natural shyness and to my total inexperience of women, it is perhaps not surprising that she was, to start with and for several years, more a friend who happened to be a girl than a girlfriend as we would understand it today. She was herself recovering from an unhappy love affair. I had little idea then that she would later be, for fifteen years, my wife and, until she died in 2003, one of my best and closest friends. For the rest of my time in college we did everything together. Constance was excellent company, highly intelligent with a gift for noticing the funny side of what people said or did. She was extremely slim and graceful in her movements with high cheekbones and fine features. She lived at the time with her father and stepmother in a very suburban house near Dun Laoghaire, six miles from the centre of Dublin. It was a strange and strangely depressing household. I occasionally went for tea there and we would end the evening curled up on the sofa after the parents had gone to bed. Constance's stepmother, Mima, was a Northern Irish countrywoman whose idea of entertainment was all of us singing hymns around the piano. She would suggest this and Constance would dismiss the idea quite sharply. A shadowy figure; I have no idea what she and Constance can possibly have found to talk about. I have no memory of Constance's father talking to her at all; he had all his meals by himself. He had married her, the sister of one of his parishioners in the County Tyrone, in the shock of losing Constance's mother, but the marriage was obviously a mistake from the start. Constance's mother had died tragically of, I think, appendicitis when Constance was seven. She had been by all accounts a highly intelligent woman with a lot of character. Shortly after her death and his remarriage I think Constance's father had some sort of mental breakdown; he was obliged to retire and came south to Dublin. Mima must have hated the move. She would have had nothing in common with her neighbours, who were, mostly, suburban Dublin Catholics. She must have been dreadfully lonely and it's not surprising that, years later, she developed the psychiatric illness that caused her to be incarcerated and to spend the rest of her life in a mental hospital.

Constance's father, Willie Conner, came originally from Cork and had Huguenot refugees among his ancestors. He had a degree from Trinity, like all Church of Ireland clergy, and was interested in Irish history among other things. He was of course absolutely devoted to Constance and she was certainly fond of him, though she did tell me once that he used to lose his temper with her quite violently. I think he accepted me because my father was a Cork man. We talked about Cork or else he would tell me long-drawn-out anecdotes about student life in the School of Divinity in the nineteen twenties. I think as a young man he could well have had a bit of the Cork blarney and been amusing company. Now, he spent most of his time in his bedroom, reading books about theology or the history of Ireland or of the church. He wrote all over all of his books, covering the text with scribbled details about himself, stereotypical remarks about life in general and, only very occasionally, comments on the text itself. When he died none of the books could be sold because of this, so we brought them to my parent's house and put them among the firewood logs. The heavy theological tomes didn't burn very well but we used to enjoy the reaction of the parents' friends when my father would say, "Throw another book on the fire, Brian, it's getting chilly."

Of Constance's mother's family I knew very little. There were two, kindly but very intimidating, aunts, and a favourite uncle, who came on occasional visits to Dublin and with whom I would be invited to have tea in some up-market café in Grafton Street. They all lived, together with another, vehemently Orange, uncle and a couthy grandmother that Constance was very fond of, in a large very prosperous house with a huge garden just outside Portadown in Northern Ireland.

Evenings that Constance and I spent together would end with my seeing her on to the last tram at Nelson pillar. If we missed the last tram, which happened from time to time, I would take her home on the crossbar of my bicycle. One night when I was returning from leaving Constance home like this I had a curious adventure. Pedalling wearily through the very middle class area of Ballsbridge at about two o'clock in the morning I was accosted by a man waving an ashplant. I stopped and then I saw that he wasn't alone; there was a large black cow standing in the middle of the road.

"Wouldja ever give me a hand," he said, "dhriving her, the road's too wide, she's wandhering every place."

Unwisely I agreed, and for the best part of an hour I did my best to help him chivvy and coax the reluctant, and probably terrified, creature along the main road into Dublin. The man was right; the road was too wide; even with two of us it wasn't easy to stop her from going up side roads or trying to go back the way we had come. Where he had come from – he had a Wicklow accent - and how far he had travelled with the animal, I can't think. And I can't imagine where he thought he was taking her. I understood from what he said - he was far from articulate - that they were going to market. In half an hour we had covered about quarter of a mile. Then, somewhere opposite the Royal Dublin Society, we came past a large bourgeois residence with a big front garden. Unfortunately the gate was wide open and the cow galloped in through it, ploughed its way across flower beds, printing its proud hooves in the manicured tennis lawn and started nibbling at the rose bushes. We rushed in to drive it out, the Wicklow man shouting all sorts of imprecations. And then an upstairs window in the house opened and a classy, English-sounding, voice could be heard saying: "What the hell do you think you're doing?" I decided then that I had done enough, so, when we had got the cow out onto the road, I said goodnight to the cow-man. He pleaded with me, offering to pay me the pathetic sum of two shillings if I would help drive her all the way to market, but I refused and rode away feeling very guilty as I did so. I often wonder what became of him, and his unfortunate cow.

During my first year at Trinity I took singing lessons with Brian Boydell for a time. Brian had another singing pupil, an attractive young woman called Mary Jones. The main reason why I gave up my singing lessons was that they got married and moved to a new house outside Dublin. It was at their wedding party, in 1944, that I met and got talking to a smiling clergyman called Adam Lamb. He asked me if I could play the piano and I told him I could strum out a hymn tune, so he invited me to be the organist in his church at Julianstown, near Drogheda for a few months while his regular organist was away. I think I actually went to see Joe Groocock at St Columba's about this, as though it were possible to teach a very indifferent pianist how to play the organ in one lesson. Joe's advice was discouraging but at least he did tell me a certain number of things to avoid, or more precisely not to attempt, which was, in the event, just as well. My first weekend at Julianstown started characteristically. I took the train to a place called Bettystown, but it was much further to walk to Julianstown than I had realised, and, when I eventually found Adam's rectory, it was eleven o'clock at night. Most of the lights were out so I didn't like to ring the doorbell. Instead, I settled down and slept in the shelter of some laurel bushes as I was in the habit of doing on my bicycle journeys. This, and my arrival at breakfast time, furnished material for anecdote when the temporary organist was later being introduced to the parishioners.

Julianstown rectory was then a beautiful Georgian house surrounded by an ornamental garden. Adam Lamb lived there in considerable comfort. He had two servants, both Catholics and unrelated to each other, James, who looked after the house and grounds, and Mary, who did the housekeeping. Since he had an extensive parish he had a small petrol allowance and drove a car. The house was furnished with antiques – Adam knew a lot about furniture and had very good taste - and there were books in every room. He himself had some vague family connection with Bernard Shaw. He was good company, intelligent and amusing, and took himself very much less seriously than most clergy. He was also, I quickly realised, a covert, or latent or merely repressed, homosexual which probably explains why he liked having me around at weekends, though he never gave even the slightest indication that there was any emotional dimension to our friendship. We never discussed the subject, though we used to talk freely about all manner of things. I was aware that an unspoken personal drama existed which he had once discussed, he told me, with the actor Michael McLiammoir. I realise now that he must have suffered a lot from the loneliness felt by many gays in those days, exacerbated in his case almost certainly by feelings of guilt. His religion can only have made things worse. He took his vocation very seriously, though. Steve remarked, when I brought him down for a weekend, that, "He's not just reciting the stuff. He says it like he really believes it."

Adam's parishioners were either what remained of the ascendancy landlords of the locality, living in shoddy gentility in vast under-heated houses, or else the remnants of the servants and hangers-on of these people. When she heard that I was going to Julianstown my mother told me that this was where she had been recruiting for Cumann na mBan in 1920, and that these big houses, where Adam and I sat on the edge of our chairs making conversation, were the places she had been told to be wary of. Not everything had changed: after the church service Miss Pepper, who lived in a converted castle across the river from Julianstown, would give me letters to post in Dublin because, she said, of the Sinn Feiners in the village.

The other parishioners, the hangers on, were most of them, embarrassingly deferential. Some of them were strongly Evangelical, and would keep asking Adam for Salvationist hymns to be included in the church services. Chief among these was a lady called Mrs Kane, who was not only the most regular attender on Sundays and the most powerful voice in the congregation, but also pumped the organ. When, occasionally, she did get one of the hymns she liked she would let her voice ring out, not unmelodiously, to full volume, heavy with sincerity. Unfortunately, to do this she had to let go of the pump handle and the rich diapason tone of the organ – it was a very nice little instrument – would be replaced by a most unmusical wheezing noise and then die. She would have to break off singing in mid-verse and return to pushing the handle up and down.

Obviously, neither category of parishioner had much to offer in the way of conversation. Sometimes on Sunday evenings we would go and call on a doctor of Adam's acquaintance. He lived, another solitary bachelor, well outside the parish, in another Georgian house with beautiful furniture, and would serve mulled wine in crystal glasses. There would usually be two or three other people there, always men, local farmers or professional people, and the talk was often wide-ranging, lively and entertaining, much more so than it would have been with either group of Adam's parishioners. Adam enjoyed the company, and so did I; and they clearly held him in high esteem. There was only one thing, unusual for the Ireland of the day, the doctor and his friends were all Catholics. This may explain some, but only some, of the warmth of the doctor's welcome; he and his friends were obviously tickled as well as flattered by having a jolly Protestant minister's company to joke with on a Sunday evening. It is true Adam was sometimes a little uneasy about what his Bishop might think of these Sunday evenings, and he asked me not to talk about them.

His relations in his parish with the Catholic Church, which, in conversation with me, he always referred to as "the Italian Mission", were cordial but distant. He was in fact very ecumenically minded. He took me once into St Peter's Catholic Church in Drogheda to show me, among other things, the embalmed head of Blessed Oliver Plunket, who was then on his way to being made a Saint. On our way from inspecting this gruesome object, coming down the steps of the church, three little girls suddenly knelt down in front of Adam, who as usual was wearing his clerical collar. "Will ye bless us, please, Father?" they said. Adam hesitated for an embarrassed moment. Then he held out his arms and waved them solemnly over the three little girls. As we made our way somewhat hastily down the steps – there was a danger that some narrow-minded Catholic priest might have seen and taken offence – Adam turned to me and said, "Well I don't think I can have done them any actual *harm*. And it would have been rude to say No."

He told me that once an old man, a local man and a Catholic, had come to him with a problem. He had been left unexpectedly, by a relation who had died, a substantial sum of money. He came to Adam and asked if he could take care of it for him, since he "didn't trust banks." Adam told him that it wouldn't be right for him to take the money and that he would do best to talk it over with Father so-and-so, the parish priest. He learned afterwards, by Mary, who knew everything that happened in the locality, that the old chap had followed his advice and that the priest's reaction had been to say, "Sure what would an old man like you be doing with all that money?" and to persuade him that the best thing he could do would be to give it to "God's Holy Church." Which he did and when, some years later, the old chap died there was no money to pay for his funeral.

The year 1946 was an important one for me: I acquired my first motorbike and I went abroad, not just once but twice. The bike, physical expression of a passion that rode high in my imagination for ten years, and in which Conor followed me. (Having the enthusiasm in common made a pleasant change from our usual dissension.) My machine was not in itself a very charismatic piece of machinery. A pre-war 250 cc two-stroke with a hand operated gear change it came all the same from a prestigious stable, being a Velocette, the make that Stanley Woods had ridden to victory in the TT in 1937. I bought it by cashing in savings certificates I had been given as a child; even so it cost more than I could really afford. It had a top speed of about fifty miles an hour which, with no rear springing, was faster than it was comfortable to go on most road surfaces at the time, but as I banked over to take a corner at forty I could imagine that I was Jimmy Guthrie or Harold Daniel weaving their way over the mountain on the Isle of Man. More realistically, averaging thirty miles in an hour instead of ten as on a bicycle meant that Ireland had shrunk to a third of its size at the stroke of a kickstarter. The Burren of Clare was now only half a day away and I covered in one weekend the entire itinerary of one of my cycling trips with Michael.

But riding the machine was only part of the pleasure that this initiation into the motor cycling world afforded. There was the satisfaction of taking the engine to pieces, finding something that could be adjusted or cleaned and getting it working again, with luck running more smoothly than before. I found the two-stroke engine, with no valves or camshaft and only two moving parts, a most ingenious, intellectually satisfying, device. Also, its very simplicity meant that there was very little harm that could be done to it by a novice, even as ham-handed a one as I was. By trial and error, and mostly error, I learnt some of the basics of automobile engineering, knowledge which paid off in later years. There was also a challenge to one's ingenuity specific to the post-war situation. Spare parts were virtually unobtainable; often the only solution was to adapt a part made for some other machine picked up in a scrap yard, drilling or filing or just bending some fiddly little bit of metal.

There was no driving test in Ireland in those days, nor was there one for many years after. My mother taught me to drive, to change gear and give hand signals as I rode in circles on the quiet side of Stephen's Green. Then I went and bought my licence, in the Post Office in Kildare Street. I held out my ten shillings and said, "I want a licence please." The woman looked at me and asked, "Is it for a car or for a dog you want it?" "For a motor bike," I said, and signed the declaration at the bottom to say that I was not blind nor subject to epileptic fits. When I went to France three years later, with a much more powerful machine, I obtained an international licence in the same manner. I only passed a driving test after several years in France when I took out a French insurance policy. By that time I had covered many thousands of happy miles. I have never learned to drive. I might have been a better and more considerate driver if I had.

Constance Conner (left)

Conor Farrington.

On the other hand there is nothing like a motor bike for sharpening your awareness of how well your tyres are adhering to the road. I learnt where the limit lay from one dramatic skid on an icy road in Wicklow which I managed to control more or less, so that both Constance and I, she was on the pillion seat, just landed uninjured in some bushes at the road side.

It was in her capacity as Chairman of the Trinity Players that Constance received in 1946 a surprising communication from the *Studenten Tooneel* of the University of Leiden, in the Netherlands, inviting four of our members, at very short notice, to attend the first night of their production of *The Playboy Of The Western World*. Constance was an obvious first choice to be one of the four. One would have thought everyone would be keen to take advantage of this unusual invitation. As it happened very few of our stick-in-the-mud fellow students were interested in a first trip to the Continent. In the end Constance was struck down with jaundice and couldn't go, so I went, with three others: Kingsley Scott, who was an old Columban, Audrey McDaniel and Mary Hamilton.

I had some claim to be chosen, since I knew quite a lot about Synge, but of the four of us only Mary was a really active member of Players. Gifted with a very expressive voice, she had played the main part in a successful production of

Synge's rarely performed *Deirdre Of The Sorrows*, which we had put on in Dublin's Peacock Theatre a year before. Travel was not easy in 1946; we none of us had passports, and we needed them in a hurry. Then Constance remembered a recent graduate in history who had joined the Department of External Affairs, so we went to see him. His name was Conor Cruise O'Brien. He was still a very junior civil servant but he pulled some strings and the four of us walked out of the Government Buildings two hours later with shiny new passports. A short week passed and we were boarding the Mailboat in Dun Laoghaire. I found the whole journey exciting, even the crossing to Holyhead and the Irish Mail to London. Though London itself, which I had seen on my earlier childhood visits as some sort of technological fairyland with its traffic lights and escalators, where everything was clean and posh, I found now to be, not only shockingly bomb-damaged, but also disappointingly dog-eared and tatty.

At the Hook of Holland two male students were there to greet us and take us by train to Leiden. The old fashioned Continental courtesy of their welcome was tempered by only half-concealed embarrassment at discovering that two of our foursome were female. They were quite appalled at this. How had such a situation occurred? Who were these two girls? Surely all the members of D U Players, like those of their own Dramatic Society must be male. We were shortly to learn that even male actors were only second-class members of the Tooneel, the Dramatic Society, and female actors were not, and could not be, members at all. We obviously thought this was absurd and couldn't resist saying so. It created a problem for our Dutch hosts however; and on arriving in Leiden there was an awkward hiatus while they hunted around for female accommodation. Mary and Audrey were eventually taken in by two girls who made room for them to sleep on their floor and shared with them their breakfasts of buns and cheese and once, when questioned, talked of the quite recent past when there had been nothing to eat but tulip bulbs.

Though we were horrified by the bomb-damage we saw passing through Rotterdam, Leiden in contrast seemed to us surprisingly spruce and even prosperous, especially considering that this part of the Netherlands had still been occupied by the Nazis less than twelve months before. There was probably some rationing but we were not aware of any serious shortages. The students that we met had plenty of stories to tell of the Occupation and of their, largely passive, resistance to it. They were all from very middle-class families of course but we were struck by how intensely patriotic they were, and, as was natural, intensely anti-German. One of us, Kingsley Scott, who spoke German, made the mistake of speaking it to buy something in a shop. Fortunately one of our Dutch friends was with him and quickly explained to the shopkeeper that this was a visitor from Ireland. The one or two young people we met who had played a small but active part in the resistance preferred not to speak of it, treating the horrors they had lived through as part of a nightmare that was best forgotten.

Occasionally someone would criticise Ireland for having been neutral in the war; we soon learned to point out that the Netherlands had been neutral also until they were invaded. Personally, though my opinion was that Ireland could not have been anything but neutral, I felt very humble when I heard what these young men and women had been suffering while I was happily cycling around Galway with Michael.

The first night of the Playboy, entitled *Der Ster van Het Westen*, took place at the beginning of our week in Leiden. I had no difficulty in following it since I knew most of the text by heart having been to several performances of the marvellous production at the Abbey with Cyril Cusack and Brid Ni Lynch a year or two earlier. This Dutch student performance was surprisingly good. In particular the boy who played Christy, - Hans Van Loonen I think his name was - was as sensitive and lively a Playboy as most of those I have seen since and certainly a much better actor than the chap in the awful Abbey Theatre production we saw in Sligo in 2004, who shouted and gabbled his lines at the same maximum volume from the first scene to the last. I can't think why the Leiden students should have chosen the Playboy for their first production after the war, though I shall always be glad that they did.

The performance was followed by some sort of ceremony at which the president of the students' union made a speech to which the chairman of the drama society replied with another speech, both of them as smooth and self congratulatory as the officers of the "Hist" in Dublin or the Oxford or Cambridge Union, with the same sort of bitchy urbanity. The same high achievers preening themselves in preparation for the top jobs they saw themselves as heading for. The actual producer of the play was of course nowhere in all this. He probably, like the female actors, wasn't even a member of their "Tooneel". Though middle-class people ourselves we found many of the Dutch students we met very bourgeois, and student society in general seemed to us to be shot through with arcane and objectionable hierarchies. For example Hans, who acted the Playboy so brilliantly, was "only" a first-year student and therefore the others felt it incumbent upon them to keep putting him in his place. Also, they frequently spoke about what they called "our colonies", meaning the Dutch East Indies, what is now Indonesia, revealing an attitude that savoured to us of old-style imperialism, of bearing the white man's burden. On the other hand we liked the Indonesian restaurant they took us to where we were introduced to *baami* and *nassi goreng* and other highly spiced specialities.

One day a group of students took us out along the dunes, along the huge barrier of sand hills, part natural part artefact, which separates that part of Holland from the sea. Quite unselfconsciously they stood and sang to us a song about the dunes, comparing the mountainous waves on one side and the flat peaceful fields on the other and ending with the refrain, "I love you my nether lands, I love you" which struck me as the first and only entirely respectable expression of patriotism ("last refuge of a scoundrel") I had ever heard.

That day we were to be joined by two French girls. As we went to meet them the Dutch students said to us, "It will be more polite if we all speak French today," assuming that we could switch languages as easily as they could. None of the Dutch were language students, they were all doing law or medicine or history. But their French sounded to us almost as good as their English which was of course excellent. We all floundered, even Kingsley and I, who were students of modern languages. Fortunately the two French girls in question were very dull and monosyllabic and not at all interested in talking to people from Ireland.

Our hosts were most assiduous in taking us around and showing us things of interest. A little too assiduous in fact; after a day or two we all felt a desire to wander around, exploring this, to us, unusual little Dutch town by ourselves, without the ciceronian presence of a Dutch student to choose and point out the things we should look at. It was difficult to explain this to our hosts; it was Mary who hit on the solution which was to insist that we wanted to go shopping. We later learned that the Dutch were puzzled by what they called the Irish passion for shopping. But for us on our very first visit to continental Europe the things that we wanted to look at were, not the museums and bits of history that they wanted to show us, but the ordinary details of everyday life which were all so different and new. It was the street markets, the odd shaped little single-deck electric trams, packed with people and with a notice forbidding you to talk to the driver, the canals with no railing or kerb to prevent you from falling in. And then there was the Christmas card quaintness of everything, the streets narrow as corridors, made up of amazingly tall amazingly narrow houses each consisting of tiny rooms like little queerly shaped boxes piled up on top of each other and linked by cramped awkward little winding staircases, the whole thing so economical of space that it seemed that there wasn't a cubic inch going to waste. And then, at the edge of the town, there was this huge windmill, again like something on a Christmas card, but when its sails were set and it was turning it made the strangest, most beautiful sound: the wind soughing in the sails and the wooden machinery creaking and groaning, and I suppose the water it was pumping, rushing through sluices down below.

On the way back to Dublin I spent a few days in London, visiting relatives of my mother's and just walking around. I stayed with three delightful old people called Chubb; I don't know how my mother knew them, they weren't relations at all but they were most entertaining and spoke with cockney accents which I often found hard to understand. They were full of anecdotes about the Blitz, putting the accent always on the funny side. As, for example, when they described the biggest bomb that hit St John's Wood, which landed in the cemetery across the road from their house. "We were picking bones up all over the place for days afterwards," they said.

On one of my walks, somewhere behind Piccadilly, I was approached by a lady in a fur coat. I thought she was wanting to know the way or the time, but then she asked me quite clearly if I would, "Loike te kem along with me for a short whoile?" I still didn't twig what this was about until she flashed her fur coat open for a second revealing that she had practically nothing on underneath. I fled, inarticulate with embarrassment. But the incident reminded me of an errand I had to carry out.

All forms of contraception being forbidden in Ireland at the time, any student going to England or even Northern Ireland would be plagued by his friends and acquaintances to bring back condoms, what we still called French letters. Most of my friends were probably virgins, as I most certainly was, never having got beyond what was still called "heavy petting," but an obvious way of boasting that things were otherwise was to require me to bring them back half a dozen or more of the little packets that were still surrounded by an aura of secrecy and guilt.

I knew that they could be purchased in chemists' shops but I had no idea that all I had to do was walk in and ask. I probably thought, such was the mentality in Ireland at the time, that the chemist might ask me to prove that I was married. Paralysed with guilt and embarrassment I walked up and down outside chemists' shops but the person serving behind the counter always seemed to be female, another problem. And then on my last day in some slightly scruffy district of south London where I had gone to buy a spare part for the motorbike I saw a shop entitled PHELPS CONTRACEPTIVES. No need to be embarrassed here, though I was. I walked in but then I didn't know what to ask for. The word condom was unknown at the time; I couldn't very well ask for French Letters or FLs as we called them. I stood there and mumbled. "How many do you want sir?" said the smiling, somewhat sleazy, man behind the counter, so I said I wanted twenty. That wasn't the end of my embarrassment. He produced twenty condoms, not in packets but, so to speak, raw, and laid them unrolled full length on the counter. Then he took the first one, and, to test it, fitted it on a sort of nozzle behind the counter, turned a tap which, with a hissing noise, inflated the thing to a grotesque, obscene, size. He did this with every one of the twenty and then produced a sort of wooden phallus-shaped object, fitted each condom onto it, rolled it up and popped it into its packet. As I paid and stuffed the parcel into my pocket he leaned over the counter, leered at me and said: "You're going to 'ave a noice little 'olidye at the week-end."

My first sight of France was from the Newhaven Dieppe boat on the 14th of July, Bastille Day, 1946. John Heuston and I were going to Paris for a month to attend a *Cours de Vacances* at the Sorbonne. As the boat approached the French coast the crew suddenly hoisted strings of flags in recognition of the French national

John Heuston

holiday. And then, as it sidled in to the quay wall there came to my nostrils, from the army of porters in blue overalls waiting on the quay, a first whiff of caporal tobacco, the smell of France, a distinctive and never-before-experienced odour. That it struck me so forcefully that day is a bit as though Proust had written pages about his madeleine the very first time he'd tasted it.

I have only vague memories of that first month spent in Paris. We stayed in the *Pavillon Franco-Britannique* of the *Cité Universitaire*, a vast complex of student residences on the *Boulevard Extérieur*. Meals were served in the Central Refectory; food was in short supply, and we had to procure ration cards containing tickets for various foodstuffs, which we had to hand in at the refectory. We were pleased when we found we were allowed to keep the wine tickets for our own use. The refectory meals, however, were frugal and unappetising in the extreme. I have a memory of a stew consisting largely of the necks of ducks or chickens and of large quantities of white noodles, totally lacking in any flavour.

The classes were held in a lecture room in the Sorbonne, to which we went every morning in the Metro. Walking down the Boul' Mich one morning, we chanced to find a *boulangerie* that sold small rectangular slices of some indeterminate, slightly sugary, composition called "*poudingues*". They weren't very appetising – God knows what they were made of - but they were cheap and off the ration. Nourished by these we were better enabled to profit by the, agreeably varied, pabulum provided by our tutor. She was an attractive, slightly dumpy, but lively young woman called Mademoiselle Cueilleron, who would say "*Bonjour mes élèves*," as she came bouncing in every morning, her chignon bobbing up and down as she spoke. I can't remember what her classes consisted of except for the songs she taught us the words of which are still in my memory. The classes were, as I said, agreeably, even disconcertingly, varied as when for example she asked John to prepare a talk about Corneille and then forgot to ask him to present it.

The classes were conscientiously prepared, but what I remember best are the excursions she organised. We went to Versailles and to Compiègne and even picnicked in the forest of Fontainebleau where the Italian member of the group was reluctant to sit down for fear of snakes. She took us to a somewhat sleazy nightclub in the Latin Quarter with obscene caricatures on the walls, where those of us who could danced the tango, which was very popular in Paris at the time. And also to the *Caveau des Oubliettes*, a *chansonnier* housed in what had once been the dungeons of the *Petit Chatelet*, where two or three characterful performers sang *vieilles chanson paillardes,* unaccompanied, but with great gusto. And, most unusually, though I didn't realise it at the time, she invited the whole group - there were about a dozen of us - to her home in the *rue de Vaugirard* where we were served drinks and nibbles and met her parents. Continental academics, I discovered long afterwards, never normally allow their home lives and their professional lives to mix.

One outing that we had independently of the Sorbonne was when we were invited by Cognon, who was an exchange student in Dublin, to his home in Mantes. In the train from St Lazare I watched a young couple in the compartment, recently married I suppose, though they were, if anything, younger than we were. The wife who was very smartly, even elegantly, dressed in a discreet pink *tailleur*, sat straight upright with her hands folded in her lap. When the train started the husband, at a word from her, got a bag down from the rack, from which she took some knitting tidily wrapped in a patterned cloth. She unfolded this cloth and spread it out on her knees and then proceeded to knit, occasionally making a remark to her husband which mostly consisted either of telling him to do something, like sit up straight, or to stop doing something, like comb his hair with his fingers. As we approached Mantes she folded the knitting up neatly, with precise hand movements, and put it away in the bag. The whole scene, unimaginable in Ireland, made me feel that we came from a nation of slobs in comparison.

The Cognons gave us an excellent lunch, a welcome change from the *nouilles napolitaines* of the *Cité Universitaire*. Afterwards they took us for a drive across the Normandy countryside which still showed signs of the battle that had raged there only two years before, in the form of temporary wooden bridges, a ruined village and, here and there, the rusting remains of tanks and field guns.

I suppose I must have explored most of Paris either on foot or in the fascinating Metro but my memories of that first visit are overlaid by so many other memories of Paris that I find it hard to remember what it was like to see for the first time. I certainly walked a lot; John on the other hand, more worldly wise, more self assured and certainly more *débrouillard* (enterprising) than I was, probably got much more from the month in Paris than I did. Also his French was much better than mine. One day, in a little café on the *rue des Écoles*, a man got talking to us. He was unkempt, probably a tramp or *clochard*, and we had some small difficulty getting away from him. As we walked away I remarked that I had found him hard to understand. "He was talking very simple French," said John. The put down still stung years later when my French had become so fluent I could pass myself off as a native speaker.

Typically it was John that found a cinema in Montmartre showing the resistance film *La Bataille du Rail*, and above all it was he that discovered, on only our first or second day, that Eisenstein's masterpiece *Ivan the Terrible* was showing in some obscure *quartier* not far away. A powerful expressionist film it was a dramatic change from what we were in the habit of seeing in Dublin picture houses. At the moment in the film where popes in bizarre vestments and with outlandish beards, to cure Ivan who is mortally ill, lower a huge Bible over his face, and Ivan stretches his head up towards it with his eyes popping out and his beard sticking up, John leaned towards me and said, "I never did like reading in bed."

On a somewhat different cultural level John celebrated his birthday by taking me to the *Folies Bergère*. The show was so spectacular and the special stage effects so amazing that it didn't seem to matter that we couldn't understand much of what anyone on the stage sang or said. The main point anyway was the rank upon rank of beautiful dancing girls doing their high kicks and of course the celebrated *danseuses nues* though unfortunately our seats were too far back fully to appreciate these, which was in the event probably just as well. Jules Romains, in *Eros de Paris,* vividly described the frustration and discomfort provoked in a sex-starved provincial adolescent, not very different from what we were, as he wandered about *la ville lumière.* "I am counting," John said, as we eyed these sylph-like creatures, "The number of my relatives who would never speak to me again if they knew I was here."

A few months before my finals, in 1947, I developed acute appendicitis. I suddenly had a sharp abdominal pain which rapidly got worse. I then developed a very high temperature, feeling more ill than I had ever felt in my life. My mother called our doctor, Millington Synge, who immediately got on the phone to Baggot Street hospital where I was conveyed in an ambulance with bells clanging. In no time I was installed in a large public ward, in the bed in which the previous occupant, who, I was later told, had been a "very decent old man", had died an hour or two before. Peter Gatenby, a childhood friend with whom I used to go on cycle rides around Dublin a few years before who was now a house surgeon in Baggot Street hospital, greeted me and gave me an injection. When I woke up it was all over and I had a stitched up wound which made it very painful to laugh or cough.

I stayed in hospital for ten days, ten days which were an education. There were about 20 beds in the ward though I only got to know the men in the five or six beds nearest to me. Beside me there was an elderly man with a broken femur. He had been a tram driver - there were still trams in Dublin then - and told me all about driving a tram, explaining the sort of cow catcher affair under the front of the Dublin trams, which was designed to pick up anybody who got knocked down before they could be injured by the wheels, and the magnetic track brake which could stop the tram dead but so violently that the passengers would all be thrown from their seats if you applied it. He knew a lot about canaries and once, walking in some park, he'd caught a canary in his hand that must have escaped from some one's house. He won several prizes with it as a cock canary and then, "Didn't it lay an egg on me."

In a bed at the end of the ward by the window was an old Dubliner with a moustache who both looked and sounded like a character out of O'Casey. He talked a lot and would always start his anecdotes with somebody's name. "There was a man I knew, one-time, mendin' the roads, Hennessy was his name..." Whereupon someone else in the ward would say, "That wouldn't be a Peter Hennessy, a big man from the County Cork now would it?" Then other people would chip in, describing Hennessys that they had known, and the rest of the anecdote would remain untold. I would remember this in later years, when I lived in the anonymity of Britain or France, where it is automatically assumed that everyone is a stranger to everyone else.

He suffered greatly, the O'Casey character, at not being allowed to smoke. He tried lighting up under the bedclothes, which might have worked had he been smoking cigarettes, but what he smoked was plug tobacco which he cut off the plug with a penknife and then shredded into his pipe. There was no way the dark clouds of rank smoke that leaked out from between the blankets could be concealed so we managed to open the window by his bed in the hope it would blow outside. Alas! there was no fooling the dragon of a Sister who thundered in, confiscated pipe, plug tobacco and penknife, and shut the window.

She was an unpleasant woman. On one occasion a youngish man further down the ward had an operation to amputate part of his leg, which was gangrenous. He was dreadfully upset when he awoke to find that they had removed almost all of his leg, but she just scolded him – we could all hear her – saying. "Shut up with yer whingin' and cryin' like a big baby!"

The most likeable, and most memorable, person in the ward was a red haired Dublin postman in the bed opposite mine. He dominated almost every conversation, though I can remember very little of what he said except when, on one occasion, he talked about a brief training period he had spent with the Irish Army. They had taken him down into the Wicklow Mountains for firing practice. A true urban Dubliner it was the only time he had been outside the city. "Gor, it was beautiful, I'd no idea there was scenery the like in Ireland." Sadly it was unlikely he would ever see it again. Peter Gatenby confided in me, when I was able to walk and he took me around the hospital, that, when they had operated on the postman they could not remove the cancer but that, for some reason, they had not been able to break the news to him. I hated knowing this as I listened to him talking to the others, advising them or reassuring them, or simply showing an interest in what they had to say, and, as I listened, my liking for the man grew. At times we would all play a sort of game, trying him with the names of obscure Dublin side streets and back lanes, but we never managed to catch him out and he would answer, citing odd and amusing bits of information about lesser known parts of the city. An intelligent man who had left school at fourteen, he was very devout. It was he who had instituted and who led the Rosary which they all recited every evening at six o'clock. As they gabbled their way through this, to me, strange ritual I would try in vain to make out the words they were saying. Absurd and outlandish as this mumbled rigmarole seemed to me I could not help admiring the sincerity that rang out in the postman's voice. I could not, and cannot, help hoping that his faith worked as a comfort to him and gave him strength in the end. When I left we shook hands and he wished me good luck. I couldn't think of anything adequate to say in reply. But I shan't forget him, ever.

The conversation in the ward ranged from the pleasure of children's growing affection to remedies for constipation. I didn't participate much, embarrassed lest my middle-class accent might set me apart, and I didn't want to be set apart. In fact those ten days spent lying on my back in that disparate group of fellow Dubliners started the process of unlearning the patrician attitudes that I had picked up at St Columba's, by which we regarded the plain people of Ireland, the "papist snullers, " to employ a Columban expression, as alien and inferior. Increasingly from that time onwards I came to reverse Jonathan Swift's famous declaration and say that, while I could conceive a hearty dislike for "John, Peter, Thomas and so forth," regarding "that animal called man" I felt mostly interest, concern and often admiration.

# English and French Schools

# 5

AFTER THE EXCITEMENT of Mod, i.e. finals, and graduation, I stayed on in Trinity for the rest of the term, editing the student magazine *TCD*, though I was no longer technically a student at all. I spent quite a lot of time in the library, actually reading some of the books that I had skimmed through in Philistine utilitarian haste in preparation for Mod. I remember in particular *Vanity Fair*, *Du Côté de Chez Swann*, and *Le Père Goriot*, which I endeavoured to read this time in French. All my friends had got their feet on the bottom rungs of some career ladder but I had no idea what I wanted to do with my life. I had had some, typically, wise advice from G.K.White of Columba's to whom I had written asking for a reference and who knew of my desire to write poetry. Like Geoffrey Taylor he had seen that I had some talent but that my poems were not about anything very important. So he said: What I needed to do was get out into the world and do some living. I could see that he was right, only I couldn't see what the first step should be. And then one day in December, over the breakfast table, my father broke a silence that he had been observing for quite some months and asked me bluntly how long I was going to sit around at home doing nothing. It seems strange now when I think of it that neither he nor my mother had expressed any concern that I should have so little idea of what I wanted to do when I "grew up". They probably saw that, for all that I was 22 years old, I was such a prickly self-conscious adolescent as to be impervious to parental advice however well-meant. Anyway, stung by my father's question, I picked up the *Irish Times*, found an advertisement for a teaching job in an English prep school, applied and was accepted, all in the space of a few days.

Why England? And why teaching? Those two decisions affected my whole life, but I didn't attach much importance to them at the time. With regard to the first, what I had seen of England, The Netherlands and France had given me an appetite for new and different places. I wanted to go abroad, for a time anyway, and an English private school was as good a start as any, since the pay, for a totally untrained teacher, seemed quite reasonable. The second choice, of teaching as a profession, was more important, since I have been a teacher of some sort all my working life. And yet that initial decision was made for the vaguest and most negative of reasons. Since I had never been anywhere but school and university, education was the only work environment I knew anything about. And my experience in both pointed to the cocksure conclusion that teaching was something that "anyone could do." I didn't enjoy discovering that school teaching is one of the rare exceptions to the principle I had learned from Joe Groocock and is, when done badly, absolutely not worth doing at all, and no fun. I fortunately didn't have to do it for long and escaped to France after six months.

This, my first experience of paid employment, took place at the Leas School, Hoylake, an English prep school situated at the end of the Wirral peninsula, looking out over the sands of Dee. Considering my total lack of experience of any sort of employment, and my almost total lack of success as a school teacher, it is hardly surprising that I should not have been happy there. But I had solid reasons for disliking almost everything about the Leas. It is true, also, that they, the two headmasters and their senior cronies who, I quickly discovered, owned the place and ran it as a business, didn't have much time for me. We had nothing in common, we shared no interests or enthusiasms, and they made no allowances for my naivety or lack of experience. They didn't, for that matter, make any serious effort to find out anything about what I could or could not do. My first encounter with school football can serve as an example of the sort of difficulties I had to contend with in other fields.

Glancing at the timetable for the first full day of term I was alarmed to discover that I was down to "take" second year soccer practice. I had never ever played any sort of football, I didn't even know, or want to know, the difference between rugby and soccer, but I was so concerned not to create a bad impression right at the start of my teaching career that I could not confess this ignorance to anyone. When lunchtime came I found some excuse, rushed into Hoylake, and asked in the newsagents if they had a book containing the rules of the game of football. Miraculously they were able to come up with a scruffy little pamphlet the contents of which I endeavoured to commit to memory sitting in the lavatory. When the moment came I trooped out with 22 boys to the field, got them to divide themselves summarily into two teams and blew the whistle I had been given to start them off. I then ran up and down the field after them, hoping that some at least of their superior knowledge of the game would end by rubbing off on me. There soon came a nasty moment, though, when there were cries of, "Oh! Sir, he was offside," and I didn't dare pull out my booklet to see if it contained an explanation of what on earth "offside" could mean. It became immediately obvious to both teams that I was totally deficient in all knowledge of football, knowledge which, to them, being English nine-year olds, was as basic as knowing how to chew or to pee.

I disliked the Tory politics of the senior staff, the anti-Semitism of my junior colleagues, the aggressive competitiveness that the school encouraged in every field, the phoney religion that each day started off with, the flagrant admiration of ill-gotten wealth that was expressed constantly by pupils, masters, and parents. And then there was the wealth itself. Many, most for all I know, of the parents were rolling in money, if only to judge by the cars they rolled up in to deposit their offspring at the start of term. The whole place was emblem and epitome of what the socialist, humanist, philosophy I was moving towards regarded and regards as the enemy: the ruling class. I had simply neither encountered nor seriously thought about the reality of it until then. This was true also of the boys, though it would be unfair to work up an ideological *odium* against small boys, however obnoxious some of them were. Most of them, to be honest, were, on the contrary, quite pleasant and fun to talk to. There was the son of the multi-millionaire owner of a well-known football-pool firm, a pleasantly stolid, not very articulate lad. I used to see his name in the newspapers thirty years later, celebrating the purchase of yet another racehorse. There were the two sons of the owner of a big steel mill somewhere in North Wales, the elder of whom possessed, or so he boasted to me, a million marbles. He was, actually, a not-un-likeable boy, very clever with his hands, who made model aeroplanes, not from the polystyrene kits that later became popular but out of balsa wood, which actually flew. Though how he found time for this activity in the overcharged school timetable I used to wonder.

The manifestation of the competitive spirit driving the school that I found most offensive was the weekly reading out of class marks. Marks, scores, call them what you will, dominated all academic activity; they had to be dished out, calculated, added up all the time. That would not have bothered me unduly: little boys like scoring off each other and it turned the lessons in French, which had to be taught as though it were a dead language with no spoken component, into a not disagreeable game in which the acquisition of these numerical absolutes was the main reason for learning French. I had more difficulty in English where I was reprimanded for rewarding such unquantifiable entities as imagination or humour. The trouble with all marks was that they had to be handed in at the end of each week and the totals for each class added up. And then, on the following Monday morning, the headmaster would read out the class lists to the assembled school all of whom would wait in fear and trembling for the turn of their own class. He would run his eye down the list and then, noticing the name of some unfortunate whose score was lower down the list than he thought it ought to be, he would scream: "Barnes," or "Laidlaw" or whatever the child's name was, "Stand up so everyone can see you!" He would then berate the wretched Barnes in a paroxysm of simulated indignation in which the child's character, his hobbies, his untidy clothes and even his love of trains would all be sneered at and the unfortunate ten-year-old would be held up as a sort of monster of spineless self-indulgence until, as often happened, he broke down in tears whereupon the headmaster would proceed to the list for the next class. I say simulated indignation, because the only piece of advice the head ever gave me was to tell me that you kept order in class, not by getting angry but by pretending to be angry. But, deciding that his face would not have been so red if all the anger had been simulated, I concluded that he must have got some complicated sexual kick from these embarrassing exhibitions.

I probably got the job at the Leas because it was, mistakenly, assumed that, having been at St Columba's, I would have absorbed the public school ethos and would approve of the system in general. In fact I knew very little about it. In Ireland at that time there was no state secondary education *per se,* so the distinction between state schools and private schools, so important in England, had very little meaning for me. My knowledge of English schools, all English schools, came mostly from reading school stories in periodicals like *Wizard* and *Hotspur*. When, after living for years in France and working at several levels in the French educational system, I came finally to live in Britain I found this dichotomy, which has been described (by George Walden, a Tory minister no less) as "the British educational apartheid", to be one of the most undesirable features of British society. In France under the first Republic and the Directoire the system of Grandes Écoles and Écoles Normales provided ladders, still in existence, by which intelligent and ambitious boys, and, later, girls, of the most modest and humblest origin could climb, with the blessing of the State and fully financed all the way, to the highest *échelons* in society. Nothing comparable happened in the early 19th century in Britain. On the contrary, while the French were making good the achievements of the Revolution, the development of the so-called public schools simply confirmed and consolidated the privileges of the ruling class.

The Leas School Hoylake was of course very different from Rugby or Harrow. And it could hardly fail, it must be admitted, to share some of the features that I liked about Columba's: the small size and the sense of community. There were so many of these small private prep schools all over the country that some at least must have been places to which thoughtful parents wouldn't mind sending their offspring. Though I must say the very idea of a prep school, an establishment to which, at considerable expense, parents would send their male children away just when they were on the point of turning into interesting people, seemed and seems as daft as it is inhuman. Remembering the pain I suffered my first term at Columba's my heart went out to two little boys, barely 7 years old, that I saw at the beginning of term, sobbing in corners.

I didn't know of any particularly humane prep schools and the ones I did know about were, if anything, more uncongenial than the Leas. There was another prep school just down the road, which we played matches against, where the headmaster was an obsessive fundamentalist evangelical. A few miles away my friend and fellow Columban Godfrey Sullivan taught in a prep school where the classrooms were equipped with hidden microphones so the head could supervise his staff in secret. All in all I was lucky that all I had to put up with were things like the self-important phoniness with which the Leas aped the famous public schools, flaunting a sorry travesty of their, admittedly, rich traditions. As for example in the school motto: *Deo parere libertas*, which, if I understand the Latin correctly, would seem to imply that the place was some sort of seminary dedicated to God rather than to Mammon, or the school song, the refrain of which went:

> Courage is born of freedom,
> Freedom to do the right,
> Deo parere libertas,
> This be our strength and might.

We had to sing this nonsensical doggerel at the end of every term. Happily I only had to sing it twice.

In Dublin during the Easter break I met a recent Mod Lang graduate who told me about the scheme by which one could spend a year or two as *Assistant d'Anglais* in a French lycée or college, teaching English conversation, and gave me the address to write to. I couldn't have imagined anything more attractive, or more useful, than a year or two learning to speak French properly in what seemed, and turned out to be, an excitingly unfamiliar context. I never gave a thought to what this decision might lead on to. I straight away wrote in my best French to M. Renard, - that wily old fox, said someone - at 96 Boulevard Raspail, and received a, surprisingly prompt, reply to say that I had been *nommé* at the *Collège de Garçons* in the town of Lunéville, Meurthe et Moselle, to start in the following September. My father took out the Atlas and we found that there was a mountain as high as MacGillicuddy's Reeks only forty miles from Lunéville. The summer term at The Leas, and even the awful cricket, were bearable now that my future, or at least the next chapter of it, seemed to be taking shape.

French railways in 1948 still had three classes. Hewitt's Travel Agency in Dublin, where I proudly bought my, single, ticket to Lunéville, advised me that French third class was to be avoided. At the *Gare de l'Est* I lugged my suitcase into what looked like a luxurious compartment occupied by one other person, a French officer in uniform who was stretched out fast asleep on the opposite seat. The elegant cut and sleek material of his uniform, together with various stripes and ribbons, indicated a high rank but, as the train puffed slowly out through the Parisian suburbs, what I noticed most about him was the smell. Dublin slum dwellers used to smell and there emanated from Tom and Larry Byrne, where we got eggs at Ticknock, and who had no access to running water, a distinctive effluvium, but this was something quite different, a powerful rank and foxy odour suggesting that the colonel or whatever he was couldn't have touched soap and water for several months or had been working in a tannery. I realised after a while that this was the reason he had the compartment to himself and I spent a lot of the journey, which in those days took five or six hours, in the corridor. The other thing I remember about that journey, the beginning of a long love affair with French railways, was the lunch to which I treated myself in the *Wagon Restaurant,* where I encountered a globe artichoke for the first time and had to be told by the waiter not to try to eat it with a knife and fork.

Lunéville was a town of about 20,000 inhabitants with some industry and, like many towns in the east of France, with a strong military presence. There was quite a handsome chateau dominating a large formal garden, laid out, I was told, by the American army as an apology for having chewed it up with their tanks, the ensemble explaining why the inhabitants described their town as "*le Versailles de l'Est de la France.*" (the Versailles of Eastern France) The amazingly ornate rococo *Église St Jacques* contained I was told the unmarked grave of a mistress of Voltaire's who died in childbirth, but I could never find it.

The *Collège de Garçons* was a substantial, slightly rundown, building, dating I think from the end of the 19th century, just off the main square in the town. Arriving at the concierge's lodge I was straightaway conducted to *Monsieur le Principal du Collège* who was an immediately likeable, round headed, smiling, but visibly harassed, man. I learnt that he had only recently been appointed to this, his first headship. He welcomed me warmly with much handshaking and shoulder clapping, told me that he'd see me to arrange my timetable in a week or so, when I had settled in, and turned away to deal with some other more pressing matter. His friendly smile, his grubby collar and his distinct air of confident authority contrasted agreeably with the constipated snootiness of the head of the Leas School Hoylake. Someone then showed me to the room I was to live in for the next nine months. A minimally furnished chamber on the top floor, where the four *maîtres d'internat* also lived, it was heated by a coal burning stove which I had to light every morning. Winters in the east of France, I was soon to discover, can be very cold. Showing me the room the man pointed out the light switches. These were of an unusual type, you turned on the light by twisting a curiously shaped button. Seeing my surprise at this he said, enunciating extra carefully, "*Lumière électrique,*" assuming I suppose that where I came from we had only candles and paraffin lamps, or maybe gas. There were two doors to the room; one opened onto the stairs, the other to the corridor where the *maîtres d'internat* had their rooms. As I got to know them I had to discourage them from using my room as a shortcut to breakfast in the mornings.

These *maîtres d'internat*, were the people I spent most time with, both here in Lunéville and later in Orléans. The *pions* (pawns), as the *maîtres* are familiarly called, fulfil the functions carried out in our schools by prefects, supervising the playground and the canteen and also l'Étude, the sort of permanent prep that is an essential part of the timetable of French schools. The job is always part time, which makes it a very convenient way for students to pay their way through university. On my first evening I was brought down to a small dining room and introduced to the four *pions*. There were three fairly uninteresting blokes: Zert, whose father was a Paris policeman, Metz, who wore pebble-thick spectacles and talked of nothing but the camera he was going to buy one day, and Four – pronounced foor - who was a hypochondriac, always wore a thick muffler and talked at length about his fragile liver and the things he could and could not eat. The fourth, who, as he stood up and shook hands, presented himself in faultless BBC pronunciation as a student of English, was Henri Dégoutin, who became a lifelong friend.

In later years when in Aberdeen I used to advise students about their year in France I would make a point of recommending that they ask to be appointed, not to Paris or anywhere near Paris, but to a small town not too far from a provincial university as was the case with Lunéville. "You may not meet Samuel Beckett," I would point out, "but the people you do meet are likely to be more interested in *you* than could ever be said of the average Parisian." I was certainly exceptionally lucky in meeting Henri Dégoutin but there were plenty of other people in Lunéville that were worth knowing. And from a purely material point of view they were not only worth knowing but they invited me out, often for gargantuan French Sunday lunches, meals to remember. One of my Aberdeen students who didn't take my advice and went to Paris told me that she didn't receive a single invitation in her whole year. Lunéville was a garrison town so I got used to being awakened by fanfares and massed bugle calls coming from nearby barracks and sometimes by a full Army band blaring out the *Marche Lorraine.* Coming from Ireland, where, for obvious political reasons, there has never been compulsory military service, the whole military thing is totally alien to me. I didn't therefore quite know how to behave when, crossing the main square, *M. le Principal* called me over and introduced me to two fairly elderly but visibly very high-ranking army officers, describing me proudly as, "*Mon Assistant britannique,* "and exclaiming, "*Vive l'Entente Cordiale.* "I did all the same know better than to let them know that I was a citizen of the nation that had stabbed the Allies in the back in 1916. But I was glad and proud to be referred to as *Mon Assistant* by this admirably unpompous headmaster. Things would surely have been very different had I gone to a Paris lycée.

Life as *Lecteur d'Anglais* in Lunéville was an easy and un-stressful affair, particularly since for the first five weeks I was given no teaching to do. I spent my time and energy agreeably, learning to speak French fluently and getting used to the French way of life which I found preferable in every way to life in Hoylake. For example, at the Leas I had lived with five other masters in a large featureless mock Tudor house down the road from the school. We were "looked after" by a character called Triggs who lived out the back, cleaned our rooms and polished our shoes. A servile, obsequious yet domineering, individual, he had to be tipped generously at the end of term, a custom which I couldn't help seeing as a sort of very expensive way of putting him in his place. There was nothing like this in the *Collège de Garçons*: the old man in overalls who came and swept our rooms out twice a week, sprinkling the floor with water to keep the dust down, was addressed as Monsieur, the jolly red-faced woman who served us our meals, and came out into the playground to call us down in the evening with a stentorian cry of, "*À la soupe!*", was always spoken to as Madame. Whatever about liberty and fraternity I saw this homage to equality as an admirable heritage of the Revolution. Regarding the undeniable economic inequalities in French society it was interesting to find that everyone knew exactly how much everyone else was paid, and to discover that this applied to all walks of life. You could ask anyone how much they earned, much as you could ask them if they were fond of music or sport, and, though they wouldn't always tell you, they wouldn't find the question indiscreet or embarrassing.

I had one brief excursion into a very different milieu. My father had somewhere met a French geologist who spoke of a family he or she knew in Lunéville, gave him the address and said I should look them up. Accordingly, after I had been there a week or two I found my way to a large house standing in the middle of a big garden and rang the doorbell. A maid, with a lace cap on, showed me into a large room full of heavy old-fashioned furniture where I met a very dignified oldish lady wearing a pearl necklace. I had brought several packets of coffee from Ireland because I had been told that coffee was rationed and very hard to come by, so I brought her a packet, realising as I presented it to her that I should have wrapped it up and not just pulled it from my pocket. We talked for a while, exchanging banalities but, since I had never met and knew nothing about the geologist to whom I owed this introduction, it was hard to think of anything to say, and I kept feeling as though I were a character from Just William who had mistakenly walked into a chapter by Proust.

I called there on one or two other occasions. Once Madame told me that she had just had a tooth out. The verb she used for "extract" was *arracher*, which I would translate as "uproot, tear out, rip away". I soon learned that it is the verb always used for tooth extraction, but I came away thinking this avoidance of euphemism typically French. Another time a number of people were there and Madame spoke of getting someone to show me round "their" factory. I don't know what they manufactured and I never learnt since the visit never took place. I think it was on that occasion I was introduced to a member of the family who was a lawyer. Madame had told me beforehand that he was an *Avocat*

*Général*, in other words a public prosecutor, and that that morning, in Nancy, as was required by French law, he had been present at the guillotining of a man he had prosecuted. *"On leur coupe la tête,"* (They cut their heads off) Madame explained, in her down-to-earth way, supposing that I was ignorant of the main thing that, ever since The Scarlet Pimpernel, many British people know about France. I tried to tell them politely that I thought the practice was barbaric, but it maybe wasn't very tactful. That was probably why I wasn't invited again.

Learning a new set of conventions was sometimes as hard as acquiring unfamiliar rules of syntax. The wife of the concierge of the College was heavily pregnant. I thought it was mildly witty to say that she was going to *faire des petits*, which is the expression used for a cat having kittens. One of the *pions* pulled me up immediately, telling me that it was extremely rude and offensive to use any animal term when speaking about a person.

Sometimes learning the convention meant learning some syntax as well. If we went to Nancy to attend lectures in the faculty we could have our railway fares reimbursed. For this we had to make a formal application to the Rector of the University. When the *pions* told me how this should be framed I was sure they were having me on. But No, it had to be written on what they called *papier ministre* and had to start: *Monsieur le Recteur, J'ai l'honneur de solliciter de votre haute bienveillance le remboursement etc etc.*

I registered as a student if only to get my rail fares reimbursed but I attended a certain number of lectures out of interest. I remember in particular a course on Beaumarchais which I chose to follow mostly because it fitted in with the train times. The contrast with TCD was striking. There can't have been many more students in the room than used to attend H. O. White's waffling monologues in College, but the lecturer's whole manner and style of speaking were as formal and as polished as though he were addressing an audience of several hundred. He rolled out these long phrases, dropping in audible semicolons and colons, putting in expressive pauses, asking and answering rhetorical questions, and only occasionally glancing at his notes. It was my first experience of hearing someone really making the French language talk and I found it a real pleasure to listen to, quite apart from what he was actually saying, which was interesting too. And then, a few minutes before the end of the hour there would be a dramatic change. He would terminate the lecture, usually with a resounding and memorable final sentence, step forward off the dais and light a cigarette as though to signal a change of mode. This done, and in quite a different voice, speaking very casually, he would invite questions and there would follow several minutes of quite lively, and completely informal, dialogue with the audience of students. I don't remember the lecturer's name, if ever I knew it, but, when I said I had been to lectures on Beaumarchais, students of literature told me I had made the right choice.

Not all university teachers enjoyed this degree of esteem. Many were both feared and disliked and the more I learnt about the examinations that were at the heart of the French university system the better I understood this animosity. One day in my first term I saw an example of it. On the days that we went to Nancy there was an agreement by which we could have lunch and dinner with the *pions* of the big *Lycée Poincaré*. It was a smallish dining room off the main *réfectoire* and there were usually eight or ten of these chaps sitting at tables round the wall. Sitting together, but well away from the *pions,* there would often be two quite important looking gentlemen of a certain age. I got to know them quite well by sight. One they called Bourdon, though I don't know if that was his real name, or a nickname because of his lugubrious voice. The other the students called Moïse, (Moses) presumably because of his large square beard. They were both senior members of the University, which was one reason why the *pions* resented this invasion of their territory, exacerbated by the obvious explanation that they ate there because they were just too mean to go to a restaurant.

On this particular evening there was quite a number of *pions,* not all of them from Poincaré, all sitting on one side of the room; Bourdon and Moïse were against the wall on the other side. I don't remember where I was sitting, it must have been somewhere in between. Towards the end of the meal – we had been eating some creamy sticky dessert – one of the *pions* got up to leave. When he got to the door he turned around and said, "*Bonsoir tout le monde,*" and switched off the light, plunging the room into total darkness. There was a vague rustling, splashing, sound and some exclamations from where the two elderly professors were sitting. When eventually the lights came on again the room was empty except for me, two or three puzzled-looking and obviously guiltless students, and Bourdon and Moïse, whose faces and clothes were smeared and splashed with a thick coating of the custardy dessert, copious spoonfuls of which had been fired across the room in the dark with impressive accuracy. Bourdon stood up and screamed all sorts of threats and abuse, but it was obviously a waste of breath. No one knew or would say who had been present in the room ten minutes before. When I told people in Lunéville about the incident they, and not only young people, roared with laughter. It is true that the discomfiture of others, above all important others, is a reliable source of mirth; the French are just franker than most about enjoying it. Personally I was a bit put off by what I saw as the young making fun of the old. But then I thought to myself how much I would have enjoyed pelting copious spoonfuls of custard in the dark at the headmasters of the Leas School Hoylake.

When I had been in Lunéville about five weeks I began to think that I had acclimatised enough so I went to the *Principal* and asked when they wanted me to start teaching. I think he had forgotten all about me but I was hastily fixed up with a timetable. It was far from being a heavy work load, I don't think I can have had more than six or eight hours in the week, which mostly consisted of simple conversation practice with senior pupils. It would be hard to imagine a less stressful way of spending one's time. I told them jokes and taught them songs. The only thing I remember being completely unsuccessful in was my effort, at their request, to explain to them the game of cricket. They could not make head nor tail of it and told me it was completely absurd. I had always thought playing cricket was a ridiculous way to spend one's time but some obscure loyalty to Anglo-Saxon culture and tradition turned me instantly, and to my surprise, into a zealous, though completely unsuccessful, ambassador for England's national game.

Teaching one's native language, especially for a very inexperienced and jejune teacher such as I was, is a slightly odd experience. On the one hand, being a native speaker, you are, or think you are, an absolute authority regarding any question of correct usage. On the other hand, since your knowledge of the language is entirely intuitive, you have absolutely no explicit knowledge of its grammar. When you hear a pupil saying "Last week I have gone.." instead of "Last week I went..." you have very little idea why it is wrong and you're constantly tempted to think up explanations which then turn out to be misleading, or mistaken, or both. Inevitably, relations with professional teachers who are not native speakers can be extremely tricky. The teachers know that you can easily damage or destroy their standing with their pupils, for example by criticising their pronunciation. On the other hand their explicit knowledge of the language, and of the intricacies of its grammar, is often much greater than yours could ever be. You can easily fail to appreciate this, and to appreciate the years of work that went into acquiring this expertise.

More specifically, the teacher will very naturally tend to regard as important those language mistakes which they have spent many class hours trying to teach the learners not to make. The mistakes that matter to you, on the other hand, as a native speaker, will tend just to be the ones that make the learners hard to understand. They won't be the same mistakes. I found it hard to convince French people, teachers as well as learners, that a French accent can sound both musical and distinguished to an English speaker's ear.

All this can make for a very uneasy relationship between teacher and native speaker. I was lucky in Lunéville: the principal teacher of English not only had a very respectable command of the language but she was keen to take every opportunity of improving it. I liked her very much, Madame Salvey, and I think she found me a more congenial colleague than the somewhat brash young English chap that preceded me. Maybe her being Breton had something to do with it. Her tendency to mother the pupils, which they often criticised, meant that, unlike some French schoolteachers, she treated them all as individual human beings, something that I liked and noticed straight away. It was part of a personal tragedy: her husband, who was a musician, was a permanent invalid, suffering from epilepsy, and for that reason they had no children. The drama, though, didn't prevent her from being very cheerful company. She was interesting to talk to too. She told me about her childhood in Brittany. And how, during the Occupation, she had agreed to do translating for a *maquis* group. She described how they had brought her, at night, deep into the forest somewhere in the Vosges, where they were looking after a wounded RAF pilot who spoke no French. So far as I was concerned it would have been a mean-spirited action to have fended off her slight tendency to mother me. Also, well, I was a long way from home, and she was an excellent cook.

Lunéville was on the main line from Paris to Strasbourg; it was also a railhead for several branch lines which I took advantage of to explore the mountains and forests of the Vosges. I purchased a Chaix railway timetable and spent many happy hours working out how to combine different lines, walking or cycling between different destinations. Some of the lines were still narrow gauge, and still working in 1949. The more I saw of French railways the more I liked them. I liked the rational way the whole network was organised, with the four clear categories of trains: *Rapide*, *Express*, *Direct* and *Omnibus*. I liked the sensible way in which fares were based in those days on a price per kilometre, so you could always work out the exact price of a ticket by looking up the distance in kilometres in the timetable. And then the main line trains, with their massive steam locomotives, looked so big and went so fast; shades of Jean Gabin in *La Bête Humaine*. They look bigger than British or Irish trains, partly because French station platforms are very low, but also because the trains actually are wider and higher as well, though the rail gauge is the same as the one decided by George Stephenson. While I was at Lunéville the SNCF were experimenting on the line to Strasbourg with mainline trains running on pneumatic tyres. It made for a very silent comfortable ride but I was told that at mainline speeds the tyres wore out so quickly that the idea was abandoned after a few years, though a similar technology is still to be found on some lines of the Paris Metro.

I often used to watch the big international expresses as they thundered through the suburbs of Lunéville heading towards, not only Strasbourg, but Munich, Vienna, Budapest, Bucharest and Istanbul. The Orient Express passed through every day, on the way to these, to me, exotic places. I fancied I could see, sitting by the little table lamps of the posh coaches of the *Compagnie. des Wagons Lits*, fez-wearing Turks, Caliphs in turbans, Chinamen in lampshade hats. Then, one evening, Henri and I were walking along a path beside the main line from Nancy. We came to the railway bridge over the River Meurthe, which was a metal bridge, a lattice of steel girders. I suppose we were daring each other, anyway we clambered out on the girders underneath the track when the Paris-Strasbourg *Rapide* was due to pass. It was a memorably terrifying experience which we did not repeat. Fortunately nobody was flushing a WC just at the moment it passed over us.

It was a homelier means of transport that took me to the foot of the Donon, the nearest 1000 metre peak to Lunéville and my first French mountain. In fact it was a sort of Micheline, or diesel railcar, that wobbled its way up a narrow forest-clad valley on what seemed to me an uneven and unsteady narrow gauge track. In the tiny village at the end of the valley there was a café that I returned to a number of times, partly because I liked the innkeeper and his wife and I found them easy to talk to but above all because every evening they would have a visit from an enchanting individual, an old man that they referred to as Le Georges, the definite article seeming to suggest some special familiarity or respect, I never understood which. Le Georges was blind, whether from birth or from a wound received in the Great War I don't remember or never knew, but he moved around, both indoors and out, without ever giving the impression that he was feeling his way. I used to admire the dexterity with which he rolled and lit his cigarettes exactly as though he could see what he was doing. Perhaps due to his blindness he had a wonderfully expressive way of talking which made him a pleasure to listen to. The people in the village were concerned about the damage done by wild boars to their crops and vegetable patches and had applied for permission to organise a hunt to reduce the number of boars in the locality. Le Georges entertained us with anecdotes about the devious behaviour and the savagery of these creatures to the extent that I became slightly nervous walking in the forests alone. In fact the only time I saw a wild boar it was trotting peacefully in front of me along a path in the woods, and I thought it was a large dog until it suddenly turned and disappeared into the undergrowth. The café owner promised to let me know when the boar hunt was to be so that I could come and take part but somehow it never happened.

The Donon was an easy walk of two hours or so, zigzagging up paths through the pine trees. I was a bit disconcerted on this, the first time that I had been higher than 1000 metres in France, to find that only the very top was bare of trees. The summit of Carrauntuohill, only a few metres higher, had been a far wilder place. And the trees surrounding the summit rocks were higher than the summit and obscured the view. Fortunately there was a sort of tower made of pine trunks bolted together with a ladder up one side and a platform at the top, constructed, I was later told, by the Germans watching out for signs of Resistance activity. Someone had told me that you could see the Alps from the summit of the Donon, so I clambered up this precarious structure, which wobbled uneasily under my weight, until I got to the height of the surrounding trees and could look out over the view which consisted of pine forest-clad hills in all directions as far as the eye could reach. Not that it could reach very far; there was too much haze and the Alps were invisible. Coming down into the village on my return I watched a man ploughing a field with two oxen harnessed by means of a heavy wooden yoke fastened over their horns. Later that evening Le Georges explained to me how the strength of a pair of oxen differed in nature from the strength of a team of horses, knowledge to be made redundant soon, but not yet. That year in Lunéville I hardly ever saw a tractor.

Petrol was of course still rationed in France; anyhow nobody I knew that year had a car. I had brought a bicycle over and made good use of the relatively traffic-free roads, as I had done in Ireland before I got the motorbike. French cyclists found my Raleigh "the all steel bicycle" with no gear change, absurdly old-fashioned. Once at the end of a long day, cycling to Dijon, I found a bus that would take me part of the way. There were two or three other cyclists. The driver climbed onto the roof of the bus, reached his arm down and slung each bike up in one easy movement until he came to my all steel contraption when the unexpected effort that this suddenly required almost made him lose his balance. The incident brought home to me the superiority of French bicycles which were made of a light alloy and had a multiple speed gear change, so at Easter, when I wanted to explore the southern part of Alsace and the high, granite, Vosges, I borrowed Henri's bicycle. Riding it after my Raleigh was like being gifted with a new pair of legs.

Both Alsace and Lorraine had been incorporated as part of Germany after 1940. The process of Germanisation had gone much further in Alsace where they already spoke a Germanic dialect. This may explain why I found people on the east side of the Vosges much more reserved and generally less friendly than those in Lorraine. I imagined that this was because their loyalty had recently been called in question, but it may just have been a regional characteristic. It was obvious from the number of ruined towns and villages, not only here in Alsace but also in Lorraine, that the war had raged much more fiercely here than in the regions to the west. There was another sign that the Nazis had considered the region to be part of Germany. As I stood on the summit of the Donon I could see below me in the valley to the southeast the village of Schirmeck. I knew that in the forest just beyond Schirmeck, a bare 5 miles from where I was standing, was the site of the Struthof concentration camp. Several people in Lunéville had told me about this place, I had heard of people being subjected to tortures there so inhuman that the thought kept me awake at night, and I knew that the real evil perpetrated there, the gas chambers and crematoria, were only known about after the war. I debated with myself at length, trying to decide about visiting this place. I felt on the one hand that, having spent the war years in comfortable bourgeois *insouciance,* I ought to see such like atrocities with my own eyes. On the other hand, feeling the fascination of this extreme of horror, I was suspicious of my own motives, of the element of morbid voyeurism, in the fascination itself. So I decided that it would be wrong to go and gawk at gas chambers and crematoria. Many years later, I was in the Vosges with Olivia my wife, and we did go there when the fascination had been replaced by a mature apprehension. Even then, many years after the war, it was upsetting.

Apart from these and other Germanic associations - I was often reminded of Hansel and Gretel - the Vosges were beautiful mountains to explore, in particular the Northern part of the range where the forest was denser and the occasional red sandstone crags stood out like crumbling ruins. The thick forest cover made it almost impossible to work out the lie of the land and several times I had to climb a tree to work out where I was, and I once had the instructive and not wholly agreeable experience of being totally lost and disorientated for an hour or two when I suddenly saw the sun shining from what I had thought was North. Though the *pions* tried to scare me with tales of the occasional wolves that in a hard winter would make their way across the Rhine, the only unfamiliar and faintly alarming fauna that I encountered, apart from my one sighting of a wild boar, were the snakes. I kept seeing snakes that year, both the very graceful grass snakes or *couleuvres,* which varied from a few inches to two or even three feet in length, and the thicker, shorter and more sinister *vipères.* I mostly saw both sorts as they were trying to cross a road or forest track, and I would dismount to watch them, moving very slowly and clumsily on the smooth surface, until they reached the grass verge where they would suddenly zip forward and disappear. They fascinated me, coming as I did from Ireland where Saint Patrick did us out of most of our reptiles. I have often wondered why, in later years and even in other more southerly parts of France, I never saw so many as that first year. Was it pollution, or roadkill, or was there maybe some other explanation?

I was on good terms with a number of the teachers in the Collège as well as Mme Salvey. They were relaxed and friendly, free from the devouring ambition which, as I was later to find in Orléans, made the *professeurs* in large lycées near Paris so tiresome and uninteresting from my point of view. Instead these people had other more personal interests. There was a teacher of natural science who organised very early morning nature walks in the surrounding countryside, which I sometimes went on and learnt the names of various wild flowers, fungi and insects, which I have forgotten. There was an amusing art teacher who went to weekly life classes in Paris as part of some in-service training scheme. Approached as he came out of the *Gare de l'Est* by a tout who asked him would he like to look at naked women he said that was what they paid him to come to Paris for. The tout looked him up and down and said, *"Tu es encore plus cochon que je ne pensais."* (You're an even dirtier bastard than I thought). But I spent most of my spare time with the *pions*, that is to say with Henri and one or two of the *maîtresses d'intenat* or *pionnes* from the girls' *Collège*, the most attractive of which was a lovely vivacious girl called Janine with a great head of curly brown hair. Henri and I took her camping on the summit of the Donon to see the dawn break on the distant Alps. Unfortunately the three of us sat up so late singing and telling jokes that we slept through the daybreak so the Alps had to wait. Coming down we passed a farm where they were milking the cows and Janine insisted that we go in and ask the farmer for a drink of milk "hot from the cow". It was not disgusting at all. So there was another totally new and strange experience which, for all that there were cows everywhere in Ireland, I had to come to France for.

One effect of being a foreigner, as I was in France, is the way in which one's class origins and affiliations become invisible. I had not anticipated this but I came to value it highly. I know that not everyone would feel as I did about this; some people coming to live in, for example, France will tend to look for French people belonging to an equivalent social milieu to the one they have come from at home. My situation was more complex. It is not that I was not proud of my family background or in any way ashamed of, or even embarrassed by, the Protestant caste that I could not help identifying with, but I could not help feeling that they cut me off in a way from the majority of Irish people, where I wanted sincerely to belong. I can see now, and have seen for years, that I was wrong to feel this. The feeling however was a fact, and it mattered a lot to me at the time. That being so I had done the right thing in coming to France. Because, just as French women, meeting a man for the first time, size him up, not, as would be the case in Britain, first and foremost as a tiddlywinks enthusiast or an Old Harrovian, but as a man, so the French people I encountered in Lunéville and elsewhere simply categorised me, not as Protestant or middle class but simply as a non-French human being.

I felt all this very strongly as my friendship with Henri grew, and above all when I met his family. He himself was still a practising Catholic, albeit a very independent-minded one. There was nothing we could not talk about as day after day we "tired the sun with talking and sent him down the sky". His background, his social attitudes and his opinions were in many ways totally different from mine, which made the finding of so much common ground all the more valuable an experience. In a way I suppose our attitudes to life complemented each other: though three years younger than me – something I did not discover until many years later – he was in some ways more mature, he had certainly lived more, had seen guns fired in anger, had had at least one passionate physical relationship with a woman, whereas I, for all I was still very much a virgin, had acquired, from Columba's and College, an air of sophistication that enabled me, more or less, to hold my own. On a more humdrum level of course he taught me a lot of French as I taught him quite a lot of English.

After I had been in Lunéville a month or two he brought me home to meet his parents, in his home town of Toul. It was the first of several visits the climax of which was the First Communion of his younger sister Monique. Toul, a cathedral town a few miles on the other side of Nancy from Lunéville, is better known, if only because its name figures in the history books. In 1948 however, as a result of the war, the centre of the town was still in ruins with rose-willow herb rampant on the broken walls and the cathedral a mere shell. Overlooking the town was a small hill, the *Mont St Michel*. There was a fort on the top and the whole hill was a maze of *souterrains* and tunnels, the remains of old fortifications. It was fun, though it was also dangerous, to explore these; a few years later someone fell down a vertical shaft and was killed, so all the underground passages were sealed off. There were also limestone caverns that we went exploring on the banks of the Moselle. They were dusty, much less impressive than Mitchelstown and less scary than Poulnagollum. It was the first time that something French was a disappointment compared with Ireland. Up till then everything French that I had encountered had seemed so much more so than the Irish equivalent.

Henri's parents welcomed me very warmly. His father was a clerk in a solicitor's office in the town; "*un proletaire en faux-col*" was how he described himself. He had been wounded in World War I and had lost most of the fingers in both hands. A reserved, slow-spoken man with a kindly sense of humour, he explained to me how he made the *eau de vie de mirabelle*, the plum brandy that is a great speciality of the region. I was in fact only too well acquainted with this delectable firewater, a litre of which Henri kept in his cupboard in Lunéville. He and the other *pions* had got me to consume a prodigious quantity of it as a result of which I got drunker than I had ever been in my life, or have ever been since, having next morning no memory at all of the evening before. What impressed me most about the experience was that next day I suffered from absolutely no hangover, a fact which I could only ascribe to the quality of the spirit and Henri's father's skill as a distiller.

They lived in a compact little house with a small garden where the mirabelle trees grew. As well as the parents and Henri's young sister Monique there was the inevitable French grandmother, a picturesque old crone in a long black dress. His mother, an un-effusive but very *sympathique* woman was obviously very much in charge. She didn't talk over much but what she said was always to the point and I could see her when there was company, watching people and silently forming her own, not always flattering, opinion. I was therefore very gratified that she seemed to like me. I was impressed by the formality observed by these totally unpretentious people. When a visitor – I can't remember who he was - came to the house Henri's mother poured out glasses of white wine, pointing out proudly that it was a *Côte de Toul*, from the locality itself. We sat around the table, with the full glasses untouched before us, while the visitor talked and talked, until at long last he paused and said, "*Eh bien, à votre santé*" and we all lifted our glasses and drank. Years later in Aberdeen I would tell students going to France to watch out for moments like this, and not disgrace themselves and Scotland by boorishly grabbing their glass and swigging as soon as it was filled.

Boorish is one thing that these people most certainly were not, so I was amused when, later in the year, Henri's parents invited me to an important family celebration at which certain country cousins would be present and Henri warned me that, "*Quelques-uns de mes cousins sont des 'country bumpkins'*". I found, then and later, that these farm people observed formalities that I was to recognize later in novels by Roger Vailland. The important family celebration in question was the First Communion of Henri's sister Monique and, since they had learned that I had a singing voice, I was invited to sing in the choir. They knew I wasn't a Catholic; that didn't seem to matter at all. As all the music was totally unfamiliar I don't think I contributed much, but it meant I had a seat in the gallery with a good view of the ceremony, which I watched with interest never having been at a Catholic service before. The music was in fact somewhat undistinguished; I can only remember one long 19th century aria sung by a tall serious girl who lived next door, with the refrain, *"Ô, mon âme, adore et tais-toi."* But the whole experience was so novel that I don't think I even found the service boring, though it must have been quite long. And the novelty continued when the service was over and we went back to the house, where Henri's mother served up the sort of gorgeous meal that only French people have the secret of. At the end of the lunch, when the little glasses of mirabelle brandy began to circulate, people told jokes and sang songs. Did I sing an Irish song? I don't remember. I know I had a lot of success with a shaggy dog story about three tortoises, only learning long after that the reason they found it so funny was that I kept getting the gender of *tortue* wrong. Then one of the country cousins, who was sitting beside Monique in her long white First Communion dress, told a long, hilariously funny but surprisingly ribald, joke about three peasants trying to register a birth at the Mairie. Other bawdier jokes followed; the occasion eventually concluded in an atmosphere of good humour and general well-being. All the time it was going on I was thinking to myself that something similar would happen down the country in Ireland: there would be the same religious occasion, the same family gathering, the same bucolic hilarity, probably around pints of stout in the back room of a pub, but that no way could I with my Protestant affiliations and my middle-class voice take any part in it whatsoever.

It was around this time that I decided, since I had enjoyed being an *Assistant Anglais* and had learned so much this year, to ask for a second year. And so I wrote to the Office and was appointed to the *Lycee Pothier* in Orléans. Everyone in Lunéville congratulated me on having landed a job so much nearer to Paris, assuming, wrongly as I have explained, that everything would therefore be better than in Lunéville. On the last day in the *Collège* I was invited to take part in the *Distribution des Prix* and sat with the other teachers on the stage of the attractive little theatre and helped in the operation of awarding books to deserving pupils. Constance had arrived by then. I introduced her to my French friends and together we visited some of the Christmas card villages in Alsace and, on the 14th of July in Strasbourg, we danced in the street in front of the towering Cathedral and drank *vin d'Alsace* which ever since has been my favourite white wine.. Back in Ireland my mother had rented a house at Roundstone in Connemara so I invited Henri to join us there. It was fun showing a wild Irish seaside to someone who had virtually never seen the sea, and seeing 14-year-old Una trying to get him to put his finger into a sea anemone. Henri was on his way to Huddersfield where he was to spend the year as French Assistant in a grammar school.

Orléans was a very different affair in every way from Lunéville. The town, the school, the teachers, even the *pions* were more considerable and took themselves more seriously than had been the case in Lunéville. They were all of them also much less interested in me. The headmaster, or *Proviseur*, was a remote lofty individual that I don't remember ever speaking to in the whole course of the year, though I suppose I must have been introduced to him at some time. We used to pass each other on the staircase and he obviously had no idea who I was. The principal teacher of English, Monsieur Houdret was a tall skinamalink of a man who had just that year been successful in the *Agrégation*, that terrifying and all-important competitive examination, obsession of ambitious *professeurs*. On the occasion of our only extended conversation, when he once invited me for a cup of coffee in his home, Houdret could talk of nothing else. He at least lived in Orléans. Most of his colleagues either lived in Paris or spent as much time there as they could. Classes ended at 12.30 and there was a train for Paris that left at 12.36; it was amusing to watch the helter-skelter of briefcases going up the *Rue de la République* to the station every day. Amusing but it had its disadvantages; I found I was left very much to my own devices.

That is not to say that I did not take advantage of the proximity of Paris, when I could afford it. Mark Mortimer, who had taught me French and English at St Columba's was now lecturing and teaching at the British Institute in the rue de la Sorbonne, actually just across the street from where the *Cours de Vacances* had taken place three years before, though it all looked very different now that I considered myself virtually a French resident. Mark had a room above a small bar in the *rue de Buci* and, being an extremely likeable and sociable person, had not only made friends with a crowd of interesting local characters but was an obvious person for visitors from Dublin to look up and, on occasion, sponge on. I would look Mark Mortimer up whenever I came to Paris and through him met up again with, among others, John Beckett, later to be well-known as a composer. I had known Beckett at Columba's where Brian Boydell had performed his setting to music of one of my Midnight poems. He was currently living in a hotel in the *rue Servandoni*, sharing a room with Brendan Behan, whose career as a writer had not as yet begun and who was working, if I remember rightly, as a house painter. Beckett was studying Irish folk song and would get Behan to sing, which he could do beautifully in the full traditional style with all the grace notes and flourishes that only the best folk singers can manage. Unfortunately he would only sing if he also drank, and the more drink he had taken the more the musical quality of his performance and of his choice of songs deteriorated, becoming maudlin and repetitive. Eventually this got too much and Beckett turned him out. He also used to spit on the floor, though I don't know if this bothered Beckett who was never a man obsessed by cleanliness.

I admired John Beckett enormously and envied his artistic integrity, his single-minded dedication to his music in spite of an almost total lack of encouragement from music publishers. Though several years younger than me he was already quite an intimidating person. I remember one minor incident from that time in Paris. Beckett maintained that the safest way to cross the Paris streets – this was in the days before pedestrian crossings and green men on the traffic lights – was to walk across with your eyes shut. If you kept your eyes open, he said, you would move irregularly, jumping backwards and forwards, and the cars wouldn't know how to avoid you, whereas with your eyes shut you could walk slowly and steadily and the cars would steer round you. It was fine as a theory; what was impressive was to see Beckett carrying it out, walking slowly and in a straight line across the *Boulevard Saint-Germain* and, it is true, being avoided by motorists who, this being Paris, didn't fail to shout at him, saying what they thought of him and, by implication, his theory, in picturesque terms.

The lycée in Orléans was built in the same style as the college in Lunéville but was about three times the size. It was in one of the main streets, close to the cathedral, which I found a depressing edifice, the mediaeval parts overshadowed by hideous 18th-century improvements. Between the lycée and the Loire there was a warren of very old, very narrow little streets with picturesque ancient-sounding names. The centre of the town was still a mass of ruins, destroyed I was told by American bombers in 1944. The bridge over the Loire, which they had been aiming at, was undamaged. The Loire itself, a wide, spreading, slow moving river with mudflats on each side and in the middle, was the town's main feature. I was told that the vinegar for which Orléans was famous originated when in earlier centuries barges bearing wine used to get stuck here in the mud.

As in Lunéville I lived with, and on the same footing as, the *pions*. There were ten or a dozen of these, together with various ancillary staff whose functions I never understood. I got to know two or three quite well; there were several that I never got to know at all. We all ate in a small room off the main dining hall or *réfectoire*. I was struck by the hypochondria of these evidently very healthy young Frenchmen. We were each given table napkins. (I had noticed how, whereas English people have table manners, the French always have table napkins.) These were kept in pigeonholes on the wall and I always knew how to find mine by looking for the only pigeonhole that hadn't got some medicine in it beside the napkin. I watched with interest at the start of each meal as they all got down to filing the ends from little glass capsules each containing some essential medication.

Several of the *pions* were of much more clearly middle-class origin than the four *pions* in Lunéville, as would have been evident from their expensive clothes and their slightly standoffish manner if it hadn't been revealed immediately by their political opinions. On the other hand two or three of the others were proud and enthusiastic members of the French Communist Party. It was clear that the political sympathies of the remainder, though they were not Party members, were in general very much to the left. In my whole year in Lunéville I don't think I can remember a single argument or even discussion about politics, let alone ideology. Here things were very different and I found the continual arguments over the evening meal intellectually stimulating to say the least. It was also a political education just to listen to them. I still had a lot to learn and not only on the level of ideology. For example we were served at table by a gentle soft-spoken man who to begin with we all, I suppose following the example of the *bourgeois* chaps, addressed as *Maurice*. The habits and manners instilled by St Columba's dying hard, I followed suit unthinkingly, saying *Bonjour Maurice, Merci Maurice* and *Au Revoir Maurice,* just as I used to say "Good morning Triggs," in Hoylake. Filliat and Gherardi, the two Communists, pointed out immediately that to address someone in a manner that they cannot use back to you is a humiliation for them. From then on we always addressed Maurice as Monsieur Mitten.

Politics wasn't of course the only subject of conversation; the other was, inevitably, sex. Here again things were different from Lunéville. Henri and I had talked very frankly, though I had managed to conceal from him the important fact that the only physical relationship I had known had been adolescent and homosexual. But the subject of our discussions had all the same been relationships, physical and sexual maybe, but always romantic and personal, between people. Most of the Orléans *pions*, older and more sophisticated, or merely more cynical, talked endlessly about the countless brief encounters they had in most cases provoked or brought about. They recounted anecdote upon anecdote about women accosted in the street, on trains, in buses or, though rarely, on country roads, and who had usually accorded their favours at the price of a few compliments. They would explain the techniques they employed to achieve this desirable result and I listened, amazed and only half believing in the truth of these adventures. And then a chance encounter in Paris put conventional French male attitudes to sex in a new and proper perspective. The chance encounter was with Oisín Kelly. He had replaced Brian Boydell as art master at St Columba's, which was where Mark Mortimer had got to know him, and was well on his way to fame in Ireland as a sculptor. I don't remember what they were talking about, he and Mark, sitting in some Latin Quarter café, or how it came round to sex. I probably was only half listening, and then suddenly Oisín was saying, "You know, fucking is terribly *difficult*, no matter how much practice you have you hardly ever get it right." Those would-be Don Juans in Orléans had with one word been reduced to a pack of self-deceiving insensitive buffoons.

Another thing that made Orléans very different from Lunéville for me was the motorbike. During the summer Steve had moved up to a 500 cc Triumph and had passed his 350cc Velocette on to me. With its top speed of over seventy miles an hour it was a huge change from the little two-stroke and there was no question but I must take it to France. Or rather it took me, and a friend, Paul Allen, who was going to be *assistant* at Fontainebleau. The journey from Dublin to Orléans took three days; it was my first experience of English and French roads and of long distances, and it was marvellous. Though I'm not sure how much Paul Allen enjoyed the journey sitting on the pillion seat, since the bike, as was common in those days, had no rear springing. It pelted with rain all the way through and over the Welsh hills and across the Midlands of England, so that when we eventually stopped somewhere near Rugby I don't think I had ever been so wet, so cold or so exhausted in all my life. Both Paul and I, so far as I remember, were just wearing ordinary gabardine raincoats; I don't think we can have had dry clothes to change into at all. But I do remember clearly how well I slept that night in some pub near Kilsby or Crick. I must have been out for nine hours and I have held it in memory ever since as a criterion by which all other nights' sleep can be judged.

It was just as well that I had the motorbike because once I had got settled in at Orléans I began to find the surrounding countryside oppressively flat and monotonous. To the north of Orléans the enormous wheat fields of La Beauce stretched out almost to the outer suburbs of Paris; south of the Loire the lakes and forests of La Sologne reached almost as far. Common to both was an almost total lack of any relief. It is an unphotographeable landscape, as some writer, Charles Péguy maybe, has observed. You could turn your gaze through 360° round the flat rim of the horizon without encountering the slightest hump or irregularity. As the year went by I came to see a virtue in this unfamiliar flatness, to appreciate the strange quality of the light in the Loire country and the way in which buildings, Chartres cathedral or the *Chateau de Sully*, stood out and could be perceived from many miles away. And, in *La Sologne* I was glad to explore the landscapes so evocatively described by Fournier in *Le Grand Meaulnes* which I had read at school with Peter Allt. But to start with I longed to see hills in the distance and I hankered after all that they symbolise and represent. The non-Communist *pion* at the lycée that I found easiest to talk to was called Tabèze and came from Aurillac in Cantal. Listening to him talk about his home region set me thinking; I looked out the map and found that the nearest mountains to Orléans were the *Monts d'Auvergne*. As soon as I could fiddle myself a few days free from teaching I got on the bike and set off southwards. There is a significant moment, somewhere south of the town of Montluçon, where the road comes to the top of a small hill and you can see, sticking up on the skyline, the unmistakable shape of the Puy de Dôme. It was a moment I looked forward to and enjoyed a number of times during the year. The *Puy de Dôme*, which is more than 1000ft higher than Carrauntuohill was the highest mountain I had ever climbed, and, thanks to the road corkscrewing round and up it, I got to the top in minutes on the Velocette, in second gear.

Ownership of a powerful British-built motorcycle, of prestigious TT-winning make, made me eligible for membership of the Orléans motor cycle club which I joined at the suggestion of Monsieur Mitten who came to work every day on a smart little Peugeot two-stroke and with whom it was pleasant to discuss the advantages and disadvantages of the two-stroke engine. Meetings of the club, which were held at the back of a café, tended to consist of endless discussions of things like the club's participation in some federation or other. Things brightened up however, when the winter was over and it became incumbent upon club members to support a local champion in grass track races and scrambles, which they called *Moto-Cross*. The champion in question, a very handsome and very charming chap called Robert Moury, had a shop in the centre of Orléans where he sold the ubiquitous French Mobylettes and was an agent for Jawa motorcycles, made in Czechoslovakia. He was very friendly, though I suspected that it might be because he hoped I might get him customers among the *professeurs* at the lycée, and I did enjoy this, for, as a rider, he certainly was a star. We would all meet somewhere at the edge of the town and zoom off together in a string towards wherever the *Moto-Cross* was to be held. Mine was I think the only British bike, though there may have been a few ex-army BSAs. All this was of course long before the Japanese came on the scene; the only possible rivals to British motor cycles were the German BMW and a few Italian makes. I remember chatting with a fellow club member, comparing my Velocette with his Moto-Guzzi when a French-made 500cc Terrot went past, pinking as it accelerated. "*Ça,* "said my companion, unpatriotically, "*C'est de la belle merde!*" (beautiful heap of shit).

The racing was often quite exciting and I liked it when I was asked to be a marshal and help keep spectators off the track. Moury didn't always win, though he was usually placed in the first three or four. He was certainly more audacious than most of the others. And his Jawa, which was a two-stroke with an unusual double-piston engine, was very powerful for its class. But what really impressed and fascinated me was the speed with which, between races, his technical team of two or three mechanics dismantled and reassembled his machine, changing the sprockets on the chain drive or, most extraordinary of all, once taking the whole engine and gearbox out and replacing them with others for some reason, in what can't have been more than about twenty minutes. When it was all over the visiting clubs would be invited, before riding off home, to a *Vin d'Honneur* where liberal quantities of white wine would be poured out and consumed. "*Buvez, mon ami,* " said one of the hosts to me, "*Cela améliore la conduite.* " (Drink up, makes you drive better). Also, only the racers wore what we called crash helmets, and then only when they were actually racing. If anyone suggested we should wear one on the road we would reply that the place to wear one's helmet was inside one's head. The past was (is?) a different country indeed.

One of the ancillary staff in the lycée who ate with us most days was a lean intellectual-looking man with a high forehead and a large nose - he told me once that he looked like Henri IV – called Jacques Souviron. He was another Communist and took a prominent part in the frequent political discussions, arguing more forcefully than the others thanks to a lawyer-like skill at remembering facts and quotations and producing them at the crucial moment. I warmed to him when, exceptionally, he lost his temper with a conservative-minded smoothie called Babinet who spoke slightingly of the *Résistance.* I had little idea then that he, and his wife and children, were to become my closest friends and to remain so for the rest of our lives. Recently married and father of a little girl he was living alone in a hotel room, his wife and baby being with her parents in Bordeaux. He was spending all his spare time tramping the streets and ringing doorbells in search of a flat so that they could join him in Orléans. His wife, who was still on maternity leave, was a *professeur agrégé* of French and classics in the girl's lycée.

As in Lunéville I was housed together with the *pions* on the top floor of the main building of the lycée. I had been given the choice of either a large cavernous room at the end of the corridor or a somewhat pokier one round the corner. I was still trying to decide which one to settle in permanently when it occurred to someone – I like to think it was me - to suggest that Souviron move out of his hotel and install himself in the larger of the two rooms. This he did with alacrity, bringing with him a few articles of furniture that he and his wife had acquired including an armchair and above all a radio, a record player and a large collection of records. The room rapidly acquired an appearance of bourgeois comfort that contrasted agreeably with the austerity of the lycée décor. It was in this setting that started one of the most significant friendships in my life. We were very different, Jacques and I, and it did occasionally occur to me to wonder what he saw in me, apart from the slightly exotic attraction of my Irish origin. We had in common our combination of middle-class origin and left-wing opinions and affiliations which set us apart from all the other *pions,* though both elements were more strongly marked in Jacques's case than in mine. Though Jacques's father had been a painter he had had a very conventional religious and bourgeois upbringing against which he was still in fairly violent reaction of which his communism was the most obvious sign. The scientific, slightly bohemian, flavour of my background gave me in contrast a certain detachment which I think he admired, as I admired his single-minded dedication to an ideal, and above all to a cause.

I have a clear memory of the first time we talked about politics. I had started criticising the British Labour government for some pusillanimous action or attitude and went on to explain how in my opinion a resolutely socialist policy was surely the best defence against communism. Jacques interrupted me by bursting out laughing - he was somebody for whom the expression was literally exact, when he laughed his whole face would become as it were illuminated with mirth - with a cry of, *"Mais pourquoi, diable, veux-tu tellement t'en défendre?"*(But why the hell should you want to be defended against it?) That started the first of many arguments. All our lives we argued, sometimes hitting upon a difference of opinion within 10 minutes of meeting for the first time in several months. Normally I tend to avoid conflicts of opinion or ideas, mostly because I tend to lose, but an argument with Jacques presented an intellectual challenge that it was hard to turn down. And I found that my own ideas and opinions, beaten out on the anvil of his mind, became clearer, more coherent and made more sense. In a way I suppose our friendship had therefore a certain dialectical quality that proved, if proof were necessary, the validity of the Marxist approach that he advocated so eloquently. And I also learnt a lot by noticing the way in which, in an argument, he would listen more than he talked, asking questions to draw out his opponent, and then remembering what the chap had said, the better to confound him with his own inconsistencies. He certainly found plenty of inconsistencies in my muddled ideas.

I had never really encountered a Communist and I had a very caricature-like idea of the Marxism to which people like Picasso, Louis Aragon, Joliot-Curie and Bertholt Brecht, not to mention my uncle Benjamin who I did not yet know at the time, were committed. Whatever image I had in my mind of the typical Party member it was certainly very different from this engaging individual with his sense of fun and his enthusiasm for mountaineering, for New Orléans jazz and for fine wines. And when I spoke of things about the Communist Party that I disliked, the parading of huge portraits of Party leaders and other manifestations of what was, years later, to be called the Personality Cult, I was surprised to find that he, and above all Marie, his wife, disliked these things as much as I did. It is true that I found his attitude to such things reminded me at times of the embarrassed, dismissive way in which clever Catholic intellectuals would talk of things like the "Holy" pictures to be seen in Catholic Repositories. But then his adherence to party doctrines was never a hundred per cent. For example, he didn't share my liking for the music of Verdi and Puccini. One day he had been talking enthusiastically of going to bullfights, because, at a bullfight, in the midst of that lively, variegated, crowd you really "felt you were part of the people". So I told him about going to *Madam Butterfly* and sitting in the "gods" of the Gaiety Theatre in Dublin, surrounded by the plain people of Ireland. Hearing this Jacques told me that I was more "*dans la ligne du Parti*" than he was.

His explanations of Marxist philosophy, shot through as they were with humorous examples and precise references to contemporary politics, made immediate sense to me. I had been travelling towards socialism for some years, and the narrow-minded, anti-Semitic right-wingers at the Leas School had helped me to conclude that, in the crudely divided world in which we lived, there was only one possible future to be envisaged and that had to be some form of socialism. All arguments to the contrary seemed to be pessimistic, backward looking and wrong, when they weren't cynically based on a selfish or unthinking desire just to conform to the status quo. But socialism, as I had imagined it before meeting Jacques, was a vague humanist affair. Marxism replaced this woolly ideal with a theory that seemed rigorous, scientific and intellectually attractive. I was used to thinking, and saying, that for a socialist there can be no enemies to the Left. In 1949 in France, at the height of the Cold War, I thought and still think, that it would have been difficult to see things otherwise if one was not to adopt an attitude that was objectively, as I learned to say, reactionary.

Of course Jacques's main aim in all our arguments and discussions may have been to make a Communist of me, but there I don't think he could have succeeded. I am just not a joiner. Though over the years I have known and admired many Party members, and though I found that I could go along with most of the Marxist theory which Jacques explained so lucidly and with such enthusiasm, I could never give to it, or for that matter to any other doctrine, the degree of commitment that would have been called for. I don't regard, this attitude necessarily as something admirable, it just happens to be the way I am. Of course Jacques had not only lived through the Occupation and fought with the French army in the last stages of the war, risking his life every day, while Marie's brother had been killed fighting with the Maquis. I, in comparison, had no personal experience of any extreme situation at all. I had had, and have had, a very easy life.

As Christmas and the end of term approached Jacques got more and more desperate in his search for a flat. He finally decided that he was wasting his time and that the only solution was for him to go to Bordeaux and with Marie and the baby to live with her parents. So he started to organise the transfer of his and her jobs, and to arrange the removal of the furniture from our joint room. Meantime I had heard from Henri. He was enjoying life in Huddersfield less than I had enjoyed Lunéville. For one thing he did not appreciate the tiresome rule in English schools that all members of staff are expected to be present in the school all day. French schools, being much less of a community, only require the staff to be present while they are actually teaching. Henri had to be in school from 9 till 4.30 and the only place in which he could work for his exams was a small noisy staff room full of teachers talking about cricket. He was keen to return to France for the Christmas holidays and invited me to come and spend Christmas with his family in Toul. I would of course go there on the Velocette so he decided to come with me, on the pillion. Accordingly, he turned up in Orléans just as I was saying goodbye to Jacques outside the lycée. I remember, Jacques had procured some sort of wheelbarrow to convey his few pieces of furniture to the station and was loading it up. We said goodbye very warmly and then Henri and I rode off.

Jacques & Marie Souviron

It was freezing hard and I still didn't have any proper clothing so it was a bitterly cold 400 km. This matter of proper or, rather, of appropriate clothing was an aspect of the French way of life that I had not become aware of at the time, though I had noticed that the other members of the motor bike club, though they were riding much less powerful machines than mine, were always kitted out in black leathers and high boots as though they were competing in the TT, the only article missing, as I have mentioned, being the crash helmet. Later I was aware that I was being made fun of on account of my eccentrically inappropriate dress, but then I for my part was beginning to find ridiculous this French mania for correct clothing. It meant, I said, that a Frenchman won't go fishing if he hasn't got a fishing hat, fishing trousers, a fishing jacket and probably fishing underpants on as well. It is all part of an all or nothing attitude which is one of the most admirably exasperating aspects of the French character, and a reason why *les anglais aux sports d'hiver* (The English at winter sports) are a standing French joke.

Christmas in Toul was the friendly gastronomically splendid affair I would have expected, and after it Henri and I went off on the bike and called on his country cousins who had a farm somewhere not far from Verdun. The farm was the classic Lorraine farmhouse, a big square building incorporating living quarters, cowsheds and barn, with a huge farm yard in front where, it seemed to me, one walked ankle deep in cowshit. That was why at the door there were rows of wooden clogs for walking outside and bedroom slippers for indoors. Once inside, everything was scrupulously clean and there was an air of almost bourgeois comfort. I can't remember what we ate but I do remember that this was where I learnt that cream, which up till then I had only known as an accompaniment to strawberries, really comes into its own when poured over potatoes. That night Henri and I shared a bed with a huge goose feather quilt under which we were if anything too warm, though in the morning the water in the wash basin was frozen solid. We talked until late into the night discussing one thing that Huddersfield and Orléans, otherwise very different, seemed to have in common, namely an almost total lack of agreeably disposed female company.

When I got back to Orléans the first thing I heard was that Jacques Souviron was still there. Apparently, minutes after we had said goodbye at the door of the lycée, there had been a phone call about a two-roomed flat not far from the school. So he, Marie and baby Hélène, were now installed in what was, considering the housing crisis in Orléans, a reasonable approximation to domesticity. What they had was two large rooms, a bed sitting room with, directly underneath it, a kitchen-dining room, in a large very bourgeois residence reminiscent of the factory owner's mansion in Lunéville. The rest of the house was rented out to a colonel in the American army with whom Jacques and Marie were on cordial but very distant terms. The Cold War was reaching its peak. The colonel must have known, if only from the torrent of Russian music that often came echoing up the stairs, that he had the ideological enemy living in the basement. If he did there was nothing he could do about it. And Jacques would retrieve from the dustbin piles of appalling American comics which he would distribute to the comrades at Party meetings as examples of what in the United States passed for culture.

The first of my many visits to that welcoming if exiguous dwelling came shortly after they were fully installed. Marie's parents had helped them to move in and, to feed this extended family, Marie had purchased *des quantités industrielles* – to use a favourite expression of hers – (industrial quantities) of provisions, far more than was needed. This was in the days before refrigerators so what could be better than to invite "*ton nouveau copain irlandais*" (your new Irish friend) to come and help finish up the excess. That was the first of so many gorgeous repasts in their company where the variety and quality of the fare vied with the liveliness of the conversation. A few months later, when my father came to Orléans I brought him there and Marie persuaded him to sing and he did a number of Irish songs I had never heard him sing before, his voice ringing out up the stairs which must have been a change for the Americans above in the house. Walking back to his hotel he told me that I seemed surer of myself, and that, when speaking French, I tended to finish my sentences properly and not just let the utterances peter out. I was vaguely aware of this, as I was conscious of not being quite the same person when I was in a French context. At Lunéville, because Brian was a name unknown in France, when asked what my Christian name was I had given instead my second name, Francis, which is as common a name in France as it is with us. Ever since then I have been Francis to my French friends and I can't help feeling that my French *persona* is in some way or other different from my English-speaking one. I once, in Aberdeen, asked a group of students, newly returned from their year abroad, if they had ever felt the same thing and I was surprised at the number who said that they had, all of which suggests that part of learning a new language consists of learning to be a different person. On the other hand it may well be that those people who get to speak a foreign language with a certain degree of proficiency, but who could never be taken for a native speaker, have an instinctive objection to this idea of turning into a French, or Italian or whatever, version of themselves.

There were two things that my father wanted to see in France, both of them in the *Massif Central*. One was the newly discovered cave paintings at Lascaux, the other the quaternary volcanoes in Auvergne. The obvious solution, which would not have occurred to everyone, was to visit these places on the back of my motorbike. So he took the train to Limoges, where I picked him up and we rode to Montignac in the Dordogne. Lascaux, which had been discovered during the war by two boys after rabbits, had just been opened to the public. We were taken round the cave, which had been only partly *amenagée* for tourists, by one of the very boys who had found the way in and had been first to see the extraordinarily lifelike paintings of animals on the walls. The mysterious and, I think, still unexplained– though there are plenty of theories – painting of a comparatively crudely drawn human figure was not then visible, since it was at the bottom of a vertical shaft. I found the sight of these paintings, at least five times as old as all recorded history, and the various conjectures as to how and why they should have been made, strangely moving. In Paris, as a sort of preparation for Lascaux, we had visited the *Musée de l'Homme* where Tony explained the different stages of the Stone Ages, pointing out that the time-scale indicated by the labels and diagrams in the Museum was now considered to be grossly under-estimated. They were all, as Lascaux was, very much older than had been first thought. It all fitted with what I had been reading in Friedrich Engels about human history. History is not, I had learnt there, the story of kings and battles but of the changes in society consequent on the development of the means of production. And it all took so much longer than anyone could have believed.

After Lascaux we rode eastwards over a maze of bumpy roads on to the *Massif Central*, stopping, as a concession to my interest in caving as distinct from cave paintings, to visit *Le Gouffre de Padirac*, the biggest show cave in

Europe which had been first explored by a hero of mine, Edouard Martel, the first speleologist, early in the twentieth century. There, after descending the immense pot-hole in a lift – Martel had had himself lowered on a rope – you walk down a winding passage for half a kilometre till you arrive at an underground river where a most un-Charon like character checks your ticket and takes you a trip on the subterranean water. Years later I was back in *Padirac* with my son Paddy aged about ten. When we were about half way down the passage the lights suddenly failed which gave us the disagreeable, and rare, experience of absolute, total, darkness. Since it was the end of the afternoon, and we were alone in the cave I did wonder uneasily for the quarter of an hour the blackout lasted if we hadn't been forgotten and the people at the surface hadn't maybe gone home. But the lights came on again and when we got to Charon down below we all had a good laugh.

The whole of the Northern part of the *Massif Central* is volcanic; as my father and I rode up into it the landscape grew increasingly tormented and strange. To stretch our legs we walked and scrambled to the top of the *Puy Mary*, which is obviously a crater plug, like many of the peaks in the region, and looked across the valley at the *Puy Griou*. The volcanic rock made that unlovely mountain look like an enormous slag-heap, which in a sense it is. From the top of the *Puy de Dôme*, another plug, you look down on a series of small volcanoes, their craters now grass-covered but the shapes clearly distinguishable. We walked over several of these, evidence of relatively, in geological terms, recent activity. As we headed back towards Orléans I was thinking how, with Lascaux, historically so old, and Auvergne, geologically so recent, the circuit we had done gave a good example of the difference between the two time-scales.

With Constance, at Easter I had ridden across the whole central massif, from North to South. To save money we stayed in youth hostels. These somewhat inhospitable constructions were deserted this early in the year, and with good reason, since it was bitterly cold. We discovered, as we arrived shivering and frozen in one small town after another, that the public space in French Post Offices is maintained at a comfortable temperature, whereas in railway stations, though the ticket staff are centrally heated behind their *guichets*, the public space is as cold as the street outside. Accordingly when we arrived in St Flour or St Chély or Mende we would head first for the Post Office to warm our hands on the radiators, before setting out to cross another stretch of bleak windswept plateau. However the very austerity of Auvergne and Cantal and later the Causses made the eventual descent towards the Southern plains all the more dramatic. As we made our way down the narrow, steep-sided valleys of the Cévennes, where Stevenson had travelled only seventy years before with his donkey, the season seemed to change with every half-kilometre until, approaching Nîmes and Montpellier, beech gave way to olive trees and we began to see almond in blossom and even, here and there, a mimosa. "You can imagine,"

My father in Auvergne

said Constance, "What the garrisons from Hadrian's Wall must have felt when they got here on their way home."

When I look back on those times from the enlightened viewpoint of fifty years later I find it hard to remember how Constance and I managed the physical side of our relationship. I imagine that younger readers nowadays would find what I can remember of it hard to believe. There was nothing particularly unusual about Constance's and my chastity; all the couples we knew observed the same or a similar restraint. We had been together for over five years. We had had various adventures, had camped, sharing a tent. We had slept in barns and bothies, in haystacks and in the open air. In French hotels I am sure we didn't have enough money to pay for separate rooms. All of which implies quite a degree of closeness. There was however, and for a long time, a clearly defined limit precluding any real sexual intimacy. Like other young women, it was Constance that fixed this limit, but I, like other young men at the time, put up with it. The limit of course shifted gradually over the years. I find it hard to place at precisely what stage our increasing familiarity with each other led us to achieve penetrative sex. It was certainly a new experience for us both; but I can't recall when it happened, though I fancy it would have been around this time. And it would have been a stage in the development of what was always more of a deeply affectionate friendship than a love affair.

# 6 Paris I

IN THE AUTUMN OF 1950 I returned to France. All through the year in Orléans I had wondered uneasily what my next step was to be. And then Sheehy Skeffington in TCD suggested that post-graduate research might be a cure for what he saw as post-graduate *désoeuvrement* (unease, indecision), and recommended that I register for a Doctorat de l'Université in Paris. This was a university qualification which, since it was restricted to foreigners, had no rigorous entry requirements and was consequently regarded by some as an extension of the French tourist trade. Unfairly, since some brilliant and highly thought of research was sanctioned by the DUP, though it is true there was also a lot of dumb-cluck word-spinning pedantry. And, as for a subject, Skeffington suggested that, since I spoke so enthusiastically about the *Massif Central*, I should work up a thesis about a regional writer from that part of France. Accordingly I found myself embarking upon the intensive study of the works of a certain Henri Pourrat whose novels and short stories celebrate and describe the landscapes and people of Auvergne. The fact that he was still alive, I was relieved to discover, did not disqualify him as a subject matter for a *doctorat* at this level.

Literary research is a highly specialised field and I have never been fully convinced either of the usefulness or the interest of much of it. I leafed dutifully through the writings of Henri Pourrat wondering what on earth I could find to say about him that would be of the slightest interest or use to anyone, apart from declaring that Auvergne was a nice place and you could learn all about it by reading his books. Broadening out the field of investigation was no solution, it only made things worse: as I acquired more and more knowledge about regionalism, regionalist literature, *les Félibres* and other representatives of different tendencies and schools, I felt whatever enthusiasm I might have experienced at the start for the writings of M. Pourrat drain away. But I wish I had realised there and then that, whatever may be said for the academic study of French literature,

I just wasn't cut out for it. As it was I felt that I had failed to engage with a literary phenomenon on its own terms and I was vaguely ashamed and embarrassed by what I saw as a defeat. As time went by I found excuses to spend less and less time in libraries reading about French regionalism.

I was able to finance my first few months in Paris by using my share of what the parents always described as Aunt's money, or what was left of it. Anne Frances Synge was my mother's father's sister, and she lived in some sort of posh guesthouse near Hastings in England. A wealthy woman, she never came to Ireland but we were constantly aware of her as a distant brooding presence through my mother, who was in awe of her and referred to her, sometimes, as Aunt Frances, but usually as just "Aunt". I only met Aunt very briefly twice, and each time it was enjoined upon us that we must be on our very best behaviour. On one of these occasions Aunt asked my father to say grace before lunch, the only time I ever heard him perform this rigmarole. Family folk-lore had it that Conor had somewhat spoiled the effect by asking, "What is Daddy saying?" Aunt would send us birthday presents of books which were often quite expensive but had obviously been chosen by the bookseller, and the text of the obligatory thank you letters that we had to send off on receipt of these offerings was always very carefully vetted by my mother. Not without cause, because once Aunt wrote to her saying, "I thought that Una was eight years old but judging by the handwriting on her letter it seems that she is much younger."

Sometime after the war Aunt's letters stopped arriving. At first this did not surprise my mother unduly, but when she received no reply to her own letters, she began to be worried. After all Aunt, who was now living in a nursing home, was her only remaining close relative. So she decided, as she hadn't been in England since before the War, to go over and visit the various Synge relations. Travel was still difficult and to go to England you had to have a permit, so she applied for this, giving as her reason for the journey her need to visit her "aged aunt in a nursing home." There was the usual delay of about a month so my mother wrote to Aunt to say she would be coming to visit her a few weeks later. Some days after posting her letter she received a telegram announcing that Miss A. F. Synge had died, and that the funeral would be in three days time. It was typical of the Catholic Ireland of the time that, while it took over a month to get a permit to visit a relative who was ill, a permit to attend the funeral of a dead one was dished out immediately.

The parents saw this as no more than a tragic coincidence, but my mother's old friend Dr Helen Boyle, a hard-headed professional woman, who was at the top of her profession of psychiatry, was immediately suspicious. Dr Boyle, who lived in Sussex not far from the nursing home, went and interviewed the manageress of the home, and talked to various people in the locality. Following this encounter she put forward a much more sinister explanation of Aunt's never replying to my mother's letters and of her dying just when my mother was coming to see her, an explanation which was made more plausible when it was revealed that Aunt had not only left all her money to the manageress but had given her a succession of expensive gifts, including a luxury motor car. However, Aunt's solicitor pointed out that it would be impossible to prove that a crime had been committed, a view justified ten years later by the interminable and inconclusive trial of Dr Bodkin Adams on a similar charge. Instead, he advised my mother to contest the will. This she did and the parents went over to London for the hearing. At the end of the first day, which already cost a small fortune, the manageress's lawyers proposed a deal: either we agree to accept a fairly small proportion of the estate or they would continue to fight until the whole estate was consumed by lawyer's fees. "Learned counsel" offered, at a price, his advice, which was that my parents should accept the offer. So the manageress, in our opinion, got away with murder, and the parents returned to Dublin, richer, when all expenses had been paid, by a few hundred pounds of which my share, if I remember right, was about £150.

In the event I didn't have to use much of this money because, after a few months, thanks to Mark Mortimer, I got a job teaching at the British Institute where he worked. The Institute was a curiously amphibious sort of institution in those days, a private fee-paying set-up that existed on the fringe of the University of Paris. It contained an important French Section, supported by British universities, and which ran classes and lectures for British, and also some American, students who were putting in their residence in France. The English section had two quite different functions, both of them fee-paying. On the one hand literature, and above all language, classes at university level were organised for, and much appreciated by, students at the Sorbonne where, as was common in French universities, individual attention and regular marking of written work were almost unknown. At the same time the Institute accepted students who had no formal qualification but who had a grounding in the language, and prepared them for the Cambridge examinations in Proficiency in English. In this way it offered an attractive solution to anyone wanting or needing a good knowledge of everyday written and spoken English, who was either put off by the dry-as-dust atmosphere, and the huge failure rates, of the Sorbonne, or who wouldn't have been accepted there anyway. The social mix in these, Cambridge, classes was very varied: hardworking students, secretaries or scientists, rubbed shoulders with social butterflies. At some of the daytime classes it felt a bit as though I was teaching in a sort of linguistic finishing school for young ladies of upper class Parisian society. The presence of a large number of these, often stunningly attractive because beautifully dressed, creatures was due, I learned, to the humdrum fact that the *chiffre diviseur* which decided the final figure of their fathers' income tax was favourably affected if he had children in full-time education. It hardly mattered to me; the Institute offered a raw but well meaning amateur like myself the opportunity to obtain teaching and lecturing experience easily and in a fairly congenial atmosphere. From the start I found teaching adults who were fairly highly motivated and, in the case of the University students, often highly intelligent, unlike school teaching, a challenge I could handle. The literature seminars in particular were child's play to prepare and quite enjoyable.

The other members of the teaching staff were on the whole easy to get on with and interesting to talk to. They were all of course, like myself, expatriates. Some were there temporarily, finishing a thesis. Others, who were in France because they had French husbands or wives, were to some degree integrated into French family life and French society. The rest of us, I couldn't help feeling, were misfits of one sort or another. We inhabited a sort of no man's land where we both belonged and did not belong. Visitors from home saw us as Parisians, whereas Parisians tended to see us as tourists who had never gone home. The ambiguity of our situation, working in France but not belonging there, put us in what I could not help feeling was a false situation. As the years went by I felt increasingly that many of my colleagues in the Institute, like myself, had chosen this as the easy way out of some problem. We were all in fact running away from something and, by setting ourselves up as teachers of English in France, we had found an enduring, if provisional, way of concealing this from ourselves. Two things exacerbated the phoniness of our situation as I saw it. One was that our being native speakers of English gave to us a false sort of authority, at once respected and resented by some French university teachers of the language, as I have described earlier. The other was that our situation as lecturers and teachers of English was given no administrative recognition whatever by the French authorities. We could never for example be appointed to any decision-making committee or exam board. We couldn't even have our car - if we had a car - insured advantageously by the MAIF, the French educational insurance co-operative. All this I felt increasingly as the years passed and when I went on to teach, not only in the Institute but at the *Institut des Études Politiques* and later at the *École Normale Supérieure de Saint-Cloud*.

For the first few years, however, none of this worried me seriously. I had got myself a reasonably interesting job and was living in Paris, and this was certainly more fun than the places most of my contemporaries had got to. Accommodation was a problem. To begin with I lived in a tiny room in the servants' quarters on the sixth floor of the building César Franck had once lived in, on the Boulevard St Michel. The room was attached to the flat belonging to a Gaullist Senator called Debu-Bridel, an interesting man who had been in the *Résistance* and had just published a book about, of all things, Emily Bronte. The room was bitterly cold and I managed to keep myself from freezing at night by filling wine bottles with water which I heated up with a methylated spirit stove. The window looked out on *La Maison des Examens*. This was a vast soulless building which was always either totally deserted or swarming with students. They came there to pass one or other of the, often competitive, state examinations which dominate the French educational system. Georges Filliat, one of the Communist *pions* from Orléans, a working-class chap who had just achieved his ambition of getting into one of the *Grandes Écoles*, came to this room and when he looked out of the window and saw *La Maison des Examens* he told me that that was where he had spent his childhood ("*Voilà, c'est là que j'ai passé mon enfance*!") Not exactly *Le Grand Meaulnes*.

I moved from this bleak little crow's nest as soon as I could afford to, first to a hotel on the *Île Saint Louis* and then by a stroke of luck to a room in a fine old building in the *rue de Grenelle*, opposite the Russian Embassy. The room, which was situated on the internal staircase of a large rambling apartment belonging to a doctor and his family, was small, not very comfortable and had no window to speak of, but there were other advantages. To begin with there was no rent. Instead I was to pay for my accommodation by helping the eldest son of the family with his English. He, Jean Élie Boltanski, had already distinguished himself by obtaining a degree in philosophy but had decided to concentrate upon English instead. He was highly intelligent, much cleverer than I was in most ways, but a singularly troglodytic, cerebral individual. He knew everything about life but hadn't done any living of it at all, all his knowledge coming from books - he was impressively well read - and from the cinema. In fact it was in a cinema that I had first seen him, in a small studio cinema in Montparnasse. There, on certain nights, after the main feature, they would have a sort of quiz with large black and white still photos as prizes. The lights would go up and the manager would fire questions in rapid succession at those of the audience that stayed on. The questions were always highly specialised: "Name two films in which Myrna Loy goes in a boat," and the handful of *cinéphiles* who answered them displayed an astonishingly encyclopaedic knowledge of all sorts of film. One in particular stood out by the readiness of his response to the most recondite questions; he struck me as a somewhat tadpoley little chap with pebble spectacles: it was my future pupil, Jean Élie Boltanski.

As time went by I came both to like him a lot and to admire the quality of his intelligence. Certainly paying my rent by talking to him was never a chore. But the whole family were remarkable, in different ways. Doctor Boltanski, a silver-haired early sixty-year old with considerable presence, was of Russian extraction. His elderly mother lived upstairs; she spoke French with a strong Russian accent. I learnt that, being Jewish, they had come to France when the doctor was a child to escape from the pogroms taking place in tsarist Russia at the turn of the century. Madame Boltanski, the doctor's wife, on the other hand, who must have been a striking beauty when she was young with her raven black hair and flashing eyes, was half Breton and half Corsican. She was an extremely sophisticated *parisienne*, knew all about avant-garde painting and sculpture and had always read the latest books. She had a passionate temperament to judge by the rows that I could occasionally hear echoing up the staircase and I was terrified of her. The doctor, for that matter was not a model of equanimity either. Because once, I was told, when he had protested at Madame's cutting a slice off the roast they were having for lunch to give to the cat and she had leant across the table and accused him of being mean, he had jumped up in a rage crying, "*Bon, je vais vous montrer si je suis avare!*" (Right! I'll show you how mean I am!) picked up the whole roast on a fork, went out to the courtyard and fed it to the concierge's dog.

Jean Élie had two younger brothers. The elder of the two, whose real name I never knew or have forgotten, was always called Toto. He was about twelve or thirteen and was on his way to becoming an indoor intellectual like his brother. The younger, a singularly beautiful little boy of about six, with a mop of curly jet black hair and black eyes, was called Christian Liberté because he was born at the time of the Liberation of Paris. In later years, long after I had lost touch with the family, I would see his name. He became internationally famous as the artist Christian Boltanski, Director of the Centre Pompidou in Paris.

Things had not been easy for them during the Occupation. They had lived in constant fear that Dr Boltanski, as a prominent Jewish medical man, would be arrested. But then, with remarkable foresight, in the very early days of the Vichy regime the doctor and his wife had got a joiner to construct a habitable space between the ceiling of their bathroom and the floor of the room I now lived in. The doctor had lived there for two and a half years, only coming out in the evenings. This self-imposed incarceration started dramatically. On the day that the persecution started in earnest, when the police came to arrest him Madame Boltanski very fortunately looked through the window and saw the gendarmes coming across the courtyard. She rushed downstairs and out the front door and immediately threw a scene. "*Maman a fait un cinéma extraordinaire,*" said Jean Élie. She pretended that her husband had already been taken, sobbing and crying out, "*Mais où l'ont-ils emmené?*" (Where have they taken him to?) She did this so convincingly that, in the end the two police officers, consulting their notes, concluded that there must have been some administrative mistake and they took their men away, thus giving the doctor time to get into his hiding place.

Madame Boltanski also told me how once Toto, who was then a toddler, had got out of bed one night when the doctor was in the salon, and had chanced to catch sight of his father. So, knowing that the child would probably babble about what he had seen to people about the building, they invented a complicated game in which Jean Élie would dress up in the doctor's clothes and pretend to be him. In that way they would have had a ready explanation if anyone heard Toto saying, "*J'ai vu mon papa.*" Unfortunately, this was not enough, since a friend of the concierge's daughter, who happened to be in the police, got suspicious and threatened Madame Boltanski, probably with a mind to blackmailing her. She told me herself how she had managed to find out that, like many Paris *flics,* the policeman had Corsican roots. So she played the card of her half-Corsican blood and, citing the names of some well-known Corsican families, she painted a terrifying picture of the merciless vendetta that would be wreaked not only on him but on every single member of his family if the slightest thing were ever to happen to her or to any of her family. This so frightened him that they never saw him again.

They were a peculiarly united family; they seemed to me to do almost everything all together. I would be working with Jean Élie on a translation when Toto would call up the stairs, *"Jean Élie, tu viens acheter du jambon en voiture?"* (Jean Élie, are you coming, we're off to buy ham in the car?) and they would all zoom off in their big black Citroën. Though the doctor was of Jewish extraction, they were practising Catholics, albeit of a very sophisticated, left-leaning nature, since they numbered among their friends members of the Communist Party and gays, including as it happens a Hungarian painter called Basil Rakosi who I had met in Dublin with Brian Boydell. Their togetherness extended to their living arrangements, which puzzled me for quite a time. The apartment which was on two floors didn't seem to me to contain any bedrooms. Dining room and kitchen were on the ground floor, as were the doctor's consulting room, laboratory and patients' waiting room. Above these, looking out on the courtyard, was a large richly furnished salon where Madame Boltanski spent most of her time stretched out like Madame Récamier on a *chaise longue.* I supposed that two doors which I saw on the opposite side of the salon from the entrance led to two bedrooms. When I had been living there for about six months Madame announced that the children were in need of sunshine and they all departed in the car for the Midi at about two days' notice. Alone in the apartment I couldn't resist the temptation to explore the rooms on the far side of the salon but I was surprised to find that the doors were not rooms at all but just cupboards. When I had got to know Jean Élie a little better I managed to ask him, without, I hoped, seeming too inquisitive, and he told me that they are all slept in the salon, his parents on the large divan in the corner and he and his brothers in sleeping bags on the floor. He didn't find this strange or embarrassing to describe.

This somewhat claustrophobic arrangement fitted in with the way they lived when on holiday, and their holiday travels were quite extraordinary for the time. In the early nineteen fifties travel was not easy: you could only take a car across national frontiers if you had a complicated *carnet de passages en douane*, there were insurance difficulties and many countries required a visa which was not always easy to obtain. In spite of this they seemed to have been almost everywhere: to the North Cape, to Morocco and Tunisia and even across the so-called iron curtain to Eastern Europe, and they did this by driving in their big *traction avant* (front-wheel drive) Citroen. When I said something to Madame Boltanski about hotels she informed me that they didn't stay in hotels, instead they camped. I found it hard to imagine these very indoor urban characters contending with tents and groundsheets so I asked Jean Élie about it and he explained that they all slept in the car. The parents slept on the back seat, he told me, which had been adapted so that it folded down. Christian slept on the front bench-seat, while he and Toto lay on planks which went from the dashboard to a shelf under the rear window and were carried in the daytime on the roof-rack. When I remarked, conversationally, that the great advantage of camping was that it made you free to sleep anywhere you chose, enjoying the countryside, Jean Élie told me that No, they always slept in a town or village. *"D'ailleurs,"* he said, *"Maman n'aime pas la campagne"* (doesn't like the country). Apparently, as they whizzed along – the doctor drove very expertly and very fast – Madame Boltanski never looked at the view or anything, instead she would read novels, mostly detective stories, all the time, and when she had finished one she would throw it out the window as they went along. When they had visited Britain they were impressed more than once when a policeman came up and spoke to them as they were installing themselves for the night, not to tell them that they couldn't sleep there but concerned for their comfort and safety. This happened, of all places, or so they told me, in the car park of Charing Cross station in London. When I asked Jean Élie how they managed about washing and so on he just told me that it was not a problem since they had Eau de Cologne.

This wasn't the only thing that surprised me about them. Whenever I went home I would ask if there was anything they would like me to bring them back. The only thing this extremely sophisticated Parisian family asked for was large quantities of what they called *la sauce anglaise.* There would be a debate about the varieties of this, to me, totally uninteresting, unexotic, condiment: *La meilleure c'est la sauce Ash Pay n'est-ce pas? Moi je n'aime pas la sauce vorstersheer, moi ce que je préfère c'est la daddeez sauce.* And so on.

They turned up in Ireland once, on Achill Island where my parents had rented a cottage, actually the same house that Michael and I had stayed in with Brian Boydell, years before. My father came in and said, "There is a very foreign-looking car outside on the road with some amazingly foreign-looking people in it. They can only be friends of Brian's." When we invited them in Madame Boltanski announced that our cottage was too far from the road for her to walk – it was about fifteen yards – so we all met in the pub in Keel. They had done a lightning tour of the country, which they described as *"La Bretagne en plus moche"* (Like Brittany only worse), in the course of which they had twice hit a seagull on the windscreen, the only time I ever heard of this happening. I can only suppose Doctor Boltanski was driving at a speed that Irish seagulls weren't used to.

Cooking facilities were extremely limited in my little room so I ate out most of the time. At first, while I was still a student, I would queue up in one of the student canteens, where you pushed along a metal tray with a series of large dents in it for large women to ladle quantities of not very appetising chicken neck stew into the dents. Later I would go to one of the small restaurants frequented by colleagues from the Institute. This was one of the pleasantest things about living in Paris, for me at least. Eating out was, in Ireland in the nineteen fifties, quite simply not a thing one did, unless there was some reason why one couldn't eat at home. For example, I don't think my parents ever ate out for the pleasure of it in their whole lives. Whereas in France, and above all in Paris, it was a regular part of one's existence.

Among the characterful *gargotes* we went to was a place a few doors down from the bar where Mark Mortimer lived called *Le Bouillon*. It was, or rather it had once been, a very basic workers' restaurant. I had in fact been in a number of similar eating places, brought by my Communist friend Georges Filliat, who enjoyed introducing me to bits of Parisian working-class culture, as much as I enjoyed being introduced to it. There, as in *Le Bouillon*, the talk would rebound about the room, lively, richly metaphorical and often, for a foreigner, very hard to understand because laced with that racy parallel vocabulary that some French people manipulate so readily.

Two things distinguished *Le Bouillon* from other working-class eating places that I had been in. One was the Naudin family that ran it, in particular Madame Naudin who did the cooking, presiding over an enormous gas range that you had to squeeze past coming in from the street. She was a big woman in every sense, with a powerful voice that resounded in repartee or commentary on whatever was going on in the room. Her husband, a short round man of few words, but cogent ones, served the wine, which was red, in litre bottles. He had been deprived by a wound received in World War I of certain essential functions which were, or so it was said in the *quartier*, now performed by a stand-in, in fact by the man who acted as waiter, a silent moon-faced individual whose name I never knew. There was also a son, a strikingly handsome young chap who was on his way to becoming a champion cyclist. The food that they served in this memorably basic restaurant was excellent but also memorably basic, consisting essentially of different sorts of steak or chop with chips and salad. I can't remember anything else, though you could probably have an apple or a little cardboard box full of nuts and raisins as dessert.

The other thing that distinguished *Le Bouillon* was the clientèle. When I first started going there with Mark Mortimer most of the others eating there were locals, people who worked in the street market or in one of the small shops down the *rue de Buci*. And, almost always, there would be a number of men in the blue overalls that French workers wear all day. Occasionally there would be one or two men in suits accompanied by elegantly dressed women. These bourgeois patronised the place, as the nineteenth century bourgeois used to patronise the cafés of Montmartre, because it was fashionable to *s'encanailler un peu* (go slumming). And then, as time went by, there were gradually more and more of these slumming bourgeois, and the blue overalls took themselves off and went to eat elsewhere, in more congenial company. But this only slightly diminished the quality of the place as a meeting ground where different cultures and social classes could interact and clash interestingly. As was shown by one incident that I remember.

It was caused by a bourgeois middle-aged couple, who had apparently come on the recommendation of a friend. The wife obviously did not appreciate the distinctive atmosphere of *Le Bouillon* from the start. She complained that she couldn't read the menu, which was scribbled somewhat illegibly on a blackboard in the corner, and when it was read to her she protested at the prices charged. She went on grumbling and in the end, as her embarrassed husband paid the bill, she walked up to Madame Naudin and complained about the décor, the cooking, the service and everything. Madame Naudin's response was to tell her in colourful terms what she could do with her custom. The husband by this time had escaped into the street, so she called out to him, asking him if he was going to stand there and listen to her being insulted by this *grosse bonne femme* (fat old bag). He however had more sense than to take on the Naudins. He took his wife by the arm and hurried her off down the street. But Madame Naudin was not to be done out of the last word. Standing in the middle of the street, waving her frying pan, she shouted after the retreating couple so that the whole street could hear, "*Grosse bonne femme, tu peux parler; toi-même t'as un cul a avoir chié la colonne Vendôme!* ("Fat old bag, is it, and you with an arse on you that could have shitted the Vendôme pillar!")

It was at the *Bouillon* that I met Brendan Behan again. He had been brought along one evening by Mark Mortimer. I had met Behan years before, when he was first released from prison; he was to be found in a number of pubs around Grafton Street in Dublin in the company of other IRA ex-prisoners. They had all been amnestied from the Curragh camp, largely thanks to "Pope" O'Mahoney, that lovable Cork lawyer, who I was told received small thanks for his efforts on their behalf. At the time I had found Behan a bit of a loud mouth though, it was true, a very entertaining one, mostly through the graphic and inventive obscenity of his metaphors and catch phrases. He was now on what was, I suppose, his second visit to Paris, but this time he was no longer working as a house painter, having started a successful career as a writer with articles and broadcasts. He had in fact been sent officially by the Irish government to represent us at some cultural jamboree at UNESCO. His journey to France had not been uneventful. The government had paid his air fare, but he had cashed the tickets, spent the money and travelled overland, forgetting that he was still *persona non-grata* in Britain. Things went well until he reached the passport check at Newhaven, where he was arrested and had to call, yet again, on the 'Pope' O'Mahoney to come and get him out. In the end the magistrate, showing a spark of humour, fined him a sum of money exactly equivalent to the difference between the air fare and the overland ticket.

At *Le Bouillon* Behan was amused by this supposedly working-class restaurant, especially as it was that evening full of bourgeois diners, some of whom he commented on so volubly and obscenely that Madame Naudin told Mark Mortimer not to bring him there again. He and I ended the evening drinking in a bar in *Saint Germain des Près* where I was impressed by his ability to talk easily to all and sundry, while making next to no concessions to the normal rules of French grammar and vocabulary. It was Saturday night and I had been invited to dinner the following evening by a couple of English colleagues from the British Institute. It occurred to me that it might be amusing to bring Brendan with me, so I fixed up to meet him, thinking that he probably wouldn't turn up. But he did; it was a remarkable evening.

Peter and Jean Wexler were among the brightest of my colleagues at the Institute. Peter was just finishing the doctoral thesis that was to make his name in the field of French lexicology and which was the reason they were in France in the first place. Jean was, I think, the only person working in the Institute who was a trained teacher. She was very intelligent, energetic and highly motivated. They stood out among the Institute people in several ways, but for me the most important distinguishing feature was that they were both active members of the British Communist Party. It was an affiliation that they were understandably discreet about, though they made no secret of their opinions on current issues. Apart from, or perhaps because of, their Party membership they lived very conventional, un-bohemian, lives in a meticulously clean and tidy little apartment in Vincennes. I had had many heated but friendly arguments with them in which they reproached me with what they called my middle-class, "*petit-bourgeois*" romantic, attitudes. That was why I thought it would be a good idea to introduce them to a real member of the working class in the person of Brendan Behan.

Brendan and I travelled out to Vincennes in the Metro. I remember that Brendan was interestingly apprehensive, nervous even, at this very ordinary means of transport. Whenever a train was approaching the platform he went and hid in a corridor until it had stopped moving and the doors were open. The first time he did this I thought he had changed his mind about coming but he reappeared and boarded the train though with obvious misgivings.

As we went along I filled him in on Jean and Peter, explaining how Jean was an excellent cook but a vegetarian though a very broad-minded one. In the event I think we had a roast chicken. But, as we approached the Wexlers' apartment, I began to wonder apprehensively how they were going to react to Behan's line of talk, larded through as it was, not only with picturesque obscenities, but also

Peter Wexler

with a plethora of what were then called four letter words. This was, it must be remembered, 1952, when even manuals of linguistics, explaining the phenomenon known as Taboo, could not actually print the words (fuck, shit etc) that they were discussing. Some of the words and expressions that Behan used were unknown to me and I later looked them up in Partridge's Dictionary of Slang and Unconventional English. Even there they were to be found with the vowels replaced by prurient asterisks.

I need not have worried. From the moment we arrived Brendan put on an act that could only be described as brilliant. The talk ranged through politics to ideology to literature. Brendan made it clear he was no doctrinaire anti-Communist, having been friendly with Party members when he was interned, but he challenged Peter to defend Soviet literature, telling him why he ought to write novels with titles like 'Cement' or 'Girders'. He recounted anecdote after anecdote about his earlier life most of which I was amused to find again when I came to read his early autobiography, *Borstal Boy*. One hilariously funny story, which was probably only partly true, concerned the Christmas Day sermon preached in Parkhurst prison by some soft-spoken Jesuit. It was far funnier when he told it than in the written version, since he put on the Stonyhurst accents of this upper-class ecclesiastic - he was an excellent mimic - to explain how "We Christians are not puritans, as we tear the tender flesh of the turkey, as we relish the rich flavours of the pudding.." and so on, to a congregation of old lags slavering at this feast of adjectives but with nothing to look forward to but a bowl of some tasteless gruel.

As he talked and as I recalled his earlier performances in McDaids Lounge Bar in Dublin and my concern about his language I realised that something quite interesting was happening. Jean Wexler was certainly no prude but she did have a certain primness. One of the charming things about her, for example, was the way she blushed if she was embarrassed. She would I am quite sure have been shocked to hear many of the words and images that Brendan bandied about so freely in other places. But, all through the evening, like a kettle that is prevented from boiling over but is kept, as the phrase goes, "on the boil", Brendan managed never to shock Jean, but to keep her, so to speak, permanently "on the shock". It was a masterful if totally synthetic performance, the stage Irishman *par excellence*.

When we left Brendan borrowed two or three books that had been mentioned, large hardback copies, if I remember rightly, one of them being T S Eliot's Essays, of all things. Ten years later, when I met Peter Wexler in Manchester, he somewhat optimistically asked me to remind "your friend Mr Behan" to return his books to him. A somewhat forlorn hope.

In addition to classes and lectures for university students the British Institute ran correspondence courses in language and literature. These were subscribed to by quite a large number of students, and not only those living some distance from Paris. Marking the translation exercises and literary essays that this operation produced constituted quite an important part of my work load. I spent many hours every week at this lucrative and not disagreeable drudgery, the work being quite generously remunerated. In those days you could sit undisturbed for a whole morning or whole afternoon in the upper or back room of one of the cafés in the Latin quarter for the price of one or two cups of coffee, so I would try to get through the wodge of forty or more literary essays in one or two sittings. The work was less tedious than it sounds, since some at least of the essays were intelligent and interesting to read, and I enjoyed exercising the sort of anonymous authority that the setup bestowed upon the comments I put in the margin. I realise now that in doing this I may well have been misleading many of the less gifted students. They were all the same preparing for a French style examination in which more importance is given to the way ideas are organised than to the originality of the ideas themselves, but I didn't know that.

After a while I found that it made the work more interesting if I kept a brief record of the comments I put at the end of each individual essay. I did this first to avoid the embarrassment of my remarks repeating or, worse, contradicting, something I had said to the same student a week or two before, but it also meant that I began to see the authors of these not always inspiring disquisitions as individuals. They certainly appreciated it as soon as they noticed that I seemed able to remember what I and they had said from one week to another. In my second year of doing this work, this personalisation brought about a somewhat curious situation.

A year or two before, when I was *Assistant* in Orléans, I had made a disastrously unsuccessful attempt to get off with one of the *maîtresses d'internat* of the girls' lycée, an attractive student of English with a lovely head of light brown hair called Armelle something or other, I forget her family name. I had encountered her at various social occasions and had never managed to get talking to her, or else I had made awkward attempts to speak to her, had said the wrong thing or showed off, and had been rebuffed, I don't remember exactly. What I do remember, and the memory is disagreeable even now, is the time I met her on the train to Paris. I suppose I had been influenced by, and was trying to imitate, the Lotharios of the boys' lycée with their interminable anecdotes of attractive women they had successfully picked up on trains. It may well be that she was treating me as such-like bores should be treated. The experience was no less humiliating, for she reacted to my over-persistent attempts to engage her in conversation by telling me bluntly, in a loud voice, and to the ill-concealed entertainment of the other passengers in the compartment, that she didn't know me, - though of course she did – that she didn't want to know me and would I shut up and leave her alone.

The memory of this incident was still green and unpleasant when I opened the package of correspondence course essays in the first week of the semester and found her name on one of them. There was no mistaking it: Armelle whatever, *Lycée de Jeunes Filles*, Orléans. So I read her essay, underlining the various infelicities of style and language mistakes a little more conscientiously than was usual and adding a standard comment at the end. The following week there was another and so on to the end of the semester. As the essays succeeded each other, as we went from *Macbeth* to *Tom Jones* and from *Gulliver's Travels* to the *Lyrical Ballads*, and, as I read her, somewhat conventional, ideas and opinions about the panjandrums of English literature, my comments became longer, and less perfunctory. As a result, I had to give more time and attention, not only to her work but to the whole operation, re-reading bits of Shakespeare and Milton and checking up on standard works of criticism. Also, when I came on awkward, French-sounding, turns of phrase or language mistakes I could not help writing out a suggested or correct version instead of simply underlining the words in red, and, having started to do this for her, I felt it was unfair not to do the same by the others. In this way everyone in the group benefited from my desire to overwrite the disagreeable memory of my last meeting with Armelle with something more dignified than the conceited inarticulacy of yester year. She, of course, had no idea whose handwriting was scribbled in the margin of her weekly *dissertation*.

Enjoying as she did, without realising it, an abnormal amount of individual attention it would have been surprising if she had not continued the course in the second semester, and, sure enough, her essay on Jane Austen was prominent in the pile awaiting me in the first week. And so I continued as before, scrawling remarks in the margin, but checking my records before commenting at the end of each essay, so that there should be continuity in what I said. I was careful now to leave her contribution to the end, partly because I was always tempted to spend too much time upon it, but also because reading through forty odd compositions about Coleridge's *Ancient Mariner* or *Oliver Twist* inevitably set me thinking so that my own ideas on the subject became progressively clearer and more insightful as I worked through the pile, and consequently I wrote more substantial comments on the later productions than on the earlier ones. I naturally preferred that she should be among the ones to benefit by this amelioration.

As the weeks went by and as the weekly essay subjects came to deal with modern or near modern authors I began to notice a difference in the way the students approached this literature, and Armelle was no exception. They were now writing about books some of which they had actually enjoyed reading, consequently their judgements and opinions became more personal and more interesting to read about. Inevitably this called for longer, more comprehensive and more personal comments from me at the foot of each last page. Unfortunately, as the essays got more interesting to read they took much longer to mark and I could no longer get through the packet in one session at the back of *La Chope Parisienne*, my preferred café. I was increasingly tempted to indulge various hobbyhorses, to remark upon the way in which English novelists are content to observe and describe the often quirky behaviour of their characters without indulging in the French desire to categorise and explain what they call their *psychologie.* Or to criticise the French tendency to read E M Forster or Graham Greene as though they were really trying to be Flaubert. In the case of Armelle my comments developed into an increasingly personal dialogue in which I advised her about books to read and went on to suggest ideas she might explore. On her side she began to add various notions of her own, and not only on strictly literary matters, asking me what I thought. The Correspondence Course had turned into a correspondence *tout court* (full stop). All the extra work and individual attention paid off in a sense for, on the last page of Armelle's last essay I found a personal message in French. In it she said how *sensible* (appreciative) she was regarding the care with which I had read her compositions and how my comments and opinions had not only been *une aide précieuse* in her studies but had also given her much to think about regarding life in general. Supposing that that was the end I felt I had achieved something, though exactly what I would have found it hard to say.

But it wasn't quite the end. When the results of the examination for the

English literature part of the *Licence d'Anglais* came out I was pleased to see that she had passed and was relieved to think that I wouldn't have to repeat the experience for another year. And then one day shortly after the results were put up I was in the Staff Room of the Institute and a message came up by phone from downstairs to say that there was someone wanting to speak to the tutor in charge of the literature correspondence course; she wanted to thank him or her personally. It was of course Armelle. She was a year or two older but she still had the head of lovely brown hair. She was carrying a small package which was obviously a book, nicely wrapped up. "*Oh*!" she cried as soon as she saw me, "*C'était vous!*" She had the grace to blush to the roots of her hair. I didn't know what to say, but I knew I must stay in control of the situation. "*Oui mademoiselle*," I said. "*Ce fut moi. Mes sincères félicitations pour votre résultat.*" And, leaving her holding the book, I smiled and said, "Good luck and goodbye!" and turned back into the Staff Room. I never saw or heard of her again. But then I suppose I didn't need to. I've often wondered what the book was.

BF & Constance after the wedding

# Chatenay

# 7

CONSTANCE CONNER and I were married in January 1953. Though it had been implicit in our relationship for quite some time, marrying me was not without problems for Constance, since it meant giving up her job and coming to live in France. Leaving her job in the University Library was a considerable sacrifice, since she had had to work very hard to pass the Library Association exams and qualify as a librarian and we quickly discovered that she could not use this qualification in a library in France. Also, she was worried about her father, about his health and about how well he would cope with living on his own. At the wedding he had been visibly very shaky: she had had to support him when he was, supposedly, leading her up the aisle. She had made a lot of arrangements with local friends and neighbours who were to come in and look after him. In the event, and probably due to the emotional strain of the occasion, he only survived the separation from Constance for less than a day. On our second morning together in Paris we were awakened by the arrival of a telegram to say that Willie Conner had died in his sleep. Constance had to return straightaway to Dublin to organise his funeral.

Accommodation was not easy. We had only been able to get married because I had found somewhere to live, an uncomfortable pair of rooms outside Paris which meant coming in every morning to the *Gare de la Bastille* in a steam-hauled train. After a month or two we moved, to a sort of tiny bed-sit, with a kitchen in a cupboard, in the *rue du Niger*, near the *Porte de Vincennes*. It was poky, uncomfortable and inconvenient. And then a piece of good fortune brought us to Chatenay. And what was to be twelve years of collective living, one of the richest experiences of my life, began.

We had heard about this place from a friend, Cecil Jenkins, who had been going to live there with his wife, Maureen. It was, we heard, a sort of commune of left-wing people, near the station called *Robinson* on the *Ligne de Sceaux*. Cecil and Maureen were going to live there, to occupy the rooms of a student of his who was going to spend his year abroad, in Belfast. But when Constance and I got back to Paris after a trip to Périgord we heard that they had changed their minds. They said that they had been put off by discovering that the commune, if not nudist had been naturist in the recent past and that something of this remained in, for example, the large shared bathroom with no lock on the door. Also, the house rules seemed to them to impose an alarming degree of collective living, everyone cooking and eating, and generally living, together. So would we like to go there instead? We hardly hesitated, the place sounded fun and a bit of naturism was a small price to pay for a comfortable flat with the use of a large garden and, apparently, the small but distinct possibility of being able to stay on after the year. We moved our stuff out of the *rue du Niger* and set off gaily for West Cork on the luxurious Sunbeam that had replaced the Velocette. My mother had rented a curiously shaped gate lodge there for the annual holiday with my father. Somewhere on the way across South West Ireland Paddy, our first child, was conceived.

*La Cité Nouvelle* as we called it consisted, at *44 Avenue Jean Jaurès, Chatenay-Malabry*, of a large late 19th century mansion with an outbuilding and a garage adjoining it and a garden fifty yards long behind it. There were rabbit hutches and a chicken coop and down the garden there were cherry trees, apple trees and a quince tree. From the upstairs windows you looked across the valley to the hill which was called Robinson, because in the 19th Century weddings were celebrated there in a back-to-Nature setting. When we arrived at *La Cité* there were eighteen people and eight children of different ages living in the house and in the outbuilding which we called the *pavillon*. As people came and went and as families expanded the number varied slightly over the years. Normally new members were only accepted after a trial period of three months but, since we were coming temporarily, this was waived in our case. The only absolute rule for acceptance by the *Cité* was that you had to agree with the general aims of the French Communist Party. In 1953, a few months after the death of Stalin, with the Party enjoying the support of at least a third of the French electorate, this was not a problem for us.

The *Cité* had been started - founded would be too pompous a word - in the early 30s by three friends who were all recovering from TB. They had many things in common, they were all students of art or architecture, they shared left-wing opinions in politics and an interest in naturism, and also in certain somewhat cranky health theories. The main thing that brought them together, however, was a desire to find a simple solution for people of reduced vitality to the problems of everyday living. So they took out a joint lease on the house, engaged a cook-housekeeper and invited other like-minded people to join in this experiment in collective living. During the years of the Popular Front, in the thirties, the *Cité* became quite well known and articles were published in illustrated papers with photographs of well known left-wing intellectuals taking part in various social and cultural activities in the garden. It was a time of left-wing idealism, there were many allied cultural and political movements and the *Cité* acted as a centre for several of these. It was a fact noted by the police who saw it from the start and throughout its existence as a hive of sedition.

Though at the end of the war the *Cité* retained many of the features and principles of the early days, by the time we arrived in 1953 there was not much left of the idealistic *phalanstère* of the past. Of the three originators only one remained, a man in his fifties called Marcel Fredou. He was an interior decorator, an admirer of Le Corbusier, and his work was highly thought of, figuring in expensive glossy magazines, though he only undertook a limited number of contracts because he was physically diminished, having had a lung removed. Since Marcel was the named leaseholder he exerted a sort of authority and he used this in trying to maintain something of the communal ideal. But it was a losing battle. The post-war housing crisis meant that the desire to take part in an experiment in collective living was no longer uppermost in the minds of those who chose to live there. Instead, young couples, desperate to find somewhere tolerable to live, decided, as Constance and I did, that they could put up with any amount of collective ideology if it meant they could have a roof over their heads. Inevitably this brought about a change, both in the sort of people living in the *Cité* and in their attitude to the collective ideal: it was no longer something that they, we, had actively chosen. But there was a more important change.

The three who started the *Cité* were all professional people, by definition middle class, for all their left-wing opinions. I don't know how many working-class comrades there were in the early days but I suspect they were in a minority. When we arrived the composition was approximately half and half, workers and intellectuals. Two or three years before our arrival the comrade who acted as cook and housekeeper, and who was presumably paid or otherwise rewarded for her services, left to get married. Marcel of course wanted to replace her, but the working class members objected, making the obvious point that they did not earn enough to pay for the luxury of a domestic servant. The question had not been finally decided three years later when we arrived but it was settled by default. The different ménages did their cooking individually in the large kitchen. We ate then, sometimes all together in the big dining room, sometimes individually in the kitchen. When Constance and I heard what things had been like before the cook left, we were glad of the change. Because, as we learned, the originators of the *Cité* had been enthusiastic followers, of an eccentric diet guru called Dr Carton, to whose ideas they ascribed their successful recovery from TB. Before the departure of the cook everybody had to eat together, the food being prepared by the cook according to strict Cartonian principles. The only Cartonian rule that I can remember concerned the cooking of vegetables, these must be boiled several times in different waters in order to remove harmful salts. There were other principles equally strange that I have forgotten, which Marcel still observed faithfully. I never met anyone outside Chatenay that had ever heard of Dr Carton.

The change from communal to individual cooking meant that, though regular meetings were still held to discuss practical matters of common interest, the *Cité* was really no longer a commune, properly speaking so much as a sort of cooperative boarding house. At least this would have been so but for one important detail: the bathroom, the one feature that remained of the house's naturist past. It was a large room on the first floor containing, if I remember rightly, three or four washbasins, a basin for washing clothes, a bath and a shower. It should be remembered that in France in the early fifties a bathroom was a definite luxury. Until we came to Chatenay Constance and I did as I had done for years, namely visited a public bathhouse once or twice a week. Hardly any of my colleagues at the Institute had access to a proper bathroom in the various lodgings they inhabited. The facilities at the *Cité* were nothing short of luxurious for the time. With the exception of this one peculiarity: that you couldn't lock the door. There was a sensible reason for this: with eight or ten people going off to work early in the morning it would have been quite unacceptable for any one person to shut everyone else out for however short a time. Of course anyone that found this hard to get used to found that it was easy to have one's shower in the evening or mid afternoon when there was no one around. But most people got surprisingly quickly accustomed to seeing and being seen by others with no clothes on. A surprising amount of friendly chat happened in the bathroom between people shaving and showering or washing clothes. I had always found the idea of nudism as boring, and as silly, as excessive modesty; I was grateful to Chatenay for putting nakedness in its place. It was interesting too to discover, looking at the older men and women, that the part of the body that ages most and most quickly is the face and head. The rest remains unchanged until, I suppose, real old age sets in. The oldest in the *Cité* were in their mid fifties.

Another important change had taken place soon after the departure of the cook housekeeper. There had been a mini revolution in which everyone had ganged up against Marcel. He returned from holiday to find that someone had removed the cash box and account books from his room, and to be told, in the course of one long and stormy meeting, that henceforward all financial decisions would be taken collectively. Almost every member recounted these events to us, highlighting at length the part that they, personally, had played in them, and describing in detail the depravity and turpitude of Marcel. Marcel himself of course told us a different story. We managed to avoid taking sides in all this. We couldn't share the general animosity against Marcel and we quickly saw that there were plenty of other inter-personal tensions among the various members of the commune. It was obviously in our interests to remain on good terms with as many of them as possible. In time Marcel more or less accepted the alteration in his role which did all the same mean that life in the *Cité* was organised more democratically. And he retained a considerable amount of power simply by always being there, by being the person who remembered the various household obligations, and remembered them in time: ordering coal for the boiler, having the trees pruned and the dustbins put out and so on. That wasn't the only reason for the vague resentment felt and shown by almost everyone in the house towards him. He was homosexual and they tended to manifest the vulgar homophobia common among unthinking French people in those days, which was sad for supposedly enlightened left-minded people. It was an attitude that we did not share.

Marcel was, when we arrived, the only remaining "Cartonian". He was of course a very loyal Party member and it was immediately obvious that his membership was of prime importance to him. He had, however, absolutely no interest in politics and took no part in the ideological and political arguments that would rage in the kitchen over meals or late into the night, listening with half an ear and an air of amused indifference. In this he reminded Constance and me of people at home in Ireland, who were regular church goers but who would have been greatly embarrassed if you'd asked them a question about religion. Thanks to his reputation as a *décorateur* Marcel had managed to persuade the owner of the house, who was the widow of a wealthy Parisian butcher, to allow a number of structural alterations, mostly consisting of the installation of huge plate glass windows in some rooms on the top floor, which meant that the rooms thus opened up had a magnificent sweeping view over trees towards the dense woods of *La Vallée aux Loups*, but gave the front of the house a curiously lop-sided, one-eyed look. Of course his hero, Le Corbusier, who saw a house as a machine for living in, was not over-concerned with what it looked like from outside.

We found it very easy to get used to communal living. There were to begin with considerable practical advantages in living in *La Cité*. In addition to the bathroom already described we had the use of the huge garden where we could grow vegetables and the children could play, I had a garage for the motorbike, there were facilities for washing clothes and of course there was the large communal kitchen. In the big dining room there was quite a good piano. We also had the use of the telephone but only for incoming and emergency calls, since Marcel, who used it for his work, had the phone in his room. None of my colleagues at the Institute had any of these things; most did not even have access to a phone.

But the main advantages of *La Cité* were human and social. We all had more or less chosen to live together; it didn't necessarily follow that we liked each other very much, but it meant that there was always someone to talk to, and, because of the nature of the relationship, if you didn't feel like talking, you didn't have to. In a way it was a bit like a large family, except that the ties between us were much looser and nobody felt responsible for anyone else, or felt that they owed anything to any of the others. Also, unlike certain communes in the 60s, and possibly thanks to the political affinities of the inhabitants, it was a highly moral set-up, conventional even, though that was not how some of the neighbours saw it. After we had been living there for a few months my friend Henri from Lunéville came to see us. Arriving at *Robinson* he found he had mislaid the address so he asked in a café if anyone knew of a house answering the description in my letter. *Ah oui*, said the drinkers straight away, *C'est chez les Culs Nus.* (The Bare Bottoms). And directed him to *44 Avenue Jean Jaurès.*

One thing we discovered was the way a number of people sharing the same facilities tended to neutralise the tensions that can arise, for example, when just two people share a kitchen. In the *Cité* if you got fed up with X for monopolising the best saucepans you could always grumble to Y, but then you would find you were siding with X against Y because they left their laundry soaking in the bath all afternoon, and with both X and Y against Z whose grilled sardines made the whole house stink of fish. In a strange way the various minor frictions and tensions that occurred tended to bring us together more than to divide us against each other. There were exceptions of course. But the mere fact of living so close to each other from day to day generated a sort of underlying solidarity that was only apparent when misfortune befell one or other of us.

As happened one day when someone noticed that Marcel was absent. He normally got up and breakfasted quite late every morning but this day there was no sign of him and his bed had not been slept in. In itself this was not unusual; he often went and stayed with friends for a day or two. But he always told someone in the house when he was coming back, in case a possible client was trying to contact him by phone. This time he had said nothing to anyone about going away, and several people had seen him going to catch the bus to Paris. As the day wore on and he had not appeared we grew increasingly worried and finally decided to telephone the police. Their response, as soon as we had given Marcel's name and address, was immediate, unfriendly and disturbing. Marcel had been arrested and was being held incommunicado in Paris. Teddy the journalist knew straightaway what this meant: Marcel had been caught *in flagrante* committing some sexual offence. It turned out that he was accused of groping or trying to grope someone in a cinema in a not very respectable district in the north of Paris. We never knew the exact circumstances. Almost certainly, I think, it was some sort of set-up or police trap, but there was no way of proving that. Things looked fairly black for Marcel until a lawyer friend of his got in touch with us and said that it would help Marcel's case greatly if we could compose a letter expressing our friendship and esteem for Marcel and send it, to, I suppose, the relevant magistrate.

So we all sat down around the big table in the dining room and put together a document which, had he ever seen it, would certainly have brought tears to

Marcel Fredou

Teddy & Zette Chemla

even Marcel's usually dry eyes. I can't recall any of the words we used, though I can remember contributing a sentence or two, as I can also remember how we argued about the expressions to employ that would convey confidence in and admiration for Marcel, and at the same time say nothing that was in a general sense untrue. We never knew exactly what transpired except that next day Marcel was back among us. I don't think he ever talked about what had happened, but I remember him saying to Constance that he was glad he had discovered where his real friends were, and Constance replying that that was one good thing that only misfortune can bring about.

There were eighteen people living in the *Cité* when we arrived, and eight children of different ages. Our arrival increased the proportion of intellectuals, as it increased the proportion of non-Party to Party members, which had also been, roughly, half and half. In all categories there were individuals who were worth getting to know and who we could never have met but for the unusual intimacy that the *Cité* created. For example there was Teddy Chemla, a Tunisian journalist who worked in the news service of French Radio, until he was "purged" for his political affiliation. He was also a painter and a classical guitarist of distinction who gave frequent recitals on the radio. Very witty and with wonderfully expressive features he could be hilariously funny when in form. Or Gilbert Thomas, who was a *Conseiller Municipal* and had fought in the Resistance, or Roland Huet, who had come up to Paris from, I think, La Creuse, talked like a character out of Maurice Genevoix about wild life and *la chasse*, and worked as an electrician, or André Lefranc, who was a Paris bus driver and whose pictures were hung in the annual exhibition of paintings by Paris Transport workers. And there were the women, above all Zette, who came from Tunis and would organise a huge collective couscous on festive occasions and Monique, who was half Greek and half Parisian working class, vivacious, perceptive, highly intelligent and wonderfully articulate in spite, or perhaps because, of having left school at fourteen.

We had of course more in common with Cecil Jenkins's student from *Saint-Cloud*, Georges Prudhomme and his wife Annie, when they came back from their year in Belfast, since they were *anglicistes*. Georges, slow-spoken and phlegmatic with an unexpectedly quirky sense of humour, and Annie, Gallic vivacity personified, became lifelong friends.

And then there was Louis Weiss and his partner Maria Brun. Louis was Hungarian and, as a young man, had taken part in the Budapest Commune in 1919. He looked, and acted, a bit like Anthony Quinn in Zorba the Greek. He had lived and worked all over Europe and spoke fluent German which he used during the Occupation to demoralise German soldiers by telling them that their home town had just been obliterated by Allied bombing. He mostly worked as a builder with one of his sons. But he had a multitude of skills: for example once, when the dynamo of the Sunbeam burnt out and a replacement was either expensive or unobtainable, he procured the correct gauge of varnished copper wire and rewound the armature for me by hand. He told me how, in the *maquis*, he had made Molotov cocktails with the saltpetre that crystallised on old walls and used them on one occasion to attack a German armoured car. (*Ça hurlait là dedans*, he said. You could hear them screaming inside.) Though he and Maria, more than anyone else in the *Cité*, lived as though the heroic values and simplicities of the Résistance still held, he was all the same more open-minded than many Party members of the time. When various leading figures who had been executed under Stalin, in particular Bela Kun, leader of the Budapest commune in 1919, were rehabilitated after Stalin's death, he openly expressed his satisfaction, declaring to me that he had never for a moment believed they were traitors. Maria, on the contrary went round telling anyone who would listen that Stalin *avait un visage qui respirait la bonté* (had a face that simply radiated goodness).

Having lived in the wild, and clandestinely, for long periods, all over Europe, Louis had a rough and somewhat brutal side which was probably why most other people in the *Cité* disliked him. He had, for example, once in a rage called Annie Prudhomme *une petite roulure* (a little tart) and we had seen him threaten Marcel with an iron bar for criticising work he was doing on a window of our main room. Somehow we found it easier to forgive these excesses because we liked the aura of wild nature that he brought with him. As for example when he told us how to make yoghurt. We had just bought an antiseptic device for doing this but Louis explained in detail that the way to make yoghurt was to kill a young lamb or goat and then squeeze the contents of its stomach into a bucket of milk. If you did that, he explained to me, the milk would keep for a week.

Our friendship with Louis started from one distressing incident. Constance, who always loved cats, had adopted a stray grey tom that she named Grey-Malkin. We were living at the time on the ground floor of the *pavillon* and the cat used to climb in through our window and sleep on our bed. Constance had got in the habit of putting milk out for him and when I came back from work she would talk about his doings and his ways. She was six months pregnant with Paddy at the time; maybe that meant that she felt particularly maternal towards this, admittedly handsome, creature. One evening I returned to find her in floods of tears. Louis, to whom Grey-Malkin was just an anonymous stray pest, had found him eating some meat he had put in the cellar to keep cool. So he had strangled him, hanged him to be precise, because Constance had come upon Grey Malkin's body hanging from a branch behind the house.

We were both very upset at this but from the start Constance, typically, said there was no point in being angry with Louis. So next day she went, called him aside and talked to him quietly and at length. I don't know what she said but I know that she brought it home to him that he had offended her deeply but, and this was the most important thing, that she, we, didn't hold it against him. I think he saw that in this we were unlike certain other people in the house, who were capable of nursing a resentment against him over the years. He came up to me a day or two later and told me he was sorry for killing what he called Constance's pet cat, but that if she and I had seen some of the things he had had to witness we would not be so easily upset over a cat. Which was certainly true.

His partner, Maria Brun, was a phenomenon of a different order. Outwardly affable she was unpleasantly sly and manipulative and largely motivated by what I can only call a political holier-than-thou attitude which made her detested by almost everyone in the house. In our first years in Chatenay, when Party militancy was still at its height and the Twentieth Congress of the Soviet party had not started to sow misgivings among the comrades, she was by far the most energetic and committed member of the local branch where she spoke with an authority strengthened by her undeniable Resistance record. She had in fact been imprisoned and held as a hostage, which meant that at any moment she could have been picked as one of a group to be taken out and shot as reprisal for some Resistance action. Her trading on this did not help to make her liked. Not that this would have worried her at all. She got her kicks, so to speak, from putting people at a disadvantage. One morning, to give a typical example, I greeted her with "Lovely morning, Maria." She replied," When I see the sun shining like that I can't help remembering the comrades condemned to death in Greece." Our common political commitment made this an easy point to score; it didn't do much to get even the most committed comrades to like her. To that she was indifferent.

But it wasn't only in the field of politics that she enjoyed producing put downs like this. She cleverly manipulated the simplest everyday situations to put you on the moral low ground. A trivial example, from among many: on summer evenings I had taken to sitting reading on the doorstep of our *pavillon*, under the room where Maria slept. Coming across to bed she remarks on how pleasant it must be to enjoy the cool of the evening reading out of doors, and I agree. "What a pity," she adds, "That the light you're reading by shines on the ceiling of my room and keeps me awake." That was the end of my reading out of doors. But a year or two later, when Maria had left the *Cité* and Paddy was sleeping in that room, I checked and saw that of course the light didn't shine on the ceiling at all. She had just said it to put me quietly in the wrong.

Everyone in the house could tell of a multiplicity of similar incidents. So there was a ready audience to enjoy Constance's modest triumph over Maria's petty malevolence. It happened not long after we had arrived when Constance had made some plum jam in the kitchen. She found she had made more jam than she had prepared pots for, so she took two jars she found on a shelf and put the excess in them. Of course it turned out that they belonged to Maria and next morning there was a note from Maria (she was always leaving little notes for people) saying, "*Constance, les pots que tu a pris pour ta confiture sont à moi. Je les avais achetés, moi.*" (The jars you took for your jam are mine, I had bought them for my own use.) With any of the other women in the house it could have been the start of a loud row in which Maria would manage to get, and stay, on the moral high ground. But Constance was well able for this. She went straightaway and knocked on Maria's door and said, very sweetly, "*Mais Maria, tu n'a pas compris. C'était pour te faire cadeau d'un peu de ma confiture que j'ai pris les pots. Si tu en veux.* (But Maria, you don't understand. I thought you might like to *have* some of my jam.) Maria was forced to say Thank you. She never tried it on with Constance again.

Long years later, in a British university I had a senior colleague who, though outwardly very smooth and affable, was cordially, and not so cordially, disliked by almost everyone in the Faculty for the manner in which he seemed to get some obscure pleasure out of using his authority to put people at a disadvantage. He did it to me once or twice, to my intense annoyance and then I ended up by getting on quite well with him. I had been there before: he was just Maria Brun all over again.

Few of the Communists that we met either in or around the *Cité* were as narrow-minded or, to use a modern term, as fundamentalist as Maria. We were struck by how different most of them were, what a huge range of differing sorts of people either belonged to or were close to the Party, and we found most of them extremely likeable, though it is true that this did not always hold for all the Party officials we chanced to meet, though it did for some.

Writing about the political sympathies and enthusiasms of those years half a century later it is hard to separate hindsight from memory, hard to admit, or even to believe, that so many intelligent, thoughtful and well-meaning people, and ourselves with them, were complacently content to ignore the cruel dark side of the Soviet regime. Of course the Cold War explains a lot. If the gulags had not existed American propaganda would have invented them. So we naturally assumed that it had.

Two things decided my attitude. One was the discovery of Marxism, in particular as developed in the writings of Engels, which seemed to me then, as indeed, broadly speaking, it seems to me even now, the truest, because scientific, basic explanation of the most of the workings of human society. The second, and probably the most important, was the admiration I felt for a number of individual Communists, their commitment, their rock-solid faith in humanity, and in the future. There was the rationalist humanism of my uncle, Benjamin Farrington, Georges Filliat fighting a personal proletarian battle to obtain an education, Jacques and Marie Souviron in Orléans and their passionate loyalty to the ideal that Marie's brother had died for: there were many such examples to look up to. One example taken at random was Pierrot Lacoste, a retired metal-worker who happened to be staying with relations in the Pyrenees when one of De Gaulle's referenda was called unexpectedly, and who spent a substantial slice of his meagre pension travelling all the way up to Paris to vote, because to do so is the first duty of a *militant de gauche*.

And of course in France in the fifties the dark shadow of the Occupation years was never very far away. The rooms that Constance and I inhabited in the *Cité* had been the home of a young architecture student called Jacques Woog (pronounced Vug). His children, a boy and a girl, teenagers, used to come to the *Cité* on Sundays; the older comrades in the house had some sort of responsibility for them. Their father had been arrested when the Party was banned in 1939, for sticking up Communist posters. He was still in prison when the Germans invaded, which made him a victim of the retroactive legislation that the Vichy regime passed when the first attacks against the Nazis occurred. Woog was executed, in fact he was guillotined, in the prison de la Santé, like a common murderer. After his death the *Cité* – I found this hard to believe but it is true - received a bill, an invoice for *frais d'execution* (execution expenses) which Marcel had kept. I don't know if it was ever paid.

Facts like this and people like some of those mentioned above meant that we tended to regard the aberrations of French Party policy as of lesser importance. Such things as, for instance, the Party line on birth control – against it – which was obviously blatantly wrong, and the line on the *Paupérisation Absolue,* which said that French workers were being worse and worse paid every year, which you had only to look around you to see was totally untrue. What counted, and counted above all for me, was that we were accepted as part of a huge mass movement, and a mass movement which, whatever about party discipline or the crazy policies described above, was made up of people who might well have made a life-defining, dedicating, choice but had, most of them anyway, surrendered nothing of their individuality. In the words of the Resistance song:

*Ici chacun sait,*
*Ce qu'il veut, ce qu'il fait,*
*Quand il passe...*

I felt this above all on the occasion of the big annual *manifestations* on May 1st and July 14th. Then a dense crowd would line the pavements all the way from the *Place de la République* to the *Place de la Bastille* to watch the parade go past: group after group, each proudly holding up their banner. There were trade-union branches, many wearing the distinctive marks of their trade or profession: miners in helmets with lamps lit, scientists in white coats, firemen in uniform, steel-erectors with their welding goggles on their foreheads, nurses in white overalls, and group after group of civil servants or teachers in their best clothes. There were local and regional groups, Auvergnats playing *vielles* (hurdy-gurdies), Bretons with bagpipes, people from Provence and Alsace in regional costumes. There was a group of concentration camp survivors wearing the striped pyjamas of Auschwitz. There were groups of fellow-travelling, "fraternal" organisations. And, dotted around among the marching groups, were various celebrities if you could recognise them: Yves Montand and Simone Signoret, Louis Aragon and Elsa Triolet, and Frédéric Joliot-Curie, France's foremost atomic scientist who had just been hounded from his job under American pressure. Someone said Picasso would be there but if he was I never saw him.

As the last of the parade passed up the Avenue de la République the crowd on the pavements would flood the roadway and follow it, converging eventually on the Place de la Bastille, a vast sea of people, the biggest crowds I had ever seen, to be addressed through a hundred loudspeakers by Maurice Thorez. "*Camarades*!" his distinctive and undeniably warm voice would thunder out. I disliked almost everything I knew about Maurice Thorez, and the more I knew the more I disliked the stultifying Stalinism that he imposed and maintained on the French Party, so different from the open-minded humanism of Togliatti in Italy. But the effect of that word, coming from him, in that place and above all to that crowd, was, to me at any rate, electrifying. To feel at one with that huge variegated concourse of people, united, not only by a supposedly scientific ideology that made cogent sense, but by a common belief in the cause of socialism, and its power to change the world for the better, was to experience the ground-swell of something more powerful than sex, that which the Jacobins, rating it on a level with Liberty and Equality, had called *La Fraternité*.

When I described all this, for example to Steve, he dismissed it as a lot of bovine tribalism and accused me of behaving like the crowds at the Nuremburg rallies or the twelfth of July. He said he had never experienced anything of the sort, which may or may not be true. But it was not thoughtless, nor was it something that I only experienced in political demos or in large crowds of people all shouting the same slogan, as he suggested. I felt the same heart-warming emotion when I went to buy wood for bookshelves at the sawmill near Chatenay. As soon as I was recognised as someone from *La Cité* it would be a warm handshake and "Salut camarade". It wasn't until some years later, and after I had left France, that it occurred to me that, powerful and heart-warming though the emotion was, it could only be generated by a feeling of solidarity with a group of human beings in the face of an opposing force. And the opposing force was always, could only be, other human beings. As I read and thought about the theory of evolution and the behaviour of our closest simian relatives I realised that, if politics was maybe not just "weasels fighting in a hole" in Yeats's phrase, it was essentially super-chimpanzees ganging up against other super-chimpanzees in defence of pieces of ideological territory. Coming to this conclusion changed nothing in my estimation of the truth or validity of Marx's analysis of society. But it did mean that I had gained in self-knowledge.

Though our, my, first parenthood was planned and a delight from the start I wasn't ready for it and as a result, after the birth of Paddy, in 1954, I went through a rough patch, a sort of nervous crisis that lasted several months. A direct result of the novelty of being a parent, it only happened this first time. When, two years later, our daughter Shevaun was born I had completely recovered. One symptom was an intense and obsessive hypochondria, which was made much worse by my being ashamed of it. Convinced that I was suffering from a throat cancer I went from doctor to doctor in Paris and Dublin, too embarrassed to spell out what was worrying me, and ashamed to be so preoccupied by myself when Constance had all the worries of first time motherhood to think about. After about six months of this our GP sent me to a throat specialist who examined me briefly, saw there was nothing wrong and said bluntly, "I suppose you're worrying because you think you've got cancer." I could feel the worry dissolving as he explained how the throat muscles can tighten as a result of psychological stress or worry and how the effect is made worse by bottling it up. Though generally I have a high opinion of doctors, that was the only time I ever walked out of a surgery completely cured in five minutes.

The experience had had one good result, however. One day during the long vacation, when the worry was at its worst, I was working in the Trinity College library in Dublin. When the medical student in the next seat went out for coffee I had a look at her *British Medical Journal*. There I chanced to read the first report by Drs Doll and Hill on the relation between smoking and lung cancer. It was so convincing that smoking immediately ceased to be a pleasure and I gave it up straightaway and never smoked seriously again. It took me a few weeks to detoxify myself and then a few months to unlearn all the smoking-based habits and gestures.

Parenthood had another inevitable effect on our lifestyle: the motorbike no longer sufficed to carry us around. But I was so devoted to the Sunbeam that, instead of taking the logical next step and getting a small car, I attached a sidecar to the Sunbeam. It made sense up to a point, since the sidecar I got, of German design and the same as was used by the men delivering evening newspapers around Paris, could be attached and detached in minutes, which meant I could use the solo bike to go to work, only attaching the "chair" for excursions *en famille*.

That said, it would be hard to imagine a more absurd and intrinsically dangerous contrivance than a motorcycle and sidecar. A lopsided three-wheeler with no brake on the outlying wheel, with steering that pulled constantly to one side, you had to use a slightly different technique to steer it towards or away from the sidecar which, if it was empty, could suddenly lift and render the whole contraption totally unsteerable. I drove it around for a year and a half until, towards the end of a journey several days long from the Alps to Dublin, with one year-old Paddy asleep between Constance's feet in the nose of the sidecar, I dozed momentarily and woke too late to stop us from crashing into the back of a caravan. The caravan's splintering plywood softened the shock so there were no serious injuries, but that put an end to motorcycling. We graduated to a 2CV Citroen which was in fact very much like a motorbike with four wheels.

The *deux chevaux* was a typically French triumph of unconventional ingenuity. I admired the air-cooled engine, smaller than the one on my Velocette but designed for continuous running at full throttle and sparking on every piston-stroke to save the expense of a distributor, the inboard brakes, the amazingly soft, linked, front and rear springing, the windscreen wipers that worked off the speedometer drive, and the overdrive which you could use when going downhill or when you had a strong following wind to go a little faster than the car's normal maximum of 35 mph. I had three of them and only abandoned the model when Citroen started fiddling with the basic design, spoiling it by putting in a more powerful engine.

From the moment we started having children several advantages of collective living that we hadn't thought of became apparent. There was the obvious usefulness, for first-time parents, of having, living in the same building, other parents of small children, whose reassuring advice was always available, though we didn't always take it. There were occasional interesting culture clashes, as for example when the other mothers in the house were appalled at the way we would put the baby to sleep in its pram out of doors so long as it wasn't actually raining. Assuming that we were either mad or criminally negligent they would rush out and bring the infant in to the safety of a stuffy centrally heated bedroom. Gradually they came to accept that we weren't wrong, just different. In fact it was interesting to compare the advice given by our two parenthood bibles: Child Care by Dr Benjamin Spock and the handbook issued by the French Health service, which was obviously aimed at a rural public. The French booklet, after insisting that small children should not be given water with wine in it to drink, laid great and continual emphasis on the necessity of sterilising absolutely everything touched or consumed by the child, by boiling it or dipping it in boiling water. In contrast the American manual, obviously addressing obsessive bacteriphobes, would say things like: Don't worry about a few germs, they'll help build up his immune system.

Another good thing about living in a commune was that there was almost always someone to keep an eye on the children, letting us out for an evening, a service which we were glad to render in return, though the offer was only rarely taken advantage of. Baby-sitting as practised in Britain or America was virtually unknown in France at the time; all our French friends, if they ever went out in the evening took their children with them. If they couldn't take the children and if there was no accommodating grandmother living with them, they quite simply didn't go out. As a couple, that is; husbands may have enjoyed a freedom that wives and couples did not. Living in the *Cité* meant that Constance and I could go in to Paris to the cinema unlike most French parents.

And then, as our children grew older there was the great advantage for them of having other children to play with who were intimates but not family, and who were always there. For us of course there was a linguistic dimension to this. Children brought up in a bi-lingual environment can be confused and their development slowed down, especially if they are surrounded by people who sometimes speak one language and sometimes the other. At worst the children can end up speaking an incoherent mixture of both languages, muddling the syntax and using a vocabulary full of gallicisms and anglicisms. The most satisfactory bilingualism comes when each language is used by, and associated with, a different set of people. This was our case: we always spoke English to each other and to the children. When they were small they probably saw the English language as some sort of family dialect. On the other hand, since, outside the immediate family circle, they spoke French with almost everybody, and, particularly once they had started going to school, they quickly became more articulate in French, speaking it better than they spoke the English which was, all the same, their mother tongue. It's clear that "mother tongue" and "native language" are not necessarily or always the same thing.

You don't have to be a linguist to find the first utterances of small children as interesting as they are amusing. When Paddy first started to string words together his English contained a lot of French syntax, ("Why you were so long time?" *Pourquoi tu étais si longtemps?*"). This was fairly soon replaced by normal English. His French, however, was from the start free from anglicisms, so far as we could judge. And I found it fascinating to see how quickly he acquired an intuitive grasp of aspects of French grammar that I had found it so hard to learn. While still quite small he never failed to use a subjunctive where one was called for, and his nouns and adjectives always agreed both in number and gender. The gender of nouns, in fact, was the area of French grammar where I found small children's linguistic competence - to employ a Chomskyan term I would not have understood at the time - most amazing. I used to test it by inventing nonsense nouns to see if I could work out how he assigned the gender to them. I would tell him that there were *gruflots* down the garden, and then when he replied, "*C'est quoi un gruflot?*" I would ask him how he knew it was *un* and not *une*. But of course he had no idea. I remembered all this years later, read up the relevant research and designed a software package to help learners of French acquire something of French speakers' skill with this most exasperating feature of their language.

At the age of thirty one I had never seen a dead body. No one close to me, either friend or relative, had died. In fact the nearest I had been to death had been my time in hospital where, though the others talked a lot about people dying, it had never actually happened in the ward while I was there. When our little daughter Shevaun was drowned Constance and I quite simply could not believe that such a thing could have happened to us and that she, someone so close to us, could be dead. Her death changed absolutely everything in our world. And yet nothing could have been more banal and ordinary than the set of circumstances leading up to the accident that cost her her little life. I was sitting at my desk writing a lecture one afternoon and I could see through the window Shevaun playing by herself in the yard at the front of the house as she did every afternoon before going up to Chatenay with Constance to the shops. She was trying to spin a hula hoop and with every try she would call out "*Allez*!" When I didn't see her any more I supposed that she and Constance had gone out together.

It was February and for several months the children had played only in the bushes round the front of the house and in the yard, coming in whenever it rained or got too cold. Shevaun, though she was naturally very adventurous, never normally went down the garden. But unfortunately we had had several days of bright sunny weather so, exceptionally, the day before, they had all been down to where an old tyre had been hung from a branch to make a swing. That was where she had gone. But, with no other children around, the swing was of no interest, so

she started to explore, came on the goldfish-pond and fell in. She drowned in about ten inches of water. She was not quite two years old.

Shevaun

Shevaun was an exceedingly lively, sociable and characterful child for her age and a great favourite in the house. Very pretty, with her dark brown hair and deep brown eyes and totally un-shy, she loved people and interacted vivaciously with all and sundry, making amusing use of the handful of words she had learnt or invented, as all small children do. Like many little girls she had an instinctive and immediate liking for animals and would pursue, not only cats and puppies but the most unpleasantly pugnacious-looking dogs, ignoring their unfriendly growling as she tugged at Constance's or my restraining grasp to stroke and caress them. The summer before the accident I had managed to get a photograph of her setting off across a field in Donegal, stretching out her hands towards an enormous and intimidating black cow. "Dee-dee," she would cry – it was her word for any creature large or small, cow or chicken, horse or rabbit. It was a prehensile tenderness that she extended also to the family of teddy bears that peopled her bedroom, and above all to Gogwog, a little black golliwog that some relative, mindless of its racist implications, had given her and which she, embarrassingly, adored above all other teddies and would cover with passionate kisses before dropping it indifferently on the floor. When we were clearing out Shevaun's things, putting most of her toys and clothes in the boiler, we came upon Gogwog. But neither Constance nor I had the heart to put it/him in the fire.

Don't invent consolations for this death,
or see a moral, no one has learnt a lesson,
nor doll the pointless mishap up with purpose,
to deck the bleak futility of fate
with tinsel meaning. There is no meaning here,
nor shape nor plan, to this limp gap
there is no answer but escape, and no escape,
or resignation, and I'll not resign.

This perfect daughter will not try our love;
stilled forever in her happiness
she'll never mourn us, fail us or grow old,
coarsen with age or cheapen with distress,
dry up unmarried, tragically die
by accident or cancer at nineteen.
And what's the comfort? This is the fact I hate;
it is my grief that she can never grieve.

Absence follows me round in house and road,
silence calls in my ears, an emptiness
filling a space beside me haunts my sight;
her image catches the corner of my mind
and sudden imagined echoes of her laughing
jar on my ears about the table still;
all cause for worry gone, cut off from care,
my amputated love goes on and on.

The world is weighted against any young;
and yet of all love-trammelled children she
had been hedged in from beckoning accident,
the staircase maelstrom and the murdering roads,
and men had built a dyke against disease
behind whose massive wall we had played safe,
and yet not safe enough; for her and me
O Grave, your idiot victory is complete.

Civilisation taught us suffering,
gave us leisure to love and love to lose,
whittled desire to a point, extended hope
into the bright dominions of our dreams;

and, now this hope's cut off, have I the right
to make more fuss than any Asian father
grieving the normal one child lost in three?
what right had I to love my children more?

My little shining daughter, some time soon
I'll have forgotten all your fetching ways,
your hands, your quick prehensile tenderness,
the smell of you, your bracken-coloured eyes,
your happy wayward spirit, how you danced,
till death, grotesque and final, dragged you down,
short-circuited the spirit out of sense
into the nonsense of eternity.

And, yawing sickly to this drag of grief,
my heart rights to reason, diminishing
the ancient spectre to a hideous fact
bodied in this once dear familiar flesh;
O death may haunt me, but no deaths appal
now this virginity of the ungrieved is lost;
life is more than lives and carries on,
Death from this is dead with my Shevaun.

# 8 Paris II

NOTHING COULD HAVE UNDERLINED the resemblance of the *Cité* to an extended family more tellingly than the accident to Shevaun. Almost everyone in the house had known her and played with her, so that they felt our loss almost as acutely as we did ourselves. But sudden death is so rare a phenomenon nowadays that it is not surprising that few people know how to react to it. Some of our friends, and indeed some of my immediate family, were rendered so inarticulate by our misfortune that "not knowing what to say" they said nothing, and did nothing either, thereby implying, mistakenly, an indifference which I am sure they neither meant nor felt, but which all the same we found, unjustly, hard to forgive. My sister-in-law, Conor's first wife, Meryl Gourley, on the other hand, reacted immediately, and in character, by cabling flowers. Had the florist known these were for the burial of a child I suppose the flowers would have been, conventionally, white. As it was, the burst of colour on the little coffin said more to us, and for us, than words could. Unsurprisingly it was the few country people living in the locality whose reaction brought us the simplest comfort. Titine, an old peasant woman that used to do ironing for Constance, and Berthe, who had a market garden down the road and sold vegetables from it which she trundled around in a sort of wheelbarrow, these women, schooled in the time-honoured ceremonies of peasant life, just came and sat with us for a moment, hardly saying a word but mopping away a tear which, whether it was sincere or simulated, was entirely appropriate.

Least helpful of all were the one or two acquaintances who presumed to offer us some form of crude religious consolation, telling us for example that God in His wisdom knew what He was doing, or insisting that our daughter was playing happily in heaven and that we would meet her again someday. It was hard to see what solace there could possibly be in the vision that this conjured up, of Constance and me, in our 70s or 80s maybe, hobbling through the Pearly

Constance and Doreen Shevaun

Gates to be greeted by a half-forgotten two-year-old. Our only practising Christian friend, Joan Horgan, who was a devout Catholic, kept a discreet and dignified silence, voicing instead the wise and very relevant truth that what had happened was no one's fault, and that children have to be free to explore the world. She and Mark Mortimer were the only people Constance would have at the funeral, because, like Shevaun, they were Irish. Constance through all this retained something, if not of her faith, at least of a religious way of thinking. For me the tragedy served but to confirm my conviction that the whole idea of a personal god that could be in some way involved in our affairs was so absurd as to be totally irrelevant.

A little over a year after the accident to Shevaun, in 1960, our second daughter, Doreen, was born. Though our friends, inevitably, saw her as a replacement for the child we had lost, it was clear while she was still a very small baby that she was quite a different person, gentler than her sister, and with none of Shevaun's self-willed obstinacy. Where Shevaun used to actually stamp her foot in anger when prevented from doing something she wanted to do Doreen quickly learnt subtler ways of getting her own way, by negotiation and sometimes by manipulating the adult world. Unlike her sister she had no interest at all in animals, only noticing them when, as with large dogs, they frightened her. While still quite young she developed a feeling and a talent for music that decided the direction that her life would take. On the other hand she was like her sister in being physically very tough and adventurous, walking long distances without complaining and putting up with intense cold. When only six years old she raced me all the way up the down escalator of a London Underground station.

Like Shevaun Doreen was born following the method of painless childbirth that had recently been brought to Paris from Russia by Dr Ferdinand Lamaze. I don't know if Dr Lamaze was a member of the Party, quite possibly he was not, but the success of the method of *accouchement sans douleur* that he popularised had an obviously political importance in the ideological tug-of-war in which we all participated at the time. Basically it consisted in applying Pavlovian principles to the process of childbirth so that the mother, by understanding exactly each stage of the process, could be in control of events and could take an active part in the birth of her child instead of remaining passive like an animal in the hands of a vet. Putting her, so far as possible, in charge, and arming her with the full knowledge of what was happening and what to expect, meant that the mother felt very much less pain, and sometimes the whole birth went through with no pain at all. That was certainly the case at the birth of Doreen; Constance was smiling confidently most of the time. I was of course present, the active presence of the father, who was trained to perform certain functions which I have forgotten, was an important part of the method. I went back to Chatenay and told 5 year old Paddy that he had a sister. "That's exactly what I wanted," he said.

One of the most valuable perquisites that came with having a job teaching at the British Institute was the possibility of putting in hours teaching at various prestigious Parisian institutions, where it was considered more in keeping with the status of the establishment to engage suitably qualified native English speakers than professional French teachers of English. By "suitable qualification" nothing more sophisticated was indicated than the simple possession of a first degree. To my knowledge none of my colleagues at the Institute had any teaching qualification, any more than I had. This did not prevent them, us, from being hired at extremely lucrative hourly rates to organise classes at the *Banque de France*, at UNESCO, at the *Institut des Sciences Politiques* (*Sciences Po*) and even at the *Ecole Nationale d'Administration*, the *Grande École* at which France's top civil servants are trained.

In this context I taught for several years at *Sciences Po*. I found it an intimidating place; the *Salon des Professeurs* was peopled by imposing or self-important men in double-breasted suits, captains of industry, ambitious professors of economics, high-ranking administrators. I definitely didn't feel that I belonged in this distinguished-looking company, arriving in my enormous crumpled motor-cycling greatcoat dotted with pop fasteners and stained with oil. I remember having difficulty finding a peg strong enough on which to hang this unlovely garment. Then, on the hour, a group of uniformed functionaries would arrive: *les appariteurs*. Their role was to herald or otherwise manage your *apparition*, i.e. your appearing in front of your students. Each one would call out the name of the *prof* for whose *apparition* he was responsible, which is how I knew on one occasion that the double-breasted suit I was sharing the lift with, together with our two *appariteurs*, was Monsieur Georges Pompidou. (This was, of course, some years before his political career began. I only noticed, and remembered, the name because it sounded to me like a character out of Dickens.) Arriving at the door of the classroom or lecture hall the *appariteur* would walk in and, like a footman at an Ambassadorial reception, would announce you in stentorian tones: *Messieurs, Votre Professeur* and the assembled students would all stand up. I don't know how Georges Pompidou felt, but I couldn't help finding that the ceremony was a bit excessive to herald the arrival of B. Farrington, genned up and all as I was with explanations about the correct use of *since* when translating *depuis*.

The students were all bright enough, since the entrance exam was fairly stiff and, being very bourgeois, they were extremely polite and embarrassingly deferential. Also, since they had all visited England on numerous occasions, their spoken English was quite good, so getting them to summarise or discuss leading articles taken from *The Times* or the *Observer* was not very demanding work, though it could hardly be described as intellectually stimulating or even interesting in a general way. But their attitudes were so bourgeois and their opinions, with very few exceptions, so extremely right-wing that it was very difficult to avoid getting into interminable arguments in the course of which I found that, while I couldn't conceal my left-wing sympathies and loyalties, I had no talent for defending them in terms of day to day politics. The situation was made more difficult by the start of the Algerian war, which most of the *Sciences Po* students didn't consider was a war at all, deceiving themselves, as did most French people at the time, by calling it *une pacification*, and trying to pretend that Algeria was as much a part of metropolitan France as Burgundy or Provence. Fortunately I didn't have to remain at *Sciences Po* for too long. My friend Cecil Jenkins, who had come to live with us in Chatenay and had been for several years working at his thesis on Andre Malraux, got a university job in Northern Ireland and, in 1956, I was able to replace him as *lecteur* (Foreign Language Assistant) at the *École Normale Supérieure de Saint-Cloud*.

*Saint-Cloud* was an infinitely more congenial environment, for me at any rate, than *Sciences Po*, though the work the job involved was very much more challenging. It consisted in teaching translation from French to English in preparation for the *Licence*, the French equivalent to a British honours degree and also, my main commitment, for the *Agrégation,* which is a *concours* or competitive examination pitched at an extremely - absurdly in my view - high level of difficulty, and which guarantees admission to the teaching profession at secondary and university level. This meant searching through French literature from the 17th century onwards for the most difficult passages I could find and then producing a fair copy of a translation into English that I could dictate sentence by sentence as we worked through the passage in class. All this was easier than it might seem at first sight. I quickly learnt that the type of difficulty that the examiners of the Agreg respected was above all lexical. There was little point in trying to render Bossuet into 17th century English, or working out an English way of representing French philosophical abstractions, or turning Proust's layer upon layer of subordination into readable English. Instead, I looked in Balzac or the Goncourt brothers for paragraphs containing lists of furniture or types of buildings or different shapes of trees. Long descriptions of herbaceous borders, of the rigging or manoeuvres of sailing ships were welcomed by these, all the same highly intelligent, learners as something well worth getting their teeth into. In the process I learnt a lot of French myself, as well as acquiring a knowledge of a large number of recondite and not very useful English words. But I enjoyed it; vocabulary is the part of language I have always found most interesting.

And the "*cloutards*" were a joy to work with and a pleasant change from the *fils à papa* (rich kids) at *Sciences Po. Saint-Cloud*, like the larger and even more prestigious *École Normale Supérieure* in the *rue d'Ulm*, was a *Grande École* on the model established under Napoleon. That meant that the students were selected at the age of 17 or 18 by means of a very rigorous *concours* (competitive examination). Once successful in this ordeal and admitted to the *École* they became in fact salaried civil servants, and remained so to the end of their career. The *École* therefore presented a convenient and effective ladder by which a bright *lycéen* (schoolboy) could, from a very modest social origin, climb to a senior academic post. At *Sèvres* and *Fontenay* two similar *Ecoles Normales Supérieures*, founded much later, catered for girls. My friend Marie Souviron, for example, was a *Normalienne*, from *Sèvres*. Most of the "*cloutards*" came from the provinces; their parents were primary school teachers, postmen, railwaymen or something similar. Naturally, seeing the social origin of the majority, though a wide variety of social attitudes were represented, a generally radical, if not necessarily left-wing, view tended to dominate. Almost without exception I found them highly intelligent, thoughtful, courteous and fun to work with. For my part my newly developed interest in and knowledge of English phonetics, added to my being a specialist in English literature, made the changeover from Jenkins easier for me, since his major preoccupation had been his thesis on Malraux.

My father and mother in Paris

One curious little detail that I frequently noticed about these lively, quick witted young Frenchmen, selected as they were by the unusual ordeal of the *concours d'entrée*, was that, almost without exception, they all had admirably clear and legible handwriting and, when, for example, they were taking notes at a lecture, they were all able to write fast and at an even speed without stopping listening. This I could never do, I either wrote or listened; what was more I wrote jerkily with my fingers clenched so tight that my hand got tired. It was as though I suffered from some sort of scribal stammer. I clearly, had I been French, would never have got into the *École Normale*.

As I have said most of my year's work was preparing students for the *Agrégation*. This curious and uniquely French institution, gateway to the top jobs, not only in the field of education but in public life generally, merits description. The examination itself was in two parts. Success in the first, written, part meant that you were *admissible* to the second, which was a sort of very formal oral interview conducted by a board of examiners. The written part consisted of translations into and out of English, my main interest, and an essay in English and one in French in answer to questions about the syllabus, which changed each year and consisted of eleven classic literature texts, ranging from Chaucer to T S Eliot. The unusual thing about this part of the exam was that there was no choice, the candidates were just given a little slip of paper on which was *one* question about *one* of the eleven authors on the programme. They were then shut in for no less than seven hours to compose their answer. Unsurprisingly, on the day of the examination, a significant number of candidates, on reading the exam paper, simply walked out, since they hadn't concentrated their preparation on that particular author.

In later years, when, in Scotland, I had done some research on techniques of testing, had learnt some statistics and above all when I had become accustomed to the way in which university examinations were conducted in Britain with external examiners, double or even triple marking of students' scripts and so on, I found the random, elitist, nature of the *Agrégation* extremely shocking in retrospect. At the time I tended to take it for granted, as did the candidates themselves, that it was impossible to predict which of the fifteen or twenty *Agrégatifs* would be successful. To tell the truth the simple fact of being *Normaliens* meant that they had all been subjected already to so elaborate a series of selection processes that it was probably a huge waste of time and money trying to choose between them at all, so the exam could usefully just have been abolished. It was, and for all I know is still, such a sacred cow that it was probably just as well I never gave voice to such an opinion. I did however, when I was leaving, tell Monsieur Canac, *Sécretaire Général of the Ecole Normale*, a man whose sense of humour I appreciated, that I had over the years endeavoured to detect some pattern in the successful candidates in the light of which I could adjust and adapt my teaching but had failed. Had it been, I said, the most, or even the least, intelligent that tended to succeed, or the most or the least hard-working and deserving, or the Catholics or the Communists, or the Bretons or the Parisians or the chaps with red hair, I could at least have known which qualities to encourage, but year after year there would be one or two candidates of every conceivable category, both among the successful and among the failures, so that it was hard to avoid the conclusion that the highly esteemed and greatly feared (and highly paid) jury of examiners might as well have drawn the names out of a hat.

Whatever about the exam itself I found the work that it gave me a stimulating and rewarding chore. Turning selected key texts and purple passages from French literature into English in the company of a roomful of highly educated, and often very critical, Frenchmen was a constantly interesting activity in itself and I learnt a lot from it. Over the years I built up quite a collection of tried and tested fair copies. I was amused to learn, years after I had left *Saint-Cloud*, from one or two Cloutards that I was still in touch with, that copies of some of these texts, with my translations, were still going the rounds, turning up in distant Faculties, where my ex-students were now *maître assistants* or professors. But *Saint-Cloud* was also important to me for another, quite different reason.

*****

Roy Johnston, a fellow Old Columban who later became one of my closest friends was, in the nineteen fifties, in Paris finishing a PhD in theoretical physics. One-day I had chanced to say to him that I was embarrassed by my ignorance as to how the wireless - as it was called then – worked, and asked him to recommend a book explaining it. Roy can hardly have realised the effect that the advice he gave me would have. In fact it was an important component in the process by which, from being a lecturer in English Literature in a second rate job in France, I became a specialist in Educational Technology in the North of Scotland. "Don't be bothered with books," said Roy, "Build yourself a low-frequency amplifier; that'll teach you the principles." I got hold of some popular electronics magazines containing cabling diagrams, purchased a soldering iron and a quantity of capacitors, resistances, and (this was 1956, remember) valves, and got down to puzzling out how to put these strangely fascinating elements together. I got some help from a friendly Romanian electronics engineer who lived round the corner and I was lucky, for immediately I connected one end of this assembly of half-understood components to a record player and the other end to a loudspeaker and plugged it into the mains the first movement of Mozart's A major Piano Concerto came singing out so loud it could be heard the other side of the garden.

It was a time when the earliest tape recorders were making their appearance, ponderous machines manufactured by Telefunken or Grundig which people would switch on during dinner parties and then listen to, amazed at hearing what their own voices sounded like to other ears. I constructed a tape recorder myself, which worked more or less, and a radio which didn't work at all. Then I managed to repair the radios of several friends by the simple expedient of replacing some of the valves and the larger condensers thus giving people the impression that I understood a great deal more than was in fact the case. The nuts and bolts knowledge of elementary electronics that I acquired by these activities, together with the spurious reputation that they earned me, came at the right moment, coinciding as they did with my starting at *Saint-Cloud*.

Several years earlier the *École Normale de Saint-Cloud* had become the centre for an important, government-sponsored, project whose aim was to slow down or stop the decline of French as an international language. The way that was chosen to achieve this end was to produce a simplified, or more exactly a reduced, version of the language that would be easier to teach and to learn but which, unlike the Basic English of Ogden and Richards for English, could act as an easy introduction to normal spoken and written French. This reduced version, known as *Français Fondamental* (Fundamental French), was based on the statistical analysis of a large number of recordings of everyday spoken French. The vocabulary of *Français Fondamental* was in this way reduced to the two thousand most common or most frequent words. The grammar was simplified in the same manner. For example, of the many ways of forming an interrogative in French only one figures in *Français Fondamental*, namely putting *est-ce que* before a sentence.

The CREDIF, the centre responsible for the *Français Fondamental*, was located in the main building of *École Normale* and a modern annexe just beside it housed the *Centre Audio-Visuel,* which was responsible for disseminating audio and visual aids in French lycées. It was hardly surprising that *Saint-Cloud* became a centre for what was not yet known as Applied Linguistics and that one of the first, if not the very first, language laboratories in Europe was installed there. I had not been at *Saint-Cloud* long before I found myself collaborating there in the production of the first French language lab course in English to be entitled "Lend Me Your Ears".

If ever there was a false dawn or a white elephant in the field of language learning it was the Language Laboratory. I shall have more to say about this expensive and unnecessarily complicated device and the half-baked linguistic theories that were cooked up to explain how it should be used. Suffice for now to say that, well, for me anyway, bliss was it in that false dawn to be alive, to talk frequencies and stimuli and responses instead of prose composition and essay-writing. I could even fancy I was turning into a scientist, at the price of believing, if only for a time, - but I'm afraid I did - that to learn a language all you had to do was listen to a recorded voice and repeat what it said, parroting every conceivable permutation of a set of expressions. We had a visit at *Saint-Cloud* from the high priest of behaviourism, B F Skinner himself, who explained in an entertaining lecture how, by using simple stimulus and response techniques, he had taught pigeons to perform quite complicated tricks, the assumption being that we had all learnt our native language in the same way and that the process could easily be applied to the teaching of a foreign tongue. Did it occur to anyone to object that human language was a somewhat more complex phenomenon than the coloured beans the pigeons were selecting? I don't remember. But I brought Francis Scarfe, newly appointed Director of the British Institute, out to *Saint-Cloud* to see the Language Laboratory and I advised on and supervised the installation of a small broadcast lab in the Institute itself a few years later. The effect that all this could have on my future career never occurred to me.

The time I spent at *Saint-Cloud* meant that I had to reorganise my teaching at the British Institute which was, all the same, my principal employer. The simplest solution was to take on work that no one else wanted to do, at unpopular times. So for five years or more I gave up literary seminars and taught mostly commercial English, and did so in the evenings and Saturday afternoons. The commercial English classes at the Institute were geared to an antediluvian exam organised by the British Chamber of Commerce in which the unfortunate candidates had to translate back into English a set of sentences that quite clearly had previously been translated, and not very well translated, from English into French. Obviously, teaching the English for *comptabilité en partie double* and *commissaire priseur* (*double-entry book-keeping* and *auctioneer*) was not very exciting intellectually, but it wasn't very tiring either. And it was easy to leaven this useful but unattractive pabulum with the occasional joke, something that was gratifyingly appreciated by the students, who were mostly hard-working secretaries and under-managers, people that I found worthier and, on the whole, more fun to teach than the social butterflies upstairs.

One evening sometime in the fifties Constance and I, having been to the cinema somewhere around Montparnasse, were having a drink in one of the big cafés on the boulevard. She had been to the Ladies – our reason for being in the café in the first place – and as she sat down beside me, she said, "Do you realise who is on the bench behind us?" I looked and recognised Jean Paul Sartre, Simone de Beauvoir and an American. We strained our ears trying, unsuccessfully, to hear what they were saying. Sartre was speaking in a lowish voice, as though he was talking to himself, and Beauvoir was translating, or trying to translate what he was saying into English for the American. She spoke confidently with a lot of mistakes and a strong French accent. I don't know who the American was; could it have been Nelson Algren? At any rate after a while they got up to go and, as they headed for the door, Beauvoir turned and said, "*Sartre, et votre imperméable?*" Sartre picked up his raincoat and that was the end of the incident. What struck both Constance and me was the formal, old-fashioned, manner of speaking that these inspiringly radical thinkers used when talking to each other. Like the aristocrat in *La Grande Illusion*: "*Je dis vous à ma femme, je dis vous à ma mère.*" (I say *vous* to my wife and I say *vous* to my mother).

It wasn't the first time we had been struck by seeming inconsistencies in French modes of address. Among the *camarades* in *La Cité* we all addressed each other as *tu*. There was one couple, however, with an unimpeachably proletarian background, who nevertheless, while saying *tu* to each other, addressed everyone else, always, as *vous*. And, stranger still, in our first six months there was a couple who had the only car in the *Cité*. She, Simone, was a doctor, I don't remember her husband's name or what he did. They were both narrow-minded Party members and, of course, used *tu* when speaking to other *Camarades*. But we used to hear them getting the car out in the early morning. "*Braquez*," she would say, "*Braquez encore, mon ami,*" using the formal *vous* to her husband.

One agreeable perquisite that being Irish in Paris in those days procured was the occasional hospitality offered by the Irish Embassy, a much friendlier and more laid-back setup than the toffee-nosed crew from the British Embassy, who would occasionally visit the Institute. I had got to know people from the Embassy in 1950, when I chanced, with Mark Mortimer, to meet a First Secretary called Scantlebury. He was complaining that he had to go to a ceremony in *Père*

*Lachaise* in memory of Oscar Wilde. "Do you know anything about Wilde?" he said. I told him how I had once been on an athletics match to Portora Royal, Wilde's old school. On the wall of the dining hall there I had seen the names of old pupils who had distinguished themselves, glimmering in dingy gold letters. One name stood out: Oscar Wilde. The headmaster explained that, at the time of his disgrace, the name had been erased from the *Tableau d'Honneur*, but that, years later, it got so embarrassing to explain the gap in the list that they had had to put it back again. Only, now, against the faded gilt names of generals, judges and QCs, Oscar Wilde's name shone out bright and new. "God that's great," said Scantlebury, "Do you want to come with me?" In *Père Lachaise* we stood in the rain, among a small group of distinguished-looking elderly French men of letters, in front of Jacob Epstein's famous monument, on which the brazen genitalia had not as yet been vandalised away. Several people spoke. It was actually very moving and the Portora anecdote, which Scantlebury told very well, added a necessary note of humour. I had established myself as a representative of Irish culture.

The Irish Ambassador, Con Cremin was a bluff hearty man with a West Cork accent and, as befitted his job, a commanding presence. His wife was a charming, refined and most elegantly dressed, lady with a surprising taste for salacious gossip and risqué stories. Once when I called at the Embassy to leave in some papers they invited me in and plied me with whiskey. Then, having heard somehow that I had a voice they invited me to sing. So I sang one or two songs from the Herbert Hughes collection which were unfamiliar to them and then Ambassador Cremin followed on with a rendering of The Dear Irish Boy and one or two other songs. I'm not sure that one or two of the First Secretaries of the Embassy who were also there weren't called upon to perform in their turn. It all seemed a little strange in this dignified Second Empire décor, but very pleasantly Irish.

In return Mark Mortimer and I would give lectures or talks on Irish literature to various cultural clubs and associations that had applied to the *Services Culturels* of the Embassy. These used to have names like *Le Club de Diffusion Artistique* and their meetings were held in the back or upstairs room of some café chaired by a somewhat shady would-be impresario who was usually the founder of the club and chief animator of its activities. He also, so far as we could see, pocketed the membership subscriptions. I gave talks in French to groups like this on Synge, on Yeats and on Irish culture generally. There was never any fee of course; the reward was the goodwill of the Embassy, which was well worth having, as I have shown. Once, however, a slightly more sizeable set-up whose name I forget applied to the Embassy and they arranged for Mark to give a lecture on Swift. This took place in a hall in the *Musée de l'Homme* and was chaired by a shadier than usual would-be impresario called Zurini. There were about fifty people there, a bigger crowd than usual for this sort of occasion.

Mark Mortimer and BF at a Yeats lecture

After the lecture, which went quite well, this Zurini thanked Mark, and, with somewhat portentous discretion, presented him with a sealed envelope. A few days later, out of curiosity, I asked Mark how much they had paid him for the talk on Swift. "I didn't open it till I got home," said Mark. "It was empty."

He had a distinctive and very personal lecturing style, Mark Mortimer, which, since it was so different from the polished oratorical performance put on by French speakers, was appreciated by most Parisian audiences: they liked it because it was so unusual. He would address an audience of fifty in exactly the same relaxed easy-going, slightly hesitant, manner that he would use talking to two friends in a café, only raising his voice as much as was necessary. Students told us that they found both him and me easier to understand than most English speakers; this was probably due to our mild Dublin accent, with its post-vocalic /R/ in words like *garden,* and its tendency not to diphthongise the vowels as people from England do.

Of a different order altogether, and much more intimidating, was an invitation to do a presentation about W B Yeats to a prestigious association called the *Cercle Paul Valéry,* the meetings of which took place in an amphitheatre of the Sorbonne. Mark and I were summoned to a meeting with the *Secrétaire* of this *Cercle,* who, a change from Zurini, was a great barrel of a man with a strong Russian accent who introduced himself as Monsieur Genghis-Khan. We agreed that the evening would consist of a lecture on Yeats, illustrated by readings of the poems. Mark would deliver the lecture while I would do the readings. We saw from the start that this was going to need some preparation so we went to several meetings of the *Cercle Paul Valéry*. The first one we went to was dedicated to the work of the innovative Canadian film maker Norman McLaren and consisted of a very abstruse lecture on the theory behind McLaren's work, followed by projection of some of his films which were, so far as I remember, all animations of an unusual kind and much more entertaining than the lecture had been. At the end Monsieur Genghis-Khan got up and said in his Russian accent *Le grant artiste est touchours au-dessus des foules* (a great artist is always way above the crowd).

The second meeting we went to was even more intimidating being addressed by a celebrity, no less than Serge Lifar from the National French Ballet. His talk, which he illustrated by producing a ballerina in a tutu and standing her up on a table to demonstrate various movements and gestures, was accompanied, or followed, I don't remember which, by someone reading *L'Âme de la Danse* by Paul Valéry and reading it beautifully. Then Monsieur Genghis-Khan got up and ended the evening by pronouncing again that *Le grant artiste est touchours au-dessus des foules.* It was clear that we were going to have to pull all the stops out. I did my part by studying the poems we had selected intensively, and then trying out different readings with Constance's help, recording them on a primitive wire recorder that the Institute had just acquired, and comparing different interpretations. I discovered again the amazing variety of styles in Yeats's poetry that I had noted years before with Peter Allt, some poems (*September 1913*) asking to be declaimed dramatically, while others (*The Wild Swans*) called for a reading that was slow and meditative, hesitant even, and some (*Innisfree*) were best spoken in a manner that underlined the music of vowels and consonants. Some poems (*Easter 1916*) even combined a variety of styles so that reading them expressively underlined the complexity of the poem.

When the day came and we stood up in this large amphitheatre I found the presence of so many people - there must have been at least a hundred, probably more - more a stimulus and an encouragement than anything else. And of course the words I was speaking were Yeats's words and not my own. Mark, on the other hand, was, uncharacteristically, not at ease. Either he had over prepared or underprepared his lecture, whichever it was the result was an uncharacteristically wooden performance, so, in order to save the situation I spoke the poems in an even more dramatic style than I had been used to in rehearsal. When it was over and Monsieur Genghis-Khan had said his piece (*Le grant artiste est touchours au-dessus des foules* yet again) people came up and complimented me. One of them was Prof René Frechet, who I knew of as a specialist in Anglo Irish literature, and he introduced me to one or two Celtic scholars whose names I don't remember, one of whom thanked me effusively for having given them *une belle et mémorable soirée* (an evening to remember). I felt that their praise was justified; for the first time in my life it seemed to me that I had brought something, if not to perfection, at least somewhere near it, and that I had discovered one thing that I knew for certain that I did well.

Reading poetry aloud looks at first sight such an easy thing to do, when in fact it calls for a lot of thought and preparation, that it is hardly surprising that it should often be done so badly. Many actors for example, when invited to read a poem, make no allowance for the unusually concentrated use of language that is the essence of poetry, and they read, usually too fast, without thinking carefully enough about the many possible meanings of the words they are going to say, and how they might best be spoken. Many poets, when reading their own work aloud, betray a depressing indifference to the sound of words, and to the many ways in which different modes of expression can alter or underline their meaning. It's clear that these poets write more for the eye than for the ear. This is most certainly not true of Yeats, and if I have had some success on various occasions in reading his poetry aloud it is because I have always had this in mind. It was most certainly not borne in mind by most of the people invited to read at the recent – I am writing in 2008 - Yeats exhibition in the National Library in Dublin. With one or two honourable exceptions (Ulick O'Connor, Seamus Heaney) these display an astonishing insensitivity to the distinctive quality of Yeats's verse. The singer Sinead O'Connor in particular reads the hauntingly beautiful *Wild Swans at Coole* as though she was explaining to a blind man what was written on a notice board, and she turns *Easter 1916* into monotonous doggerel. I wrote to the organisers of the exhibition to complain about this but received no reply.

The last 10 years or more of my time in Paris were dominated by the Algerian war. This horrific conflict, which many French people denied was a war at all, meant that French soldiers, some of whom had an honourable Resistance record, found themselves in the same situation that the SS had been in in France only 15 years before, and carrying out similar atrocities. This was brought home to many people in France by the death of Ali Boumendjel, a young Algerian barrister well-known by Parisian lawyers, who, having been arrested by French paratroopers in Algiers, managed to kill himself by jumping out of a window because he knew he could not trust himself not to speak under torture. Pierre Brossolette, a hero of the French Resistance, had done exactly the same thing, in Paris in 1944, when arrested by the Gestapo.

The war couldn't fail to have a special significance for anyone from Ireland, if only because of certain similarities with our own national struggle. I wrote one or two articles about it for Irish papers, in particular I wrote a review article for the *Irish Times* about *La Question*, the book that Henri Alleg, editor of the newspaper *Alger Républicain,* wrote containing an account of being tortured by

French paratroopers, which was banned by the Government in France. Constance on the other hand did something very much more useful.

For a few years in the late fifties or early sixties a tall dark-haired young teacher of English called Micheline Pouteau had come to live in Chatenay. We saw her as an intelligent, lively companion who knew a lot about cinema and talked interestingly about the various shows on in Paris at the time. Constance in particular saw quite a lot of her; I don't think she thought much of me. We had disagreed about someone coming to the *Cité* and I had argued pompously, taking on, as she said, *un air de grand seigneur*. Anyway she found a flat near the lycée where she worked and moved out.

In common with several other people in the *Cité* Micheline had grown increasingly critical of the attitude of the French Communist Party to the Algerian war. When France had been at war with the Viet Minh in what was then Indochina, the French Party had organised campaign after campaign against *la sale guerre* (the dirty war) with women lying down on the rails to prevent trains full of conscripts from leaving. However, now that the French government was carrying on a much dirtier war, on France's own doorstep as it were, the issues, as seen through Party eyes, were much less clear. The war had no clear East versus West implication, and the FLN (*Front de Libération Nationale*), the principal movement fighting for Algerian independence, was not a left-wing movement and had a significant religious, Islamic, component. Also, it must be said that there was quite a lot of anti-Arab racism in the French working class. As a result the Communist Party's attitude to the war was ambiguous and indecisive. Active opposition to the war was above all to be found among people of the non-Communist Left, most of them middle class intellectuals. Prominent among these were Jean Paul Sartre and Simone de Beauvoir and the monthly journal *Les Temps Modernes*. By publicising and denouncing the generalised use of torture and other war crimes and abuses of human rights it could be said that these and others like them did something to save France's honour. But there were some that considered that this was not enough.

Francis Jeanson, a friend of Sartre's and his biographer, had come to the conclusion that, since the French Left was powerless to stop the war, the only logical alternative was to help the Algerians to win it. He was not alone in this. In all it has been estimated that there were over a thousand French people actively helping the cause of Algerian independence, organised in a number of secret underground networks. The network that Jeanson organised and ran for several years was composed of intellectuals, teachers, artists, writers. There were many women among them. Micheline joined some time after leaving Chatenay. Their activity in support of the FLN consisted largely in providing safe accommodation for Algerian members and above all in acting as treasurers. The FLN financed their struggle very largely by taxing Algerian workers in France. Keeping this money and above all transporting it so it could be lodged in a Swiss bank was obviously an operation as delicate and dangerous as it was important to the Algerian cause. This could be, and was, more easily done by non-Algerians.

We only knew of the existence of the Jeanson network and of Micheline's membership of it when it was betrayed to the French authorities. Together with seventy nine other members Micheline was arrested by the police. Jeanson himself managed to escape. At the trial Micheline spoke movingly of the humanist values which had made her proud to be French, and explained why, in her opinion, they could in the present situation only be defended in opposition to the government of France. The trial received a lot of publicity, above all when Jean Paul Sartre himself came and gave evidence declaring that if Jeanson had asked him he would have been glad to carry a suitcase full of money wherever he was told.

At the end of the trial, which was bitter and acrimonious, Micheline and nine others were given the maximum sentence of 10 years. They were incarcerated in the very old-fashioned prison of *La Petite Roquette* on the north side of Paris. Constance used to go and visit Micheline there, taking Paddy aged six with her. On one of these visits Micheline asked Constance to bring her a lot of pairs of nylon stockings the next time she came, which she duly did. Some time later we were amazed to read in the newspaper that Micheline and five other members of the network, all of them women, had escaped from *La Roquette.* Later we learned that they had managed to climb out of a lavatory window and get into the prison yard. Then the FLN had got someone to throw a knotted rope in over the exterior wall of the prison and got them out into the street. An hour or so later they were over the Belgian frontier and safe. They had got down from the lavatory window on a rope made of.... nylon stockings.

Micheline was eventually amnestied. Until that happened and she could return to France, 10 years or more, she worked in a bookshop in Italy I believe. She won't ever have known how much I admired her for what she did. E M Forster said that if he had to choose between betraying his country and betraying his friend he very much hoped that he would betray his country. Things are rarely as simple as that, but I can think of nothing more heroic than to turn one's back, not just upon country or friend, but upon both friends *and* country, as well as family, culture, background and all, simply in the name of a conviction that that is the right thing to do. Examples can be found in recent Irish history. Conor O'Brien and Erskine Childers made a similar, difficult, choice as in fact did my mother when she ferried Countess Markievicz around Dublin during the War of Independence. As did Roger Casement, who paid for it with his life. I am only glad that I never had to face such a choice. I doubt I would have had the courage to choose right.

# 9 Mountains

Hills in the distance have always had a special significance for me. When I was small at Ticknock it was a sign of fine weather when you could see the Mourne mountains clearly, 60 miles beyond the haze over Dublin. Then, on the edge of the Mournes, there was Slieve Gullion from whence, in Standish O'Grady's version of the story, the Enchanter came to cast a spell over the High King of Ireland and his court on Tara hill. I was glad that in my first view of the Alps, when I at last managed to see them from the Vosges, they stood out in a thin lacy line, high above the horizon of haze, like a distant, dangerous, fairyland. It was daybreak, a winter's morning, on the summit of the Hohneck. I had scrambled up the screes in the dark but the sight more than made up for the twisted ankles and scraped knees. The time I had spent reading Coolidge and Whymper and Leslie Stephen meant that I had no difficulty in recognizing the Wetterhorn, the Eiger, and the Jungfrau. The desire to turn this distant vision into an approachable reality, to get in among those jagged skylines was immediate. Only I had no idea how to go about it. It wasn't obvious for a solitary impecunious Irish youth. Of course I could have joined a climbing club; it might have been better if I had. But that sort of solution never occurred to me. As I have said: I am not a joiner. I looked at the mountains and wanted to get into and up them, alone.

In the end I climbed my first 3000 m peak, not alone but with Jacques Souviron and a guide, one year when our families shared a chalet not far from Chamonix. We had scrambled up a number of minor peaks together, some of them involving some easy rock-climbing. The obvious next step was to take a guide and do a real mountain. It was a pleasant introduction to the high places. The guide we were allocated – in France you don't choose, you get the next on the list – was an oldish man, and, as we set off up the approach walk, Jacques remarked to me that his breath smelt strongly of wine. He walked all the same so quickly that we had difficulty keeping up with him. He was a slow spoken

Savoyard, a native of the valley, had been a guide all his life and pointed out landmarks, telling us anecdotes about them with obvious local pride. Next morning, in the dark, he took us up to the *Glacier de Trélatête* and, as dawn came, across the ice, showing us how to negotiate crevasses, up some steep snow and finally along a fairly narrow ridge of broken rocks with a big drop on either side. There we encountered another party whose guide was everything that ours was not: young, handsome, loud-voiced, and clearly very pleased with himself as he joked and jeered at three slightly nervous girls and their father. The summit, a thing called *Le Mont Tondu*, was a not very clearly marked high point on the ridge, but the view looking back at *Le Dôme de Miage* and the S W face of Mont Blanc was almost literally breathtaking. And, unlike other guides I have known, our man didn't try and hurry us down by inventing threatening clouds on the horizon, but let us sit and enjoy the sight for a reasonable time. Then, when we got back down to the hut, he took what was left of the food we had brought, bits of bread, cheese, a few raisins, everything except the chocolate, and crumbled it all into the soup. I did the same on hills for years, as it were in memory of him.

It is a strange profession that of the mountain guide. In France it is organised into something like a trade union. In Chamonix, unless you have a clear mountaineering reason for choosing a particular guide, you must take the next on the list. In Zermatt, in Switzerland, on the other hand the guides seemed to hang around street corners offering their services, rather as though they were asking if you would like to meet their sister. Was it this that gave me the idea that climbing with a guide, paying for companionship on a mountain, is a bit like paying for sex? Perhaps. At any rate it was not something I was able to afford in my early years in the mountains. The few times I did hire a guide, though I learnt a lot about ice and snow and how to abseil, and though I got taken to places I could never have got to alone, I found that having someone to show you the way took away almost all the sense of achievement and with it most of the fun.

I suppose I would have returned to the Alps next year and maybe scrambled up some more challenging peaks than the Tondu. But next year I followed the Souvirons to the Pyrenees and a hotel at the foot of the *Pic du Midi d'Ossau*, a dramatic isolated little Pyrenean Matterhorn. Jacques and I drove into Pau and bought ourselves two pairs of climbing breeches (very French, this) and a rope. Thus appropriately attired and equipped, we climbed *l'Ossau*, the easiest way up which is defended by two moderately tricky chimneys. From the narrow, agreeably vertiginous, top of its *Pointe d'Espagne* I gazed eastwards at a choppy sea of peaks and was filled with a desire to explore their, still slightly mysterious, complexity. Mysterious, because the only maps obtainable then were muddily printed, full of errors, and left the Spanish side of the frontier blank. All this added to the excitement of exploration, and for more than thirty summers, though I did visit other mountain ranges, I returned year after year to the

Pyrenees. I was lucky to have discovered these 'Delectable Mountains' when I did, before tourism had developed, before the, necessary, and desirable, National Park had been formed.

I could have wished at times that the Pyrenees were higher, but apart from that they were a bit like what the Alps were at the beginning of the century, that is to say there weren't many people there. In the Pyrenees I found that whenever you met other climbers you tended to be glad to see them, and sometimes a bit relieved as well. In the Alps already, in my experience, they were either queuing up in front of you or, what was worse, queuing up behind you. Then, like the Alps in the old days, the Pyrenees were a *place*, the people you met there, once you got up to about 1000 m, were all autochthonous, they belonged there. Shepherds, rain-gauge inspectors, smugglers, muleteers, poachers, no one was there to sell you the landscape. And most of the climbers I used to meet, French or Spanish, lived within sight of the mountains I met them on, and knew them intimately, winter and summer. This wasn't the playground of Europe, it was their place, and I liked that and respected them for it.

Then, these were mountains with another side to them. The range stretches from Atlantic to Mediterranean, a high unbroken wall separating two nations, two climates, and, in those days, two cultures and two stages of civilisation. The passes are all called *Port*, *Brèche* or *Pas*, their names all mean "gate" or "breach"; they aren't *cols* or *jochs*, mere dents in the skyline, they are ways through. Some mountaineers are indifferent to this, or think they are. But who has ever breasted a ridge without some feeling of curiosity for what is to be found on the other side? And a dose of disappointment when it is exactly the same as what you have left behind you? I so well remember that feeling, staring down at Courmayeur from the *Col du Géan*t, and discovering that it was the spitting image of Chamonix.

Well, when you climb up out of France at Gavarnie you leave below and behind you a lush humid valley, rich with vegetation and noisy with falling water. Behind you there stretches a fairly thickly populated valley, the vegetation comes fairly high, the sky is busy with clouds, there is an Irish moistness in the air. As you get near the top of the celebrated *Cirque*, an enormous glacier corrie with the highest waterfall in Europe thundering into it, you are on scree and *nevé* (snowfield) but the lumpy mountains to the north might be Wales or the Lake District. The passage to Spain goes through the *Brèche de Roland*, a fantastic doorway broken through a wall of cliffs over 300 feet high. It is on the threshold of this apocalyptic wicket in the mountainside that the contrast hits you. The other side is totally, bewilderingly, different. You look down a valley of the shadow of death, leading to a flat arid plain of snow and stones, with weird *nunataks* of limestone sticking up out of it, desolate as the moon, with, far beyond it, canyons of polychrome cliffs and beyond that the vaporous distances of Spain. The first time I was there two vultures were slowly circling as though

Breche de Roland, Pyrenees

Paddy in the Pyrenees

suspended in the sky. "Beyond the Pyrenees," said Victor Hugo, standing at this place, "Africa begins."

In those days the contrast was even more marked than it is now. Leaving France you left behind tarred roads and 220 volt electrification. In the Spanish village of Sallent the light was from candles, there were no shops and the man who sold us wine had to put it in a goatskin bag since he had no bottles. On a patch of ground by the village we watched a group of men threshing with flails. And very much in evidence were Franco's *Guardia Civil*, in their old-fashioned uniforms looking as though they had typewriters on their heads. They were not very friendly, particularly if you met them anywhere near the frontier. And, as the French ordnance survey maps left the Spanish side blank, and Spanish maps were non-existent, it wasn't always easy to know which side of the frontier you were on, and you could be shot at if you weren't careful. All that has gone, and none of it is to be regretted.

Over the years I ended up by climbing almost all of the major peaks and many of the minor ones, some of them several times, with different companions, or alone. The first time that I took Paddy we climbed the *Pic du Midi d'Ossau*, my third ascent, *Pallas* and *la Grande Fache*, two big granite peaks and, above the *Cirque de Gavarnie*, the *Casque de Marboré* where we scrambled up a vertical cave, potholing in reverse as it were, to emerge from the iced tunnel in the middle of a snow field. It was all a somewhat hairy excursion for a little boy of eleven, especially our attempt on Pallas where I picked the wrong couloir and we ended up on an alarming razor edge ridge with no feasible way forward, but it was a good start. As years went by and we both grew older our roles were gradually reversed and in the end it was he that led me up the North faces of *l'Astazou* and the *Pic du Midi d' Ossau* and over the *Flammes de Pierre* on the *Petit Pic* as well as up some big Alpine peaks.

In the course of all this I had various minor adventures. Something rarely encountered on Irish hills, frequent in the Pyrenees, were the thunderstorms. Spectacular when seen from the valley they produced various strange effects on the heights, and could be quite alarming even when several miles away. Metal objects would start emitting a sinister buzzing sound and you could feel a strange sort of tension in the air as the static charge increased until the lightning struck. It happened once when I was on a peak near Gavarnie with my niece, Una's daughter Sarah, who had longish blonde hair. The tension built up as we were hurrying off the crest of the mountain. I looked round at Sarah and her hair was standing out like a sort of golden halo, looking for all the world like a painting by William Blake.

One strange thing occurred when I was alone for several days. I had set out to climb the *Mont Perdu*. Not without some difficulty I had picked my way up the East Wall of the *Cirque de Gavarnie*, and over into the hanging valley on the other side. It was a beautiful desolate place, the *Vallon Glacé,* with a frozen lake in the middle, a jagged row of peaks down one side and the North face of the *Mont Perdu* on the other. In a gap between two of the jagged peaks was the *Refuge de Tuquerouye*, a tiny climbing hut perched in a dramatic situation at the top of a steep couloir of ice on each side. That was where I had decided to stay for two or three days. The hut was a bit dilapidated but its roof was still sound and it hadn't been used as a lavatory. Next day I made an unsuccessful attempt to get up the *Mont Perdu*; it was late in the season and I couldn't get across the *rimaye*, the gap between ice and rock face. So I spent the two days exploring the valley and climbing the peaks on each side of the hut. It was a beautiful but very lonely place to be. Even from the summits I couldn't see any artefact or other sign that humanity existed. Very different from Chamonix where all day and all night you'll hear motor horns and trains.

The strange thing that occurred was this: as I was cooking my supper on the second evening I kept hearing voices. One way to the hut was up the ice couloir, so I assumed it was coming from there. So I went and shouted a greeting down and then went and tidied my things to make room for the newcomers to sleep. No one came and eventually it got too dark and I think I stopped noticing any sound. The next evening the same thing happened. This time it seemed I could definitely hear what they were saying. They sounded quite different from the wind, which I could also hear in the crags above the hut. There was nothing scary or spooky about all this, what I seemed to be hearing, and hearing quite clearly, were the jokey remarks that climbers make to each other as they make

Refuge de Tuquerouye

their way up a difficult pitch. Again I went repeatedly and looked and called down and this time it seemed I heard someone replying. Because the top of the couloir was icy I even offered a top rope, because it sounded as though they were in difficulty. But again there was nobody. I cooked my food and went to bed. On the next day I had no food left so I waited till the afternoon when the snow in the couloir was soft and went down and scrambled back to Gavarnie and my car.

Next day I called on Léon Gassan. He was a delightful retired philosophy professor in his 80s that I had got to know through Marie Souviron and whose wry, pithy, comments on current affairs, on politics, on his neighbours and on life in general, uttered in a sort of cavernous whisper, were always worth hearing. I first heard of him when I was with the Souvirons in a refuge hut above Cauterets. It was raining so we were leafing through the log book of the hut which contained terse factual descriptions of routes climbed, interspersed, and it seemed to us disfigured, by the usual idiotic facetious remarks. Suddenly we came on two lines in black ink, of precise, squiggly, handwriting, where we read: *On dit que l'altitude stimule l'intelligence. En lisant ce livre je suis navré à la pensée de ce que doit être l'intelligence de certains au niveau de la mer.* (They say that altitude makes you more intelligent. Reading this book I am appalled at the thought of what some people's intelligence must be at sea level). "That," said Marie, "Can only be Léon Gassan." So we went to see him in his lovely old house smelling of apples in the valley above Lourdes, and in the course of conversation he described mountaineering as *le ciel visitable* (a way of visiting the sky), a description that I have always liked.

When I told old Gassan about Tuquerouye – he knew the *Vallon Glacé* and the little hut – I thought he was going to tell me that I had been taking myself for Joan of Arc, hearing voices. But he laughed and said, "*Ah oui. C'est normal. L'homme n'arrive pas à penser qu'il est seul dans l'univers. Et pourtant c'est vrai.*" (Man is incapable of thinking that he is alone in the universe. But he is.)

I had started climbing high mountains in my thirties, round about the age that ace climbers give it up. I often wished I had started ten years earlier at least, when I thought nothing of cycling from Galway to Dublin in a day. I could have used the legs I had then and that reserve of stamina in the hills. On the other hand there were advantages in starting late, as I discovered talking to my cousin Owen Clarke, Nancy's son, when he came to see us in Paris. He had done really hard alpine routes and had led at Very Severe standard but was now giving it up because he could no longer make any progress, doing harder and harder things. Since I could never have done those routes anyway 35 was quite a good age to start on more modest adventures. Listening to him talk fired me with a desire to know some big mountains before it was too late. And when he told me that anyone who could climb Grade 3 could get up the Matterhorn I knew straightaway what I wanted above all else to do, to have done.

I spent 10 days in Zermatt in the very *sympathique* Bahnhof Hotel whose proprietor or manager - I never knew which – Bernard Biner had been a leading Zermatt guide. A marvellous raconteur, impressively fluent in all the languages of Switzerland as well as English, and a most likeable man, he gave plentiful and very useful advice about all the Zermatt peaks. I asked him to recommend a guide for the Matterhorn and foolishly stipulated that I absolutely must have someone who spoke French. The reason was that, some years before, I had wasted a week trying to learn to ski in Austria where the instructors spoke only German. It never occurred to me that all the Zermatt guides spoke English as well as their native German and my insistence on a French speaker limited the choice so that I got taken up the mountain by a pleasant enough, but very *sportif*, young chap called Norman something, with whom I had almost nothing in common, when I would have much preferred an older man with a wider range of interests and knowledge.

He was certainly an impressively agile climber, Norman, though. Guides won't take you up the Matterhorn until they are sure you can cope with the exposure. So we took the rack railway up to the Riffelalp and scrambled up the Riffelhorn, a modest rock peak overlooking the Gorner glacier. It wasn't very difficult but I was amazed at the speed and ease with which Norman moved over the rock, reminding me of Lionel Terray's description, in *Les Conquérants de l'Inutile,* of Lachenal climbing: *des prises naissent sous ses doigts* (handholds seem to materialise beneath his fingers). At the top the view on all sides was stupendous, with Monte Rosa, Castor and Pollux and the Breithorn, all snow and ice, looking down on us to the South, the Matterhorn across the valley and the beautiful pyramid of the Weisshorn to the West. It all made the little peak we were standing on seem insignificant. It seemed less insignificant when Norman pointed over the edge and said, "Now we go down here." Climbing down is harder than climbing up but, though it was nearly vertical, there were plenty of footholds and things to hold on to, so I was surprised, when I looked at the map back in Paris, to discover that I had had the height of the Eiffel Tower between my boot-soles and the glacier down below. At the time the whole experience was so exhilarating that I hardly gave it a thought. As I wrote later in a poem: "The build-up is too gigantic to care if it kills you or not." When I got near the end of the rope I stopped on a small ledge and Norman came scampering down like a man running down a staircase. We climbed horizontally along for 50m or so and then back up to the top and Norman told me what I already knew: that the Matterhorn would not be a problem. However, I had to wait. By the end of my ten days, though I got up a number of lesser mountains on my own, the weather still had not cleared and the high peaks were all white with ice and snow, so I returned to Paris very disappointed.

A year later, in September, a few days before term started, we had a week of very hot clear weather. At six o'clock on a Monday evening it occurred to me that I would just have time to do it before work started. An hour or two later I was in the sleeper and next morning I was in Zermatt, looking up at a dark Matterhorn, almost completely free of snow. I contacted Norman and arranged to meet him in the Hörnli hut. Next day I walked up there. Usually people take the cable car but I thought it might help to acclimatise. It probably did, but not at all enough. It was a long walk, gaining nearly 5000 ft in altitude, but a good path with an easy gradient. After you pass the upper station of the cable car the path zigzags up onto the Hörnli ridge and you're looking down onto the glaciers on both sides. Then I was in the shadow of the Matterhorn, like a great black finger across the sunny slopes of the valley. I began to feel the cold and the altitude. The mountain looks terribly steep when you are just under it, or else it seems to be falling away backwards; the foreshortening does strange things to the height; it doesn't look high at all and it is hard to realise that there is more than twice the height of Donegal Errigal in the distance from the hut to the top.

The Hörnli hut is a palatial affair for all that it is at 3200m, a three-storey building made of wood and stone with kitchens and dormitories and all. I met Norman who was there before me. He had already done the mountain the day before. The sunset was a marvellous sight to see, it always is from these high huts, probably because it is so unusual to be safe and relaxed at that altitude and at that time of day. When the sun had gone down it became dark almost immedi-

[FOLLOWING PAGE]
Fixed rope on the Matterhorn

ately and the stars were of an extraordinary brightness and I looked across the glaciers to Monte Rosa and the Breithorn and other mountains all glimmering strangely in the starlight.

We were up at four thirty and off before five. Breakfast was a summary affair. It was pitch dark outside so we put the rope on when still inside the hut. There was one other pair ahead of us and two climbers off to do the mountain by the Zmutt ridge which is very much more difficult than the Normal route we were taking. Behind the hut a path led up onto the ridge, and then down and across some snow on a little saddle, and ended at a bluff of cliff about five hundred feet high. From then on there was no path, no place where our foot didn't have to be set down a fair distance above the last step. We scrambled up the first few slabs of the cliff, then round and off the ridge and onto the east face of the mountain, the left-hand side in the standard Christmas card photo. Most of the way went up this face, zigzagging here and there, clambering over masses of boulders at first, now and then climbing a nearly vertical outcrop of a few metres. It wasn't very steep, about the same angle as the sea face on Slieve League. From time to time the route we took brought to us out onto the ridge itself and there I could feel the height more. But it was still dark; there was only the greyish light of before dawn and I had difficulty in seeing where I was putting my feet. I didn't feel very bright or steady at all; I had a slightly sick feeling and a headache. When we stopped at last for a break I had a brief chance of looking out to the East. I wish I had had more time to look for it was extraordinarily beautiful. The valley below was quite black except for the lights of Zermatt almost underfoot. Then the outline of Monte Rosa was dark with, above it, a line of intense deep colour. Every time I looked round the colour had changed a little. It was like the colours on steel being tempered, straw yellow tingeing into deep deep blue. There wasn't any sound anywhere.

Just when the light was breaking and the tip of the Matterhorn above us was tinged with pink from the rising sun we moved off the face, which had become vertical, and started to climb up the ridge, and I looked down on to the Matterhorn Glacier below the North Face. This side of the mountain is practically sheer from the shoulder down, a monstrous precipice over a mile high. Because it was the end of summer the glaciers had hardly any snow on them and they were all a greeny blue colour and the crevasses were wide open. You could see down into deepening blue in the widest ones, even though they were so far below. The ridge was now a proper one man's pass with great towers, "*gendarmes*", on it and sometimes we climbed round the edges of these on narrow ledges and once we went over the top of one. Then we went out on to the east face again and there were the first few rope lengths of really vertical climbing where we had to go one at a time and there were a few passages that seemed to me quite difficult, though nothing as awkward as the hard way up the big rock on Three Rock Mountain at home. After three rope lengths of this we came to the Solvay Hut.

This is a tiny wooden box perched between two cliffs, right on the ridge which is supposed to be used only in case of accident or bad weather. Four bunks, a table, tins of paraffin, a stretcher and a smell. Behind it with typical Swiss meticulousness a little lavatory. This was at 4000 m, higher than I had ever been. I felt awful, my head was aching, I felt sick and shaky and terribly worried that I wouldn't be able to get to the top. We had done 800 m in an hour and three quarters, which is fast going. It would have been better for me if we had gone much more slowly.

After the Solvay Hut the mountain gets much steeper and the rock changes. Now it was all a sort of slatey stuff with a smooth surface and the shape of the mountain was different, for the ridge we were following tilted upwards and after a while we were going up a very steep edge indeed and of smooth unbroken rock. This is where they have fixed ropes and chains, and you can easily see why, for even then, in September, at the end of a hot summer, there were patches of ice. We were coming to the Shoulder, the foot of the great triangular block at the top of the Matterhorn, and there was a tricky place with a thick fixed rope on it where the route goes out onto the North Face and turns up to the left towards the summit. From now on the climb should have been at its most exciting. Straight under us the North Face sloped down and then fell sheer for a mile onto the Matterhorngletscher, and to one side we looked back down onto the knife of the long ridge we had followed all the way up. It should have been exciting, I say, but I was feeling worse and worse, like a sick man climbing in a nightmare, like the worst hangover you could imagine. I just slogged on, my legs were working all right but I had no enthusiasm at all, and I fumbled with the rope and let Norman do all the thinking as I concentrated all my efforts on just pushing myself forward. It seemed very long, this last part, and the top of the mountain seemed to get further and further away so I stopped looking up.There were some hard bits here that would have been fun to climb if I had felt myself. There were few actually vertical passages but a lot of places where you climbed out and up a very sharply tilted spine of rock with the view on both sides and down as an encouragement to keep going. This was the place where the famous accident occurred on the first ascent, because there were iron bars here and there , with ropes or bits of chain, but I hardly needed them, even in my distress, and often didn't touch them. After this the slope eased a bit and we started just plodding up some very steep scree. The summit seemed infinitely far away and I started counting steps and said to myself: I won't look up until I have counted 300. Then, when I had counted 80, there suddenly wasn't any ground above me.

The top of the Matterhorn is the most exciting place I have ever been, a sort of chisel point so narrow you can't sit down anywhere, a line of snow and ice and rocks shattered by lightning, a gappy razor edge between the two crosses marking the Swiss and Italian summits, with abysses falling away on every side. The view is vertical and enormous; Mont Blanc stands out, seeming only half a mile away, with, near it, the Grand Combin and the Gran Paradiso. The sky is a deep cosmic blue and the air a thin diluted gassiness that only half fills your lungs so you breathe like a puppy, and there is the marvellous feeling of having overcome the difficulties and whittled away a mass of mountain two miles high until it is reduced to a point the width of a man's foot... well I didn't feel any of all that at the time; I just leaned over the lacy edge of ice and threw up into Italy. I do remember it now, though.

It was my misfortune, and my fault, to have got mountain sickness as a result of attacking the mountain without sufficient acclimatisation. Scrambling down wasn't much fun, but once we had got past the Solvay hut I began to feel better. The weakness and nausea had gone by the time we reached the Hörnli hut and, in high spirits, I practically ran down the path to Zermatt.

On reflection, though I learnt a lot from it and gained some valuable experience, (and was not above boasting on occasion about having climbed the Matterhorn), I could not in my secret self feel that it was a particularly glorious enterprise. I have felt prouder of having got guideless to the top, or near the top, of other far less prestigious mountains. The ice coated summit ridge of *La Barre des Écrins*, or the final couloir on the *Petit Pic d'Ossau*, these called for more commitment and for more nerve than anything on the Matterhorn; I was even more pleased with myself the day when, in my sixties and feeling in cracking form, the weather fine and the ground frozen hard, I raced to the top of Ben Hope by the North Ridge and got back to the car all in well under three hours. As I have written elsewhere, the great thing about mountaineering is that you are competing only with yourself. No one else knows how much the peak cost you, or if it cost you anything at all. And the achievement, the *dépassement de soi* thing, is only part of the point of doing it anyway.

## PYRENEES

Pastures to pines to alpine roses to scree to snowfield to rock;
Horizons recede, your eyes fill up with sky,
Step by step, level by level the earth falls away,
The foothills that loomed last night have been trampled into the haze.

Escape to simplicity: nothing is less like ordinary living,
There are only extremes up here, in the brilliant wilderness;
Food and water and warmth are desired with Neanderthal passion;
The achievement is merely will-power, the choices are always clear.
The route turns into a route, then peters out.

The perils are huge and serene: stones clatter to the abyss,
The mist prowls below, the way is a maze of brinks,
Yet the danger is somehow dwarfed by its own paraphernalia;
The build-up is too gigantic to care if it kills you or not.

And when you have thrust the world down into the tawny shade,
Gouged out the couloir, tapered the shoulder off,
Shaping and making the mountain, whittling it out to a point,
That's all the point there is, a spike driven into the sky.

The sky is all around you and above you and beneath,
Familiar accessible sky, visitable heaven,
Earth falls to a formless muddle of slopes and plain,
The best of the view is the bit you are standing upon.
Like Balmat, first up Mont Blanc, you can say if you like,
I am the statue this pedestal was awaiting,
*Je suis la statue qu'attendait ce piédestal.*

But the world soon follows you up, homo can be tristis here too;
It is later than you thought, your breath returns with the cold,
It's on the way down that accidents usually happen;
Mediocrity rises as evening comes up to meet you.

This patient passion and triumph then are futile,
A muddle of means and ends, but so for that matter is love.
Where better send this poem, then, but to you,
With whom I've come slowly back from high places,
At peace with the bothering world, and, yes, on the whole,
Glad to be in it again?

# Olivia IO

A JOB THAT LECTURERS at the British Institute had to do twice a year was to supervise the examinations for the Cambridge Certificate of Proficiency in English. It was a pleasant enough chore, and was quite well paid. This being France you had to go round the room checking the identity of all the candidates to make sure that none had persuaded, or bribed, their clever cousin or sister to sit the exam in their place. I was pleasantly surprised, on turning up one day in 1958, at the lecture room that had been hired for the purpose from the Sorbonne, to find that my colleague for the day was a new arrival at the Institute, an electrically attractive young woman called Olivia McMahon. I knew that Mark Mortimer had recruited her when she had come to his lectures on Joyce, that she was of Irish extraction, but I don't think I had ever spoken to her. It was easy to make up for this once the exam had started, seated as we were on this huge dais looking down on a mass of bent-backed students all scribbling away. She had an English accent that sounded, to me, melodiously fetching. I learned, however, that, in spite of this she had more autochthonous Irish antecedents than I had, her parents both coming from families of small farmers in County Clare. When the morning session was over she announced that she had been invited to lunch by *des gens* in Montparnasse, three kilometres away. I saw straightaway that this was almost certainly going to make her late for the afternoon exam and consequently land me with the job of dishing out sheets of paper single-handed, so I persuaded her to have lunch with me instead. I can have had little idea then of the changes in my life that all this would bring about.

I had had very little truck with glamorously attractive women until then, viewing them from afar as alien beings that could only be communicated with by means of a language that I did not speak. And my relationships with women, apart from my deep friendship with Constance, though not perfunctory, had been brief, and unsatisfactory if only because so short-lived. But now one of the most enchanting women I had ever seen was not only marvellously easy to communicate with, and interested in the things I felt like talking about, but obviously, and this I found hard to believe, seemed also to be attracted by me. Of course the age difference between us counted for more when she was in her mid twenties. Had I realised that in some years' time I would regard her as an intellectual equal, and superior in some fields, I would probably have been too intimidated to say anything at all. As it was she was marvellously entertaining company, quick-witted, perceptive and funny, as when, for example, she would imitate some of the more eccentric of our colleagues.

In the weeks that followed we saw more and more of each other. It was not difficult since we were working in the same place. We both chanced to be allocated literary seminars, studying the same text which was E. M. Forster's *The Longest Journey*. Within and around the framework of discussing Forster's novel I learnt more about Olivia, learnt that she was Catholic, had been brought up in a very devoutly Irish Catholic background in the North of England, that her brother was even then training to be a priest in Paris. All this could have held us apart had it not been that she had suffered a recent tragedy. She had been engaged to be married to a young French officer who had been killed in Algeria. Her fiancé, Jean Bayet, a nephew of Professor Albert Bayet, a leading figure in the defence of secular education, had been at the start of a distinguished military career when he was killed in action at Sakhiet. We had thus, both of us, been forced abruptly to come to terms with the terrifying banality of death. The consequent questioning of all previous assumptions, which we both were going through in our very different ways, brought us together, just as it underlined the troubling, fascinating, differences between our worlds: Protestant middle-class Dublin on my side, Catholic Lancashire and Clare-Galway on hers.

Within a very few months I knew that I was, and for the first time in my life, wholeheartedly, obsessively, incredibly, in love and, most incredible of all, the infatuation seemed to be mutual since, such was my good luck, it appeared that Olivia had never happened to meet anyone quite like me. *Les amoureux sont seuls au monde* (lovers are alone in the world) went a French song of the period, and for a few delirious months, and for both of us, the rest of the world sank into a background of photograph grey. The greed for each other, which we indulged on every possible occasion, and often in the most grotesquely, ridiculously, comically, unsuitable places, seemed insatiable. Whatever the cost, I said, we said, "all the dreaded cards foretell..." I, we, absolutely must have this. So we had it. We didn't foresee that the passion would become an addiction, that it would go on and on, and that it would change everything in both our lives. Nor did we foresee what the cost would be, something that weighs heavily on my conscience even now. But it couldn't have been otherwise.

Years later, in a letter, I wrote a poem describing Olivia.

LOVE POEM

I love you because I love you, because
I love *you*.

Preposterously concerned and unconcerned.

Vain as the Pompadour in the most unpompadourish places,
(kneeling in jeans in the flapping tent, titivating your eyes).

You slept six years in a bed without turning the mattress.
How is it you're always clean and never seem
to be washing or scrubbing or fussing about the laundry?

Casual, deft and abrupt, you move through the mess you make
like a train gliding straight over a scribble of rails,
your sleeve never catches, you never knock anything over.

Free as the mountain waterfalls: no point in trying
to argue them back up, or point out a better way down.

Prone to inordinate scunners;
a sucker for praise, but tearing the snapshots up;
unphotographeable, like waterfalls, flames or the sea.

I caught you,
in a half-made dress with your mouth full of pins,
arched in a strutting curve between two mirrors,
and you moved from yes to yes, from now to now. .

and your hands, cleaning the sparking plugs of your car

Olivia in the Tarn Gorge

At the start the apparent total impossibility of any future to our relationship, which made it all the more poignant, also made it excusable, in our eyes at least. Meanwhile we were both concerned to conceal it from our colleagues in the Institute. Clandestineness added an obvious spice, with the inevitable narrow escapes. For example we used to go and have lunch outside Paris, in a small village called Chateaufort, preparatory to making love in the woods Racine used to walk through on his way to school at Port Royal. Once, after this, Olivia had to get the train in to Paris to take an evening class. We drove to Massy and I asked the way to the station of two women. They said they were going there themselves, so I offered them a lift and they talked energetically to us and to each other all the way there. Next day one of the secretaries at the Institute told me, with a hint of you-can't-hide-anything-from-me in her voice, that she had espied me in Massy. On hearing this my heart sank. And then she said, *"Oui, vous étiez dans votre voiture, avec toute la famille* (You were in your car with all your family). Those chatterbox women had unknowingly provided us with a cover.

On the other hand our affair was no secret from Constance. I couldn't have concealed it, even if I had wanted to. Though, like most men I suspect, in matters of sexual morality I have found it hard to be honest with myself, I have a strong principle, a remainder of Protestantism, against telling lies. I certainly did not "deceive" Constance, nor was I "cheating" on her, to employ the conventional clichés. We had both, before our marriage, read and discussed our Simone de Beauvoir and agreed that absolute fidelity was a bourgeois convention and that there had to be room in a marriage for *des amours contingentes*. In fact, looking back, I can see that, selfishly, thoughtlessly, I used to tell Constance much more about Olivia than she wanted to know. Though it was not easy, and was in the end very painful for her, she realised that I was living through an entirely new and intoxicating experience. Her self-possession and her very strong character enabled her to view the situation philosophically. Men, it is often said, are like little boys. They start by finding a mother figure, stay with her till they have grown up and then go after a much younger daughter figure. That, I think, was how Constance saw things. And there was some truth in it, at least at the start. Also, though extremely sensitive and warm-hearted, she had a way of distancing herself from events that touched her personally. In this her character and her attitudes owed much to the loneliness and the unhappiness of her childhood, and to her relationship with her father whom she certainly loved but whom she also found it difficult to respect.

Like me, like Olivia, Constance took refuge from the possible implications of Olivia's and my passion for each other in the seeming impossibility of there being any future for it. Any end to our marriage seemed unthinkable, given my deep affection for her, which was never in question any more than what I felt for Paddy and, later, for Doreen. In any case, since divorce was legally impossible in Ireland, an Irish person could not divorce in France. For her part Olivia never imagined that our relationship presented a danger to my marriage with Constance. To begin with it was out of the question that she should ever marry a divorced man, for this, she felt, would break her parents' hearts. But also, stability, settling down, the conventional 'suburban' preoccupations of most young women in those days, were very low on her list of priorities, if they figured at all. What she wanted above all to do was to write. But then for that matter so did I. We would sit in cafés discussing our different attitudes to our somewhat similar inability to actually do it.

For several years we all went on living happily enough. The fact of being colleagues as well as lovers gave to Olivia's and my relationship a substance without which it might not have survived, had it been nourished solely on romantic self-indulgence. We had prescribed texts, grammar problems, teaching strategies to discuss, as well as having other colleagues, interesting or eccentric, to gossip entertainingly about. The life I shared with Olivia was therefore distinct and separate from Chatenay and from Constance and the children. I managed all the same to spend a lot of time with them, and enjoyed it. Constance and I would eat out most weeks in a favourite Italian restaurant in the Latin Quarter. My time was divided between picnicking and rock-climbing with the children in Fontainebleau on Thursdays, lunching in Chateaufort, and of course teaching in two different institutions at opposite ends of Paris. And Constance had a life of her own too. Around this time she became friendly with an influential, though very elderly, French political personality called Charles-André Jullien. I only met him once. She gave him English lessons – he called her *ma maîtresse* anglaise (my English mistress) - and he got her the job of translating into English a book that was very important at the time: Franz Fanon's *Les Damnés de la Terre,* with Introduction by Sartre. Her translation, taken over by Penguin, had a world-wide circulation but she never made much from it, as she had failed to sign a regular contract with the first publisher.

Olivia was a much more interactive teacher than I was and, as a result, much better and more successful at teaching spoken English. The trouble about teaching spoken language, however, is that people tend to regard what you are doing as "just" conversation and consequently something that "anyone could do". One way of resisting this tendency to underrate what can be, should be, a highly skilled activity is to incorporate in one's teaching a knowledge of Phonetics, something the uninformed regard with respect, since their ignorance of it makes it into a mystery. Was this the reason that Olivia was drawn to what is in fact a science, or did I suggest it? I don't remember. We both got interested in Phonetics at about the same time. It happened that one of the best language teachers at the Institute, if not the best, was a woman called Madge Truffert (she was married to a Frenchman). Madge had followed a course in Phonetics at London University and she ran classes in English pronunciation. She actually had a marked Yorkshire accent herself but she used her knowledge, and a genuine enthusiasm for Phonetics, together with various ingenious procedures she had devised herself, to train people who had a special difficulty with certain English sounds to articulate them correctly. It seemed an obvious thing to take advantage of this expertise *sur place*. So Olivia started attending Madge's classes and I followed her.

From the start I found Phonetics a very satisfying sort of knowledge to acquire, though I was never as good at it or knew as much about it as Olivia. Spend two hours translating a paragraph by Proust with a group and at the end, though you can be sure you have all spent the time in a highly civilised manner, it would be hard to say for sure exactly what, if anything, anyone has actually learnt. When teaching literature or doing literary translations you are dealing all the time in imponderables. Whereas, and most unusually as regards anything to do with language, applying this new expertise was as positive an act as a dentist crowning a tooth. Armed with a handful of knacks, you could take someone who was physically incapable of articulating the vowel in a French word like *dure* or an English R sound and send them away after a few sessions, pronouncing the sound like a native, and marvelling at their own new-found skill. In addition a knowledge and understanding of the way in which the nuts and bolts of language functioned and interacted made it possible to attach a precise meaning to impressionistic expressions like *accent, brogue, dialect, tone of voice* and so on, and to understand exactly what it was that differentiated people when they spoke.

Through the very superficial knowledge of Phonetics that I acquired, and my experience with Language Laboratories, I became increasingly aware of the existence of Linguistics as a body of scientific knowledge about which I knew hardly anything. Though the audio-lingual theory on which Language Laboratory methods were based has been almost completely discredited, it had all the same a claim to be scientific. The view of language held by almost all my colleagues at the Institute, both French and British, was in contrast essentially literary, subjective and anecdotal. My growing dissatisfaction with this amateurish attitude became part of a general dissatisfaction with my situation as a teacher, and as an expatriate. Though I was teaching language I was increasingly conscious of my lack of any genuine expertise. And then my uneasiness at being an expatriate, living in France but not really belonging there, which I have already mentioned, was finally getting me down.

It was possibly an Irish thing, this uneasiness, as well as being personal to me. I had met other Irish people in France who felt something similar, as it were a sort of guilt complex. There was a man that I used to meet at the St Patrick's Day party at the Irish Embassy who would say, year after year, "Well I'm definitely going back next year." And year after year he would be there again. I never met an English expatriate that felt this. So was it Ireland home and mother that we were fleeing from? I don't know. In his case it was likely to be mother church. Regarding myself, I simply don't understand the reluctance I felt in those days to face the idea of returning to my own country. It certainly wasn't just a question of money, though it is true that with my two jobs I was earning very much more than I ever could have been paid in any conceivable employment at home. I think that part of it was possibly a matter of identity: for some reason I felt, quite wrongly, out of place in Ireland. But if I didn't go back to Ireland where could I go, where would I want to go? Deeply dissatisfied with the life I was leading I balked at envisaging any alternative to it. The *angoisse* got worse every year.

In a way my starting a love affair with Olivia could be seen as a sort of displacement behaviour, or like a drug that enabled me to forget or to escape from the main problem that preoccupied me already. It certainly worked in that way for a time, but then, inevitably perhaps, we just grew too attached to each other, and what had been an escape from the impasse that I felt myself in turned into another, similar but more painful impasse, and soon both problems merged into one. At the same time my dissatisfaction with the work I was doing at the

Institute grew. I wouldn't have felt this so clearly had not Henry Quick, one of the senior tutors there who I liked and admired a lot, said it to me bluntly. "Get out now," he said, "You have a fine mind; here you are stagnating in mediocrity." (He himself bitterly regretted having returned to Paris after the War). Things weren't much better at *Saint Cloud.* Though the *École* was still pleased with my work, it remained that I could only have a yearly contract there, so the salary remained stationary, whereas the French colleagues I had there, one or two of whom had actually been my students in my first year, saw their pay and their grading improve every year. As regards the money this didn't really matter, the École found a way of paying me very generously for the extra hours I did, "Out of the roofing budget," M. Canac jokingly told me. But there was no solution for the annual loss of status. It was clear that I couldn't stay there indefinitely; I would have to move, but where to and how I could not see. Or I couldn't face the decisions that any change called for.

After a year or so the happy delirium of my relationship with Olivia came to be increasingly overshadowed by the seeming impossibility of any future to it. This mattered above all to Olivia who grew increasingly conscious of the contradictory nature of the situation she found herself in. While she could not help resenting the marginal role she was playing in my life she found that she could not bring herself to consider any of the conceivable alternatives. So, more than once, we agreed to separate. One occasion in particular I remember. We used to walk in the evenings in the forest of Fontainebleau in those days, before going back to eat in Olivia's little flat. This time we walked for ages in the *Gorges de Franchard*, first talking about the situation we had got ourselves into and then, tearful and speechless, at what seemed the only possible way out. It was raining, the end of a beautiful autumn day, and the dripping, blazing red trees seemed like a mirror of the vertiginous doom of separation that faced us. "Right," I said. "We'll go back and have onion soup and I'll walk out of your life." But of course, though we tried, it wasn't possible to ignore each other, working as we were in the same place and meeting every day. After a miserable week or so we were back together again. Another time we tried living together through a long vacation. I was ostensibly working at a book of exercises so we rented a flat in a small provincial town called Figeac and tried to set up house together. But then almost immediately everything went dead, our desire and our affection for each other, even our appetite for food. After ten days Olivia went back to Paris and I drove on South to the Pyrenees. A month or so later we were back in Paris and it had all started again.

Ashamed as I was of my indecision, I didn't feel that I could confide in anyone. And, because my relationship with Olivia was central to my dilemma, the old guilt regarding anything to do with sex made me even more inhibited. I became increasingly self-conscious and hypersensitive, and fearful of the censure of friends. Rightly in fact, since the one or two Irish or British friends

I did manage to talk to were maximally unhelpful. And then one day, after a dreadful clash with Jacques and Marie Souviron in Orléans I broke down and told them tearfully why I had become so prickly and disagreeable, told them about Olivia and how I was, and for the first time in my life, passionately in love. I expected them to come up with a mixture of sympathy and disapproval, but Marie just sat thinking for a while and then she said, *"Évidemment, il n'y a rien que tu puisses faire."* (Obviously, there's nothing you can do about it.) It was as though I had announced that I was suffering from an incurable illness. I was strangely reminded of Peter Allt explaining Racine to us, saying how, when Nero announces that he is in love, the passion is absolute and that it would be as unracinian for someone to tell him to just pull himself together as it would be for him to exit pursued by a bear. Thank God for France, I thought.

"*Even the wisest man grows tense / With some sort of violence, / Before he can accomplish Fate, / Know his work or choose his mate,*" wrote Yeats in one of his last poems. In the end, if I eventually managed to uproot myself, and the roots were many and painful to tear out, it was first of all because Olivia acted decisively. In September 1963 she left the Institute, left Paris and registered for a course in Teaching English Overseas (TEO), at Manchester University. After a few months she found the theoretical side of the course so interesting that she decided to put herself down for an MA in General Linguistics in the following year. She wrote to me describing her discovery of the world of Linguistic Science and the new ideas about language that she was encountering, and comparing all this with Paris and the British Institute. "How long are you going to stay there," she asked in a letter, "Among all that dead wood?" I realised that if I didn't break loose from the paralysis of indecision that beset me I would forfeit her esteem, and that this was more than I could bear. I handed in my notice at the Institute and at Saint Cloud. Circumstances helped a bit. My one-time colleague Peter Wexler had come on a visit to Paris earlier in the year. He was now a Senior Lecturer at Manchester University and he had told me about the Course in General Linguistics that had recently been started there. This was obviously the course that Olivia was intending to follow. So I wrote to Professor Haas to apply for a place on it and was accepted.

Only then did the problem occur to me of how all this change and upset in our lives could be financed. I had been so concerned by the emotional implications of leaving France, of leaving Constance and leaving the children, that I had given hardly any thought as to what we were all going to do for money. Then, by a stroke of luck, I heard that at the British Institute they were desperately looking for someone to handle a correspondence course in commercial English. It was work that few were qualified to take on, and that no one wanted to do. The years that I had spent teaching the unappetising jargon of British business suddenly paid off, and I managed to persuade the Institute to let me run the course from a bed-sit in Manchester. It involved quite a lot of work. Once I got established there this voluminous parcel, full of translation exercises teaching the English for things like *bon de commande* and *dommages et intérêt,* would arrive every Friday, so that, after a week passed trying to make sense of Generative Grammar, I would spend all of Saturday and Sunday going through the painstaking efforts of hard-working Parisian secretaries, underlining and correcting their mistakes. This monumentally boring labour was, however, reasonably well remunerated and the francs it brought in, like the sale of the car and various other bits and pieces, supplemented our much reduced French income. Things were easier when Constance got a job in the *Musée Pédagogique.* Looking back, though, I find it hard to work out quite how we managed. If we did it was in no small measure thanks to Constance, her generous heart. I am glad to think that through all those difficult years and our separation and divorce we never once had an argument about money.

# Manchester II

SUPPORTING MYSELF in Manchester was less difficult than maintaining the family in Chatenay. With Olivia's help I managed, almost immediately, to get some hours teaching English Composition to "Mature Clerical Officers" – who, I was surprised to learn, were native speakers of English - in evening classes in a College of Further Education. This brought in just enough money for me to live on. Looking back I wonder what on earth they can have made of me, the Mature Clerical Officers, for I was such a fish out of water in Manchester. Apart from the shortest way from Holyhead to Dover I knew hardly anything about England, and what I knew, which was mostly limited to unfriendly Bed and Breakfasts in places like Folkestone, I didn't much like. The North of England, which seemed to be peopled by motherly women with Lancashire accents who called me Luv, and folk like the Clerical Officers, was certainly much nicer, but it was all very strange. Fortunately there were all the Irish immigrants, so that if you got on a bus and were able to recognize the conductor's accent and ask him how things were in West Cork or Galway there was a good chance you wouldn't have to pay the fare. Not that I could afford to take the bus much. For the first time in my life I walked everywhere to save bus fares. It was reassuring to discover how cheaply you can live when you have to.

Our difficulties weren't only financial. The change from Paris and my life there was so complete that it's not surprising I found it extremely traumatic. I was homesick for France; I missed Paddy and Doreen dreadfully. Also while I felt very guilty at leaving Constance, at the same time I couldn't help missing her, the sensible reassuring presence that had been a part of my life for so long. And Olivia had psychological problems of her own, the complexity and importance of which I failed to appreciate, being too wrapped up in mine. She was in fact confronted by decisions just as difficult as those that I had faced before coming to Manchester, though I did not realise it at the time. It meant that we lived in separate bed-sits for the first year. In our different ways we were, both of us, having to come to terms with a lot of everyday reality. Also, as regards our relations with each other, well, in the circumstances the course of true love could hardly be expected to run smoothly, and it didn't. We were certainly neither the first, nor the last, to find it hard to turn a romantic love affair into a permanent commitment, but, if there was nothing original about the difficulties we faced, that didn't make them any less painful to overcome. There were some very distressing moments, several definitive separations and some dreadful rows. Looking back I tend to forget all these and to remember instead the bright moments and the laughs we had. If we "came through" - D H Lawrence's expression - it was because there were plenty of those too. It was also because, through all the tensions and troubles, we loved one another.

One thing that was a hundred per cent enjoyable from the start, however, was the course in Linguistics. It was marvellous to discover how much easier, and how much less tiring, learning is than teaching. Whereas in Paris I used to sit up late at night preparing the next day's lectures or seminars, now all I had to do was turn up in the lecture room with a blank notebook and a pencil. There were whole afternoons spent in the library browsing my way through Reading Lists as the fog of ignorance gradually cleared. And I found Willi Haas's main lectures to be exactly what I wanted: he gave a straightforward methodical exposition of the basics of linguistic and semantic analysis which was down-to-earth and commonsensical, while at the same time showing sensitivity to the imaginative power of language. He was Czech but, though he had taken over many of the ideas of the Prague school of Linguistics, he had come to the subject through philosophy. One of his best-known publications is an article on Translation which ends up with a brilliant metaphor for the translation process by which he compares it to what happens when a dancer is taught a new dance, the disembodied entity, the dance, which is conveyed from one dancer to the other being compared to whatever it is that is conveyed between languages when you translate.

A few weeks after the course started a note came round the Department announcing that an American linguist called Noam Chomsky, whose work had been causing a stir among theoretical linguists, would be giving a lecture in Leeds. Though we knew nothing as yet of Chomsky but the name, Olivia and I drove over the Pennines in a memorably dramatic thunderstorm to hear him. It was a remarkable performance: at great speed Chomsky covered a huge blackboard with what looked like an acre of tree diagrams. When we got back to Manchester the Department organised a sort of workshop at which those of us who had been to the lecture pooled what we could remember, and what we could understand, of what Chomsky had said. It was just before, or just after, publication of his second book, in which he developed the theory of Deep Structure. In his lecture - I am simplifying grossly here - he had shown how this idea could be used to explain things like, for example, the difference between two sentences such as *John is easy to please* and *John is eager to please*. According to traditional grammar, which can describe only the Surface Structure of a sentence, there is no difference, since *easy* and *eager* are both adjectives describing *John*. But they are not the same, since you can turn the first sentence round – transform it - to say *it is easy to please John,* but you can't do this with the second one. With this and other examples Chomsky had shown how the concept of what he called Deep Structure could explain this difference.

At the lecture in Leeds, when the time for questions came, Haas had got up and read out two sentences: *He danced with his wife* and *He danced with his sister*. Since you can say *He danced with his former wife* but not **He danced with his former sister,* does this, he asked Chomsky, mean that the Deep Structure of a word like *wife* or *sister* must contain an almost infinite number of possibilities and impossibilities? I can't remember, and anyway I couldn't understand, Chomsky's answer to Haas's question; it was long and extremely technical. But I don't think it was convincing. Haas, like other members of the Manchester Department, was suspicious of the choice of the word Deep, with its implications of superior profundity, and was consequently sceptical as regards the whole notion of Deep Structure.

The other memorable teacher that we had in Manchester was no stranger. Peter Wexler had been a colleague in Paris. (He often spoke about the evening with Brendan Behan that I have described). At that time the thesis he was writing- on the development of a railway vocabulary in French - seemed to me a prime example of academic futility, of the passion to know more and more about less and less. Now, however, as I learnt to approach language scientifically, I found that the aspect of language that interested me most was the lexicon, in other words vocabulary. I quickly discovered that it is a much more complex, and even more fascinating, phenomenon than I had realised, since it is at the interface between language and society. I was therefore glad to be able to include French lexicology as part of my MA in Linguistics.

But it was not only the subject that was intellectually exciting. Wexler had a most original mind and was a highly unconventional teacher. Out of interest I sat in on some of his undergraduate lectures on the history of the French language, though lecture is hardly the word to describe these unusual sessions. He would distribute around the class, of about 30 students, a foolscap sheet containing 25 or more citations, dating from the 15th to the 20th century, and all containing the same keyword which would be a word of obvious historical or cultural relevance such as *bourgeois, nation, industrie* or *patrie*. The quotations were chosen to illustrate the way in which words change in meaning with the passage of time, and therefore to show how there is no such thing as the "real meaning" of these or, for that matter, any words. Instead, the meaning of a word is an unstable, fluctuant, thing depending always on the use that is being made of it at any given moment, which careful study of the context will show. But Wexler didn't tell the students any of this, he got them to discover it for themselves by just asking them why they thought he had chosen each quote, and then firing very brief but very cogent questions at them about their responses. His own utterances were minimal in the extreme and often quite witty.

Of course some of the students didn't take very kindly to this unusual mode of instruction, they disliked being made to discover knowledge for themselves, preferring it to be spoon-fed to them in the conventional fifty minute monologues. Wexler himself was modestly dismissive regarding the original nature of these sessions and talked of replacing them with some even more radically experimental approach. Personally I thought that his method was admirably suited to the original way he was getting his students, among whom I included myself, to view as it were the micro-history of the language. Etymology, instead of the dry as dust study of where the form of a word originated, became the history of a word between two dates, as made evident by the contexts it occurred in. To examine closely a score of contexts spanning several centuries in which a word like *bourgeois* occurred was to look in a most revealing and down to earth way at the history of French culture and society. *Bourgeois*, for example, which to start with simply referred to the inhabitants of a town, at the end of the Middle Ages began to take on the added meaning of a social class. In contexts, taken from 16th to 20th century texts, in which *bourgeois* occurs, it is possible to trace the changing perception and magnitude of that category of people, and the changing attitudes to them – approving, admiring, scorning or despising etc –thus throwing an unusually instructive light on the way French society saw itself over the years.

Another thing that Wexler's undergraduates had to do was to find neologisms, new French words or acceptations as yet unrecorded in any dictionary. At first this seemed to me an impossibly difficult task for the poor kids, while being all the same an excellent way to get them to take a very close look at the language they were supposed to be studying. However, when I tried it myself I was surprised to find that it wasn't too hard, in a few pages of newsprint, to come upon ten or a dozen cases where a word was used in a way, or with a meaning, that no dictionary had caught up with. What he was getting them to do in fact was look for the points, the green shoots so to speak, at which the language was growing.

People speak of the Eskimo's supposed large number of words for snow. Wrongly as it happens, since the Inuit languages have apparently no more words for snow than other North American tongues, and modern skiers have at their disposal very many more words for different sorts of snow than any Inuit. What is interesting, instead, is the way the skier's terms for snow, for example in French *la poudreuse, la tôlée, la glacée* (powder snow, crusted snow, iced snow), were all coined very rapidly in the last half-century or so. New words appear in every language as people become more aware of any new, or newly relevant, reality. And the process by which meanings settle around a word, and by which its new acceptation is gradually, or eventually, adopted by society, is complex and interesting to study.

All this set me thinking of an area of French vocabulary that interested me personally The initial study of this gave me matter for my MA thesis, and it has occupied me on and off for many years since. The subject is the topography of high altitude landscapes, the words that describe features of high mountains. I had started thinking about these words some years before as I scrambled up the cliffs above Gavarnie in the Pyrenees, the climbing guide book in one hand and my ice axe in the other. I was struck then, and seriously inconvenienced, by the imprecision of the terms in the guidebook. Was the cleft in the rocks above me a *couloir* or a *cheminée*? What was the difference between *une vire* and *une corniche* (two sorts of ledge)? As I puzzled my way up the nearly vertical labyrinth, luckily without mishap, I couldn't help wondering about the process by which words had got associated with, and had thereby defined, the not always obvious features of a shattered mountain-side. I was fortunate to have started mountaineering in the Pyrenees, since several of the routes I had followed were first described in detail as early as the 18th century by a most engaging individual, Louis François Ramond de Carbonnières. Reading, in his measured 18th century French, descriptions of ice gullies and slanting ledges that I had myself scrambled up or along two centuries later was a real and unusual pleasure. In his writings, and in those of his, rare, contemporaries, it was easy and interesting to learn about the early history of mountain exploration as I traced the uncertain, hesitant, process by which what is now a technical terminology came into being.

I had in fact hit upon an unusual, and, to me, unusually interesting, field. Other linguists had studied the evolution of vocabularies describing new technologies and inventions: new words for new things. But the mountains, obviously, were not new, the words I was interested in referred to something that had always been there, the only thing that was new about the features I was studying was the way they had begun to be noticed. And unlike, for example, terms such as *locomotive* or *aeroplane,* the words that interested me did not designate objects that were clearly singled out to start with by their inventors. In early maps and descriptions even the mountains themselves hardly figure as such. In the first French dictionaries most of the examples listed for the word *mont* – such as Mont Cenis – refer, not to a mountain at all, but to a pass. The distinction between mountain and mountain-pass was not recognised. To most travellers in fact the mountains were an irrelevant vertical wilderness, and the summit was not a mountain top but simply the place where the road began to go downhill again. "I should like the Alps very much," wrote someone called John Spence in 1730, "if it were not for the hills."

It is an amazing fact, when you think about it, that it was not until ten years after James Cook's voyage in search of the austral continent that anyone had sufficient courage and curiosity to investigate a *terra incognita* that could be clearly seen from the streets of one of the great cities of Europe, namely the heights of Mont Blanc. I had found a complex reality, therefore, which had had to wait to be structured by language till the eighteenth century, when the hills were first described by valley and plain dwellers, earlier peasant frequenters of the mountain fastnesses having left no written record. It was my good fortune that the language spoken by most of the earliest mountaineers was French.

It was not, maybe, a vocabulary of earth shaking historical importance, but no one had thought of examining it before me. As I started work on the somewhat superficial MA thesis that started my long love affair with French mountain words, I felt like stout Cortez on that peak in Darien. I wrote to my father describing what I was doing, noting and comparing the words that 18th and early 19th century travellers had found for the vaguely perceived features of the awesome landscapes that they were the first to describe, he wrote back to me saying, "Now you know what it feels like to know more about something, however small and unimportant, than anyone else in the world." I didn't think for a moment that the familiarity I was acquiring with the changing meaning of a handful of French words could be compared in importance and usefulness with his knowledge of the boulder clays of the Liffey valley, but his approval of what I was doing meant a lot to me, particularly since I knew that, being very fond of Constance, he had misgivings about the change in my life.

Peter Wexler did me another service in addition to opening my mind to the complexities of French lexicology. He had been invited to spend a year in the States and managed to arrange for me to replace him in the French Department as regards his language teaching for the second year of my MA. That meant an immediate and welcome solution to our financial problems and also gave an easy, and on the whole agreeable, introduction to the world of French Studies in the United Kingdom. It is true I found it a strange milieu. My new colleagues were, on the whole, kindly disposed towards me, but I never got to know them socially and was never invited for so much as a cup of coffee by any of them over the year. But, obsessed as I was with homesickness for France, and remembering the wide-ranging and impassioned arguments in Chatenay or at Saint-Cloud, I couldn't fail to find the unFrench atmosphere of this Department of French Studies curiously synthetic. One of the senior lecturers for example, a nice man and interesting to talk to, a Welsh nationalist actually, once said to me that he thought it a great pity that so much of French literature was not really suitable for students to read.

If the French Department was a bit of a nonstarter from the social point of view this was not true of the Irish community in Manchester. I made contact with them immediately through the local branch of the Connolly Association and, for the two years I was in Manchester, I took part in most of the activities of the branch, above all in helping to sell the Association's paper, *The Irish Democrat*, around the pubs where Irish people tended to congregate. It was a totally unexpected and heart warming experience to be welcomed by a community of working class Irish socialists, and campaigning with them put an end to the guilt I used to feel at the political futility of my life as an expatriate in France. The penury in which I lived, above all in my first year, walking to save bus fares, living in a tiny, shabby, bedsit, put me on an equal footing financially with most members and supporters of the CA.

The Association's headquarters were in London where *The Irish Democrat* was edited by Desmond Greaves, biographer of James Connolly. A charismatic scientist turned historian and left-wing campaigner, Greaves imposed his personality and his ideas upon the Connolly Association. His views were, fortunately, much more enlightened and intelligent regarding Ireland than those of most other Communists in Britain at the time. I had written my *Emigrant of the Hundred Townlands* poem, of which more later, for *The Irish Democrat*, and Greaves had liked it. He had in fact heard a building worker singing it to a tune of his devising in a London pub. The Association's policies were fairly simple and straightforward. First and foremost we were publicising and protesting against the multiple injustices of the current regime in Northern Ireland. To some extent it would be true to say that we foresaw the troubles that were to come. We certainly believed, as I still believe, in the ultimate aim of a United Ireland. But with hindsight it is easy to see now that, if we were naive in thinking that the Unionist majority of people in the province could be persuaded to see the desirability of a United Ireland, we were certainly wrong, I was certainly wrong, to imagine that it could, or should, ever be imposed on them against their will. At the back of our thinking was the belief that successive British governments had held, and were holding, on to Northern Ireland for strategic reasons related to the Cold War. The idea was probably Soviet-inspired, by the medium of our Communist members. We certainly didn't realise, nobody then knew, that this reasoning was already completely out of date. It is common knowledge now that for years every British government, Labour or Tory, would have been glad to be shot of the whole Ulster problem, if only a trouble-free way could be devised to bring this about. In addition to campaigning about Northern Ireland we tried in the *Irish Democrat* to convince Irish workers, who were mostly in the building trade, that they would be better off if they joined a trade union.

We held weekly meetings which I attended regularly and a monthly "social" but, as in Chatenay, I found that I had very little talent for, or interest in, discussing policies or politics, preferring to leave that to others. However I did try to contribute to the branch's activities as much as possible: I gave talks at branch meetings and once I even tried speaking from a soapbox in Platt Fields, the park in Manchester where this sort of behaviour was tolerated. I wasn't much good at this, though it was an interesting experience, above all for someone studying Linguistics in the British tradition. To British linguists what is called "the implication of utterance" is of paramount importance; it is axiomatic that, since language only exists in a social context, it must be studied in context. You don't make up synthetic examples, you study bits of real language, someone speaking to someone else.

What struck me as strange about the soap box experience was that, to start off with, there is no context. We would find a suitable place within earshot of the dog walkers and one of us would get up on the box - which wasn't actually a soap box but a little platform made of boards someone had nailed together – and start speaking, to thin air. It didn't matter what you said, since there was no one to listen, you just had to keep talking and the context would create itself, something like the way the residual magnetism in the field coils of a dynamo starts it charging as it were from nothing. After a while a few people would gather and you would start addressing them directly. Not too directly; it was different from lecturing in this because if you overdid the eye contact they would be embarrassed and shuffle off and your audience would disappear, but directly enough to start a dialogue which could turn into a useful argument. I didn't enjoy this much, professional talker and all as I was. When I confessed this to Sean Redmond, who was General Secretary of the Association and a brilliant and powerful speaker, he said, "The trouble with you academics is that you can only perform in front of a captive audience."

My main contribution, and Olivia's, was selling the *Democrat*. I have always enjoyed this sort of grass-roots activity. Here it consisted in taking a bundle of papers round the pubs frequented by Irish immigrants on Friday and Saturday evenings. We usually did it in pairs starting around seven or eight o'clock. Between then and closing time we would usually manage to take in thirty or forty different establishments ranging from fake Tudor lounges – not many of these - to sawdust boozers. On the whole we were well received and it wasn't difficult to sell five or ten papers in almost every pub. Greaves had had the clever idea of including on the back page of each issue the words of four or five traditional Irish songs. We knew that many people bought the paper simply for the songs but we also knew that they provided a convenient "alibi" for any one showing the typically Irish discretion about their political opinions. "I do buy it for the oul songs" was something we often heard from the mouths of people who we happened to know were politically sympathetic to the cause.

I was amazed to find how many pubs there were catering for an almost exclu-

Tom and Aine Redmond

sively Irish clientele in the localities that we worked. You could usually tell if it was worth taking the *Democrat* in by the music you could hear from outside the door. If there was a piano going and you could hear them all singing "Down by the old Bull and Bush" there would be no point in going in there at all. On the other hand the variety and quality of musical talent in the Irish pubs was surprising. There was one pub I remember that had two brilliant flute players and, so long as they kept playing, their pints were on the house and, when closing time came, they would hand their instruments to the barman who would keep them safely till the next week. Other places had singers with guitars or bodhran drums and there were even a few fiddlers.

There were pubs where you met only Northerners and others full of Galway men or Cork men. Several times I came across a group speaking Irish. The people who bought the paper came from all over Ireland, with the majority, or so it seemed to me judging by the accents, coming from the Western counties, but most of our active members in the Manchester branch came from Northern Ireland, though the secretary of the branch, Tom Redmond, Sean's younger brother was a Dubliner. A highly intelligent, well-read chap with a great sense of humour and a lot of charm, Tom was a Party member with an impeccable

Dublin working-class background. He spoke with a broad Dublin accent which I analysed as a Phonetics exercise for the Linguistics Department. He and his wife Aine (pronounced onya), who had a pleasantly clear singing voice which she used very expressively, kept virtually open house in their apartment above a bank in Moss Side. In the storm and stress I was going through consequent upon my leaving Constance, leaving France, leaving a well paid job with no clearly defined future before me, the Bank Chambers, as it was called, was a very welcome and much appreciated refuge.

One of the most agreeable activities of the CA branch was organising what we called "socials". This meant hiring an upper room in a pub and inviting as many of the local musicians as we could persuade to participate. The evening then more or less organised itself. Since we had quite a lot of support from the local Irish immigrant community there was never a shortage of performers and there were some genuinely gifted players and singers who came regularly, together with several individuals with more self-assurance than talent who had to be tactfully but firmly discouraged. Among the former I remember Eddie Lenehan, a tall thin man with high cheekbones who had a fine, distinctively husky, voice, and a wonderful sense of melody. Eddie had fought in the War of Independence and in the Civil War. He used to sing, among other things, the ballad about the Manchester Martyrs, "*The Smashing of the Van*", so expressively that any time I hear anyone else sing that song it seems to me that they have got the tune wrong. And there was Barney Watters, by far our oldest member, who not only played the violin with great style, incorporating technical tricks like double stopping in his performance of traditional Irish tunes, but would discuss the playing of other musicians, admiring or criticising them in well-chosen words according to the purity of their style of playing and how far they resisted the all-pervading rhythms of rock music. Barney had such a refined critical ear and obviously knew so much about music - I used to see him occasionally at concerts of the Hallé Orchestra - that it never occurred to me that he was entirely self taught. I made the mistake once of asking him to play me an F so that the song I was going to sing would be within the range of my voice. He took up his fiddle and played an arpeggio that was no more F than it was B-flat. My embarrassment was nothing to the admiration I felt on discovering that he could play so beautifully without ever having learnt to read music.

Another musician who came occasionally and played at the Connolly socials was a picturesque character by name of Felix Doran. A fine looking man with a distinctly bohemian air, he looked something like the portrait of a Spanish gypsy by Goya and was a tinker; in fact I believe he made quite a good living dealing in scrap. He was famous among people in the know as one of the finest, if not the finest, Uileann piper alive. We were extremely pleased and proud to have him, and to hear his piping, though we could have done without some of his hangers-on who tended to be obstreperous and to get involved in, or cause, fights. But I remember one occasion when there was some sort of row among our other musicians, one group accusing the other of trying to lay down the law as to how a tune should be played. Things were getting quite nasty when Doran strode across the room and onto the little stage. "You know who I am," he said, "I'm Felix Doran. So pack it in." There was a short silence and then the music started up again.

Of course all our musicians played and sang purely for the pleasure of it, and most of them could probably be classed as genuine folk singers, to the extent that the term can be precisely defined, since their music was played, and belonged, to the community it sprang from. But this was the early sixties and the fashion for so-called "folk", which wasn't folk-song at all, as performed professionally to paying audiences by singers like Joan Baez and Ewen McColl, was at its height. There were several folk clubs in Manchester patronised by students and other young, mostly middle-class, people, where songs of the type popularised by these singers could be heard, as well as some traditional music. It was at one of these clubs in fact that I first heard Eddie Lenehan singing.

The two types of folk music came together in a remarkable family from the Falls Road in Belfast called McPeake. There were three generations of McPeakes: the old father who I seem to remember singing in a quavering but tuneful tenor, his son Frankie, the dominant musical personality of the group and Frankie's son and daughter. They all sang and played several instruments and had a huge repertoire of songs some of which had originated with them. Though genuinely talented they had never seen themselves as professional musicians, but played and sang to brighten, and to express, the everyday life of the Republican West Belfast working class, with its constant humiliations and permanent unemployment. But then when the boom in folk music started they quickly became, deservedly, famous. They received invitations to perform by folk clubs all over the country and they would travel from one to the other of these venues all crammed into their large rackety old car. I don't know when or how they had become close friends of Tom and Anne Redmond but, any time they were performing almost anywhere in the north of England, when the concert ended they would make their way to the Bank Chambers in Moss Side, Manchester, where they would arrive, sometimes at two or three in the morning. They would then usually stay a day or two and we would all have the pleasure of their company. When Paddy, aged 12, came to visit Olivia and me and we went round to the Redmonds, Frankie took out his Uileann pipes and played, of all things, the Marseillaise on them, in Paddy's honour.

He was a marvellous talker, Frankie McPeake, and it's a great regret of mine that I never managed to record him on tape, though he probably would have been self-conscious if he had known he was being recorded. Even so his account of their two international trips, one to New York and the other to Moscow would have been worth preserving. I fancy it was because he never read newspapers or listened to the radio or watched TV that his description of those two so different cities, and his stories about the people that he met there, were so fresh and spontaneous. And then there was the story of the time that Joan Baez came to call on him in Belfast. What had happened was that she had been singing a song of the McPeakes, the *Wild Mountain Thyme* (Will ye go, lassie, go?) and her agent and whoever published the McPeake records were at loggerheads over copyright. Baez, who was giving a concert in some concert hall in the city, came down the Falls Road in her enormous limousine to tell Frankie that, whatever about the agents and their lawyers, she would see that he got whatever he was due if she sang his song. "Ai tooled 'er," said Frankie, "Thut she shud navver huv come doon the street un thot cawr. They'll hov the whayls off of ut."

1965 was the centenary of Yeats's birth. As a member of the Connolly Association I was used to being chivvied into taking part in activities I hadn't bargained for, so I wasn't much surprised when Desmond Greaves, rang up with the bright idea that we mark the occasion with a lecture in London on Ireland's archpoet. I was, naturally, flattered when he said that the person to deliver this lecture should be me. I gave quite a lot of thought to the lecture, and more thought to the rather scruffily printed little monograph that I wrote afterwards, which was based on it. This was called *Malachi-Stilt-Jack*, after the title of one of Yeats's last poems, and it figured among Connolly Association literature for some time after. While expressing wholehearted admiration for most of Yeats's poetry I criticised the social and aesthetic attitudes and views which lie behind it, and which most readers and critics choose to ignore. After the lecture one or two speakers pointed out that the way I read the poems showed an admiration and a feeling for the poetry that was in contradiction with my critical remarks. That was certainly true but I didn't see it as a failing.

My criticisms, however, when the little book was published, offended a number of people, which I suppose is not surprising, since I described one of Yeats's best-known poems, *An Irish Airman Foresees His Death*, which figures in school anthologies, with its climax line, "a lonely impulse of delight," as a celebration of killing people for fun. The poet Austin Clarke, to whom I sent a copy and who reviewed it in a broadcast, said to me, "Your criticisms are more devastating than you maybe realise." That is probably why the poet-professor Brendan Kennelly, in the only other review the essay received – in *Hermathena*, the TCD research journal - dismissed it, I think unfairly, as "a strange mixture of ludicrous statement and perceptive insight." I was too hurt by his criticisms to see that most of his remarks were simply a matter of his opinion. Also, he failed to see that I didn't just express a vague admiration for Yeats's poems, I spelt out, arguable but explicit, reasons why I also considered, and consider, Yeats's poetry superior to that of any of his contemporaries. The little book remains, so far as I know, short and superficial as it certainly is, the only Marxist view of Yeats, though that is not immediately apparent since I avoided almost all the obvious Marxist buzz-words.

I was grateful to Desmond Greaves for having organised the Yeats centenary and for having got me to write *Malachi Stilt Jack*. I owed a lot to him indirectly also, as do many others, for the way he ran the Connolly Association. This was in spite of his having a curiously sexist blind spot. Women members were practically invisible to him except as organisers of fund-raising jumble sales and the like, though there were several women in the CA who were in every way as active as the men. In the various political campaigns that I have supported since leaving Manchester I have had reason to be glad of the experience gained militating with the CA. I learnt there to watch out for well-meaning but divisive leftist ideas, I learnt to listen to potentially supportive fellow-travellers, to pick out what is positive in their ideas and not alienate them by banging on about our own. I learnt to look for short-term objectives that could be achieved. Above all I learnt not to underestimate the influence a small group of dedicated people can have, quietly working away. Several of our members were influential later in the formation of the Northern Ireland Civil Rights Association.

Desmond Greaves had invited Hugh MacDiarmuid to come and speak after the Yeats centenary lecture, but at the last moment he went to Cuba. Instead an Irish poet I had often admired, W R Rodgers, came. When it was all over Rodgers and I were put up in a friend's spare bedroom. We talked late into the night, Rodgers reminiscing about his friend Louis MacNeice, who I had never met or even seen, but some of whose poems I knew by heart, and who had rescued Rodgers from his early life as a clergyman. At one moment we were talking about contemporary poets. He seemed to know, or know about, a large number of these. And then, referring to a group of quite well-known names, he said, with the scorn of the full-time professional for the Sunday amateur, "Yes, but they all have *jobs*." I pointed out, that until he became a Senator, Yeats had never had a job in his life. "You're right," he replied, "Neither he did. He was the real thing."

Having or not having a job was something that loomed ever more menacingly as my second year in Manchester proceeded. Olivia had been appointed to a lectureship in Linguistics at the University of Salford. I answered various advertisements but as I drew blank after a blank I realised that my age – I was 41 - was against me. As the months passed and the end of my temporary post in the Manchester Department drew near I began to despair. In early 1966 there were only two remotely possible posts advertised: one was for teaching English with the British Council in Tunis, which would have meant going back to the ex-pat life I had escaped from. The other was in the University of St

Johns, Newfoundland. I was trying to decide which of these unlikely solutions to my problem to try for when a miracle happened. The French Department of the University of Aberdeen needed someone to manage the newly acquired Language Laboratory. I applied immediately, even before looking in an atlas to see exactly where Aberdeen was.

I had written to Francis Scarfe, my boss in Paris, to ask for a reference but he had replied, thanking me for the "lively essay on Yeats" which I had sent him, but saying that he could not recommend me to a university French department since he considered that I had no knowledge of French literature. I therefore didn't give his name as a reference so the only references I had were from Prof Haas in Manchester and Monsieur Canac in Saint-Cloud, who wrote, characteristically, to say that he "*attendait de pied ferme*" (was standing by) to give a good account of me. In the event I don't think in Aberdeen they bothered either him or Haas. All Prof Diverres did was to telephone Scarfe, who he had known in Glasgow, and I suppose Scarfe must have spoken highly of my knowledge of electronics because I was straightaway called for interview. *Malachi-Stilt-Jack* probably counted for something too, after all Scarfe had himself written a lively little book on Auden and his contemporaries. So I flew up to Aberdeen and was reassured to learn that I was the only candidate for the post. Armel Diverres, to whom I took an instant liking, showed me round the Department and introduced me to several members, who, I was pleased to find, were about twenty years younger than I was. The general atmosphere seemed much less stuffy than Manchester. The actual interview went well but so much depended on it for me that I found it nerve-racking and, when they called me back in and asked if I would accept whatever the salary was that they offered, I had difficulty stopping myself from just saying Oh Yes, Please.

# Aberdeen 12

When I told my father I had got the job in Aberdeen, he remarked that, since they move about all the time in British universities, it would do for a year or so while I got my bearings. I thought the same as I walked around Aberdeen shortly after arrival. It all looked very grey and forbidding; the inhabitants I talked to, and the town itself, seemed curiously provincial as compared with other cities in the UK. After Manchester I missed all the Irish and the Caribbean immigrants, and the tandoori restaurants and Pakistani grocers' shops, and I found the tartan and haggis honky-tonk of Scotland a poor substitute. I took a bus to one of the outlying suburbs and walked into the country but instead of the railway lines and canals and closed-down coal mines, all the left-over artefacts of the industrial revolution that I had found so fascinating in Lancashire, there seemed to be nothing but interminable fields of turnips. It is true there was the harbour and the sea, one thing Manchester didn't have. As I stepped from the train on my first day I was assailed by the smell of herrings and the sound of the cries of seagulls.

Turnips and herrings: there were of course cattle also. But as I walked about I was reminded, improbably, of Dijon. Jacques and Marie Souviron had recently moved there from Orléans and grumbled interestingly about the prosperous but stick-in-the-mud nature of the inhabitants, a bourgeoisie whose unchanging wealth came from centuries of producing and trading almost uniquely in food. Though mangel-wurzels and kippers may sound less romantic than Maille mustard and Nuits-St Georges, the prosperity resulting from their production had much in common with that of Burgundy. In fact it seemed to me more marked here in Aberdeen. On the west side of the city a vast area is taken up with street after street of large houses, all expressive of the same staid 19th century opulence and all built of the same cut granite. You could walk around this district, as I once did for a whole afternoon, without ever retracing your steps and without ever once seeing a corner shop, a newsagent's or a pub. The silence, the lack of passers-by, and these rows of costly mausoleum-like dwellings; the whole place reminded me of the *Cimetière de Père Lachaise* in Paris. If you continue in a westerly direction these somewhat dated mansions give way to more modern single-storey constructions, similarly pricey, made of the same cut stone and described, by Aberdeen solicitors - there are no estate agents here - oxymoronically it seemed to me, as granite bungalows.

Granite: the city is justly proud to be built of it, though the stone itself, having less mica, doesn't sparkle like the Wicklow granite of the Government Buildings in Dublin. This means that the more recent buildings, where the stone has been cut with a saw, often look as though they were built out of breeze blocks. The granite itself came, for the most part, I was told, from a single quarry on Rubislaw hill. I couldn't wait to see this phenomenon once it had been described to me: "the biggest hole in Europe." Not knowing that it was still being worked, and that there was an easy access on the other side, I scrambled over a barbed wire fence and through a thicket of brambles and very nearly fell into it, which would have been unfortunate since it is over 400 feet deep and the sides are sheer.

A few years later, when my niece, Una's daughter Mary Brown, came to visit us and I took her to see Rubislaw quarry, the gate at the top of the stonecutters' access chanced to be unlocked. We climbed down flight after flight after flight of a rickety staircase; it was a long way down. We eventually came to the top of the final ladder where I thought it was wiser to stop before the men working below saw us and shouted at us. But the view from near the bottom of this enormous hole in the ground, far bigger and deeper than the Gouffre de Padirac, was as spectacular as it was strange. And it was even stranger to think that, where Mary and I were standing, near the bottom of a hole on the top of a hill which was 200 feet high, we were actually 200 feet below sea level. Sadly, no one can experience this any longer (2010). They stopped working the quarry some years ago and the City Council is letting it fill slowly with rainwater. It will soon be just a boring pond of unsuspected depth.

As I have said, in 1966 I was struck by how remote and provincial the city of Aberdeen seemed. Driving north, the dual carriageway came to an end soon after Edinburgh or Glasgow. Coming by rail the Flying Scotsman ceased to fly once it was over the Forth Bridge; I suspected them, probably wrongly, of changing the locomotive in Edinburgh. And Aberdeen airport was not much bigger than the little private airport of Toussus near Paris. All these things tended to make Aberdeen seem even further North than it actually was. A stone grey city, stuck in its ways and dedicated to the production of food. The harbour was dominated by the fishing industry and the largest ship was the boat for

Shetland and Orkney. There seemed to be little left there of the seaport that a hundred years ago had built the Thermopylae, sister ship to the Cutty Sark. Even the local patriotism, which I admired, seemed to have a small-minded, parochial flavour. Once, in a shop I was mystified as to the function and purpose of a spirtle (porridge stirrer) and said to the girl: "What's this?" She answered, "It's £1.20." So I said, "Yes, but what's it *for*?" "I just told you," she said. "It's for £1.20." She was so unused to strangers to the City she couldn't imagine any other sense to my question. We were advised to do our Christmas shopping in November, as the shops never ordered enough of anything interesting and the shelves would be bare of toys long before Christmas. In any case in Aberdeen then Yuletide was still only a minor festival as compared with Hogmanay, and many shops didn't even close on Christmas Day.

All this was to change, was already changing out of all recognition as the provincial backwater was transformed into the, per capita, wealthiest town in Britain and the silver city with the golden sands for Glasgow holidaymakers became the oil capital of Europe. But, though the change was fast, it affected our everyday lives so little that we were only half aware of what was happening all around us. It is true the invasion of foreign oil-men was not all that noticeable since the Americans kept themselves apart, with their own stores and clubs and schools. But there were plenty of other changes. Old-fashioned family department stores closed down and characterless retail parks took their place, underused churches were taken over, tarted up and occupied by insurance companies or turned into night clubs, ethnic restaurants appeared in every street, and the surrounding countryside was rapidly transmogrified into subtopian housing estates. Any of these changes could be seen as representative of the whole. To end with a trivial example. In Belmont Street, a few yards from Aberdeen's main shopping thoroughfare there used to be a particularly dreary butcher's shop. On dingy shelves in the window were displayed strips of tripe and strings of pallid sausages and mealie-puddings, an insipid local speciality consisting of pig-fat and oatmeal. And then, some time in the 1980s, the drab shop front was suddenly transfigured. Glossy black paint and bright red zig-zag lettering drew the attention of passers-by to a display of sexy underwear. From mealie-puddings to "Naughty Knickers" in 20 years seems as good a symbol as any of the transformation of the local culture.

All this was, in 1966, still in the future. I soon came to see the advantages of living in a medium-sized city like Aberdeen as it was then and, to a great extent, is still. I learned to appreciate the distinctive character and culture of its inhabitants and, eventually, to understand something of the strongly marked dialect of Scots that they speak, which is not always immediately comprehensible even to a native of Edinburgh or Glasgow. Scotland itself, which I quickly learned to see less as a region with a chip on its shoulder and more as a potential nation, I found to be a very satisfactory solution for the permanent ex-pat Irishman I seemed to have become. This was largely because I considered myself, and liked the Scots to consider me, as a foreign visitor, unlike certain of my English colleagues in the University, who tended to speak of themselves as though they were marooned in some remote and semi-civilised province of their own country. And there were things that I liked immediately. For example I found Scotland much more democratic, more egalitarian even, than England, and in this more like France or Ireland. Certainly there seemed to be a much wider and more radical social mix among the students at the University than had been the case in Manchester. This was probably because the educational apartheid that fuels so much snobbery in England hardly exists at all in Scotland, save perhaps in Edinburgh.

The slightly jaundiced eye with which, at first, I had looked at Scotland in general and Aberdeen in particular certainly didn't extend to the University. I felt at home there immediately; the relatively small size as compared with Manchester made it much less intimidating. I liked the mixture of ancient and modern buildings and the University's situation in the old town which was then, before the oil came and changed everything, at the very edge of the city, so that in 20 minutes' walk from my office I could find myself in fields surrounded by cows. Colleagues in Manchester had told me that Aberdeen was a university famously generous with things like travel expenses. "It's so far north," they said, "Otherwise no one would want to go there." I experienced an example of this generosity soon after I arrived when they offered to make up several months of pension contributions that the Finance Officer in Manchester had argued his way out of paying. So much for the fabled Scottish meanness, I thought to myself. And then there was Gordon House, a palatial piece of Scottish baronial extravagance, which the University had purchased to house newly arrived members of staff like me. I managed to get a place there after I had been in Aberdeen a month or two. My second experience of collective living but a very far cry from Chatenay. Though it was fun too, in its way.

One-time residence of Lord Aberdeen - and possibly built for him, I don't know - the University had apparently bought Gordon House cheap from someone who had intended to turn it into a hotel but had found that the local residents wouldn't allow a licensed bar anywhere in their granite paradise/wilderness. When I first caught sight of it with its steep roofs and pepper-pot towers I thought it looked more like something out of *Snow White and the Seven Dwarfs* than a residence for University staff. Unsurprisingly the University ended up, some years after I had left, by selling it off to be a nursing home. For the time being, bizarre and excessively luxurious, it was quite a good place to live. The only disadvantage was that the bedrooms were so immense they had to be shared. I managed to avoid this by getting them to give me a sort of cubbyhole under the stairs, which I preferred. There were domestic staff; breakfast and dinner were served every day in a large dining room with five or

Francis Synge

six to a table. That was when we tended to meet, a random mixture of academics of every age and variety. There were a couple of very high-powered medics, a charming Italian *lettrice*, a few entertaining talkers, some talkers who were not entertaining and one or two interesting-looking men who turned out to have nothing to say at all. Someone would bong a gong and there would be a tricky moment as we would all go in. I quickly learnt the importance of arriving when about half the others had decided where to sit. Arrive too early and there was a chance the bores would come and sit beside you. Arrive too late and the only vacant chairs would be beside them.

I was introduced to Gordon House by my cousin, Francis Synge, who had just been appointed to a lectureship in geography. I had known Francis since we were children, his father, Millington Synge, had been our family doctor, and I knew that Francis had collaborated with my father in research on the geomorphology of the Wicklow mountains. My mother had tended to see him as someone who always arrived to discuss geology with my father at odd and maximally awkward times of day, when we were on the point of eating or going to bed. I hadn't realised that he was a researcher with an international reputation, having published something like forty articles. Unlike most of the other denizens of Gordon House, however, Francis was driven, not by a desire for status or promotion, but simply by an overpowering hunger for more and more knowledge about his subject. He couldn't bear to hear of some interesting fieldwork being done without going to see it for himself, wherever it was. This meant driving his rackety old Ford car sometimes incredible distances week-end after week-end. Conversation over meals in Gordon House would often turn to travel, since it was clear that for these academics a lot of prestige depended upon their "having to go" to Birmingham or Bristol to some "important" meeting or other. Francis didn't play this game, mostly because he saw the distance he had to go as the least interesting thing about a trip, though he travelled further and more often than any of them. He knew quite a lot about academic status though. I remember once, when a group of us were discussing a rather obnoxiously ambitious fellow-resident, Francis saying in his very slow, slightly drawling, manner, "Ken is what you think of if you're wondering what unpleasant professors can have been like.... when they were young."

One winter's day, while we were still at Gordon House, Francis and I went hill walking. He was amazingly tough and a very strong walker and I had the greatest difficulty keeping up with him as he strode up the steep East ridge of Morven. "God, Francis," I panted, "you're a terrible walker." "I know, I'm sorry" he replied, misunderstanding my Dublin colloquialism completely, "I'm not in good form today." A similar misunderstanding happened two hours later when we got back to his trusty, and rusty, old Ford. He had earlier explained how he had had the heater removed because he thought it made him sleepy. The window on the passenger side was half open and, as soon as we drove off, a slitting blast came in. I tried desperately to wind it up but it seemed to be jammed. Francis looked across, saw me struggling with the winder and said, "Oh it'll open all right if you give it a bang," and promptly did so. Well I suppose the fresh air kept us both awake.

Francis had worked, among other places, on Baffin Island in the Arctic, where he had narrowly avoided an encounter with a polar bear. But his main interest was in Ireland, where he eventually returned to join the Irish Geological Survey, my father's first employer. Some years after we had both left Gordon House he was married to Margaret Lancaster, a fellow geographer. Sadly he died of a cancer when he was barely sixty and now lies buried, close to my father's grave, in Calary churchyard, under Djouce Mountain, among the Wicklow hills he knew and explained so well.

Olivia had remained in Manchester which meant some long-distance commuting for me, which I managed to pass off, over dinner in Gordon House, as important professional travel. At Christmas I took Paddy for a week skiing in the Alps. We avoided the seasonally overcrowded trains by travelling to Saint-Gervais on Christmas Eve and back on New Year's Eve. That way in each direction we had a compartment to ourselves. Olivia meanwhile was at home with her parents where she went down with an exceptionally nasty dose of flu. She was so ill for 10 days or more that she stopped smoking and decided, when she had recovered, not to start again. At my first free week-end in January I took the train south and she met me in York. As we drove out of the town, realising that there was something different about her and knowing full well the importance of remarking upon it, I racked my brains to decide what it could be. New hat? New hair-do? New coat? We were halfway across the Pennines before I realised that she hadn't had a cigarette.

I had consulted a solicitor in Manchester and had learnt that before Constance and I could obtain a divorce I would have to establish residence in Britain and reside there for a year. My move to Scotland, which in the eyes of the law is a different country, delayed this by a further year, though it was otherwise advantageous, since the Scottish legislation was simpler and better in several ways from our point of view. Divorce can never be a pain-free process but the pain of our separation had been partly alleviated for Constance, and my feeling of guilt eased slightly, when she formed an attachment to an old friend who was living in Chatenay called André Ramillon, whom she later married. "Ram," as we called him, was a primary school teacher from a small village near Orléans. He had a wide range of interests, an encyclopaedic knowledge of natural history and a distinctive, entertainingly elaborate, style of writing. He became extremely fond of both Paddy and Doreen, as they were of him. In a way it could be said that Constance and my separation meant that Paddy and Doreen, ended up, to some extent, with two fathers instead of one. For example Ram took Paddy fly-fishing and duck-shooting, activities that he could certainly never have experienced with me. Ram's political affinities - he had been in the Resistance and was a Party member for most of his life - counted a lot for both Paddy and Doreen too.

It was thanks to Ram and Olivia's forbearance and general generosity of spirit that Constance and I were able, not only to remain friends, but to see quite a lot of each other as time went by. When Olivia's and my children, Tadg (he spells his name without the h) and Roisin, were growing up we had several holidays in Donegal, sharing my mother's house there with Constance and Ram together with some, or all of our children. There were occasional tensions but on the whole the time was spent happily. Ram took Tadg fishing off the rocks where they had the unusual adventure of Tadg catching a seagull. (Ram had the greatest difficulty getting the hook out of its beak). Constance invented games to teach Tadg and Roisin French words. Ram and Constance looked after Roisin when Olivia and I and Tadg were climbing in the Pyrenees with Paddy. Tadg once turned up out of the blue, in Paris, asking to be put up. "Constance is the only person I know," he said, "Who panics slowly." But all this was still in the future.

Once the divorce had been agreed upon, and my Scottish residence had been established, the only thing that held us up was the antediluvian complexity of the legal process and the unbelievable inefficiency of the firm of Edinburgh lawyers that Constance had, quite how or why I never learnt, been given to represent her interests. They would communicate with my solicitor in Aberdeen to the effect that the process could not move forward until they received some document from Constance. I would telephone her and she would put it in the post immediately. I learnt after several months of prevarication that the only thing to do then was to bombard them with phone call after phone call saying Will you please open the flipping letter that I know you have received and reply to it. The delay went on and on and Olivia grew increasingly concerned. There was a reason for her concern. Once the legal process was started we had thought it would only take a month or two for the divorce to be declared, since there was no opposition. It was some time before we realised the full extent of that sling or arrow of outrageous fortune, i.e. the law's delay. And in the interim another process had started: Olivia, who had left Manchester in 1967 and was now working in Dundee, found she was expecting Tadg, our first child.

Therefore, wishing to cause her parents as little distress and embarrassment as possible, with a mind to relations back in Ireland, and the *qu'en dira-t-on* (what will people say?) in a small village in County Clare, she phoned one evening and told her parents that our marriage had taken place that day. As proof of this we put on our best clothes and had a "wedding photograph" taken by an Aberdeen photographer and sent it around the family. And, since we were now "married", it was normal that Olivia's parents should be invited to visit us in Aberdeen, in the little house we had just bought in Orchard Place. It was June 1968, the visit was a great success but we would have enjoyed it more if, at the back of our minds, knowing that the legal term was coming to an end, we hadn't been increasingly worried that the divorce wouldn't be heard in time, and that our real marriage might have to wait till the end of the summer vacation. In the event the case was fitted in, and only just in time. It actually took place while Olivia's parents were still staying with us. Constance flew over from Paris to Edinburgh, and Tom and Aine Redmond, essential witnesses of my adultery, came up from Manchester. I didn't of course have to appear, but I drove down from Aberdeen, telling Olivia's parents that I had to go to a meeting in Edinburgh. Creeping out of the house at five o'clock in the morning so as not to wake them, with a bottle of whisky I had bought as a present for Constance to bring to Ram, I dropped the bottle on the doorstep. Olivia had some difficulty explaining how the broken glass and the smell of whisky could have been left by someone going to an "important academic meeting".

I arrived outside the law court in Edinburgh just after the case had been heard. By a curious coincidence the Connolly Association, together with other groups had got the Edinburgh City Council to agree to put up a plaque at James Connolly's birth place in the Cowgate and the ceremony took place that day. I helped by photographing Sean Redmond, Tom's brother, standing in front of the plaque. The Dublin Transport and General Workers Union had sent a brass band so it was quite an occasion. It was unfortunately noticed by the fascists of the Edinburgh Orange Lodge who tore the plaque down almost immediately and it has not been replaced. When the ceremony was over Constance and I took Tom and Aine and Owen aged three, who they had brought with them, up Arthur's seat in the car. Then they set off back to Manchester. There was some problem about Constance's flight back to Paris and I tried to persuade her to stay overnight in Edinburgh so we could at least spend the evening together. But at the last moment there was room on the plane, so she left. She was worried anyway about leaving Ram to look after Paddy and Doreen for two nights. On the way home I stopped under the Forth Bridge and went for a long walk along the shore. The tide was very far out and I looked out over desolate acres of seaweed wondering sadly if all was for the best and hoping that it was. Then I drove slowly north, back towards the future that I had chosen.

But the lawyers hadn't finished with us. About three or more years after Constance and my divorce I suddenly received a bill for over a hundred pounds – a lot of money at the time – from Constance's Edinburgh solicitors. A fee, they said, for "finalising the case and closing the account". I went to our lawyers in Aberdeen, Clark and Wallace. They agreed that it seemed excessive, and said they would take it up with Edinburgh, and I received a phone call shortly after to say that they had managed to obtain a "modification" of the bill. If I paid immediately the Edinburgh firm would allow a reduction of ten pounds. So I sent it off, minus ten pounds. But that wasn't the end. A week or so later I got Clark and Wallace's bill "for intervening in the matter of an invoice." For ten pounds.

I had been appointed to take charge of the Language Laboratory, so in the few months between the interview and my taking up the post in September 1966 I had done quite a bit of reading and thinking about this intrusion of expensive technology into the comfortably old-fashioned arts world where language learning resided. And the more I thought, though I continued to find the technology fascinating, the more sceptical I became as regards the uses to which it was being put. In truth my scepticism had started at Saint-Cloud where a programme to teach English intensively to engineers from Renault by what was now called "language laboratory methods" had run into some interesting difficulties.

The theory of language laboratory use had been largely developed by a high-powered American dullard by name of Stack. His book, which laid down the law as regards the design of materials to be used in language laboratories, was everywhere. The basic idea, which lay behind the audio-lingual theory of language learning, was that you learn a language by listening and repeating what you hear. This may seem obvious but it is only true if what you hear and say makes sense, and if it relates to some meaningful context. Stack took absolutely no account of this essential proviso. The basic exercise described in his book, a model followed in countless publications, and in language laboratories all over the world, went something like this. (The words in italics are what the learner might be imagined saying.)

> Model recording: I am having my hair cut today.
> Learner repeats, getting a word wrong: *I am having my **hairs** cut today.*
> Model proposes a change: yesterday.
> Learner tries to adapt her response: ***I am having** my **hairs** cut yesterday.*
> Model gives correct answer: I had my hair cut yesterday.
> Learner repeats correct answer: *I had my hair cut yesterday.*
> Model proposes a new change: tomorrow.
> Learner: *I will **had** my **hairs** cut tomorrow.*
> Model gives correct answer: I will have my hair cut tomorrow

And so on. Each exercise was supposed to consist of eight or ten sets of these stimuli and responses. The basic idea was that the learner would pick up the grammar automatically by repeating the various model sentences over and over again. It wouldn't need to be explained. In fact grammatical explanations were forbidden. The theory that lay behind this view, which was used to justify the expense of installing this expensive hardware in schools and colleges all over the world, was interestingly, and totally, at variance with the view of language held by linguistic scientists who, increasingly, agreed with Chomsky that whatever language was it was not a habit structure to be learnt by stimulus and response. Everything I had learned from Haas and his colleagues had reinforced my natural suspicion of over-simplified views of language. And I remembered how at *Saint Cloud* the Renault engineers had reacted against undiluted audio-lingual methods by making up their own grammatical notes. They would keep these on the backs of old envelopes under the desk and consult them surreptitiously so as to improve the correctness of their responses. Though some of these learners, since they were intelligent engineers, became quite proficient at parroting the recorded models, and even at modifying them correctly, since they didn't understand most of what they were saying, the skill they had acquired in doing this was not very useful when it came to selling and servicing cars in America, which was the aim of the whole operation..

But my first reason for querying received wisdom as regards so-called language lab methods was not the defective theory that underlay them so much as the incomparable tedium of sitting hour after hour repeating and adapting the same meaningless little bits of language. The more I saw roomfuls of students crouched over their tape recorders, repeating these boring and contextless utterances, like battery chickens with headphones on, the more I thought that this was a stupid and mistaken use of what was all the same a useful invention, namely the twin-track tape recorder.

A twin-track tape recorder is just a tape recorder with a Master track containing exercise material recorded by a native speaker and a Student track on which the learner can record his or her own voice. The only thing that is unusual about it is that the Master track cannot be erased, whereas the students can record and erase their recordings at will. Programmed intelligently, recognising its limitations, this remains in my opinion a very useful device, if not for learning a language – that is always best done with a teacher – but for consolidating what one knows, and above all for practising and improving one's pronunciation by comparing it with a model made by a native speaker. Tape recorders are currently being replaced by computers but the principle remains the same. A Language Laboratory is just a series of machines linked up to a teacher's console, which is usually equipped with a large number of sophisticated and expensive facilities most of which are never used at all.

The setup I found myself in charge of in Aberdeen consisted of two large classroom language labs, rooms for private study and a little recording studio. All this was shared by the Departments of French, German, Italian, Spanish, Russian and Scandinavian and Celtic languages. There was, when I started, a staff of two, a technician and a senior secretary. They were both 10 or 15 years older than me, which was just as well since I had quite a lot to learn about the job and they both saved me from embarrassment on various occasions. The technician, Jack Holden, - his father had been a well-known performer in Scottish music halls before the war – had been in the Royal Navy throughout the war and was still in the Reserve. Working with him, and discussing the various technological developments that we had to keep up with in the sixties, I came to appreciate the thoroughness and perfectionism that came of his naval background. A kindly man he was tolerant of my very amateurish knowledge of electronics, but we shared an interest in the new developments that were taking place, as well as a suspicion of trendy novelties. He talked interestingly about the technical side of the war against Nazi Germany. It was clear to me that he had given much thought to the issues that had been at stake then. Though we tended to avoid any subject that we might disagree about I think his sympathies and affinities were not all that far from my own. The Language Lab secretary, Alison Murray, became a close friend. An intelligent woman interested in books and cinema, in the work context she was similar to Jack by being another perfectionist, a quality that was much appreciated by colleagues who needed typing in strange character sets, Arabic or phonetic script. Having been born and brought up in Chile she spoke fluent Spanish. She also used our lab's facilities to teach herself a lot of French. Warm-hearted and friendly she was excellent company. She was also marvellous with our two children, Tadg, and Roisin, who was born three years later. Gifted with an artist's eye, she took remarkable photographs with a little Instamatic camera. Typical of Alison's sense of humour was her response when I tried to sell her tickets for a play that some colleagues were putting on. "I love

Olivia, Tadhg and Roisin. Photo: Alison Murray

amateur dramatics," she said. "I've done quite a bit and I love everything about it. I've prompted, I've stitched costumes, I've painted scenery, I've even acted at times. There's only one thing I draw the line at." "And what's that?" I asked. "Sitting in the audience," said Alison.

Programming the Language Labs for French where there were several hundred students (them were the days...) was my main job. I didn't find it difficult to replace the prayer-wheel tedium of grammar drills as described in the Stack book with something more appetising. I decided that the most profitable and interesting way of using the technology was to concentrate on improving the students' ability to understand native spoken French. So I set myself to devising exercises in structured listening. To find things for them to listen to I harnessed my own immense home-sickness for France by putting on the weekly tapes things like speeches by De Gaulle or André Malraux and songs by Brassens, Barbara or Boris Vian. I was pleased, and relieved, to find that this fare was liked and approved of by colleagues in the French Department. Most of them, that is. One tiresome Oxbridge-trained individual went around boasting how he had proved to himself the correctness of his critical acumen by disliking Barbara's best known song, *Nantes*, for a piece of what he called "typical maudlin French sentimentality". When I mentioned the striking, and musically very unorthodox, change of key in the last verse of the song, though he played several musical instruments, this character hadn't noticed it. But he was an exception, and he left Aberdeen soon after.

The formula I had worked out for the weekly Language Lab exercise came into its own when I was invited to participate in a large scale inter-university, Carnegie-funded, project to produce teaching materials for first year university French. My share in this enterprise was to devise an Audio Course to run in parallel with the written materials, and it was suggested that a team should go to France and make recordings on which exercises could be based. I quickly saw the amateurish and expensive disaster that this would be. So instead I asked that the funding should be spent on a Research Assistant and we used professional recordings taken from radio and other sources, choosing clips of varying length that were politically or culturally interesting, or intrinsically amusing, and invented exercises and activities of different kinds based on these. The recordings we used ranged from André Malraux's deeply moving funeral oration on Jean Moulin, the Resistance leader, to the Communist leader Jacques Duclos reminiscing about once having had a walk-on part in a play starring Sarah Bernhardt. Regrettably the only woman celebrity we included was Brigitte Bardot who expressed her views on matrimony, declaring "*J'adore me marier...*" (I just love getting married...).

Working with a Research Assistant was a new and entirely positive experience. I was fortunate that Catherine, a highly intelligent Parisienne, had a mentality sufficiently similar to my own to preclude time-wasting clashes of opinion, while being at the same time different enough for us to compensate for each other's shortcoming. The Audio Course we produced was still in use 20 years later, when many of the celebrities whose voices we used were either dead or forgotten.

If I felt at home in the French Department it was largely thanks to the general enthusiasm for France and things French that reigned there. It wasn't the only thing that made Aberdeen different. Years later, at an Applied Linguistics meeting somewhere in England I was chatting with an elderly Senior Lecturer in Spanish and he suddenly said "It's something I've observed countless times. Any time anyone wants to try anything innovative in the field of language learning in a British University the first and fiercest opposition always comes from the Professor of French." The most obvious proof that things were different in Aberdeen was the fact that the Professor of French there, to fill a fairly responsible position, hadn't appointed the usual standard candidate with a shiny new doctorate. Instead he had chosen me, a forty-year-old English teacher with no PhD, who knew more about electronics and WB Yeats than he knew about French literature, and furthermore had a degree in Linguistics, which in those days the world of French Studies tended to regard in the same way as 19th-century bishops viewed the theory of Natural Selection.

He was a complex, and entertaining, mixture of the conventional and the unconventional, Armel Diverres, but the first impression that I had of him, which remained dominant through the years I worked with him, was one of warmth and

Prof Armel Diverres

generosity. There was also a sort of eccentric paternalism regarding his department. "All well at home?" was his standard greeting if you passed him on the stairs. He and his wife would come round at Christmas to all members of the Department who had small children and distribute toys to them. We used to smile at this "visiting the cottagers" but there was a total lack of condescension in it. And at the end of the year he would take the entire staff, plus spouses, out to dinner in a restaurant at his own expense. I can't imagine what it cost; there were at least twenty-five of us. The paternalism went in some way with the rapid turnover in the Department; he seemed to like having two or three new young faces every year and he never made much effort to hang on to people when they were tempted to move back to England. Not a power person, though he obviously enjoyed his authority and never seemed frightened by it, unlike some professors I have known, and he was pleasantly unprudish about things like money, promotion and status in general.

He was half Breton and half Welsh, and proud of both halves, speaking fluent Welsh whenever the occasion presented itself. He had strong likes and dislikes, most, though not all, of which I shared, such as his Francophilia and his feeling that a university has a responsibility towards enriching the life of the local community at large. This was expressed by two things that the current French Department, regrettably, have no time for, or can't be bothered with. These were: his involvement in things like the Franco-Scottish Association, and the relations he maintained with school-teachers of French all over the University's vast catchment area; he seemed, amazingly, to know all their names. I shared his scorn for those French academics who spend half their time in fast trains getting back from their provincial Universities to their Parisian domicile and contribute nothing to the locality they are working in. I admired his readiness, unusual among academics, to discuss his own field of mediaeval literature with non specialists. I once travelled down to London with him in the train and the conversation, or rather monologue, ranged from Scottish mediaeval history to methods of ploughing, from lighthouses – the Bell Rock, just visible from Arbroath - to geology, from winter wheat to solid-state electronics, and always with the refreshing assumption that everyone should be as interested in everything as he was. Somewhere around York I asked him what had started his interest in the Middle Ages. That kept us going all the way to King's Cross.

It always puzzled me that someone who was such a bad listener managed to hear and know so much of what was going on. The booming voice is something that everyone who knew him remembers; he was touchingly unaware of how many people could hear everything he was saying, or maybe he just didn't mind. Once I was on a crowded railway platform in England with him and, seeing the glossy magazines on the bookstall, he started to tell me about some hardcore pornography he had chanced to come across in a telephone box. His innocence was such that he was as surprised as he was shocked by what he saw there. His appalled, graphic, and blow by blow, so to speak, detailed description of the acts of multiple fellatio portrayed in this publication, boomed out at full volume, must have given our fellow travellers something new to talk about to their wives and husbands when they got home.

My success in devising a course of interesting listening material for the Language Labs landed me with a chore I hadn't counted on: I learnt that I must sanction it with an exam. A series of fortunate coincidences meant that this somewhat tiresome requirement started me off in an entirely new, and forbiddingly daunting, field of activity in which, years later, I was able to make a small but unique contribution.

Shortly after I arrived in Aberdeen the University had purchased a new mainframe computer. It cost a million pounds and a special building was put up to house it on the top of Sunnybank hill, whence the noise of the plant that kept it cool could be heard grumbling away all day and all night. Leaflets came round the University inviting members of staff to come and be shown around this installation. I didn't see what this had to do with me but I felt all the same that I ought to know something about this new technology, so, when another leaflet came round offering tuition in programming, I remembered Roy Johnston's advice to me years before. I had asked him to recommend a book about electronics and he had said: Don't read about it, get doing it. So I turned up on Sunnybank hill with a shiny new notebook and joined what looked like an alarmingly high-powered group of physicists, chemists and engineers to learn the programming language Fortran. The tutor, a big shambling man with a Lancashire accent, was a bit taken aback when he learnt that I came from, of all places, the French Department. He was even more taken aback when he set us our first exercise, which was to program the computer to work out a fairly simple equation involving Greek characters I had never seen before. I had to tell him that I wouldn't have the first idea how to do it on paper, the sums I had learnt at school not having taken me that far. But he was a resourceful man, and devised exercises just for me that did various things with words.

I was just beginning to make sense of Fortran when I chanced to make the acquaintance of a lecturer in physiology called Morton Diament who was working on an original type of multiple choice test which they were experimenting with in the Medical School. Called an Indeterminate True False Test this presented the students with a series of sentences to accept or reject. The right answer gained them a point; a wrong answer lost them one. The unusual feature of the test was that the students could answer Don't Know to each question, in which case they neither lost nor gained a mark. Mort Diament was fighting a vigorous battle in defence of this test against colleagues who objected that a student who answered Don't Know to every question could, in theory at least, get a better mark than those who simply got some questions wrong. Whatever about its suitability for physiology - and Diament was interestingly critical of the way medicine is taught in universities - I saw that this type of MCQ was exactly what I wanted for testing comprehension of spoken French. He gave me a copy of the program he had written - in Fortran, happily, as it happened - to mark his exam and to analyse the results. I set about adapting it as a language test, puzzling my way through page after page of what, to start with, seemed totally incomprehensible code.

It is hard to believe that a mere 30 or 40 years separates our world of gigabytes and mobile phones from the huge mainframes of yesteryear. Aberdeen University's new mainframe, in its temple on Sunnybank hill, was harmless enough to look at, resembling, as Olivia remarked on one of her rare visits, nothing so much as row after row of washing machines. The user-unfriendliness of the installation as a whole was another thing altogether. You could only read programs and data into it by typing them onto, literally, hundreds of punched cards, an 80 character line at a time. You then had to hand this immense deck of cards to one of the operators, without dropping them, and the program would take its turn on the machine, sometimes a whole day later. More times than not it would fail. If there was a mistake in the programming the machine would spew out several pages of cryptic error messages and stop. Or else there would be a miniscule typing error, a space before a comma somewhere, and it would churn away, producing enough paper to wallpaper a bathroom, with SYNTAX ERROR printed three hundred times on every sheet. All this was maximally intimidating to me since, being the only non-scientist on the scene and only marginally numerate, I was sure that one of the operators in white coats was going to come up to me and tell me I was wasting the machine's time and to go away and not come back. As a result I made myself as inconspicuous as possible, hiding in a corner behind the card punches and only working in the evenings or late at night when there was hardly anyone else there.

And then a minor incident reassured me that, whatever about being computerate, literacy could be useful too. I had been working quite late several nights running, tinkering with my program, and I had been very conscious of this character at the other end of the room banging away at tremendous speed and with great brio on one of the card punches. Judging by the bits of very technical conversation with the operators that I had been able to overhear he was obviously a scientist and much more at home in the place than I was. We had never spoken; I saw him as just another scary pundit. This particular night one of the operators came in and presented him with a wodge of printout. I could hear him swearing, grunting and gasping and making other frustrated noises. Then he suddenly got up and came over to me. "Can you help me," he said. "Program fails every time... tried everything...can't see what's wrong." Fearful that my total inexpertise was now at last going be shown up I took his program and tried to pretend to understand the reams of indecipherable code. And then I saw that in the very first line of his program, where in Fortran you have to declare the sorts of numbers used, he had spelt *integer* with an "a". "Gosh," he said. "However did you spot that?" "Child's play," I felt like answering.

Had I had the slightest inkling of what the future had in store for everyone in the way of information technology I would have found it all far less awe inspiring. That huge machine, with its own building and its team of jargon-speaking operators in white coats, took nearly half an hour to carry out an operation that the most ordinary microchip can now do in milliseconds. And its 32K of memory was too small even to contain the names of the students in first year French, they had to be given numbers. Still, I wrote several programs for it, mostly calculating other exam marks, and learnt some statistics in the process. The familiarity with computers that I had acquired was useful when microcomputers came on the scene some years later. But that story comes later.

A few years before leaving Paris I had met Liam Miller of the Dolmen Press in Dublin. He had liked my *Emigrant* poem which had appeared in *The Irish*

*Democrat*. Inspired by a poem of Aragon's, *Le Conscrit de Cent Villages*, which is just a versified list of village names, I had woven around the names of a hundred Irish townlands a simplistic Marxist analysis of most of the country's major ills of the time. So I had given him a selection of poems to look at and, preoccupied by other problems, I had forgotten all about them. And then one day in Dublin I mentioned them to Austin Clarke over lunch chez my brother and he encouraged me to jog Liam Miller's memory, advising me, if Dolmen published anything, to watch out for misprints. Accordingly I rang Liam Miller and he took me off - it was ten o'clock in the morning I remember - to a pub by Baggot Street Bridge where over mugs of whiskey he went through my little collection saying Yes to this one and No to that. In 1969 when my *Emigrant of the Hundred Townlands and Other Poems* came out I wished I had taken Austin Clarke's advice to heart. One of the poems was rendered incomprehensible by a misprint.

Through innocence or inexperience I had assumed that it was for the publisher to send copies of a book for review and didn't realise until my *Emigrant* had been out for nearly a year that Dolmen didn't work that way. So the book received only the most perfunctory of notice. This didn't really worry me. I thought, as I still think, that while my best poems are as good as most of what was written at the time, there just weren't enough of them. And I had moved on from wanting to think of myself as a poet. I had in fact myself taken the advice that I gave occasionally to students who wanted to be actors or artists. This was that if you possess only a moderate amount of creative talent it is better, more satisfying and, above all, more useful to society, if you put it into everyday activities instead of hanging around the fringe of the artistic world in endless frustration and disappointment. Second-rate actors, poets and artists are all over the place, whereas society badly needs imaginative administrators, and teachers gifted with a bit of creative insight.

### THE EMIGRANT OF A HUNDRED TOWNLANDS

I stand at the gap of the year and send
A greeting back to home and friend,
Murmuring over, name after name,
The hundred townlands whence I came.

Their names, their names, they turn in my mind:
Boherapuca, Carrigaline,
Six-Mile-Bridge, Watergrasshill,
Scart, Spink, Ballynakill.

They whine like fiddles in Nad and Neone,
Nenagh, Nurney, Naul and Cloon,
Or croon like doves in Croom and Coole,
Oola, Collooney, Cloonacool.

Names with a distant alien ring:
Maas, Louisburgh, Glinsk or Bweeng,
Names that are Irish in to the core:
Caherconlish, Magherymore.

Newtownmountkennedy, Ballyjamesduff,
Names within names, and sure enough,
Horseleap, Priesthaggard, Five-Alley-Rath,
A name is a story's aftermath.

Though it's long ago and far away,
Crossmolina, Portballintrae,
Borris-in-Ossory, Ballinafad,
I'll not forget the times we had.

The school was cold, the paint was green
Daingean, Rathangan, Ballyporeen,
The teacher beat us for climbing the wall,
Crolly, Kinnitty, Golden-Ball.

When we were lads in Mullingar,
Camolin, Timolin, Swanlinbar,
Camps, Claudy, Ring and Glin,
We'd rides on the floats when the hay came in.

Kill, Killaloe, Killala, Killeen,
Cahernahallia, Cahirciveen,
Ballyconneely, Aherlow;
Lads kicking ball in the field below.

Where are the lads now, where are they gone,
From Courtmacsherry and Grianan,
From Penny-Come-Quick and Moneygall,
Elphin, Delphi, Valentia and all?

Gone like the horses, gone like the herring,
From Clara, Claddagh, Schull and Sperrin,
From Silvermines, Allihies, Moneymore,
For gold and for good, like the copper ore.

There's money making in Dublin town,
Naas and Drogheda, Portadown,
And never a penny ploughing back,
In Lack or Lackan, or Ballinalack.

Money invested over the sea,
But in Esker, Emly, Clonaslee,
Tuam and Tully, Cloyne and Clare,
It's the tourist's cash pays the emigrant's fare.

It's a sorry state that is torn in two,
At Pettigo, Clones and Belcoo;
Ah when will the ancient curse be laid
That milks this land of man and maid?

For then Dungannon, Dungarvan, Dunloe,
Dunlaoighaire as one together will go,
And Malin and Mizen, Linnhe and Lene
In one coherent land be seen.

T'will be Clane and Prosperous, Trim and Clear,
Edenderry and Golden there,
And my hundred townlands peopled again
With a power of children girls and men.

The year 1969 saw not only the publication of my *Emigrant* but also the performance of what I still think of as Conor's best play, *Aaron Thy Brother*, at the Peacock Theatre in Dublin. One of a series that he wrote based on episodes of Irish History, *Aaron Thy Brother* tells the story of how, after the failure of Robert Emmett's rebellion, John Philpot Curran, Ireland's leading lawyer and an influential opinion-former, was blackmailed by the English authorities into declining to act in defence of Emmett and other nationalist leaders. By threatening to have his beloved daughter, Sarah, who had been in love with Emmett, arrested and tried for treason, they silenced what would have been a powerful voice speaking for Irish freedom. In his play Conor made very effective use of a chorus of Irish soldiers serving with the United Nations in Africa whose simple devotion to duty, boring or dangerous, contrasted movingly with Curran's effective betrayal of the national cause.

Both Olivia and I found *Aaron* a very moving piece of dramatic writing, made more powerful in performance by being written in a sort of loosely structured blank verse. This, while it heightened the dramatic effect when spoken on the stage, gave a distinctly off-putting appearance to the printed text.

Whether it was this, or simply that Conor's whole approach was out of tune with the style of play-writing then in vogue, the play had been turned down by the Abbey Theatre. When it was put on in the little Peacock, it only ran for a week and received only a few somewhat indifferent notices. It was the sixteenth stage play he had written, the only one I ever saw performed, and his, in the opinion of many people, totally undeserved lack of success with it was sadly typical of his career as a playwright. I wasn't alone in thinking that he had a very considerable talent as a dramatist and that Irish literary culture is the poorer for not having recognised it.

Conor was, as I have said, a very much more single-minded and dedicated person than me. While still at school he had decided that his future would be in the theatre. So, shortly after graduating from TCD, he joined a travelling theatre company in order to gain practical experience. The company, which was run by Geoffrey Kendal and his wife, parents of the actor Felicity Kendal who was then still a baby, had found a niche for itself presenting popular and classical plays to expatriate British communities overseas. Shortly after Conor had completed his two years with them the company was made the subject of the Merchant Ivory film *Shakespeare Wallah*. The film describes the fortunes and misfortunes of the Kendals' troupe, which was called *Shakespeariana*. They toured India and Pakistan presenting, not only *Macbeth* and *Hamlet* in schools and colleges, but also modern farcical comedies such as *Charley's Aunt*, to the leftover hangers-on of the recently dismantled British Raj. Conor returned to Ireland in 1954 and joined the Radio Eireann Players. He became one of the best-known and admired actors in the company, performing in radio drama and also in popular radio soaps like *The Foley Family*. He had a major part in the production of *Bloomsday* when Radio Eireann presented the whole of Joyce's *Ulysses* in one non-stop 24 hour radio drama marathon. Thanks to his understanding of radio drama he wrote a number of successful radio plays which was some compensation for his lack of success in theatre. In 1993 Olivia and I were in a police station in Kerry, handing in a tourist's wallet we had found. Hearing the name Farrington the burly Garda sergeant immediately asked was I any relation to the Conor Farrington he listened to regularly on Radio Eireann. I was proud to be able to say that I was Conor's brother.

Personally I have sometimes wondered if the reason for Conor's failure to break through to success as a playwright didn't lie in the very purity of his artistic integrity and his refusal to compromise, to meet as it were the exigencies of popular taste half way. If that was so it is possible that his marriage to Patricia Martin who was an experienced actor with many friends and acquaintances in theatrical milieux might have enabled him to escape from his artistic isolation and to work more collaboratively. But unfortunately a few years into his very happy second marriage he developed the inoperable cancer that was to blight his last years and he died tragically when only 66 in 1996.

Conor [Above]
Peter Wexler

After I had been a few years in Aberdeen the nature of the set up I was in charge of began to change. From being a small unit giving technical support to the academic language departments it was turning into a centre providing language services of different sorts to the University as a whole. In view of this a new building was put up with purpose-designed accommodation, a properly equipped recording studio and other facilities, and I was made Director of what was in fact a Language Centre, though, through the ignorance of a senior professor, we were obliged to keep the discredited misnomer, Language Laboratory, for some time. I was given funding to invite departmental lecturers and, seeing that it was an occasion to make some sort of mark, I gave quite a lot of thought to the choice of a first lecturer. So I invited Peter Wexler. The occasion turned out to be more memorable than even I, knowing P. Wexler, could have expected.

I wish I could recall the title that Peter suggested for his "talk" and which figured on the leaflets I sent around the Senior Common Room. All I can remember is that it consisted of one, somewhat tantalisingly ambiguous, sentence designed, I could see, to stimulate curiosity about linguistics. It succeeded in this; quite a number of people turned up, and not just linguists. Several were standing around in the room when Peter and I arrived, obviously undecided as to where to sit. Lecturers, like students, almost always prefer to sit at the back. When Peter started moving chairs around and then moved himself two or three times, so that no one could be sure where the back and the front of the room were, I realised something unusual was going to happen. I had asked him what he would like me to say by way of introduction and he had said, "As little as possible. Two, three words." So, as soon as he stopped moving around, I just stood up and said, "Well, here is Dr Wexler," and sat down.

Peter stood up, beamed at the expectant audience, and pronounced just one sentence. It was something like, "The thing about being a lecturer is that, whenever he opens his mouth, what comes out is a lecture." And then he stood there, saying nothing, looking around him, unperturbed, deadpan. There followed a silence: total, bizarre, acutely embarrassing, interminable. It went on and on, unbelievably, for one minute, two minutes, all of five minutes I think, though it felt like more. Knowing Peter I knew straightaway that it was intentional. The others did not have this advantage and the atmosphere grew more and more tense and uncomfortable until at length a kindly Senior Lecturer in English, obviously thinking that Peter had been struck by some sort of aphasia and wanting to throw him a lifeline, said, "Well, um, supposing you tell us what you mean by a lecture." Peter glanced at him, looked around the room and said, "Me, tell you?" Somebody else, the tension having relaxed somewhat, spoke then, rather pompously, and again Peter picked a key word from his remark and threw it back, again with a querying intonation. There followed a most extraordinarily interactive session which lasted the best part of an hour. Provoked as much by Peter's responses as by his silences, speaker after speaker came out with statements, ideas and opinions, some thoughtful, some idiotic, some totally irrelevant, to each of which Peter's reaction was instantaneous, thought-provoking, and often quite witty, as for example when he said, "Teach people? The trouble with "teach" is that it's too transitive a verb."

From my memory of his lectures in Manchester I could see what Peter was doing. The main idea behind this performance was that if you teach something to students by conventional methods you make it impossible for them to discover the knowledge for themselves. But, instead of spelling out this idea in the usual 50 minute monologue, he was trying to get this roomful of academics to discover it for ourselves. He succeeded in this, with the more intelligent and sensitive members of the audience. On the other hand some more conventional colleagues couldn't take it at all. A Senior Lecturer in Education walked out in the middle slamming the door, though the Professor of Education later rang me to say how much he wished he had been there. One man, a lecturer in Forestry, announced in a loud voice that it was such a waste of time that he didn't know what he was going to say to his wife to explain why he was late home for his tea. And one of the Professors of French, not Armel Diverres, missed the point completely. He went round telling everyone afterwards that Wexler either just hadn't bothered to prepare his lecture or else had lost his notes. But in the weeks and months that followed Peter's visit thoughtful colleagues, and, in several cases, people I hardly knew, usually scientists, would come up to me and say things like, "Extraordinary business that non-lecture thing you organised..Really made me think....Who is this chap Wexler?"

One morning in 1972 I was surprised to receive an invitation from the Scottish Exam Board to serve as a visiting examiner in French for the new Sixth Year Studies exam. It came from my friend Bernard Swift, an Aberdeen colleague who had recently moved to Stirling and was now a Chief Examiner for the Exam Board. I had once entertained him with stories of oral examining for the Cambridge Proficiency in English exams in Paris. I didn't think this was really my cup of tea, and I told him so. "The thing is, Bernard," I said, "I just find it very hard to decide how good or how bad someone's French is." "That," replied Bernard Swift, "Is precisely why I want you on the team." I could hardly refuse after that. So started a collaboration which lasted happily for nearly 25 years and which enabled me to explore and to get to know the Highlands in an unusual way, and at an unfashionable time of year.

I filled in some forms and received some weeks later a list of schools in or around Aberdeen accompanied by a page of schoolmastery instructions reminding me to make my travel arrangements "in good time" with an invitation to attend a standardising meeting in Edinburgh. Here I met the other examiners. When I entered the room they were comparing each other's "marching orders". "Plockton," one was saying, "How on earth am I to get there?" "That's nothing," said another, "I have to go to Stromness, of all places." "Oh Stromness in Orkney," said a third, "Last year I found that if I got an early flight I could get back in time for tea." I said nothing as I listened to all this, but next year, when the form came round, I scribbled across it that I had no objection to staying away overnight and that I preferred the Highlands and Islands. As a result every year for twenty years or more I spent a number of days driving across the beautiful wild wastes of Northern Scotland from one small town to another at the expense of the Scottish Exam Board, punctuating, and justifying, this tourism with, on the whole, pleasantly varied conversations in French with intelligent teenagers, who, into the bargain, were usually girls, and often managing to get up a mountain or two on my way home. And all this at a time of year when there were no midges and no tourists.

The actual exam itself was essentially a simple test of conversational French. Discussion of the coursework the students had done was supposed to be an important feature but, while this added an obvious note of academic seriousness, since you had to tell them before it started that their actual knowledge, or ignorance, about the syllabus was not being tested, it just meant that they came into the room with an idea of what they were going to start off talking about. Sometimes the conversation took an unexpectedly personal turn, which was not altogether surprising since the poor kids were all the same under some emotional strain. I had to remind myself that my role was limited to noting things like adjective agreements and that I was not paid to give advice on domestic crises. I'm afraid I interpreted some of the Board's instructions somewhat freely, but I was reassured to learn, after I had been doing it for a few years, that my grading correlated with the general performance of the candidates more closely than that of the rest of the team.

On the whole, though, I liked and approved of the instructions we were given, in particular the reminder that even the weakest candidates should not leave the room with a feeling of total failure and that the strongest should feel that they had been stretched by the test. Since these could, as occasionally happened, be girls with French mothers or actual native speakers of French, this wasn't always easy, and I would be hard set to flummox them or at least frame questions that would give them an occasion to show off by using literary vocabulary or arcane subjunctives. At a lower level I found it easy to think up strategies that would help me to decide between Satisfactory and Good. For example I would ask candidates what they *would* have done – *qu'auriez-vous fait si* - if they had been Thérèse Desqueyroux, to see how they handled the Conditional and other similar tricks. Another thing I liked about the exam was that there was no Pass and Fail, and, since only pupils with a definite interest in French stayed on for a sixth year, there were very few inarticulate stumblers and the job mostly consisted in grading them somewhere between Satisfactory and Very Good, keeping Excellent for the near-native speakers.

I was impressed at the quality of the French of these Scottish teenagers which was if anything better than the English I had been used to in Paris. I remarked on this once to the Head Teacher in one small Highland town where I had just met two girls the fluency of whose French had surprised me, since they had never been to France and the school had no French *Assistant*. He said to me that French and German tourists often drive too fast along the single-track Highland roads. They meet something coming the other way, pull to the right and end up in the Cottage Hospital down the road. "Whenever this happens," he said, "I send our Sixth Year candidates along to talk to them and interpret for the nurses. Works very well some years."

In Paris interviewing a long production line of candidates could become exceedingly *fatigant*, in both senses of the word, and it was often hard to find different subjects of conversation. In Scotland there were rarely more than four or five candidates in a school and when I had seen the last one, and chatted briefly with the teacher I would have twenty, or thirty (or fifty), miles to drive through Highland scenery before seeing the next batch. And the schools ranged from ultra-modern, open-plan, to incredibly antiquated as at Stromness where the Head Teacher, Mr McInnes, told me that his buildings were in demand by BBC for filming things like *Nicolas Nickleby* or *Jane Eyre*. He, McInnes, was a favourite of mine. He was a man with no small talk at all. Where I would normally be greeted by Headmasters – there were very few Headmistresses – with banalities about the state of the roads, at Stromness I would walk into his office and he would look up and plunge straightaway into a conversation about clouds or missionaries or Marco Polo or some other subject equally unexpected. For years I thought of getting in first with some similarly Byzantine opening, as for example when I read somewhere a description of Camembert cheese as "tasting like the smell of God's feet", I thought immediately of surprising Mr McInnes with it. But I never managed to.

All this had, however, an inauspicious start which very nearly made me resign after two years. At a school in the West Highlands the room I was given to interview the three candidates in was beside the somewhat self-important Head Teacher's study. I had just started talking to the third, a very nervous girl if I remember rightly, when an angry voice could be heard through the wall from the next room followed by an ominous silence, and then, unmistakeably, the sound of six strokes, of a cane I supposed, though actually what was used was, I believe a specially designed leather belt. I terminated the examination, reassuring the girl who was I think less shocked than I was by the experience, which told me something about the school. I left as quickly as I could. If I hadn't been so new to the job and to Scotland I would certainly have created a scene. But I still felt myself very much a foreigner, and for all I knew this was an everyday occurrence. So I scuttled away, ashamed at having remained silent and wondering what had happened to the young man who, twenty years before, had argued with a French *Avocat Général* telling him that his guillotine was a barbarity. Happily nothing like this ever happened again and a few years later all physical punishment was prohibited in Scottish schools, and none too soon.

Of course this oral examining wouldn't have been at all the same had I lived in or near a large city like Glasgow or Edinburgh. It was the distances I had to cover to reach places like Gairloch or Thurso that I liked about the job. I also found the candidates in small towns tended to be more interesting to talk to. And then I decided that it would be easier and suit me better if I camped in the car instead of staying in hotels or B & Bs, which were in any case thin on the ground when the examining happened, in February and early March. As the years went by I managed to find places all over the Highlands where it was possible to get the car off and well away from the road in the dark. Olivia and I found that the Austin Maxi suited this solution exactly and we had several of them. As a piece of automobile engineering the car was distinctly second rate but it was the fastest double bed on the European furniture market. Also you could transform the seats into a bed without opening the doors, which was a great advantage when it was snowing, as quite often happened. Olivia would be preparing for bed in Aberdeen and I would depart. Two or three hours later I would be in my sleeping bag among the alder trees or by a favourite lake in the hills above Inverness. I learnt to be wary of lakes, since the water level can vary suddenly because of hydroelectric schemes. Once when I had parked on firm ground but very close to the water's edge I woke at about four in the morning alarmed to hear "lake water lapping with low sounds" round the car. Happily only a few inches deep.

I decided that it would be best if the officials of the Exam Board, friendly and all as they were, knew nothing of all this. So I had a problem when it came to declaring my expenses. I was afraid that if I claimed for nothing it might seem odd, on the other hand if I put in a full claim someone might suggest I was camping in the car out of simple pecuniary greed, in order to pocket the, actually quite generous, overnight expenses, in cash. In the end I didn't claim and no one found it strange. Of course if I was away several nights running I had to adopt a more orthodox solution anyway, so that I could have a bath. Otherwise I much preferred to go my own way, though I am afraid the Exam Board might not have considered my sleeping arrangements to be in keeping with the dignity of my function.

As for example the time I had parked on waste ground at the foot of a huge high-tension pylon. There was snow on the ground and a hard frost when I arrived and all night I could hear it crackling on the insulators above me. The sun was just rising next morning when I got out for a pee. Since I had a very warm Alpine sleeping bag and I'd have been too hot in pyjamas I never wore them. I stepped out onto the crisp snow, enjoying the sudden bite of the sharp air on my bare skin, like a cold shower. Then, turning to look at the sunrise, I chanced to nudge the open door of the car and it slammed shut, locking me out into the landscape, which suddenly became less picturesque. As I frantically checked all the doors and windows a car went past, a police car actually I think, but I crouched out of sight, imagining what the local paper would make of this odd behaviour on the part of a representative of the Scottish Exam Board. And then I remembered that, backing clumsily into one of those black and yellow posts that used to ornament the Station car park in Aberdeen, I had dented the lock of the boot so it didn't close properly. I managed to get it open and clamber in. An hour later, dressed in my sober suit and tie and wearing my serious face, I was greeting the Head Teacher of the local Academy.

Or the time I had taken seventeen-year old Doreen, who was on holiday from her French lycée, on one of my examining trips. I was due to oral three pupils at Oban on the West coast at nine in the morning so we arrived as usual the evening before. I had never examined in Oban but I was sure it would not be difficult to find a scenic spot to park and camp somewhere along the coast. Unfortunately, when we came out of Oban's indifferent Chinese restaurant, it was not only pitch dark but raining heavily. We drove around for miles but the dark and the rain made prospecting for a sleeping place difficult and we ended up some distance from the road in what seemed to be a field. It was in fact a deserted caravan-site. We folded down the seats and got into our sleeping bags.

Next morning it was still pouring but we managed to have breakfast without getting out of the car. Then I got into my suit and started the engine. But it had rained so much and the ground was so soft that the wheels just spun round. There was nothing for it but to get out into the rain and phone for help. I had to walk several miles before I found a house with a phone and got a chap from a local garage to come with a Land Rover. A surly character, he pulled us on to the road easily and then when I went to pay him he suddenly gave me a knowing wink. Realising what he was thinking I made some remark referring to Doreen as "my daughter". "Sure," he replied, the alacrity of his response compounding the innuendo by accusing me also of hypocrisy, as though to say "That's what they all say."

The last year of this agreeable labour, and the last school I visited was marked appropriately. I had taken longer than normal at the preceding school where the unique candidate had been a girl who was blind, I think from birth. The circumstances that surrounded her learning French were so unusual, and so interesting, - she had had to read the prescribed texts in Braille, looking up the words she didn't know in the unwieldy four volume Braille edition of the Harrap dictionary – and she was such a pleasant person that, though her spoken French was excellent, I'm afraid I kept her talking longer than I needed. Anyway I rang the next, and last, school to say I would be late, and the Modern Languages teacher told me that, since she would be teaching, the janitor would look after me when I arrived.

Accordingly when I arrived the janitor directed me to a room with HEADMASTER on the door. I knocked and entered and, finding the Headmaster sitting behind a massive desk, I started in on the usual conversation I was accustomed to having with headmasters, apologising for arriving late, describing the difficulty of finding the school, talking about the exam and other banalities. It's true that, as I spoke, I was thinking to myself that he was a bit on the young side, even for nowadays. Anyway after some minutes of this, and running out of things to say, I asked if the candidate would be along soon, and he replied, "But I am the candidate." I did my best, unsuccessfully, to talk my way out of having taken him for the Head. It's true he was a "mature student" in his early twenties. But I realised that it was time I stopped. I had reached the age limit anyway.

My last ten years directing the Language Centre were spent agreeably. In addition to my teaching in the French Department I developed software which is described in the next chapter, I published a number of articles on this and on my mountain vocab research, but, since my job had been redefined by the relevant national higher education authorities as having no research commitment, no one, me or the Centre or the University, was able to claim any credit for any of this. Not that this worried me. On the other hand the University began to take an increasing interest in a sideline that we had opened up.

It had started one day in the early eighties when Christine Burgess received an unexpected phone call from Shell, the oil company. Christine, who had been a student of mine and was now a York-trained language teacher, had recently joined the Language Centre. It was a miraculous coincidence that she should have turned up in Aberdeen looking for a job just when Alison Murray was on the point of retiring and we were trying to choose between the only two applicants for her post, both of them preposterously unsuitable. The nature of the job was changing. Cheap photocopying had put an end to the typing that had taken up much of Alison's time. On the other hand our activities were expanding so Christine's entrepreneurial skills, her talent for innovation and her knowledge of Applied Linguistics were to prove invaluable later, as it turned out.

Shell, we learned, were sending two engineers to Venezuela in a month's time and had just learnt that they would have to be able to speak Spanish. Could we help? Christine was on the point of saying Sorry, and suggesting they try Berlitz in London when an alternative occurred to us. So we rang Berlitz ourselves, pretending to be an oil company in Scotland, describing the problem and asking for an estimate. Berlitz replied immediately, citing a figure for three weeks' intensive tuition, six hours a day. I don't remember the amount, which would be meaningless today anyway, but it was for what sounded to us like a very large sum of money. The University Spanish Department, as a result of a recent wave of cuts, had just lost the funding for their foreign *lecteur*. So I rang them and when they had got over the surprise they said they would be game for organising a three-week intensive course in Spanish for complete beginners if it would pay for a *lecteur* post. So we told Shell that we could do it here in Aberdeen for a price that was about three quarters the sum cited by Berlitz and landed the contract. It was the first of many.

Over the years we developed an extensive range of language services to industry in the North East of Scotland: interpreting, translating and training. It was linguistically quite interesting since, for example language training courses had to be carefully designed to fit in with the practical needs of the client and the time available, both of which would dictate how much and what grammar and vocabulary to choose to teach. We got quite good at designing very short intensive programs which sometimes contained very little language beyond greetings and apologies but would instruct business men going abroad how to bow and be bowed to if they were going to Japan, or, if they were invited to lunch in France, not to turn up with a bunch of chrysanthemums.

All this earned a considerable amount of money, most of which went directly to the University which was adapting itself both to the effect of reduced government funding and the prevailing economic climate of monetarism. However, though our entrepreneurial activities were approved of, since universities are not businesses, the official attitude to them was from the start amateurish. As was proved by what happened over our relations with the French oil company, Total.

In the early eighties we had secured a very lucrative contract with Total by which the Language Centre supplied a full-time tutor in English as a Foreign Language. The tutor's post, which Olivia took over in 1984, received a lecturer's salary but the fee for the contract, which Total paid, and which covered various unlikely eventualities, was for a much larger sum. Unfortunately the University was not content with this and, after a few years, got greedy. When it came up for renewal the University asked for a much increased figure, whereupon Total cancelled the contract. The whole episode reminded me of something my father told me about. After a meeting of a committee on which there were several Reverends, at the Dublin Zoo actually, this businessman said to him, "Parsons are no good at business. They think business is just cheating. So if ever they have to *do* business they just try to cheat." Aberdeen University was behaving like the Dublin parsons. I had another example when they started chivvying me saying that the Language Centre had made X thousand pounds this year and what was my "business plan" for increasing this and by how much. The row smouldered on until I retired. Of course it was true that like all British universities Aberdeen was in serious financial difficulties. But I would have preferred it if, instead of working out ways of applying the cuts in funding, British universities had tried to fight them, as I had seen French faculties doing, if necessary coming down into the street. But of course that is not part of the British way of life, more's the pity in my opinion.

The Total affair ended happily for us however. A few days after the contract with the University was cancelled Total rang Olivia and said that they had no wish to end their agreement with her personally. If she set herself up as an enterprise, they said, they would award the contract directly to her. She worked there until she retired, making a success of what was an unusual teaching situation: tutoring very high-powered French engineers and geologists on a one-to-one basis. She was able later to use the experience as a basis for her first novel "*Love as a Foreign Language*," published under her maiden name of McMahon and for books on English grammar and pronunciation for French learners which were published in France.

The Total fiasco wasn't the only example of the University trying unsuccessfully to pretend to be a business. A ludicrous instance was a one-day workshop in Management that was organised for all senior staff and Departmental Heads, to which I was summoned in the last year before I retired. A team of Management Consultants, most of them in their mid-thirties, had been brought up from England and presented to us by a senior Vice-Principal of the

University who, though he was a distinguished mediaevalist, felt he needed to describe himself to these people as Chief Executive of the University. After a keynote monologue about the need for university people to learn from the business world we were divided up into small groups and given sheets of paper containing various management problems to discuss. For example there would be a list of hypothetical academics of different ages, different degrees of specialisation, different sorts of personality, publications and so on and we would be invited to decide which if any of these individuals we would consider for promotion and why. Teaching, so far as I remember, didn't figure among the parameters to be considered. As we went from one problem to another I found it mildly amusing to see which of my colleagues entered into the spirit of this gratuitous activity, thereby earning the approval of the management expert in charge of our group, a young woman whose only knowledge of universities, it became clear, seemed to have been acquired by reading novels by C P Snow.

One of the problems on the sheet concerned the appointment of a dynamic young specialist to a post already held by a senior academic who had produced no research for years. One solution suggested by our expert was that the older person should be let go, her euphemism for giving him the sack. At this point one member of our group objected, pointing out that the Head of an academic Department did not have the power or authority to terminate a lecturer's appointment. "Well I'll have to set you right there," said the consultant, adopting a sort of Nursey-knows-best tone of voice, "That's not the case, you know." There followed a dialogue which the rest of us could not help enjoying, since we knew the objector, Maureen Shaw, and her position in the University admin. Eventually someone spoke up and said, "I think you ought to know that the person you are speaking to is the University Personnel Officer". Collapse of stout party. It was just as well it was lunch-time then.

After lunch we were divided into two groups each of which were given the same puzzle to work out a way of solving. The puzzle itself was quite interesting; it consisted of a complex jig-saw in which the pieces fitted together in a number of different ways and it wasn't clear which way up they were to go. One team, composed largely of medics was headed by a science professor who I knew to be a very effective head of department but a bit of a bully. The other, to which I was assigned, was headed by Peter Ramsey, a History professor who, though he was exceedingly intelligent, having worked as a code-breaker at Bletchley during the War, was a diffident, not very incisive but courteous man. It was later obvious that someone high up in the University must have collaborated in setting up the teams. Because the basic aim of the activity was obvious. It was clearly intended to demonstrate the superior efficiency of a closely structured line management set-up.

When the game started the difference between the two teams was audible: the science professor could be heard barking orders and instructions on the other side of the room whereas Peter Ramsey, after examining the pile of jig-saw pieces for some time, just said, "Um, don't know where to start really. Anyone got an idea?" Various people put forward tentative suggestions and we set to trying these out in small amorphous groups with different degrees of success. The band of Management Consultants could hardly have hoped to find a better example of anarchic, disorganised muddling through. Except that it didn't work out the way they had intended. Someone in our serendipitous team hit on a way of solving the problem so that we, the academic muddlers, had our puzzle finished well ahead of the line management crowd. The team of management experts did their best to conceal their discomfiture and pass this disaster off as a triumph but I don't think they even fooled themselves.

It was easy to laugh as we did at this exercise in Business expertise being imposed on a roomful of academics. As it turned out I would have much preferred the university authorities to have been content to play at being businessmen in an atmosphere of harmless amateurism. Instead, mildly ridiculous events such as I have described were a foretaste of a much more unpleasant reality. As years went by there were more and more examples, in Aberdeen as elsewhere, of universities applying and imposing monetarist principles in the most unsuitable ways. Adopting a Thatcherite view, when Thatcherism was already on the wane, some senior academics and admin staff chose to see this as a fashionable modern replacement for the humanist idea of a university as an institution dedicated to the pursuit and transmission of knowledge for its own sake. They therefore set out so far as possible to sideline the principles and ways of working that universities had pursued over the years, which may have seemed vague and woolly but which had been evolved to deal with imponderables, such as scholarship, which cannot be evaluated precisely and which call for acceptance of a wide margin of error if they are to be evaluated at all. Instead they are now endeavouring to work out a sort of Mickey-mouse cost-benefit analysis of all sorts of activities whose value commonsense had long rated as unquantifiable, seeing higher education as an industry, a business geared to production, the customers being students and the products graduates. For instance when our daughter Roisin went to university I had to fill in and sign some administrative form. On this document the box in which Roisin's name was to figure was labelled: Name of Customer. At the time I saw all this as a temporary aberration, a misguided attempt by a minority of eccentrics in power to curry favour in the world of business by aping the values of Alan Sugar and Michael O'Leary, and I was sure that a wiser view of Academia and its importance to society would prevail. But by all accounts the situation has got steadily worse in the last twenty years. I am therefore glad that I retired when I did so that almost all my memories of Aberdeen and its university are pleasant to recall.

# Language Learning by Computer 13

One morning in 1979 Christine Burgess and I received an invitation to attend a demonstration in St Andrews of a "groundbreaking innovation in the joint fields of computing and of language learning." Essentially, we learned, this was to consist of a talk by a Senior Lecturer in German from the University of Hull called Rex Last. It was to be followed – the groundbreaking part - by a demonstration of software that he had created. It was the first time I met Rex Last. He may not have been the only person in Britain to think of using a computer for language learning but he was undeniably *the* instigator, pioneer and initiator of CALL (Computer-Assisted Language Learning) as a distinct speciality in Britain. A somewhat prickly individual, this first meeting with him was notable for much the same mixture of inspiration and exasperation as later encounters. In his talk he described materials he was developing for teaching elementary German using Hull University's mainframe computer. He spoke with great enthusiasm, and often very wittily, of the future that this new technology offered. However, since hardly anyone in the audience knew anything at all about computers, there was as much mystification as there was enlightenment in the general effect. This was not helped by the way he bandied a host of technical terms about, speaking freely of things like machine code and databases without explaining what any of these things were.

When we went from the lecture room, and crowded round a terminal in the University Computing Centre for the demonstration, mystification turned, for many of the audience, to disillusion. This wasn't really all Last's fault. Because, inevitably, when he called up the Hull University computer on the telephone, not a word about learning German appeared. Instead, since he was only one user among many, the screen was filled by the usual gobbledygook of incomprehensible system messages, addressed to, or relevant to the activities of, other users. We waited as screen after screen of this stuff came and went. Several people gave up at this point and left saying that machines were obviously too stupid to do anything with natural language. Christine and I waited however, and eventually a series of questions relating to German grammar and vocabulary came up. From the start our criticisms of what we were being shown had nothing to do with the technology being in its infancy, which it clearly was, but with the language content. For example, when the system presented its first question: *What is the German for car?* and Christine typed in one of the two possible correct answers, namely *Der Wagen,* the reply came: *That is the wrong answer. The German for car is Das Auto.* More interestingly, when she tried putting in a correct noun with the wrong gender article it just came up with the same response: *That is the wrong answer. The German for car is Das Auto.* "Pretty silly to ask a question with two right answers," she remarked, voicing what was in my mind also.

Rex Last, then, got the system to come up with some grammar questions that were more interesting, linguistically, than elementary vocabulary. While I was trying to think of different ways of testing these I chanced to hear someone at the back of the group asking Last why it was that his system had only one way of responding when a student gave a wrong answer. Last replied, somewhat glibly in our eyes, saying that it was important not to confuse the learners by irrelevant complications. When my turn at the terminal came to an end I went round and got talking to the questioner. He turned out to be a Senior Lecturer in Electrical Engineering and he told me that he had for some years been using a teaching program of his own design on the St Andrews mainframe and, what was more, he offered to show it to us working. We went round to the Engineering Department and he started his program off. In the exercise that he showed us a set of related electrical circuits was described to the learner who was then asked: *What, in ohms, would you expect the resistance to be between contact A and contact B?* If the learner gave a correct answer the system simply proceeded to ask another question. On the other hand – and this is what impressed us straightaway - if the learner gave one of a number of wrong replies there would appear on the screen a whole paragraph of explanation saying, for example: *You are wrong. You have failed to take into account the voltage present at points X and Z, and what is more ...etc.* When I asked the friendly engineer how he had designed the teaching content of his system he told me that he had first of all run a version which stored all the wrong answers given by students and had then used these in selecting and formulating his explanations.

As we drove back to Aberdeen my mind was turning over ways of programming a system that would do something similar to this Electrical Engineering program, but for French, and not just at beginners' level like Rex Last's German exercises. It would, I felt, be more interesting, and also more useful, if the software could be designed for learners at the more advanced level our First Year students were at. At the time, and until very recently, the principal language learning activity in university French Departments was centred on translation, and mainly on translation into French: the very traditional prose composition exercise. The obvious thing would be to see if some way couldn't be found of using a computer to make the student's role in this activity more productive of knowledge, and to make the teacher's role, which consisted of correcting and marking a weekly packet of exercises, less of a soul-destroying chore.

The idea that I came up with was to use the computer to present a conventional prose composition exercise as a series of questions: What tense will you use for this verb? How will you translate that word? What noun will this adjective agree with? And so on. I sketched out a program to present this questionnaire using a sort of pseudo-code of my own invention and a colleague from the Computing Centre obligingly programmed this for me and got it working on the University mainframe. I managed to interest the Scottish Education Department in this, and to impress them with its potentiality. After some negotiation I received funding for a three-year project to produce teaching materials for schools based upon this simple system, which was called, unimaginatively, Teacher. The grant provided for travelling expenses for a working party of local language teachers, purchase of two Apple II microcomputers and, most important of all, the salary of a Research Assistant.

When it came to choosing someone for this post I remembered my earlier experience of collaboration with Catherine, when producing the Audio Course. I had learnt then the importance of having someone with qualities that would compensate for my own shortcomings but who wouldn't get in my hair with bright but irrelevant ideas of his or her own. I therefore turned down applications for the post from several apparently suitable and highly qualified people, for example from a native French *informaticienne* and from a young colleague with qualifications in Linguistics. Instead I chose Mary Crawford. Mary had been Secretary to the eminent Professor of Physics at Aberdeen, R. V. Jones, had a very accurate knowledge of written French and a knowledge of and interest in both languages and computing. I saw immediately that she was not only the sort of person that would keep my feet on the ground, but also, having learnt French herself in evening classes in the not too distant past, she knew much more about elementary learners' problems than I did. (I had after all picked up my very fluent but lop-sided French in the course of late night political arguments in Chatenay.) We worked very well together for the three years the project lasted, and Mary contributed several original and very useful ideas to it. Unfortunately the funding came to an end just when we were getting into our stride and Mary left.

As soon as we started working it became clear that there were important differences between Electrical Engineering and language when it came to designing software for learning. For one thing, while we found it easy to think up French grammar questions to which there was only one possible correct answer, the wrong answers that our students came up with were different from the wrong answers of the Engineering students. In our case these were never, or very rarely, the result of thought processes that it was interesting or productive to discuss, but usually just the effect of unthinking guesswork. When it came to more thought-provoking questions, to matters of translation for example, a more fundamental complication appeared, specific to language. This was the very large number of possible *right* answers that there were to even the simplest question. While the number of language mistakes that students might make when translating was on the whole manageable, even the most ordinary English phrase could be translated into French in such a multiplicity of different ways, all of them more or less correct, that it seemed to me methodologically unacceptable to prefer any one version and impose it, in the manner of Rex Last, on the learners.

The more we worked the more I came to think that this plodding interrogation, reducing as it did the man-machine interaction to a sort of wisdomless Socratic dialogue, was the wrong way of using the technology. What was needed was something much more imaginative. Instead of asking the learners a lot of boring questions with predictable answers, the ideal would be to present them simply with a text in English and to invite them to translate it into French. The problem then was how to devise some way of processing what the students typed in, so that the machine would respond usefully to anything a learner was likely come up with. A tall order, obviously, since at first sight this looked very much like the problem that the Machine Translation people had spent millions of pounds in the fifties trying to solve. They hadn't had much success. In fact, at the time, they hadn't had any success at all.

The solution I eventually came up with, though at first sight and in operation it looked impressively like Machine Translation, wasn't anything of the sort. In one way it was much simpler. Whereas a proper automatic translation system would have had to produce an acceptable translation of any text read into it, Mary and I were working with prepared texts, and a sentence at a time. On the other hand our need was for something more complex. While a Machine Translation program would only have to produce a single version of whatever was fed in, we needed a program that could accept, and respond to, every conceivable translation that a student was likely to think of, including all the mistakes that could be expected. The solution I hit on was not an intelligent system. It was just a way of organising all the bits of language that learners were likely to come up with when faced with a given text, and then putting all this material into what was in effect a structured database, though that was not a term I used at the time. The way in which this Knowledge Base, as I came to call it, was put together, and the way students worked through it, were original. The design of it was almost certainly the cleverest idea I have ever had. The manner in which the idea came to me is worth describing.

When we broke up for the summer vacation Mary and I had been working on a simple English sentence about an old man working in his garden: *He seemed so intent on what he was doing that he didn't notice her arrival.* We had easily filled a page with all the different ways in which this banal little bit of English could be acceptably rendered into French. For example there were at least ten different ways of translating the first few words, *he seemed so intent on what he was doing*, and there seemed to be no reason for preferring one version to any of the others. For several weeks, in various places, I had been turning the problem over. I could see that, if the various target sentences in French could be broken up into bits, what was needed was a set of rules for putting these bits of French together into sentences. Then all the system would have to do, as a student typed in her or his translation, would be to check that the words and phrases figured in the right places in the Knowledge Base.

The answer came to me, quite literally, in a flash. I was out walking in Donegal with my daughter Doreen and we had come to one of those dry-stone walls that are such a feature of the West of Ireland. I don't think that it can have been the structure of the wall that set me thinking, though it is true that these walls are methodically built, with the larger stones at the bottom and the smaller ones at the top. Whether it was or not it is certainly true - and I remember it exactly - that as I started to clamber over the wall I was still puzzling over bits of French about this old gardener, but when I stood on the other side of it I had thought of a way of dealing, not just with this sentence but with any sentence at all.

It is not possible to describe the solution I found without entering into more technical details than are likely to interest most readers. The next two paragraphs may be skipped without missing anything essential.

The solution I found was in the way the Knowledge Base was constructed. This was essentially an expanded version of the Systemic Grammar developed by the British linguist M.A.K. Halliday and others. In ordinary everyday language it meant breaking the possible French sentences up into exchangeable chunks, and arranging these on four levels which I later named Word, Brick, Block and Sentence. Word level just contained all the words in all versions of the sentence. On the next level the Bricks were phrases, combinations of words. For example the different ways of translating *what he was doing* went into one Brick, which contained *ce qu'il faisait, ce qu'il était en train de faire, son travail, son jardinage* and half a dozen others. Then, just as the Bricks consisted of different combinations of words, so the Blocks were made up of combinations of Bricks and the Sentences consisted of combinations of Blocks.

There were two original features of my solution. One was the idea of expanding the grammar so that at each of the different points in the sentence structure there could be a list of elements instead of just one, as shown above. The other, which I thought of at the same time, was to identify the elements on each level simply by numbers. In that way a Sentence would consist of strings of Block numbers, a Block of strings of Brick numbers, and a Brick of strings of Word numbers. Only the Word List itself would consist of words. The whole Knowledge Base would in fact be composed of numbers, all of which would be pointers pointing to other pointers, the last ones pointing to words in the Word List. Replacing words by numbers, though it made the data files unreadable without special software, was advantageous in three ways. First, it meant that the Knowledge Base could be made to hold in a small file a number of variant translations for a single sentence running to several million, and sometimes more. Second, typing all the variant versions of a sentence into the data file could be done much more easily and much faster. Finally, since computers are so much happier with numbers than they are with words, the time taken processing what the students typed in was reduced to a degree which was, especially with the slow little microcomputers of those days, sensational. This meant that, when you typed a word in, the machine's response was instantaneous, something that astounded fellow-workers when we first demonstrated the program.

I worked out the details of this in the days that followed, but the essential ideas all came to me, mysteriously, in the few moments it took to climb over that wall. I say mysterious because I was not aware of any trying-out of hypotheses, any process of thought at all. At one moment I could only think of a disordered profusion of bits of French and at the next I had in mind a structured database of a distinctive and complex form. It was a very strange experience, but it seemed to me, on thinking about it, that I had once before experienced something similar. Only that time it wasn't an adaptation of Systemic Grammar which had seemed to come to my mind almost as fast as I could write it down, but a poem.

It was when I was seventeen years old and still at school. I had just had a very unpleasant clash with the school rugby or cricket team, I forget which, over some ill-advised remarks I had made about sports fans. I had been frightened by these bullies and, as I walked out of the school grounds and up the lane behind the school, I was still upset by this manifestation of hostility on the part of what Kipling called "flannelled fools and muddied oafs". As I went up the lane, a ballad about a social outcast being beaten up by a lot of rednecks began to take shape in my mind. I sat down on a bank and scribbled it out. The metre and even the rhymes came to me almost as quickly as if they had been dictated, and the finished poem, *Bandy the Outcast*, was one of the rather better written ones in the little collection I entitled *Midnight*. The idea of the translation program happened in very much the same way. "Inspiration" is surely a portentous word to apply either to a piece of moderately talented juvenilia or to a very minor scientific brainwave, but it's hard to think of a more apposite term, and the striking similarity between the two experiences, between artistic creation and scientific discovery, that they seem to demonstrate, may be of interest.

## BANDY THE OUTCAST

Black-hearted Bandy
was born at midnight,
born to a beggar, by a
road-worn witch;
a shouting rowdy
ballad-singer,
and an old mad tinker-woman
drunk in a ditch.

Bandy the madman,
shouting and swearing,
Bandy the outcast,
Bandy the fool,
never knew that the
world must fear him;
cowered and raved, and
drank and stole.

But ten big men from the
back of the village
went at nightfall to
find the thief;
found a wild figure
lonely and frightful
shaking a dead goose in a
raging grief.

It was Bandy, evil-faced,
angrily blaspheming,
Bandy hungry,
Bandy alone,
Bandy crazy,
wild-faced and screaming,
calling to the shadows and
cursing at the moon.

Then the ten big men took
ten big branches
beat at his body till it
screamed no more;
threw it in a ditch, all
bloody and dead, said
"That's what mad men
get round here."

When I got back from Donegal to Aberdeen Mary and I and our working party of teachers got down to constructing exercises for the new system, to which I first gave the name *Littre,* after the famous French lexicographer. The name, unfortunately, couldn't be retained when we came to publish the software, for copyright reasons. So we named it *BonAccord* instead, adopting a mediaeval password once used by the inhabitants of Aberdeen to identify themselves. A first version of *Littre/BonAccord* was produced in the University Computing Centre, not without difficulty, by Brian Robertson, who was attached to our Project, a very fortunate choice since he was interested in language and relished the fairly formidable challenge presented by what turned out to be a highly complex set of programming problems.

Then it occurred to us to make use of a feature of the design of the program to which we hadn't given much thought at first, namely the ease with which predicted mistakes could be built into the grammar. So we started putting into the data files, not only every way of translating a given sentence that learners were likely to come up with, but also all the language errors that they might make. To find out what these were the simplest way was to choose texts that had been set for examinations and then to check through all the student scripts. It was a time-consuming but very productive business, since it showed up, not only numerous unexpected language mistakes, but also many acceptable versions that none of us had thought of. It was easy then to add a file containing grammatical and lexical explanations to be triggered whenever a learner made a predictable mistake.

There was one aspect of the *Littre/BonAccord* system that I hadn't thought of at all. This was the possibility that the system, with its multiplicity of "right" answers, opened up for unconventional, investigative, learning. Since the learners worked through each sentence in an exercise suggesting or trying out words it was clear that at any point the system "knew" so to speak what all the possible, acceptable, "next" words were. It was therefore very easy to let learners look at this list of possibilities and choose from them. For example, in the sentence about the old gardener, if a student translating *what he was doing* had typed *ce qu'il,* and then clicked on Next the machine would suggest, not only *faisait*, but also *était,* which would give a hint towards the, slightly, better version: *était en train de faire.* At first sight this looked like making it possible for students to cheat, and they inevitably saw it like this to start with. But it soon became clear to them that being shown the list of possible "next" words didn't make the exercise easier. Since it put them in front of choices it usually made the work harder. Also, by nudging them towards more sophisticated translation ideas than they might have thought of by themselves, it made the whole operation not only more challenging but also more interesting. Encouraging students to make liberal use of this "next" facility got them to use the system as a resource rather than as a simple question and answer tutorial, which was obviously a much more intelligent way of working.

As time went by Brian Robertson and I developed versions of *BonAccord* to run, first on the BBC Micro, and later on IBM PCs and, much later, on PCs running MS Windows. I developed a methodology and programmed an authoring system for constructing the data files, and finally put together a package of exercises in translation into French which was taken up and used by most British universities. It would have had much more success, above all in secondary schools, if all this had not coincided with a decision on the part of the British examining boards no longer to include translation into French as part of the A level examination. An updated version of BonAccord is still (2010) available via the Internet and still enjoys a modest success. I also produced a version of the system called Dominie which was adapted to teach, not translation into French but guided composition of English, and which has been much appreciated by students of English in Belgium. But this is to anticipate.

It was the early eighties. Suddenly there was a profusion of microcomputers on the market: Apples, Pets, Sinclair Spectrums, Newbrains, and many others whose names I have forgotten. And with them came a host of what later pundits sneeringly, and unfairly, called hobbyist programmers. Time after time, when I visited a school in my capacity as examiner, I would be led aside by the teacher, keen to show me grammar and vocabulary exercises that he, it was never she, had devised and programmed. Some of the software was quite ingenious, and the teacher's enthusiasm for this innovation possibly meant that his pupils learnt something from it even when it wasn't. As, for example, in a school near Inverness where I was taken to a classroom in which a score of little boys were seated in pairs in front of microcomputers, all of different models I noticed, and busily working away. I leant over one pair. On the screen the letters S-E-P-T appeared, one by one. The child touched the key for 3. An error message appeared on the screen: *That is the wrong reply. Try Again*. He keyed in 5. The same message appeared. "Try seven," said his companion, so he did. On the screen appeared the words: *Congratulations! You have found the correct answer in 2.357 minutes.* "What do you think?" said the teacher. I didn't want to appear unfriendly, but couldn't help expressing some doubt as to the usefulness for language learning of what I had just been watching. "Listen," he said. "It's nearly half past four on a Friday. None of them is impatient to get home. And what they are doing is French." There seemed to be no real point in disagreeing. Anyway I much preferred this chap to one or two other individuals who would speak darkly about the grammar software they were developing, explaining why they weren't showing it to me because it was "Strictly copyright". As though Bill Gates and Alan Sugar were already at each other's throats to take it over.

I couldn't help being reminded, when looking at even the best of these early CALL (Computer Assisted Language Learning) materials, of the way in which the Language Laboratory appeared on the scene just when the theory underlying its use, based as it was on an outdated behaviourist view of language, was increasingly discredited. Much early CALL software was quite out of tune with current thinking in Applied Linguistics. The post-Chomskyan concept of what was called Communicative Competence meant that teachers were giving less importance to mere grammatical accuracy and, instead, were laying an emphasis on the meaning and social function of the bits of language they were teaching. Computer exercises that insisted on exactly correct spelling were therefore, understandably, seen by intelligent teachers as largely irrelevant to elementary learners' needs. Fortunately none of this applied to our *BonAccord*, designed as it was, specifically, to teach written language, and at an advanced level.

Most CALL exercises in elementary written grammar seemed to me in fact more suited for teaching a dead language than for French or Spanish, where even beginners are keen, and are encouraged, to start speaking as early as possible. Curiously, though, I only knew of one example of CALL materials being created for learning Latin. My colleague in Aberdeen, Duncan Macrae-Gibson, produced some interesting computer-assisted materials for teaching Anglo-Saxon, using contrasting colours to indicate grammatical categories, but he was very much a loner and I don't think his work was ever published, which was a pity.

Another feature of almost all early CALL materials that I noticed, and became increasingly critical of as the years went by, was the poverty of the linguistic content. To some extent, it is true, this was inevitable in the early days at least, since they were mostly designed for near beginners, and both grammar and vocabulary had to be kept simple. But as time went by and the technology became increasingly sophisticated it seemed to me more and more that the boring banality of the language content was in depressing contrast to the liveliness and ingenuity of the presentation. It was obvious that more time and money was being spent on programming the machine than on thinking about and working out what it was going to teach. In the end I think this is one reason why computer assisted language learning where the machine acts as a tutor, though it is still around, never really caught on. Quite simply it was that, powerful and all as this new technology was, it failed to present learners with an interesting enough challenge in linguistic terms.

These ideas were beginning to stir in my mind at the first big conference on Computer Assisted Learning that I attended, in 1983 in Leeds. I chanced to remark upon the inadequacies, from a linguistic point of view, of the paper we had just heard to a Frenchwoman that I was standing beside. She thought the same, we got talking and found that we had many ideas in common as regards language and computers. I learned that her name was Françoise Demaizière and that she was in charge of the language section of the French national centre for computer assisted learning, which was located in one of the Paris universities. We exchanged addresses and agreed to keep in touch. I returned to Aberdeen pleased to have met such a highly articulate and well-informed French practitioner of this my newly acquired expertise. I was even more pleased to receive six months later an important-looking communication informing me that my name was on a list of British scientists invited to visit a French University, all expenses paid. Apparently a paper had arrived on Françoise's desk from the British Council asking if there was anyone in Britain working in her field that she would like to visit her department. So she had scribbled my name on it. It was the first of many visits that I made to the CNEAO (*Centre National d'Enseignement Assisté par Ordinateur*) to lecture or run workshops, culminating in my participation in the high-powered *Jury* that awarded Françoise her doctorate, the first doctor's degree in CALL to be awarded in France.

The CNEAO was a suite of windowless offices situated in the cellars of the University of Paris VII, at Jussieu. The language section was manned – if that can be the word – by a team of very lively and very affable young women, who were busily engaged in drafting language learning materials using an elaborate authoring system that had been designed in the Centre. (An authoring system is a sort of computer language for designing and writing, in this case language learning, software.) One of the workers at the Centre, Nicole Gandilhon, showed such perceptive appreciation of the original nature of what was to become *BonAccord* that after I had retired I persuaded her to help in building the data files. Collaborating again with a highly articulate and intelligent Frenchwoman reanimated all the admiration I used to feel at *Saint-Cloud* for the way French people learn to manipulate and exploit their marvellously expressive language.

I liked a number of things about the CNEAO, as well as enjoying the very flattering esteem in which the personnel there seemed to hold me and our LITTRE system. Above all I approved of the way they regarded the linguistic content of their software as of primary importance. This, I quickly learned, was because the Centre owed its existence to Prof Antoine Culioli, at the time one of France's most eminent linguists, and because in their method of working they were putting into practice, so far as this was possible, the theory of "*les operations énonciatives*" (meaningful utterances, speech operations) that Culioli had developed. Everyone at Jussieu was in awe of Prof Culioli, and with reason. Several important, and interesting, pieces of research in French linguistics had been done in the light of his theory. He was also, I could see, an extremely powerful man with a lot of influence in high places. But I had a slight advantage here. Forty odd years earlier, in 1945 Antoine Culioli had replaced Jean Pierre Molinier in Trinity as exchange lecturer. He had many pleasant memories of his year in Dublin, and actually, when we met in 1986, remembered me, reminding me that in those far off years I had worn a beard. I found him intimidatingly impressive intellectually as I endeavoured to make sense of "*les operations énonciatives*" but, on a personal level, he was friendly, kind, and refreshingly un-pompous.

One practical effect of the primacy of language and of linguistic theory could be seen in the way they worked in the Centre. Just as Mary and I spent hours poring over old exam scripts and noting down all the variants and language mistakes that we found there, so, before starting work on a piece of software, these Frenchwomen would give a selected group of learners a mass of exercises to do on paper. This would show up the precise difficulties learners had with whatever bit of grammar the software was going to teach, and the mistakes they were likely to make. From then on things were however very different from Mary and me in our little room in Aberdeen. In the Centre they had professional programmers who would if necessary adapt the authoring system. This meant that the people writing the materials - they were almost all women – could actually pride themselves on their ignorance of the nuts and bolts of computing, programming languages, file handling and so on and could concentrate instead on the language. There were several teams, each working on software to teach a different language. The whole setup, a National Centre for CALL, properly funded, with its own premises and staff, was totally, and interestingly, different from the scene I was used to, and at first I was very envious. In the UK, dedicated enthusiasts, like myself, dotted around in different institutions, working alone or in small isolated groups, were devising computer-driven learning materials of different sorts, trying out the results on our students. Unlike the French we were starved of resources and usually had to do our own programming. The scene was typical in every way of muddling through, DIY, British empiricism.

It is true that, sometime in the mid-eighties, a large sum of money, a million pounds if I remember right, was suddenly allocated by the Ministry of Education to Computer Assisted Language Learning. But unfortunately whoever was given the job of distributing this largesse passed over almost all the people who, like myself, had several years' experience of devising CALL software, but whose programs were written for small machines like the BBC Micro. This new round of funding was inevitably associated with the IBM PC computer. This wasn't in itself a bad thing, since PCs and Apple Macs were the future, but the short-sighted and narrow-minded way in which this large amount of money was dished out meant that the incipient notion of what could have become a distinctively British school of CALL never took shape, one in which the key-word: Learning, contrasted interestingly with the American: Instruction, and the French: *Enseignement* (teaching). As a result work like Graham Davies's innovative text manipulation programs, John Higgins's ingenious linguistic games and above all Tim Johns's groundbreaking invention of what he later called Data Driven Learning got no recognition, and no significant funding, at all. The money went instead to people with no track record in CALL but who were working, or, some

Tim Johns

of them, just said they were *intending* to work, with IBM PC computers. We had a visit in Aberdeen from a disagreeable smoothie associated with this scheme and I'm glad to say we gave him a rough ride. But it didn't do any good. I was not surprised to learn, some years later, that the smoothie in question, I forget his name, had been given a job by IBM.

Data-Driven Learning or DDL, which was in my mind the most really innovative development in the whole field of CALL, took advantage of the ability of computers to generate concordances. (A concordance is a sort of dictionary of all the words in a given text, or collection of texts. A concordance to the Bible, for instance, makes it possible to find all the occurrences of any word, and therefore to locate any quotation.) A computer concordance can therefore be made to print out every single context in which a given word occurs in a collection, a corpus, of texts. The concordancing programme that Tim Johns wrote could in a few seconds check through, for example, all the leading articles in *The Times* for twenty years to find all the occurrences of the word *persuade* and to print them out with, in every case, the context consisting of four or five words before and after the key-word, *persuade*. A simple language exercise could then be constructed by printing this out but replacing the key-word with a blank and inviting students to guess the missing word with just the contexts to go on. A more complex, but very useful, exercise can be made by getting the contexts for each of a pair of words that foreign learners find hard to distinguish (*say* and *tell,* or *make* and *do*) and jumbling them so that the learners would have to work out which contexts went with which word.

There were a number of more sophisticated variants of this basic model and Tim used them to teach, and to explore, not only a wide range of vocabulary but also, by concordancing grammar words like *all* or *since*, patterns of syntax. I say teach and also explore, because it was found that the concordancer could throw up or highlight features of the language that dictionaries or grammar books tended to ignore. DDL tended in fact to turn both students and teachers into researchers into the language. I found an example of this when I used Tim's concordancer for French. A similar exercise to the *say* and *tell* one above which I designed to teach, or discover, the difference between the two French words for *know*, *savoir* and *connaître,* revealed a syntactic difference: *savoir* can be followed by an infinitive or by *que,* while *connaître* cannot. I knew this of course, but I didn't know that I knew it, and it is not mentioned in any book teaching French to English speakers that I have been able to check. Instead they try to explain the difference between the two words in terms of different sorts of knowledge.

A more significant effect of the use of DDL is the way it encourages learners to see the importance of contextual meaning. All students, and literary students in particular in my experience, tend to see the meaning of a word as a sort of ghostly figment hiding behind it. They have to learn, and some never learn, that much of the meaning of a word can be deduced from the context, and that the collocations of a word, the company it keeps, are an essential part of what you know when you know what a word means. Tim Johns, a great communicator of enthusiasm, is, sadly, no longer with us but I am glad to say that his ideas are prospering in places as far apart and as different as Limerick and Katowice in the hands of some of his disciples, (I like to imagine the huge burst of embarrassed laughter on his part that that noun would have provoked).

The climax of my years of collaboration with the CNEAO in Paris came, as I have said, when I was invited to be on the *Jury* that awarded Françoise her doctorate. It was a singular distinction, foreigners only rarely being invited by French academia to take part in such an important occasion. It was also quite an experience. In Britain a PhD viva involves at most four or five people in a small room and can result in the doctorate being refused, and the candidate failed. Here it was obvious the result was a foregone conclusion since there was an audience of about a hundred or more, most of them I supposed to be friends, colleagues or relations of Françoise's. The event, or ceremony, took place in a large lecture theatre on the top floor of the skyscraper that housed the University of Paris VII. Françoise sat in an open space in the front, for all the world like the Accused in the Spanish Inquisition, faced as she was with the Jury of five examiners and Prof Culioli. I took my place among them, looking around me in nervous anticipation. I had fortunately been warned that I would be expected to speak for about 45 minutes, so I had ploughed through the 500 odd pages of Françoise's thesis and prepared a report. The thesis, for all that it was written in French academic-speak, was a fairly easy read. I agreed with a lot of it, though I couldn't imagine myself ever bothering to spell it all out in such detail. The shortcomings that I thought worth pointing out mostly concerned practical issues that she didn't seem to consider important, or else failed to mention. Also, I wouldn't have spent so much time considering the para-philosophical implications of the dialogue between a learner and a machine.

The latter aspect turned out to be the only thing that really interested the other members of this posse of examiners. Françoise had written, fairly briefly, about the uncertainty regarding the identity of whoever, or whatever, a learner is interacting with when they are working with a computer. She described this uncertainty as "*un malaise énonciatif*". (The phrase is a hard one to translate: interactive uncertainty, ambiguity of utterance, something like that.) I had decided that the question was neither very interesting, nor really relevant to CALL. This, however, was not the way the other members saw it. One after another took up this phrase and went to town on all its possible implications. As I listened to them, abstract speculation following on abstract speculation, I realised that, if any of them knew anything about computer assisted language learning or had any practical experience of it, it was certainly not apparent. I concentrated therefore in my remarks on the simplest and most down to earth questions, things like the problem of integrating CALL into a conventional teaching situation. I later saw that a very much more relevant criticism, which I failed to make, would have been to say that Françoise, by concentrating exclusively on the tutorial mode of CALL, - individual learners interacting with individual machines -, had made no attempt to discuss, or even mention, any of the other ways, concordancing or e-mail for example, in which computers could, and would shortly, be used to assist language learning. At the time I was pleased, after it was all over, when several people came up to me and complimented me on being the only one of the examining team to have said anything about computer assisted language learning at all.

# 14 Hungary

One day in 1985 I received in the Language Centre an exotic-looking envelope containing an invitation to attend a Conference on Computer Assisted Language Learning in a place I had never heard of, the University of Debrecen, in Eastern Hungary. This sounded more fun than the usual run of things I got invited to, in places like Exeter or Lancaster, so I accepted straightaway. Particularly when I learnt that Jeremy Fox, from Norwich, was also going, since the main reason I used to go to places like Exeter and Lancaster was to enjoy his thought-provoking company. The other people invited from the UK were a curiously mixed bag and included Marie-Madeleine Kenning and her husband, joint authors of one of the first books on CALL. We were all met at Budapest airport by the Conference organiser, one Istvan Kecskes, the first of my many dealings with this egregious individual. The visit started with a 240km bus ride to Debrecen, across the interminable great Hungarian plain. That too was to become very familiar in the future, had I but known.

Debrecen turned out to be a medium-sized Hungarian town with some fine buildings all painted in the mustard-yellow that seemed to be the mark of the Hapsburg Empire. In particular Kossuth University, where we stopped off on arriving, was a magnificent edifice built around a striking open courtyard, floored with large black and white tiles like an immense chessboard. Music was playing when we arrived and some sort of dancing class or practice was going on, the dancers all dressed in black and white like the tiled floor.

We were then brought to a large hotel, palatial in the East European manner, where there was a welcome ceremony at which we were greeted by the Mayor of Debrecen, a large lady in a flowery dress. There were speeches and toasts in Palinka, a delectable Hungarian brandy made of apricots, and one of our party that I had not met before, produced the gaffe of the evening by thanking the Mayor on our behalf for her welcome and declaring how pleased and proud we all were to find ourselves in .... Budapest.

This was the only time I had ever been in a socialist country, so I was keen to form an opinion of my own, having been subjected to so much propaganda both for and against. I knew that Hungary, as a result of the 1956 rebellion, enjoyed a much more liberal regime than, for example, Bulgaria or Poland. It was, I had learnt, regarded from both sides of the Iron Curtain as a sort of Switzerland. So I was expecting to find more things to like than to dislike, and on the whole I was not disappointed. My first impressions were however distinctly inauspicious. When our plane touched down in Prague, and later in Budapest, in each place we had to have our papers checked by an unsmiling posse of maximally antipathetic police. As an un-welcome it was only equalled in my experience when a few years later I first arrived in New York. In Hungary, however, I was ready to explain it away as a symptom of the Cold War.

As a socialist visiting a socialist country I was happy to make my affinities known. This was not difficult. Kecskes had allocated a student to each one of our party to act as interpreter and guide. Jeremy and I were given two most attractive and intelligent girls, our Hungarian rhapsodies, as Olivia described them in later years. Tunde, who had the job of looking after me, was the more serious of the two. Her main subject of study was of course Russian but she spoke excellent English with very few mistakes. I got her to teach me some Hungarian which, having studied Applied Linguistics, she did very effectively pointing out how much easier Hungarian was for an English speaker than English was for her, which was certainly true as regards the pronunciation. I learnt that she was a Party member, belonged to the Communist Youth Movement, whatever it was called, and had spent several months in Moscow. In the evenings and in the breaks between conference sessions she walked me around Debrecen and we talked a lot. I found the experience, talking to a young socialist who was actually citizen of a socialist country very interesting, and not at all what I might have expected.

To begin with there was none of the campaigning enthusiasm of young left-wing people in the West. When I related anecdotes about our activities in Aberdeen, organising meetings for CND, going on marches and demos against apartheid in South Africa, it was clear she had only a very vague idea of what I was talking about. On the other hand from the freedom with which she expressed her likes and dislikes and her enthusiasms, not only as regards everyday personal topics, but also concerning matters of ideology and the interpretation and application of Marxist ideas, I certainly got the impression of a degree of personal commitment and thought and not just obedience to official dogmas.

This was particularly marked when I asked her about her visits to the Soviet Union. She launched into a critical diatribe against the Russians she had met and the courses she had followed there. They hadn't, she told me, understood

Tunde and BF, Debrecen, Hungary

the first thing about dialectical materialism, they had never read anything by Engels at all, they hadn't even read Marx, except in selected extracts, and what they had read they had misunderstood completely. And, what was worse, she said, they weren't even interested in politics. I listened to her, admiring her sincerity; it was a bit like hearing a Northern Ireland Protestant describing a visit to the Vatican. And then, walking past some official building, we saw two Russian officers on sentry duty. I had never seen Russian soldiers before and I was struck by how smart they looked, and how elegant their uniforms were, and I said so. The vigour with which she contradicted me made it clear that the vehemence of her earlier tirade was inspired, not quite so much by an enthusiasm for Marxist theory as by a simple dislike of anything and everything Russian.

I didn't think I'd ever see Tunde again. Still, meeting her was probably the most interesting thing about this Hungarian experience. So I kept in touch with her; she wrote interesting letters, and I helped her a bit with her English, sending her books, and a teddy bear to her first-born when she got married. The rest of the conference was certainly not very inspiring. However, when we got back to Budapest Jeremy and I decided that the organisers deserved encouraging, if only for their initiative. So we went to the British Council and made a favourable report on Debrecen. As a result the Council invited Kecskes to

Britain and he came up to Aberdeen and demonstrated some software to a meeting I got together. Most of his stuff was fairly run-of-the-mill, but there were some unusual exercises teaching use of the English Passive, apparently a problem for Hungarian speakers. I took him round some schools with the idea that a visit from a "distinguished Hungarian" might enhance the standing of teachers whose CALL work deserved encouragement. Putting him on the plane for London I thought that was the end of Hungary.

But it wasn't. Three years later I received notice of another CALL Conference in Debrecen. This time Kecskes had invited several really interesting people. Graham Davies, Tim Johns and Vivian Cook came from the UK. There were also three important professors from Germany: Dieter Wolff, Edith Buchholz and Udo Jung whose charming spouse was dressed with such superb, if slightly old-fashioned, elegance that she seemed to have been poured into her clothes. There were also some extraordinarily boring, but, since they came from Salt Lake City, probably very influential, Americans. And this time I found that, by flying to Vienna and continuing to Budapest by train, two could travel for less than one person flying direct. So Olivia was able to come with me and enjoy all this too. In addition, with Edith Buchholz and Frau Jung, she was able to discover the delights of an exotic Hungarian speciality: bathing in a hot spring. The actual conference was much more interesting than the earlier one. In particular Vivian Cook demonstrated a host of brilliantly ingenious programs running on a BBC Micro none of which he had bothered to make crash-proof when run by anyone other than himself. As a result their circulation was extremely limited so we felt ourselves in a sense privileged to see them.

As usual with conferences the formal presentations were the least useful and least interesting things about it. I was able to do some valuable brain-picking by talking to Tim Johns and Vivian Cook, while Graham Davies gave me some very useful and encouraging advice about publishing software as we drove back across the great Hungarian plain in this huge Russian limousine. Meeting Edith Buchholz and Dieter Wolff led later to invitations to address fairly high-powered conferences in Rostock and Bonn. And one of the Americans, a Mormon called Frank Otto, came over and delivered himself of a long spiel of fulsome praise of my presentation, somewhat invalidated by my having noticed that he hadn't been there when I gave it.

On the way home several of us stayed on for a day or two in Budapest in the course of which we went to hear *Don Carlos* in a huge modern opera house. The performance was a bit static, the actors hardly moving at all as they sang, but musically it was very powerful and, another plus point for the socialist regime, five of us got in, and to excellent seats, for the equivalent of less than five pounds. An experience that was somewhat wasted on Vivian Cook who, being a jazz enthusiast, said he found the rhythms totally uninteresting. "At least," he said as we came out, "I shall know never to go to an opera again."

Next day one or two of us called on the British Council and reported on the conference to a youngish woman who sounded sincere when she said she so missed not being able to come to Debrecen it all sounded so interesting. She spoke of taking us all out to dinner somewhere special that evening. So, with the prospect of an exotic Hungarian dinner at the expense of the British taxpayer we had a very light lunch – not an easy thing to have in Hungary – and at the end of the afternoon, after going for a boat trip on the Danube, we headed towards the agreed meeting place. Then Olivia decided it would be wiser not to accompany us since she felt a migraine coming on, so she went back to the hotel. But alas the promised exotic Hungarian banquet didn't occur. Our hostess had decided that, since we were all Brits surely what we would prefer would be home cooking. So she brought us back to her flat, where we were joined by two or three others, colleagues of hers I suppose, and were served dollops of shepherd's pie followed by rice pudding washed down with tinned beer. The conversation, over and after dinner, consisted mostly of joke-telling of the Englishman, Irishman and Scotsman variety. And one of the colleagues even seemed to know a slightly different version of each joke which he would explain and then others would join in this exegesis. As soon as we could do so politely we returned to the hotel. When we got there we learnt that Olivia's migraine had not developed after all. So she had made her way down to the hotel's dining saloon where, at the same time as we were eating our shepherd's pie, she had had a gorgeous meal of roast goose and paprika, while being serenaded passionately by handsome gypsy violinists.

Again I thought that was the last I would see of Hungary. Again I was wrong, very wrong. In 1990, the year I retired, and a month or two after my farewell do from the Language Centre, I was surprised to receive a communication from Kecskes who was now in the US, at the University of Montana. He was in fact on a Fulbright scholarship which he had been awarded, partly anyway, on the strength of a recommendation from me. His letter contained no personal news, no account of how he was finding America or anything like that. It was quite short and was simply to ask me if I would like to replace him for a year as Professor of Linguistics in a town called Szombathely in Western Hungary. At first I thought it was some sort of joke, though, from my knowledge of Kecskes, I didn't think jokes were his sort of thing. I didn't know that he had moved from Debrecen, or that he had been promoted to a professorship. It's true there were many unexpected things occurring in Hungary with the change of regime, so it was not really surprising if the move and his promotion came simultaneously with his departure for Montana. But, reading between the lines of a second letter, I could see exactly what had happened. Though he had only been in Montana for a few months the possibility of a second year there must have come up. He would have been keen to accept this and to enjoy the fleshpots of American university life, and an American salary, for another year. The only problem was his post in Szombathely, where they were expecting him back the following summer. So he must have written to the College suggesting that his friend B. Farrington replace him for the year. And the College, I suppose, though I found it strange – I still had a lot to learn about Hungarian ways – must have accepted this proposal, or at least not turned it down straightaway.

My opinion of Istvan Kecskes was to change in the course of the next few months, but at this stage, knowing what conditions were like in Hungary, I could certainly understand the situation, and sympathise with his desire for another year in the US. My first reaction was to accept. After all the proposal presented an immediate answer to the question of what I was going to do with myself now I was retired. The only problem was Olivia's job. I wouldn't want to go to Hungary unless she could come too. But then a partial solution presented itself in the form of a suitably – actually very highly-qualified - friend who could replace her at Total for the first three months of the academic year. So I wrote and told Kecskes that I accepted his offer. Shortly after this I received an important-looking document in Hungarian with translation attached, appointing me to the post of Professor for one year at Berzsenyi College, Szombathely. I gathered that there would be a job there for Olivia also.

I learned then that, largely through the help of Graham Davies, of Thames Valley University, Kecskes had applied for funding from the European Union to set up in Szombathely a Centre for Computer Assisted Language Learning for Eastern Europe, and that the grant, which involved a large amount of money, had been approved by Brussels. Hearing this I assumed that, since Kecskes would want to be on the spot running this Centre, this would be incompatible with my replacing him. I was disappointed, since I had started looking forward very much to my Hungarian year. But then it appeared that Kecskes had changed none of his arrangements; he was planning to participate in the running of the Centre, not so much by remote control as it were, from Montana, but by flying backwards and forwards at frequent intervals, and he was expecting the grant to cover his air-fares. It seemed crazy, but then I was beginning to find a lot of things about Hungary distinctly odd.

For example I had written several times to Dr Molnar, Head of the English Department – who Kecskes had described to me as a "brilliant administrator" – asking about courses at the College and in particular asking what teaching and lecturing she wanted me to do. Not receiving any reply I even telephoned her once with the same question, to be told that we would discuss that when I arrived. Since we were planning to arrive a few days only before the teaching term began, the simplest thing seemed to be to pack a case with all the notes for all the lecture courses I had ever done, together with a big bag of books, to be on the safe side. It turned out that I was wise.

Berzsenyi College, as we found when we arrived in September 1991, was a sort of glorified teacher training college hoping to become a university. It took up one side of a fine square, facing the baroque cathedral. On the other two sides were imposing public buildings whose walls were painted in the now familiar Hapsburg mustard yellow. In contrast the building that the College was housed in was a characterless modern block. It had been put up to replace another fine old building destroyed in the war and the College had only recently moved into it. Before that it had been the regional headquarters of the Communist Party, and in the front hall there was a large plinth draped with a Hungarian flag. A bust of Lenin had been removed from this a few months before. Also some of the lecture rooms had obviously been Party committee rooms and had retained the furniture. In particular there was one which was fitted out with very posh leather armchairs and a mahogany table. I did my English grammar classes in what I suppose had been where the Central Committee or Politburo had sat.

The rapidity with which the regime change had taken place had other less obviously visible effects. To begin with there was the shortage of finance. It was clear at the first meeting of the English Department that my unusual situation, having been parachuted into a temporary professorship on the simple recommendation of Kecskes, was more the rule than an exception. The Department was staffed by a strangely disparate group of people, only a few of whom were Hungarian. There were Americans, some funded by the Soros Foundation, some by the Peace Corps, an English woman funded by the British Council, several others from British universities on some scheme I never understood or have forgotten, an Austrian woman, a Canadian. The presence of these people on the staff had a simple economic explanation: the College seemed to take on anyone that came with external funding, almost irrespective of their qualifications. (I was of course in a different category, having a Hungarian salary, but, like most of the others, I was new to Hungary.)

But there were other things about the College, and about academic life in general, that seemed odd or puzzling and that were probably caused by the change from state socialism. There were animosities, and rivalries, interpersonal and inter-departmental tensions, the origin of which could have been political as well as professional. Outsiders, such as Olivia and me, navigated with difficulty in all this since we understood so little about the issues at stake. The language situation exacerbated the problem. Because we couldn't read newspapers or listen to the radio or follow conversations and arguments we were dependant on Hungarian colleagues to know whatever was going on. And, as I shall explain, I found Hungarians curiously reluctant to speak frankly about Hungary or about anything Hungarian. Instead, if ever you asked them an awkward question, either about local or national politics or about the everyday running of the College, they would come out with a string of bland platitudes, effectively saying nothing of use or of real interest.

Like most visiting lecturers I failed to appreciate the pressures our Hungarian colleagues were under as a result of the political situation and the low standard of living. Many of them were teaching in several other places, sometimes quite far away which may explain the general disorganisation and inefficiency. For example, whoever was responsible for timetabling often double-booked rooms, and not just classrooms. Several times, together with over fifty students, I was turned out in mid-lecture because the theatre had also been reserved for some other professor, more important than me. And then for First and Second Year English there didn't seem to be anything like a course or a syllabus. On arrival I had sought out Dr Molnar to ask her yet again what I was expected to teach. Her reply was so vague that I took it upon myself to sit down and sketch out a first year course in Linguistics, based on the notes I had brought with me. She glanced at it briefly and said, "Perfect. You start tomorrow." I learned that the others had been similarly invited to do their own thing, whatever that was. At the end of the semester I was asked to make out a list of students' names, grading their work on a scale of one to five. I was not told on what basis this should be done and I had to ask whether five was the top or the bottom grade.

Sometime after the beginning of term Graham Davies arrived to set up the Brussels-financed CALL Centre for Eastern Europe. He brought news of a meeting of the Steering Committee in London which had turned into a clash of Shakespearian proportions between Istvan Kecskes and the rest of the Committee. The Committee had made it clear to Kecskes that the Centre was not going to be some sort of personal empire that he could run from Montana, and that, if he was not going to be physically present in Szombathely, then he couldn't be its Director. It turned out that, not only he but also his wife, were staying in, I think, the Savoy and that he was expecting the grant to cover this as well as their air fares. The climax of the row had been when Graham, who headed the whole Project, refused quite rightly to authorise payment for any of this. Kecskes returned, furious, to the States whence he telephoned and wrote to me, presenting himself as the victim of a sinister conspiracy to do him out of his role as initiator of the project and Director of the Centre. I sat down and replied saying, as I had said to Graham and also to the Rector of the College, that I was sorry but that I agreed with the view of the Committee: his place was in the College in Szombathely and not in America. I added that I appreciated the difficult choice that he faced and said, though with some misgivings, that, if he came back and took up the post of Director, I would support him in every way. The Rector of the College, incidentally, had invited me to stay on in my professorship even if Kecskes did return. He had also offered to turn it into a permanent post. I decided that I couldn't accept this flattering offer for various obvious reasons. Anyway Kecskes never replied to my letter and we heard no more from him.

Meanwhile I had made contact with the French Department of the College which was small, French not being an important language in Hungary. There was a junior lecturer and a French *assistant*. The Head of French, I was surprised to hear, was going to be none other than Kecskes's wife. She suddenly appeared in person then, coming straight from London. I gathered that, like her husband, she was intending, or hoping, to fulfil the requirements of the post *in absentia*. She had apparently come to start the academic year off and to sort out some problems concerning their house in Szombathely before leaving for Montana.

I had met her two years earlier in Debrecen, and I remembered trying to talk French with her and finding her French very difficult to understand. Though I understood that she was the daughter of a distinguished Hungarian linguist, Professor Papp, she hadn't struck me then as being at all academic. I certainly would not have expected to find her Head of a French Department. Renewing her acquaintance, and hearing her talk French, strengthened this impression. Anyhow we heard then that the College had decided that she could not combine being Head of Department with living in America.

Talking to her before she left for Montana both Olivia and I found her, whatever about her academic qualifications, to be a warm and unpretentious person. She was understandably worried about the move to Montana which she didn't much like. She didn't seem particularly bothered about her job in the College but more concerned that their children, a boy and a girl, shouldn't grow up into Americans. I often wonder what became of her and their two, rather nice, children.

The departure of Madame Kecskes meant that the French Department was understaffed so I was invited to replace her in addition to my work in English. I never knew quite where I was with Dr Molnar, while I rather liked Istvan Csury, the young lecturer in French and his wife, who spoke excellent French, unlike Madame Kecskes. And I saw that, instead of some English grammar classes, this meant that I would be giving my Linguistics lectures twice each week. There was only one complication: the second time the lectures would have to be *in* French. This struck me as an interesting challenge.

Britain is the only country in Europe where, in university language and literature departments, the teaching is not carried out in the language being studied. In Aberdeen I was the only person in the French Department that lectured in French and I was quite proud to be doing it fairly successfully, considering that what I was teaching was Linguistics and Phonetics, subjects which students of literature tend to regard as boring. But of course I used to cheat by using a maximum of visuals, throwing up on the screen the text of everything important that I said. And I would sugar the pill by using as many funny effects as I could. And then if I saw blank looks, or the students' eyes tended to glaze over, I could always drop into English and explain. But here, in Hungary, if the students were doing French that meant that most of them knew no English. I found that lecturing, where there was no English safety net so to speak, put quite a strain on my knowledge of French, which I was surprised to find was only just good enough for this particular activity. This was because of the need, especially with this Hungarian audience, to say the same thing extra clearly and several times over in different words. Luckily I found it easy to establish a friendly rapport with the students who were not unaware of the occasional difficulties I was having and who seemed to like me the better for it.

That was one source of unmitigated pleasure in Szombathely: the students. For a long time I couldn't understand the success I was having with them. Both in English and French I was doling out a slightly simplified version of the lectures I had been giving for years in Aberdeen with varying degrees of approbation. Basically it was just Saussurean linguistics, lexicology and phonetics. Though not very sophisticated it was all the same fairly technical stuff. And yet here in Hungary there were times when they almost clapped at the end. This was all the more surprising in that my classes were often at eight o'clock in the morning and some of the students lived so far away that they had been up since five. They would arrive in the lecture theatre with buns and plastic mugs of coffee which somehow never seemed to stop them from taking notes. They were maximally attentive, responsive if I asked questions, and if ever I started to tell a story to illustrate some point there would be a sort of buzz of pleased anticipation and they would all laugh at the end. I could hardly fail to enjoy all this, and to play up to it, and after a few months I found I had got fan clubs of a sort in both English and French which was very pleasant, especially since, as always with Modern Languages, most of the students, though not all, were girls and some of them very attractive.

I found this, though agreeable, exceedingly strange, especially when compared with teaching in Scotland. The scales fell from my eyes eventually when I told a Polish professor who was visiting Szombathely about the success I was having with Hungarian students and he said "You are like all British professors. You lecture with jokes." Well of course it was true. But then you could hardly expect to hold the attention of Scottish adolescents while explaining phonetics, or the difference between Langue and Parole if you didn't make them laugh now and then. And it was easy to understand why these Hungarian students liked my stuff when I had occasion to compare it with the pabulum dished out, in somewhat ropy English, by some of my Hungarian colleagues, schooled as they were in the traditions of deadly Teutonic seriousness. But I was slightly sobered to realise that what the students appreciated was not so much my quality as a teacher but my talents as a clown.

Before my first visit to Debrecen the idea I had had of Hungary had largely been formed by a book I had read as a child, called *The Good Master*. The story, so far as I remember, was centred on a large farm run on feudal lines by this "Master". There were a lot of horses, both wild and tame, and people wore colourful traditional costumes. My idea of Hungary, therefore, strengthened by Brahms's Hungarian Rhapsodies, was of somewhere exotic. At first modern

Hungary, and modern Hungarians, seemed disappointingly conventional and ordinary. The impression was of course superficial; we soon came across plenty of examples of extravagant or unusual behaviour. But the only people that could be labelled exotic were the gypsies and they were generally looked down upon by both our students and our colleagues in a manner that could only be described as racist. This was probably the only really disagreeable, and inexcusable, feature of Hungarian society that we encountered.

One thing that was certainly exotic was the Hungarian language, and its peculiar, non-Indo-European, nature was something that the Hungarians, uncharacteristically, prided themselves on. Personally I found coping with a grammar, and above all a vocabulary, that were not related in any way with those of any other European language fascinating. One thing it did was bring home to me the power and validity of Saussurean concepts and distinctions that I had been explaining to students for years. *L'arbitraire du signe* for example. When I asked my students what the Hungarian for *happy* was and they told me it was *boldog* it seemed I had never encountered a sign so arbitrary, never heard a word so totally opaque as regards its meaning. Just thinking about the strange fact that Hungarians had chanced to choose just those sounds and letters to signify what other peoples mean by *heureux* or *glücklich* reanimated a feeling of wonder at the extraordinariness of language that forty years teaching linguistics had only partially worn away.

It's true the unique nature of Hungarian didn't make it at all easy to learn. The almost complete lack of cognates meant that to say even the simplest and most obvious things, *thank you, postage stamp* or *envelope* you had to recall an unmemorable concatenation of letters or syllables. On the other hand in several ways it was less difficult than some less unfamiliar languages. There were no serious pronunciation difficulties and the spelling, once one had got used to the sz and the cs, was regular and corresponded exactly to the pronunciation, unlike English and French. And there was a strong pressure on us to learn at least enough to manage basic social operations since very few people outside the College spoke any English and there was no culture of multi-lingualism, all notices and labels on food tins for example, being just in Hungarian. There was the day we bought, and tried to eat, a white substance that looked like cream cheese and discovered that it was in fact intended for cleaning shoes.

The East European Centre for CALL, of which I was Acting Director for a few months, meant a considerable gain for the College and not only in prestige. A large computer lab was installed, together with a certain amount of ancillary equipment, and a Director and Secretary were appointed. Then a series of workshops and conferences were organised to provide training and hands-on experience of computers to language teachers. Applied Linguists

Graham and Sally Davies

specialised in CALL came to these from Germany, France and of course the UK. Prominent among these was Tim Johns who explained and demonstrated Data-Driven Learning to an audience largely composed of language specialists from Germany and the UK.

This preponderance of non-Hungarian speakers at these conferences and workshops was something that I grew increasingly critical of. Though the meetings were often extremely interesting it seemed to me that the main purpose of the EECALL Centre was not being served by paying the travelling expenses of German and British linguists to come and talk to each other in Szombathely, Not enough, I thought, was being done to bring about the active participation of linguists. from other Hungarian colleges who, I was sure, would have had a useful, and possibly divergent, contribution to make. The reason for this lay in inter-institutional rivalries and jealousy. I was well aware of this so I should have known better –remembering Hungarian sensibilities - than to voice these criticisms forcefully at the closing feedback session of a conference towards the end of my year in Szombathely. The non-Hungarian participants saw the point of my intervention and quite a worth-while discussion ensued. But the representatives of the College, in particular Dr Molnar, were incapable of seeing my criticisms as anything other than a personal attack on themselves. The result was that I ended my year in Hungary under a disagreeable cloud and received no thanks for my year's work there.

If the EECALL Centre was regarded by the Brussels authorities as the most successful project they were financing at the time this was mostly due to Graham Davies's managerial, financial and above all diplomatic skills, his all-embracing knowledge of CALL and his contacts in related fields. There was also the amount of donkey-work he had done to make it a success. When the three years of funding were coming to an end and we were preparing the final meeting, which coincided, if I remember rightly, with the holding of the annual international Eurocall Conference at Szombathely, it seemed to me and to several others that the project should not end without some recognition of how much was owed to him personally. I saw, knowing the Hungarians by now, that this was not likely to happen spontaneously, so I asked Dieter Wolff, who, being a powerful German professor, was the most influential person on the scene, to suggest that some way should be found of expressing our appreciation of all Graham had done. Dieter agreed but came back with the response from the College that such a gesture would "not be appropriate", so nothing was said. In his speech closing the Conference and ending the Project Graham however succeeded in including his definition of a Hungarian as "a chap who could enter a revolving door behind you and somehow manage to be in front of you coming out the other side". He even managed to make it sound like a compliment, just.

# Rosbeg 10

In 1959 my father bought, for £500, the house in Rosbeg County Donegal that we all called Polladingdong after the name of a rocky creek some way along the shore. This started an association with this little seaside Donegal townland which has lasted more than half a century and is still ongoing. But it wasn't the result of a long-meditated decision on the part of my parents but of a series of chance circumstances.

In fact Donegal was outside the orbit of our usual summer *villégiature*. When Conor and I were small the parents usually found somewhere in the West or South for our holidays. We had only twice been in Donegal: once to Fintragh near Killybegs and once, a most unsuccessful holiday, to Rossnowlagh where we were housed in a maximally unpicturesque tin bungalow in a row of unpicturesque tin bungalows lined up beside the beach in what the parents ought to have known was a popular resort. Both these things, the resort and the bungalows were anathema in the parents', above all my mother's, eyes. Also it rained every day. The only good memory of the place was of Una, who was one year old, saying her first word – *wuwu*, meaning animal: dog, cow or seagull – but she could have said that anywhere. The following years we went to Cork, Kerry or Connemara.

The reason we went to Rosbeg was that the parents were offered the use of a house there in September 1958 by a friend of my mother's. I think they had already had a holiday somewhere else that year. Constance and I and our children had been in the Alps with the Souvirons in July. However, since we had not had a family holiday and my term in Paris didn't start until mid-September my mother accepted the offer. We liked Rosbeg so much that we went there again the following year, and my father bought Polladingdong. From then on we stayed in our own house.

The friend of my mother's who chanced to lend us the house in 1958 and started our long association with Rosbeg was a woman called Millicent Weir who was married to the owner of a long established Grafton Street firm of jewellers. I only learnt the romantic story behind this improbable friendship of my mother's when she was very old. She told me then how, in the early years of the 20th century, when she and her brother would spend their holidays from school at the Synge estate, Glanmore Castle, she was friendly with all the farm workers on the estate and their children. Among them was a girl called Millicent whose father kept the gate lodge at the back of the Glanmore estate. Sometime shortly before the war the eldest son of Weirs, the jewellers, was driving what must have been one of the earliest cars to be seen in County Wicklow and chanced to come down the steep and narrow hill on the road between Roundwood and Ashford too fast. The brakes on the car failed so that when he came to the sharp corner outside the back gate of Glanmore Castle he crashed into a tree. He was carried into the lodge where the doctor who was called from Dublin said that his injuries were such that he should not be moved until they had healed. So young Mr. Weir stayed there for a month or more being nursed by the keeper's daughter, Millicent. He fell in love with her and asked her to marry him.

Apparently the Synges of Glanmore Castle, with the exception of my mother, were very snooty about this match which they did not approve of. But my mother remained very friendly with Millicent who I can remember as a very gracious lady living in a very much posher house than any other of my parents' friends. When we were small Conor and I used to be brought to tea there. This was served by a maid in a lacy uniform who Mrs Weir used to summon by pressing her foot on a bell push concealed under the carpet. She was very kind to us and I remember her, when I was 10 years old, giving me my first fountain pen, a blue Conway Stewart with a gold nib which I kept carefully for years. It was on the occasion of a visit to Mrs Weir in 1958 that she told my mother about this house in Rosbeg which they had for the people working in the shop, and which chanced to be vacant that September so she asked if we would like it.

Towards the end of our second holiday in the Weir house, when Constance and I and the children had set off in our 2cv Citroen for Paris, a local man, Joe Harkin, asked my father if he would be interested in "a bit of a house I have, that's beyond". The house in question was part of a complex of rather tumbledown buildings which, until a few years before, had been known as Frick's Hotel. It had been owned and run as a hotel since early in the century by one Herr Frick who had died some years earlier. His hotel used in the old days to be patronised by relatively well-off people from Belfast and Dublin who liked to stay in plushy comfort in wild and primitive places. I knew of several such places in the West of Ireland. They were usually run by slightly eccentric proprietors, like Herr Frick, who tended to accept as hotel guests only people that they liked and approved of. This was of course in the days before there was such a thing as a tourist industry. One of Constance's uncles in fact, a prosperous Belfast

A Ramillon "Ram", Brian and Doreen

lawyer, used to stay there regularly in the Thirties. He told Constance how he would arrive by train in Glenties and finish the journey in a pony and trap. Many years later Olivia and I found horseradish growing wild in the grounds behind the hotel building. Probably a relic of Herr Frick's German cuisine.

The house my father bought was not the hotel proper, which was a large, late Georgian-style edifice, containing several magnificent rooms with great windows facing the view, but very dilapidated. Instead, the house Joe Harkin showed him was a more modest and much more recent construction tucked in behind the main building. It had no view but it was solidly built, had five bedrooms and a large kitchen-dining-room, and was not too far from the shore. We had our first holiday there in 1960, when Doreen was a baby. Year after year the parents and their friends, with the rest of our family clan: children, grandchildren, great-grandchildren, in-laws and friends, spent exuberant holidays there.

In latter times and when my mother was very old – I'm an old hag, she used to say - Olivia and I with Tadg and Roisin and sometimes Paddy and Doreen would stay there, together with Ram and Constance. They would arrive with Ram's car packed full and heaped high, not only with all Ram's elaborate fishing equipment and guns (for shooting rabbits), his bird books and insect books, but a complete set of tools of every description with which he would set about repairing things about the house which was always much improved after he had been there. His English, which he never used when talking with Olivia or me, while adequate for his needs was far from fluent, which made for long and amusing interactions in local hardware shops, this being before Ireland went metric. His knowledge and understanding of natural history together with his general way of seeing things, which was very French but non-Parisian - his uncle had been a wheelwright in a small village near Orléans - all of these things enriched the times we spent with them in Rosbeg. For example he arrived one year having constructed the necessary cages or boxes for preparing snails. He would gather these creatures on rainy evenings and, after carrying out the complicated preparation, which took ages, would serve them up for supper, an unusual variation on the customary Donegal fare. Though, to be honest, *escargots* were never a dish that I cared for, a bit too much like chewing little pieces of garlic-flavoured rubber. I appreciated much more the delicious little brown trout that he would catch in his favourite lake, Birrogue, where he would stay all afternoon if necessary until he had caught a fish for every person staying in the house.

It was clear to me that, more patient, more thoughtful and less selfish than I had been, Ram had given Constance something that I just had not been able to give, and so it would have been surprising if I had never felt a twinge of jealousy. But, since I was so happily married to Olivia and since, thanks to Olivia and of course to Ram, Constance and I were able to remain friends, it was not difficult to reason that away. Whenever I had a meeting in Paris I used to stay with Constance and Ram in their flat in Chatenay, just down the road from where the *Cité Nouvelle* had been demolished and replaced by a hideous block of flats. Constance had ended up with quite a good job teaching English in one of the *Grandes Écoles*, *l'École Centrale*, which was now situated near Chatenay. She received a doctorate for her research into one of the Communards who had visited Ireland at the end of the 19th century. Though Ram was by all accounts an outstandingly good *instituteur* he never enjoyed the job. Therefore he took early retirement as soon as ever that was possible which meant that he and Constance could spend more time in Ireland, either in Rosbeg or, for most of each summer, in Constance's house in Dublin whence, accoutred as only French fishermen can be, he would drive out to spend long days catching pike in Poulaphouca Lake.

Sadly Ram died of cancer in 1995 when he was only just in his 70s and shortly after that Constance, who was several years older than Ram, began to show signs of dementia which were later diagnosed as the beginning of Alzheimer's disease. Our two children, Paddy and Doreen, did what they could to alleviate the loneliness of her life in Chatenay after Ram's death, as did I, staying with her every time I had occasion to go to France. And then through a fortuitous combination of circumstances I spent a whole week in her company. What happened was this: I had a meeting in Paris and I had planned, after the meeting, to spend a day or two with Constance and then to go and visit various friends. But I had no sooner arrived in Chatenay than the whole French transport system, trains, buses, even the Paris Metro, was suddenly paralysed by a strike which went on for over a week. There was no way of leaving Chatenay, even to go into Paris. So I spent the whole week with Constance. We went for long walks every day in the Parc de Sceaux, in the woods of *Verrières* and the *Vallée aux Loups*. We talked of our earliest times together, putting together all sorts of half-forgotten memories: good times, such as when we had gone together, on Ivy Day in 1945, to watch a group of aged Parnellites lay a wreath on the lost leader's grave in Glasnevin, and bad times that were best forgotten, but which we could now discuss freely. We agreed that young people nowadays seemed to have a much easier time of it. Talking frankly about those two strange complicated and inhibited people that we had once been we reaffirmed what was to both of us a precious friendship. As her malady progressed and her personality dwindled I was more and more glad that that week, which could never, for many obvious reasons, ever have been arranged beforehand, had, all the same, chanced to happen.

In the end, when, in 1988, my mother died, aged 96, Polladingdong went to my brother Conor, and is now the property of his widow, Patricia. I had not wanted to inherit it. When the parents were making their wills I was living in France and I did not feel able to look after Polladingdong properly from there. So, instead, they left me some acres that they had bought in Wicklow and planted with trees. I don't know what they paid for this land, but as time passed and Dublin grew to the south the value increased considerably. Eventually this, combined with a roughly equivalent contribution from Olivia, made it possible for us to buy a house of our own in Ireland, something Olivia had hankered after for years. Since we knew and liked the local people in Rosbeg, and they had known us for so many years, it would have been foolish to go anywhere else. We were lucky in that a local woman, Teresa White, was looking to sell her house to move nearer to the church in Ardara so we bought it. The house was called Mountairy. We didn't care for the name, finding it non-Irish but we didn't want to offend Teresa, so, thinking that the name had been chosen to describe the house's exposed situation, I translated it into Irish as Ardnageeha which, I realised too late, would literally translate back into English as something like wuthering heights. It wasn't until we went to America and I looked at a map of Kentucky that I realised that all this was quite irrelevant, since Mountairy was the name of the town Teresa's American husband Sam White came from.

Olivia and BF at Rosbeg

To some extent acquiring a house in Ireland, for all that it was only a holiday cottage to be inhabited for only a few weeks in the year, meant returning to my native country, rubbing out what remained of the expatriate's *angoisse* which so troubled me when living in France. But having lived abroad for all my working life I had come to see being a foreigner as normal. And Ireland had changed so much that I hardly felt any more at home there than I felt in Scotland or would have felt in France. It's true that we had for years thought of retiring to Ireland, but by the time I retired we had two Scottish children living in or near Edinburgh and most of our friends were in Scotland. With the exception of Una all our Irish friends were the same age as myself and just as likely to drop off at any moment, whereas most of our Scottish friends were a good 20 years younger than Olivia or me.

Working on a re-edition of my essay on W B Yeats, *Malachi-Stilt-Jack*, I came to consider again Yeats's hatred of old age, and to conclude that, growing old myself, I couldn't altogether share his rage against the depredations of time. Instead, I found that there were a certain number of advantages in growing old, and I chose to concentrate my mind on these. It is true that modern technology has helped in this, since I now have a heart pacemaker, an artificial hip joint, a radio-treated prostate and a hearing aid. Without some of these gadgets I probably wouldn't still be around whereas with their help I am able to enjoy life quite a lot. But it's true that when you are old you don't enjoy things in the same way,

Olivia,
June 2009

or the same things. I remember when I was about 10 years old I saw an old lady open her front door and exclaim, "Oh, what a *lovely* day!" I remember thinking, "What is she on about, silly old bag? It's just a bit of sunshine." Well now I am myself like the silly old bag, I take a constant and repeated delight in the simplest of things, the blueness of sky the greenness of grass, the coldness of wind. And there are a lot of things that I no longer feel or notice which I can well do without. I think of Prospero in Auden's *The Sea and the Mirror* who, at the end of his life, says:

> I am glad
> I shall never be twenty again and in love,
> The fuss and fury, the conceit, the expense.

Whatever about being twenty I can happily do without being in love again. In the course of my life I have, like most people I suppose, had what Simone de Beauvoir calls "*amours contingentes*". I enjoyed these life-enhancing, unsettling experiences very much while they were happening, though I have had more enjoyment from the friendships that most of them ended up as. None of them came within miles of endangering my whole-hearted attachment to Olivia in any way. Now, looking back from the relatively impotent wisdom of old age, I wonder was it worth the amount of time some of them took up and the inevitable complications and tensions involved. I tend now to see masculine sexuality, or my experience of its tiresome dogginess, a disruptive and importunate time-waster. Yet I know that it also plays an essential part in making life worth living. One of the nice things about being old is that, at least so far as I am concerned, while this last feature is still active and functioning more or less, the disruptive and importunate aspects are of diminishing effect. Instead, my day to day interactions with Olivia, our agreements and disagreements, the changing colour and temperature of our likes and dislikes for each other's being and each other's ways, generate a complex peace of mind, a happiness, which would have been unimaginable in the stormy days of our first passion.

In the course of writing this book I have read a number of other people's Memoirs, some of them constantly interesting to read and others an extreme of bland banality. Leaving aside those that were compulsively readable simply because the events or adventures recounted were inherently interesting or tragic or funny, I found it very hard to explain why one person's account of their day to day existence should be a pleasure to read while another person's description of fairly similar facts and circumstances should seem pointless and wearisome. The answer I tentatively came up with was that reading this sort of book is a pleasure in so far as the reader identifies with the person telling the story. Wherever this is not possible, where the reader is invited to regard writer or central character and his or her activities, and admire them, as it were from outside, then only content or subject matter fascinating enough to excite one's curiosity can save the text from tedium. I saw a good example the other day in a book review by Roy Hattersley where he cited a boring sentence in the book that should have been omitted, saying that this sort of writing should only figure in Christmas letters to neglected relatives. I have tried to cut out from my text any sentence that reads like something from a Christmas letter to distant cousins. I hope I have succeeded.

Having said this I should not all the same end the book without including some Christmas-letter-style information about a few of the *dramatis personae* in my story. Olivia's second novel *Rose-Tinted Scissors* was published in 2009. She is currently working on a second collection of her poems. Of Constance's and my children, Paddy is now a Professor of Mathematics at the Open University. His partner Cathie Lloyd is a sociologist. Doreen opted to live in France and now has both Irish and French nationality. She teaches piano in a *conservatoire* outside Paris. She has given recitals in Paris including some of her own compositions. Olivia's and my two children live in Scotland. Tadg is married to Margaret Nicholson who is a primary teacher and they live in Dunbar with Molly aged nine and Ben aged six. Tadg has written the screenplay for television documentaries. His book, *The Average Life of the Average Person,* written in relation to one of these, has recently been published with some success. His

Una

sister Roisin works for a Housing Association in Edinburgh. She and her partner Clive Boag, who is a health and safety consultant, have an engagingly sociable little two-year-old boy called Fergal.

My sister Una, having lived for years in Spain, returned to Ireland where she acquired two university degrees. In her last job she was for twenty years in charge of a large National Trust property in Northern Ireland, Ardress House. She now lives in Donegal, not far from Rosbeg where she has created a much-admired garden.

Two friends that I made in my first years in France remained close all our lives. My Orléans friends, Jacques and Marie Souviron, moved several times, each move causing a problem, since what was promotion for one was never promotion for the other. They ended up near Montpellier which was almost as far you could get from Aberdeen but near to their, and our, beloved Pyrenees where we went climbing and hill-walking together. Jacques became a highly esteemed senior civil servant in the Ministry of Labour. When he died he had enjoyed several energetic years on the municipal council of the small town they lived in. Marie published research articles on Diderot. They both remained faithful to the Marxist ideals of their youth.

Henri Degoutin, from Lunéville, quickly got bored teaching English in a

Jacques Souviron [Above]
Henri Degoutin

school and gave expression to his enthusiasm for the theatre by organising among young people in his native town of Toul a lively amateur troupe, a very unusual thing for France. They had so much success presenting classical and modern plays all over Lorraine that they gradually became professional. They moved to Nancy where Henri, who had long given up teaching, ended up as Director of a theatre, *La Comédie de Lorraine*, with government funding. His very success, and that of his partner the talented *comedienne* Jeannine Vedrenne, was their misfortune. Because, having started a movement of young enthusiasts, Henri, whose political affinities were generally of the left, though he owed allegiance to no party, had retained a large audience of keen young supporters. Someone in authority in Paris got nervous at the idea of new and radical ideas circulating among young people in Nancy. Consequently they first appointed some dullard as a sort of super-Director over Henri and ended by elbowing him out of his job. Though his theatre died he went on performing and producing into old age.

When we were in Hungary Olivia and I used occasionally to eat in what was the best restaurant in Szombathely. Known as the fish restaurant because it specialised in serving a large and rather terrifying-looking type of perch called

*Fogash*, which they caught in Lake Balaton, it was a pleasant change from other eateries where you got nothing but pork. But the best thing about the fish restaurant was the menu on which the name of every dish was followed by a description in English. This was remarkable in that, though you could not find a single actual mistake of vocabulary or syntax anywhere, the general effect of every single description was hilarious. Typical among these was the description of the most famous of all Hungarian dishes. Under the word *Goulash* was written: *A Rich Soup, With Additional Material.* It seemed a good description of my life.

THE END

# Index